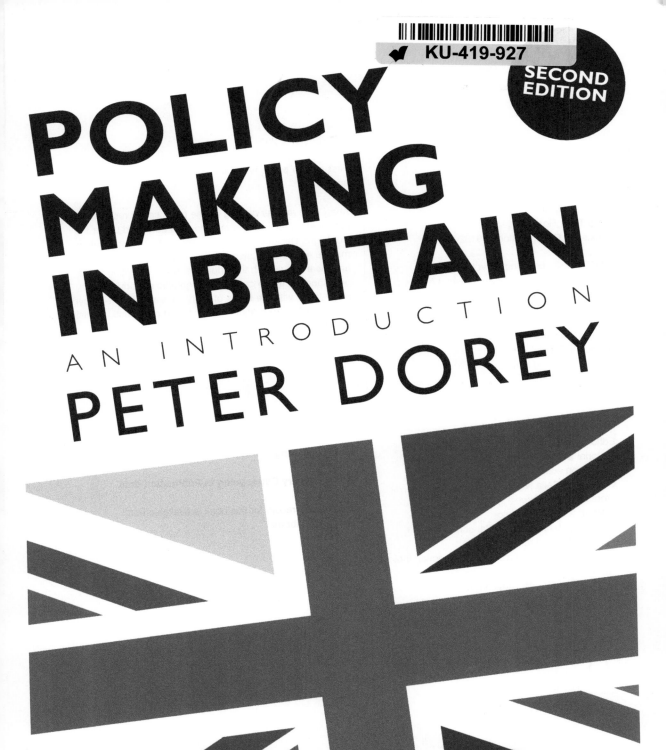

SECOND EDITION

POLICY MAKING IN BRITAIN

AN INTRODUCTION

PETER DOREY

Los Angeles | London | New Delhi
Singapore | Washington DC

SAGE Publications Ltd
1 Oliver's Yard
55 City Road
London EC1Y 1SP

SAGE Publications Inc.
2455 Teller Road
Thousand Oaks, California 91320

SAGE Publications India Pvt Ltd
B 1/I 1 Mohan Cooperative Industrial Area
Mathura Road
New Delhi 110 044

SAGE Publications Asia-Pacific Pte Ltd
3 Church Street
#10-04 Samsung Hub
Singapore 049483

First edition published 2005. Reprinted 2008, 2009, 2010, 2011 and 2012.

Editor: Natalie Aguilera
Editorial assistant: James Piper
Production editor: Thea Watson
Copyeditor: Salia Nessa
Proofreader: Jill Birch
Indexer: Silvia Benvenuto
Marketing manager: Sally Ransom
Cover designer: Francis Kenney
Typeset by: C&M Digitals (P) Ltd, Chennai, India
Printed and bound in Great Britain by
CPI Group (UK) Ltd, Croydon, CR0 4YY

MIX
Paper from
responsible sources
FSC® C013604

ISBN 978-1-84920-847-5
ISBN 978-1-84920-848-2 (pbk)

POLICY MAKING IN BRITAIN

Also by Peter Dorey:

British Politics since 1945

The Conservative Party and the Trade Unions

The Major Premiership: Politics and Policies under John Major, 1990–1997 (ed.)

Wage Politics in Britain: The Rise and Fall of Incomes Policies since 1945

Policy Making in Britain: An Introduction, first edition.

Developments in British Public Policy (ed.)

The Labour Governments 1964–1970 (ed.)

The Labour Party and Constitutional Reform: A History of Constitutional Conservatism

British Conservatism and Trade Unionism, 1945–1964

From Crisis to Coalition: The Conservative Party, 1997–2010 (with Mark Garnett and Andrew Denham)

House of Lords Reform since 1911: Must the Lords Go? (with Alexandra Kelso)

British Conservatism: The Politics and Philosophy of Inequality

To Jane – cherished wife and soulmate.

Contents

List of Figures

List of Tables

List of Boxes

Preface to the Second Edition

Harold Wilson once remarked that 'a week in politics is a long time', so the decade that has passed since the first edition of *Policy Making in Britain* seems like something of a lifetime ago. Plenty has occurred during the past ten years to warrant a second edition, but this book aims to provide more than a simple update based on incorporating more recent empirical examples – although it does contain these in each chapter. In the light of feedback from academic colleagues and students who have used the first edition, I have significantly revised and expanded this edition, with some chapters restructured and new ones added.

The first edition's chapter on organized interests has been replaced by a new chapter on 'policy advocates', in which the role of organized interests is examined alongside that of political parties and think tanks. There is a new chapter on the internationalization of public policy, which considers three aspects: Europeanization; globalization; and policy transfer. The final chapter is also new, and considers the evaluation of policies as well as the sundry problems that this often entails. I have introduced nine to ten questions or topics for seminar discussion at the end of each chapter.

This seems to be an ideal opportunity for me to thank two people at Sage in particular. First, I am extremely grateful to David Mainwaring for inviting me to write a second edition of this book, and for readily accepting my suggestions as to how the first edition should be expanded, revised and updated.

Second, I want to thank Natalie Aguilera who has been my editor at Sage throughout the writing of this second edition. Not only has Natalie offered constant support and cheerful encouragement, she has displayed remarkable patience and understanding when my progress has been rather slower than envisaged, due both to increased teaching commitments and the ever increasing administrative responsibilities that contemporary academics are burdened with.

As always, any deficiencies or shortcomings in this book are mine and mine alone.

Pete Dorey
Bath, Somerset
August 2013

Abbreviations and Acronyms

ASBO	Anti-social Behaviour Order
BBC	British Broadcasting Corporation
BMA	British Medical Association
CAP	Common Agricultural Policy
CND	Campaign for Nuclear Disarmament
CPS	Centre for Policy Studies
CSA	Child Support Agency
DEFRA	Department of the Environment, Food and Rural Affairs
DES	Department for Education and Science
DOH	Department of Health
DTI	Department of Trade and Industry
EEC	European Economic Community
EMU	Economic and Monetary Union
ERM	Exchange Rate Mechanism
EU	European Union
FCO	Foreign and Commonwealth Office
G7	Economic summits comprising Britain, Canada, France, Germany, Italy, Japan and United States
G8	As above, but with additional membership of Russia (since 1998)
IMF	International Monetary Fund
IPPR	Institute for Public Policy Research
LEA	Local Education Authority
LSE	London School of Economics
MAFF	Ministry of Agriculture, Fisheries and Food
MSP	Member of the Scottish Parliament
NATO	North Atlantic Treaty Organization
NFU	National Farmers Union
NHS	National Health Service
NI	National Insurance

Ofcom	Office of Communications
Ofgem	Office of Gas and Electricity Markets
Ofsted	Office for Standards in Education
Ofwat	Office of Water Services
PFI	Private Finance Initiative
PPP	Public–Private Partnership
PSBR	Public Sector Borrowing Requirement
RAE	Research Assessment Exercise
SDP	Social Democratic Party
SPAD	Special Adviser

Introduction

THE STUDY OF POLICY MAKING IN BRITAIN

Until relatively recently, many models of policy making assumed or implied that there was a clear sequence of stages through which public policies proceed and which therefore constituted the 'policy process'. As Figure (i) illustrates, this 'stagist' model of the policy process starts with agenda setting, and then portrays policy proceeding through a logical sequence of stages: recognition of problem; consideration of options; agreement on most suitable option; legislation or introduction of new policy; implementation.

Although there have been variations on this model, they have all reflected and reinforced the notion that policies proceed through a sequential series of stages, and that there is a 'policy process' with a clear beginning, middle and end (although to be fair, revised versions of this model have sometimes added an 'evaluation' stage after implementation, which then feeds back to agenda setting).

One famous version of this 'stagist' approach was provided by David Easton's (1965) wider notion of the political system, in which societal demands were processed inside the 'black box' of the political system, and then emerged as outputs in the form of allocation of resources, legislation and public programmes, as illustrated by Figure (ii).

In reality, of course, matters are rather less clear-cut and straightforward. For example, most policies are still being 'made' while they are implemented, and as such, may be transformed in ways that were not originally imagined or intended. Moreover, far from constituting the 'end' of the policy process, the implementation 'stage' is often

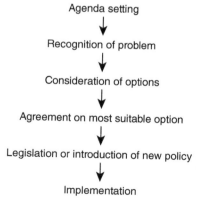

Figure (i)   The 'stagist' model of the policy process

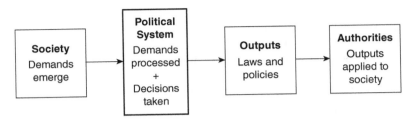

Figure (ii)   Simplified version of Easton's model of the political system

Source: Adapted from Easton, 1965.

followed by a realization that the problem(s) it was intended to solve has not, in fact, been successfully tackled.

Alternatively, implementation might itself prompt further, unforeseen and unintended problems, either due to inherent faults in the design of the policy, or because those responsible for administering the policy at local level make decisions that alter its effectiveness; they might interpret or apply the rules and regulations in a manner different to the intentions of central policy makers. When it is realized that the implementation of a policy has not achieved the intended objectives or results – indeed, it might unwittingly have caused new or further problems – then it is likely to move back onto the policy agenda and either be reformed or repealed.

Meanwhile, Parliament plays a role in both scrutinizing and giving formal approval to policies, particularly in the form of legislation, and subsequently in evaluating the impact of policies and laws. In other words, Parliament's role *vis-à-vis* a particular policy does not end when the relevant legislation 'leaves' the House *en route* to implementation, because MPs might later highlight problems with a policy. They might do so by asking the relevant minister questions on behalf of affected or aggrieved constituents at Ministers' Question Time, or perhaps by writing to, or even speaking with, the minister to convey their concerns over the negative impact of a policy. In such cases, the intention will be to persuade the minister that the policy is sufficiently flawed that it warrants reform or replacement.

A further important means by which Parliament plays a role in retrospective policy evaluation, and thus in highlighting problems that might lead to reconsideration by ministers, is through the many select committees that conduct inquiries into departmental policies and sometimes publish highly critical reports.

Another criticism of the 'stagist' approach to policy making is its failure to distinguish between different policy areas or sub-systems. It does not disaggregate or distinguish between discrete areas of public policy, or convey the extent to which different policies will involve different policy actors and modes of interaction or influence. For example, the poor have generally had rather less input into shaping welfare policy than farmers have had in shaping post-war agricultural policy in Britain.

Meanwhile, Britain's membership of the European Union (EU) has had a variable impact on departments and policies because some have been more affected than others by 'Europeanization'. Furthermore, among those departments most affected by Britain's membership of the EU, a few have actually viewed the EU positively, either because Britain's membership has granted them a new lease of life or sense of purpose, or because they recognize that many of their policy objectives can only be achieved by working with other member states – 'splendid isolation' is rather less splendid in terms of tackling transnational problems that require international cooperation.

Consequently, the 'stagist' version of the policy process has been criticized for providing an inaccurate account of how policies are 'made', because it depicts policy making as a linear process with a clear beginning, middle and end. This sequential model, its critics argue, not only grossly oversimplifies the manner in which policies are apparently initiated, developed and implemented, but also fails, crucially, to explain *how* issues emerge, *why* some enter the political system (but not others), *how* they are 'processed' inside the 'black box' of the political system (and *who* is involved and in *which* role or capacity), and *why* the policies (the outputs) subsequently encounter various difficulties, or enjoy varying degrees of success when they are being implemented.

In short, the 'stagist' model can be criticized for failing to provide either a realistic or an explanatory account of policy making (for two examples of such criticism, see Jenkins-Smith and Sabatier, 1993: 3–4; John, 1998: 25–7). Sabatier especially emerged as a prominent critic of what he termed 'the stages heuristic' – or what Nakamura more prosaically called 'the textbook approach' (Nakamura, 1987) – claiming that while it 'served a useful purpose in the 1970s and early 1980s by dividing the very complex policy process into discrete stages', subsequent research and analysis of policy making has exposed serious weaknesses with the 'stages heuristic' model of the policy process.

Not least of these deficiencies, Sabatier elaborates, are: its failure to provide *causal* accounts of policy development; the sequence of the stages is inaccurate or misleading because the 'first' stage (agenda setting) is itself intimately and inextricably affected by other stages, such as the 'final' stage (evaluation); it reflects a rather legalistic or top-down approach to policy making in which the focus often appears to be on legislation *per se*; it fails to distinguish between different types or aspects of public policy; it reflects an emphasis on government rather than the recent trend towards governance involving different actors at different levels (Sabatier, 1999: 6–7).

Similarly, John argues that:

Instead of policy being a linear sequence of intended actions, that is followed by success or failure, decision-making is characterised by learning, adaptation and reformulation ... the analyst needs to understand the policy-making process in the round.

(John, 1998: 30)

Meanwhile, a former senior civil servant in the Department of Trade and Industry in the early 1990s, who also served in the Cabinet Office during the first Blair government, asks rhetorically, 'What [policy] process?', emphasizing that:

The problem is that new policies, and policy decisions, can arise in, and are handled in, a multitude of different ways. But it is often possible to discern a number of separate stages, including research, consultation and gaining knowledge, exploring options, more consultation, and taking decisions through to Ministerial agreement. The individual stages do not operate sequentially, but overlap as policies become firmed up.

(Stanley, 2000: 44)

Yet the 'stagist' model remains popular and can still be defended as a tool or starting point, which can help us to understand some of the aspects of policy making. The fact that policy making is frequently complex or messy actually makes it even more useful to provide a simplified model, which identifies some of the constituent elements of 'the policy process', precisely so that the complex or messy reality can begin to be understood.

Indeed, the 'stagist' model has often been defended on these grounds, namely that it is best understood as a 'heuristic device' rather than an accurate depiction of policy making in the real world. A 'heuristic device' is an analytical tool or pedagogic model – particularly in the social and political sciences – designed and deployed to aid understanding (particularly for educational purposes) of an otherwise highly complex issue or process.

In this context, characterizing the policy process as a series or sequence of stages 'facilitates the understanding of public policy-making by breaking the complexity of the process into a limited number of stages', even though in the real world of day-to-day policy making 'there is often no linear progression as conceived by the [stagist or sequential] model' (Howlett and Ramesh, 1995: 12).

In other words, we would argue that the 'policy stages' or 'stages heuristic' approach is still useful in helping us to begin to understand aspects of policy making in Britain, particularly if we take on board Sabatier's criticism about the sequence of the stages. We can identify: how policy making in Britain enshrines various stages, even though they overlap; the stages are inextricably interlinked; the stages do not always occur in the sequential order that the 'stages heuristic' suggests. For example, this book treats agenda setting and the role of ideas in a separate (and prior) chapter to those that examine the roles and relationships of the formal policy makers in the 'core executive' and how they formulate public policy, but we readily acknowledge that those inside the 'black box' of central or formal governmental institutions themselves sometimes shape the policy agenda and promote influential ideas, rather than merely responding to them (as the sequential model clearly implies).

Ultimately, therefore, while fully acknowledging the limitations of the 'stages heuristic' approach, as enunciated by critics such as Sabatier (1999) and John (1998), we still believe that it can provide useful insights into some of the ways in which public policy is made or shaped in Britain and by who (or what). Without it, it would be difficult, if not impossible, to know where to start.

STRUCTURE OF THE BOOK

With the above caveats firmly in mind, this book commences with a chapter on agenda setting, and discusses how and why some issues become defined as 'problems' and perhaps prompt policies to address them, while others are ignored. The chapter emphasizes that problems are not always evident, but subject to a variety of factors, not least of which are social values and ideology – what might be deemed acceptable or normal in one era or decade might subsequently be viewed as wholly unacceptable. Conversely, an activity or lifestyle that was previously considered scandalous or taboo might become widely accepted and embraced a generation or two later. This chapter also reiterates the messiness of the policy process by highlighting some of the key models designed to illustrate how and why some problems result in a new policy or policy change, while others fail to do so.

This section of the chapter will thus outline the notion of an 'issue attention cycle', the concept of 'policy streams' (which need to flow together for policy changes to occur) and the manner in which policy making resembles either a primeval soup or garbage can. The latter two models or analogies emphasize that policies are not always made in response to a problem; they often exist *a priori*, whereupon the policy's advocates actively search for a problem to which their favoured policy can be applied. This vital factor is yet another reason for *not* viewing the policy process as a linear or sequential series of stages, with a clear beginning, middle and end.

The second chapter discusses the role of three crucial institutional policy advocates, namely the main political parties (at Westminster), think tanks and organized interests. As Britain is widely recognized as having a system of party government, it is essential to understand the core beliefs and principles of the Conservatives, the Labour Party and the Liberal Democrats, as well as the tensions and ideological 'groupings' or 'factions' within each party. This is particularly important when the party is in government, because many of the policies it pursues will depend on which 'faction' is dominant at the time.

A key development in British politics, and thus the policy process, since the 1970s has been the increase in the number and activities of think tanks, many of which have had close links with the Conservative Party and Thatcherism. Although there are method-ological difficulties in gauging their actual influence on public policy, it is undeniable that many of the policies enacted by the British governments since 1979 have been advocated by various think tanks, although these policies might well have been enacted anyway. Certainly, though, the Adam Smith Institute (ASI) was a passionate advocate of privatiza-tion from the late 1970s onwards, while the Institute of Economic Affairs (IEA) urged the 'marketization' of the public sector, and much greater responsiveness to the interests and wishes of service users.

Meanwhile, the 'New Labour' think tank, the Institute for Public Policy Research, was renowned as a keen proponent of Public–Private Partnerships, whereby private companies built or provided infrastructure for the public sector (for example, building and equipping new hospitals) and then leased these back to the public sector for up to 30 years. This enabled new hospitals, prisons, schools and universities to be built without the need to raise taxes to finance them.

The other main institutional advocates of public policy are organized interests (or pres-sure groups). These span a wide variety of issues – economic, environmental, ethical, moral and social – and seek to persuade policy makers to pursue policies that will benefit either their members or those on whose behalf the groups are campaigning.

Yet some organized interests are (or have been) much more influential than others, as reflected in their close and regular contact with policy makers at the very highest levels. The most influential organized interests have usually been those who are either economi-cally powerful (hence policy makers cannot afford to ignore them) or possess specialist knowledge and expertise derived from their profession, such as agriculture or medicine. Furthermore, such groups have not only been valuable to policy makers in terms of the advice they can offer, but also because they can assist in the implementation of policies once they have been agreed.

Conversely, groups campaigning on ethical or social issues, such as poverty and low pay, have not generally enjoyed much access to policy makers, and so have been much less influential. Most governments have either not deemed the issues that such groups campaign for to be a priority, or these groups are not considered to possess the specialist expertise that policy makers require. It is also the case that some 'social' or 'ethical' pressure groups are not ideologically compatible either with most governments or the dominant values in British society; these groups are often viewed as irresponsible, extreme or unrepresentative.

In Chapters 3 and 4, we examine how and why traditional discussions about the role of the Cabinet, ministers and civil servants in policy making have been superseded by the rise of 'core executive studies'. This draws attention to the increased role and importance of Junior Ministers, the growing significance of Special (Policy) Advisers, the changing role of senior civil servants (and thus their changing relationship with ministers), the role of departments themselves, and the increasing importance of supporting and coordinating institutions at the heart of the core executive, most notably the Cabinet Office and the Prime Minister's Office.

The concept of the core executive also places strong emphasis on the interdependence of the individuals and institutions that comprise the core executive, and challenges older accounts that often depicted relationships in terms of 'Prime Ministers versus Cabinet' or 'ministers versus senior civil servants'. Instead, we will explain how the various 'actors' in the core executive are bound together by 'resource dependency' and therefore need to interact in order to achieve policy goals. Instead of viewing individuals as having a specific degree of power, as if it was 'fixed' and predetermined, we will show how power in the core executive is relatively fluid and contingent, in the sense that its possession and the exercise of it is heavily dependent on circumstances, personalities, styles of leadership and the type of issues or policies involved.

Chapter 5 analyses the role that Parliament plays in the policy process and how this has changed in recent decades. Whereas many academic commentators have been inclined to dismiss Parliament almost entirely as a meaningful actor in the policy process, we argue that Parliament plays a more indirect role, one which its critics overlook or underestimate. For example, it may well be that the overwhelming majority of governmental measures are formally approved by Parliament, not because it is weak and subservient to the executive, but because ministers generally only pursue policies and legislation that they are reasonably confident will secure parliamentary approval. In other words, Parliament's power is often covert or latent, similar to the 'hidden face of power', which is discussed in Chapter 1.

Furthermore, since 1979, a range of select committees have scrutinized the policies of the government departments and ministries, regularly cross-examining ministers, senior civil servants, and other witnesses either involved in the formulation or implementation of a policy, or affected by it. The reports published by these select committees can themselves sometimes prompt policy change or modification. These select committees are also now increasingly involved in 'pre-legislative scrutiny', whereby 'draft Bills' are examined by MPs before being formally introduced into Parliament as a whole. The increasing use of pre-legislative scrutiny by select committees means that Parliament now has the opportunity to play a rather more active and potentially influential role in the legislative stage of policy making than it has previously, in addition to its scrutiny of laws and policies after they have been enacted.

A particularly significant development since the 1980s, which we examine in Chapter 6, is the transition from government to governance. This refers to a number of simultaneous and interlinked trends, whereby policy making has become increasingly fragmented and conducted at different levels – national, regional and local – while also involving a more diverse set of policy actors drawn from the public, private and voluntary sectors.

The concept of governance emphasizes the extent to which 'the government' is now only one of many participants in the policy process and is increasingly concerned with 'steering' and coordinating public policy, rather than necessarily determining it from the centre (although how far governments have actually relinquished control is a matter of continuous academic debate). Governance places a premium on both vertical and horizontal coordination, and greater interaction, cooperation, partnership and 'exchange relationships' between the plethora of actors now involved in the formulation and/or implementation of public policy.

During the same period, many policies have been 'internationalized', partly as a consequence of 'Europeanization' and partly because of the expansion and acceleration of globalization, both of which we discuss in Chapter 7. We will consider how policy making in Britain is increasingly shaped by developments in, and directives emanating from, the EU, and how Westminster and Whitehall have adapted to the Europeanization of public policy in several areas. However, it is also emphasized that the impact of the EU on British public policy is variable or uneven, with some policies and departments rather more affected than others. We also note that departmental attitudes towards the EU vary; some see it as a threat to their autonomy and priorities while others welcome the opportunities that EU membership offers for enacting mutually beneficial policies, often to tackle common problems that could not effectively be solved by Britain alone.

The same period has also witnessed the extension and acceleration of globalization, as partly indicated by the various transnational organizations that Britain is a member of and which themselves form a burgeoning system of international governance (but not, we emphasize, a world government). Yet quite apart from these sundry bodies, many erstwhile domestic policies are increasingly affected by globalization, particularly those concerning economic policies (due to the growing importance and power of multinational companies), although other problems also require extensive international cooperation, most notably issues pertaining to the environment/climate change and various forms of international crime.

One other manifestation of the internationalization of public policy in Britain that we briefly address in Chapter 7 is that of 'policy transfer', whereby some policies are 'imported' (with varying degrees of adaptation) from abroad, especially from the USA. This has been most evident with regard to welfare and penal policies.

Until relatively recently, implementation was considered a largely unproblematic or straightforward aspect of the policy process, representing the final part of a series of 'stages' through which public polices proceeded. However, as we explain in Chapter 8, implementation is often the 'stage' at which policies unravel or falter, as problems become apparent during the practical application and administration of them. A policy that was enthusiastically formulated in the core executive, and then formally approved by Parliament, may then encounter unforeseen difficulties when it is being applied in the real world or have unintended consequences.

What also has an impact on the success of a policy is the manner in which it is interpreted and applied by those ultimately responsible for implementation, namely 'street level bureaucrats'. Consequently, whereas implementation was previously viewed as a largely 'top-down' process that followed the policy-making 'stage', it is now widely recognized that implementation should also be seen as a 'bottom-up' process, whereby street level bureaucrats – doctors, local authorities, police officers, social workers, teachers, and so on – both shape public policy through the manner in which they apply it 'on the ground' and themselves discover problems with the original policy, which might then be reported back to 'the centre' and possibly result in the policy being amended. In other words it, it is now recognized that the implementation 'stage' itself contributes to policy making rather than merely following it: it is an integral part of a dynamic, ongoing 'process', not simply the end point.

In an attempt to overcome problems at the implementation 'stage', not least by ensuring that street level bureaucrats administer policies effectively, the past three decades have been characterized by the imposition of a new public management throughout Britain's public services, entailing much stricter top-down regulation and monitoring of professionals and front-line staff (and thus a corresponding diminution of autonomy and authority), both by general managers and by the application of numerous performance indicators and targets. To 'incentivise' public sector staff and other 'service providers', funding has increasingly been linked to the attainment of targets, thereby embedding a carrot-and-stick approach into the public sector.

We end, in Chapter 9, by examining the main ways in which policies in Britain have been subject to evaluation in recent years. We do not claim that policy evaluation is new *per se*, but that it has acquired increased importance in the last couple of decades. This is closely linked to the ministerial concerns, noted in Chapter 8, to ensure the compliance of 'street level bureaucrats' via the imposition of performance indicators and targets. These, of course, then need to be measured.

Consequently, since the early 1990s, public sector organizations and their staff have been subject to an increasing array of external audits and inspections to monitor and measure their efficiency and 'outputs'. As we note, however, these audits are themselves frequently criticized for numerous reasons, such as focusing on quantity rather than quality (the former being easier to measure 'objectively') and encouraging bureaucratic game playing or perverse incentives, whereby professionals focus primarily either on those activities that have had a target ascribed to them, or are going to be measured in the next audit or inspection. A system intended to improve efficiency can itself generate inefficiency!

In spite of such criticisms – which ministers usually dismiss as the predictable moaning of 'vested interests' in the public sector who are afraid of accountability and hard work – policy makers have become so enamoured with the apparently objective measurement and evaluation of policies that they have increasingly talked of 'evidence-based policy'. This is canvassed as a means of enacting policies that are not ideological, but are instead based on 'what works', as 'proved' through evaluation and measurement to gauge effectiveness and success. It also purports to instil greater rationality into policy making, rather than relying on merely 'muddling through'.

To gauge 'what works', a growing number of policies are being evaluated through 'pilot schemes', to ascertain their effectiveness and identify any problems prior to enacting the policy nationally or more widely. What this means, therefore, is that policies are increasingly being evaluated *before* being fully implemented, in addition to the more traditional post-implementation evaluation conducted via audits, inspection and parliamentary select committees. This, in turn, reminds us that in spite of the ordering and sequence of the chapters and topics in this book, the 'real world' of the policy process in Britain is much messier than linear or 'stagist' models suggest. This vital point needs to be borne in mind throughout what follows.

1 Problem Definition and Policy Agendas

Policy makers are faced with many demands for action to tackle a multitude of issues at any one time, so our first task must be to understand how and why only a few of those issues are likely to be defined as 'problems', and therefore prompt the development of policies to tackle them. It will also be important to acknowledge that even when a problem has been recognized as such, there will usually be more than one political perspective explaining its occurrence and underlying causes, which will thus yield different policy proposals.

As one political scientist has noted: 'Of the thousands and thousands of demands made upon government, only a small portion receive serious attention from public policy-makers' (Anderson, 2006: 87). This chapter will consider how the identification of problems, and the policies developed to address them, involves such factors as ideological perspectives, social construction, policy agendas, issue–attention cycles and policy streams. These concepts are all concerned in illustrating how and why some issues become defined as problems, and therefore lead to action by policy makers, while other alleged problems are denied or ignored.

THE ROLE OF IDEOLOGY AND POLITICS IN PROBLEM DEFINITION

Some problems will seem to be obvious or self-evident, such as high inflation, mass unemployment, or record levels of recorded crime, but even in such instances, the relevant figures or statistics will invariably be open to different interpretations, leading to political disagreements over the most appropriate policy response. Critics of a government might condemn it for presiding over record levels of unemployment, but ministers might argue that the rate of increase is slowing down, thereby implying that the numbers of jobless will soon start to fall. Or it might be claimed that Britain's level of unemployment is still lower than that of other major European economies, so that the apparently awful figures need to be placed in a broader context, whereupon they will not appear quite so bad after all. Such responses imply that existing policies will be continued rather than abandoned in favour of new ones.

A government might be faced with official statistics indicating record levels of crime during its term in Office, but ministers might seek to exonerate themselves by claiming that the figures reflect a greater willingness by citizens to report crime, rather than crime itself having actually increased.

Yet even when there is almost universal agreement over the development, existence or scale of a particular problem, there will invariably be political disagreements over the underlying causes and thus over the appropriate policies to tackle it. For example, high levels of unemployment might be viewed as evidence of a 'dependency culture' in which 'generous' welfare provision has undermined self-reliance and a work ethic. In attributing high unemployment to moral or attitudinal deficiencies among the unemployed themselves, this perspective will invariably lead to a Right-wing policy response, which both curbs social security entitlement (by imposing tighter eligibility criteria on claimants) and the financial level of benefits paid to each recipient.

Alternatively, high unemployment might be blamed on insufficient investment in economically deprived regions, inadequate provision of education and vocational training and/or failures in the operation of 'the market'. Such a critique would probably prompt a Left-wing policy response entailing an increase in the role of the state and more public expenditure, in order to create new jobs, boost consumer spending and tackle 'market failure'.

These two views of unemployment and their markedly different policy responses clearly reflect political ideologies. The Right readily blames individuals for being unemployed, depicting them as feckless, lazy and work-shy people who are happy to 'scrounge' off the welfare state and the taxes paid by the hard-working majority; in the language of Conservative ministers in the post-2010 coalition, 'shirkers, not workers', and 'skivers, not strivers'. From this perspective, what the unemployed need is tough treatment and punitive policies to make life 'on the dole' as difficult as possible.

In contrast, the Left invariably blames unemployment on structural factors, not least the failings of capitalism, which is deemed to be inherently prone to instability and thus oscillates between boom and slump, whereupon periodic mass unemployment ensues. For the Left therefore it is the economic system that needs to be reformed, while the unemployed 'victims' of capitalism deserve sympathy and support, not condemnation.

Another example whereby common recognition of a problem nonetheless leads to markedly different political conclusions about the underlying causes, and thus the most appropriate policies to solve them, was provided by the serious civil disorder that occurred in England in August 2011. Several cities were affected over four or five nights by gangs of (predominantly) young people engaging in arson, assaults, looting, vandalism and other forms of violence, with a few people being killed in the mayhem. Many inner city shops and businesses were destroyed, and many residents were left homeless; some initial estimates suggested that the total cost of the damage would be at least £100 million (Hawkes et al., 2011: 10). Inevitably, it seemed that virtually everyone, be they academics, ordinary citizens, newspaper columnists or politicians along with people commenting via online message boards and other social media, offered their often trenchant views on the underlying causes of the violent disorder, and *inter alia* the policies that they believed should be enacted in response.

One widely held view, but expressed particularly vigorously by commentators on the political Right, was that the violent disorder was a consequence of decades of excessive social liberalism or permissiveness (originating in the 1960s), which had steadily undermined respect for authority and prevented parents, police and teachers from imposing discipline, often because of an alleged obsession with 'human rights' and 'political correctness'.

This perspective also held that there had been too much emphasis by 'do gooders' on trying to empathize with sections of society who were anti-social, to the extent that bad behaviour and lack of personal or social responsibility were rarely, if ever, condemned; it was always assumed to be society's or someone else's fault when individuals or certain social groups engaged in anti-social behaviour or criminal activity.

There were also suggestions that the civil disorder was, directly or indirectly, linked to 'excessive' immigration. For example, the prominent historian and television presenter, Professor David Starkey, alleged that many white youths had 'become black' due to the influence of 'destructive, nihilistic gangster culture', which had become fashionable among many young people (*Newsnight*, 2011). For those subscribing to this explanation of the August 2011 urban riots, the recommended policy responses included: a very much stronger emphasis on law and order; tackling urban gangs; linking entitlement to welfare benefits and social housing to good behaviour; making those found guilty of causing criminal damage either recompense businesses or homeowners through deductions from their social security or be made to clean up the areas they had vandalised; bringing back national service or military conscription (to instil discipline and respect for authority); making it illegal to conceal one's face in public (a reference to 'hoodies'); repeal of the Human Rights Act; a halt to immigration.

Against this critique, many liberals and Left-leaning commentators – while condemning the perpetrators along with their violence and damage to property – nonetheless argued that the riots ultimately reflected the scale and depth of growing socio-economic deprivation and poverty in many parts of contemporary Britain, and the extent to which some individuals or groups now felt totally marginalized or excluded from mainstream society; they had 'parallel lives' to the rest of the population. This marginalization and alienation from the lifestyles, norms and values of the majority of the population was deemed to be both reflected and reinforced by lack of educational and employment opportunities, and a sense of being routinely ignored by mainstream society and politicians.

The ensuing resentment and frustration was also attributed to the scale of inequality in contemporary Britain, entailing an ever-widening gulf between the rich and the poorest, perceptions of greed and corruption among economic and political elites – MPs' expenses scandals, bankers' bonuses, telephone 'hacking' by some newspapers/journalists, and so on – and by way of sharp contrast the manner in which the bulk of the coalition government's cuts in public expenditure (to eradicate Britain's post-2008 fiscal deficit) were targeted almost entirely against recipients of welfare and citizens heavily reliant on soon-to-be cash-starved public services. For those subscribing to this critique, the proposed policy solutions included: more investment to combat social problems, and provide facilities and support for young people in deprived areas; reducing or reversing the planned cuts in public expenditure; narrowing the widening gap between rich and poor; abandoning the government's planned reduction in police numbers (which was the Home Office's main contribution to public expenditure cuts).

Of course, the different sets of policy proposals were not mutually exclusive, and many of those urging the latter range of policies nonetheless agreed that the individual perpetrators of criminal activity in the August 2011 riots should also be firmly punished. The point here, though, is that the riots prompted different explanations of their underlying causes and therefore yielded the advocacy of very different policies to prevent similar civil disorder in the future; these differences broadly reflected ideological perspectives and political values.

THE SOCIAL CONSTRUCTION OF PROBLEMS

Along with the role of ideology in defining (or denying) problems, it is also important to recognize that 'how a problem is defined depends not only on its objective dimensions, but also on how it is socially constructed' (Anderson, 2006: 83–4. See also Rochefort and Cobb, 1994: 5–7). This refers to the manner in which social or cultural values also play a major part in identifying how, why and when something or someone is defined as 'a problem', and therefore warrants attention from policy makers. At any moment in time, a particular set of social values or 'norms' (derived from a dominant ideology) is likely to prevail, providing the moral framework in which certain modes of behaviour or lifestyles are deemed acceptable or not and thus permissible or problematic.

Although these will often depict certain values or behaviour as 'common sense' or 'natural', they will often be socially or historically contingent. This is because many societal values and moral codes vary from one historical epoch to another; behaviour or lifestyles that might be deemed 'deviant', 'outrageous' or 'a threat to civilization' in one era might be widely accepted or even embraced a few decades later. Conversely, some activities or practices that were once accepted as a 'fact of life' might be judged unacceptable in subsequent decades. In other words, what is defined as 'problematic' behaviour actually varies over time, as cultural, moral and social values change. Some examples of this are outlined below.

Child abuse

The physical abuse of children is not in itself new or novel – some children have always been subject to bodily harm by certain adults – but only in recent years has 'child abuse' *per se* been identified, defined and recognized as a social problem, and so prompted policies to tackle it. What has fostered recognition of child abuse as a problem is the notion that children have certain inalienable rights, not least of which is the right to grow up free from being physically or sexually abused. This itself reflects a change in dominant attitudes in recent decades, for until the 1960s at least, not only was it widely believed that 'children should be seen but not heard', but more significantly, it was generally accepted that parents should be entitled to discipline their children as they wished; if that meant hitting their children, either with their hand, a stick or belt, it was no business of the law to intervene. How children were raised in the family home was considered to be an entirely private matter and so not an issue of public policy.

The abuse and ill-treatment of children was not recognized as a 'problem', due to the dominance of a particular set of societal norms and values that emphasized the need for discipline and obedience, and unquestioning respect for one's parents and other members of society in positions of authority, such as teachers and police officers. Hence the old aphorism 'spare the rod, spoil the child', meaning that a child would *not* grow up into a normal and socially useful adult if they were *not* subject to physical punishment during their childhood. Linked to this widely-held view was the notion that harsh treatment of children was 'character building', and would thus better prepare them for the 'hard knocks' of adult life that invariably awaited them; parental cruelty was apparently a form of kindness!

It is only relatively recently that the abuse and ill-treatment of children has been defined as a social problem, and resulted in policies to provide children with statutory protection from physical and sexual abuse, and to empower social workers to seek (via the courts) the removal, from the parental home, of children judged to be 'at risk'. Indeed, in the last decade or so, there has been occasional media-fuelled public anger and political condemnation when local authorities and social workers have failed to notice the physical or sexual abuse and ill-treatment of young children by their parents or step-parents, which has occasionally resulted in the child's death.

The rights of married women

Another example of a problem being recognized and defined by virtue of changes in social attitudes and the development of much more enlightened values, concerns the status and rights of married women. Until a few decades ago, wives were considered, in the eyes of the law, to be the property or 'chattel' of their husbands, whereupon married men were effectively entitled to behave as they wished towards their wives. Consequently, the law often tolerated such atrocities as men hitting their wives and sexual abuse, and marriage was assumed to confer certain 'conjugal rights' on the husband to the extent that a wife was always expected to accede to his sexual demands.

Indeed, it is only since the early 1990s that rape within marriage has finally been categorized as a criminal offence (like any other form of rape or sexual assault), while recognition of the crime of 'domestic violence' has led both to an expansion in the number of women's refuges and hostels, and more serious or sympathetic attention by the police. Previously, the police had often declined involvement in 'a domestic' when a wife reported her husband for assault, tending to treat such instances as a purely private matter (Hulley and Clarke, 1991: 18).

Sexual relationships

Sometimes, though, changing social values can result in a former 'problem' being re-defined, so that it is no longer considered as such by most people. A good example is provided by the history of homosexuality, for until the 1960s, sexual relationships between two men or two women were deemed to be 'deviant', morally unacceptable and socially repugnant, to the extent that it was unlawful for two men to have sex with each other, even in the privacy of their own homes (for a discussion of how sexuality is socially constructed as 'natural' or 'deviant', see Vance 1989; Weeks, 1992: 228–33, 240–6). Although same-sex relationships were decriminalized in 1967, via the Sexual Offences Act (see Dorey, 2006a), it was not until the 1990s that same-sex relationships became more widely accepted by public opinion, albeit with younger people generally proving rather much 'liberal' or relaxed about gays and lesbians than their grandparents.

Indeed, such has been the change in either public opinion or the political climate since the 1990s, that legislation has recently been enacted to allow 'civil partnerships' and same-sex marriages. Furthermore, same-sex couples in a long-term loving relationship can adopt children (although public opinion is perhaps less tolerant of this particular mode of gay and lesbian equality than it is of same-sex relationships in general).

The point remains though, that as recently as the 1980s, civil partnerships, gay marriages and gay/lesbian adoption of children would have been virtually unthinkable, and any prominent public figure who advocated such policies would have been vilified and deemed unfit or unworthy to hold public office. Certainly, when prominent political figures such as Ken Livingstone, as leader of the Greater London Council (GLC) in the mid-1980s, promoted 'gay rights' (in tandem with campaigns and policies to combat racism and sexism), he was regularly denigrated and ridiculed by many Conservatives and pro-Conservative newspapers as the public face of the 'loony Left'.

Meanwhile, other aspects of sexual behaviour and lifestyles have become much more widely accepted, whereas just a couple of generations ago, they would have been frowned upon or considered scandalous: sex before marriage (although it was always women who were expected to remain virgins until their wedding night, while men were often expected to 'sow their oats' before settling down and getting married!); divorce; living together prior to or instead of getting married ('living in sin'); and raising children without being married.

Hence, changes in public opinion or the political climate can be so profound that what is (or would be) deemed outrageous and wholly unacceptable in one era or for one generation, might not even raise an eyebrow a couple of decades later or among the next generation; it is no longer recognized as a problem by most people.

Drug (ab)use

To provide a final example of how dominant social norms and values effectively define what is deemed either desirable or deviant, and thereby socially construct who or what is defined as a problem warranting attention from policy makers, we can refer briefly to drug use in Britain. Here, as Hulley and Clarke (1991: 14) note, there has long been a clear distinction between legitimate and legal drug use, in the form of smoking cigarettes and drinking alcohol, and 'deviant', illegal drugs, such as cannabis, cocaine and heroin. Indeed, cigarettes have often been portrayed via the media as 'cool', glamorous, sexy or a sign of sophistication, while drinking alcohol has become so popular and extensive (not to say increasingly excessive) that it is those who are teetotal who have often been viewed as rather odd or unsocial.

Certainly, in many working-class communities and among many professional footballers, for example, heavy drinking has been – and still is – viewed as evidence of being 'hard' or macho and 'one of the lads', while getting drunk on a regular basis is considered almost *de rigueur* for many students; a rite of passage to full adulthood.

By contrast, those who consume other types of drugs have invariably been viewed as 'deviant' and quite possibly a menace to society. Those defined as 'drug users' are commonly assumed to be 'drop-outs' from society, and usually assumed to be unhealthy in lifestyle and unkempt in appearance, as well as probably being economically inactive, socially irresponsible, morally degenerate and even mentally unstable.

Now, one of the key arguments that has invariably been invoked against 'drugs' concerns the physical and socially undesirable consequences of using them. Cannabis is widely assumed to lead on to harder drugs (hence it is sometimes referred to as a 'gateway' drug), while many drugs are deemed addictive and can also lead to crime, as users steal in order to obtain the money necessary to 'feed their habit'. Yet cigarettes are also highly addictive, to the extent that many smokers struggle to give them up, while for some people, alcohol proves to be dangerously addictive, often resulting in marital breakdown and loss of family (as the spouse leaves, taking any children with them), dismissal from one's job, possible violence or other irrational behaviour, and, eventually, various illnesses deriving from excessive drinking. Yet drinkers are not warned: 'It might only be a couple of pints or glasses of wine now, but in a couple of years, it will be at least a bottle of vodka every day'.

Meanwhile, alcohol in Britain also fuels crime, as evidenced by the violence and vandalism evident in virtually any British town or city on a Friday or Saturday night. Interestingly, though, in other countries, heavy drinking at weekends does *not* normally result in violence or anti-social behaviour, as anyone who has visited cities such as Munich or Reykjavik will be able to testify (unless a British stag or hen party is in town). The apparent correlation between excessive alcohol consumption, anti-social behaviour, social disorder and violence does seem, sadly, to be a singularly British phenomenon, doubtless deriving from a range of cultural, historical and social factors.

The point here, though, is that what is defined as a drug or deemed a 'bad' drug to be prohibited, is socially constructed, reflecting dominant or widely-held social and moral values. These values have, at least until very recently, been widely accepted, so that alcohol and cigarettes have been widely viewed as natural and socially acceptable, and even somehow glamorous or stylish, while cannabis has been defined as a drug, with all the negative connotations that this invariably implies. That said, things do seem to be changing somewhat, as evinced by the 2007 ban on smoking in public places, and growing political concern over 'binge drinking'.

Social construction, therefore, has major implications for public policy because what is defined as 'deviant' will be subject to various laws or other sanctions to prohibit or regulate it, and quite possibly punish the 'deviants' who transgress these laws or social norms. In other words: 'How problems are defined, and who defines them, affect what response will be made to the problem' (Hulley and Clarke, 1991: 19).

THE ROLE OF POWER IN DEFINING OR DENYING PROBLEMS

Conversely, some 'issues' are *not* defined as problems requiring action by policy makers, because the dominant values or attitudes do not define them as a problem. For example, poverty and inequality have often *not* been defined as problems by policy makers, mainly because of what might be termed a 'dominant ideology' in Britain, whereby inequalities and disparities of wealth and income are widely accepted as natural, inevitable or necessary (in order to provide rewards and incentives for hard work and extra responsibilities).

Even during the latter half of the 2000s, when growing numbers of people were expressing disapproval of the six- or seven-figure salaries and bonuses being paid to many bankers and company bosses, and the consequent growing gap between the super-rich or top one per cent and the rest of the population (the other 99 per cent), there was limited sympathy for the poor *per se*, and hence little public support for wealth redistribution from the rich to the least well-off.

Instead, the dominant or most prevalent view among the British public was that many, if not most, of the poor were largely responsible for their lack of earnings or low incomes. Sundry opinion polls and the annual British Social Attitudes survey have regularly revealed that more people attribute poverty to laziness among the poor than to injustice, unfairness, greed by those at the top or capitalism itself. Furthermore, there is a widespread suspicion that many of the unemployed are 'work-shy' and could find a job if they really tried, and also that, while opportunities are certainly not equal, many of the 'disadvantaged' could still achieve more in life if they made greater effort and had stronger self-motivation – which they might do if they were not 'pampered' by the welfare state (see Dorey, 2010a; Dorey, 2011b: Chapter 5).

Some political scientists have used examples such as widespread, often unquestioned, acceptance of inequality and poverty to argue that there are 'hidden' faces or forms of power that serve to shape and constrain the definition of problems, and so shape the policy agenda in a manner that deflects or prevents challenges to the status quo or the existing allocation of resources, especially the unequal distribution of wealth and power. The 'first' and most obvious manifestation of power is when there is a visible conflict over a particular issue or advocacy of two different policies, and one policy actor's preferences or interests prevail over those of the other (see Dahl, 1961).

However, Bachrach and Baratz argued that this 'first face' fails to recognize more subtle or concealed exercises of power, because power is not only exercised when *A* prevails over *B* in a conflict of interests or preferences, but:

> ... is also exercised when *A* devotes his energies to creating or reinforcing social and political values and institutional practices that limit the scope of the political process to public consideration of only those issues which are comparatively innocuous to *A*. To the extent that *A* succeeds in doing this, is prevented, for all practical purposes, from bringing to the fore any issues that might in their resolution be seriously detrimental to *A*'s set of preferences.

> (Bachrach and Baratz, 1970: 7)

This is the 'second or 'hidden' face of power, whereby some individuals or institutions possess such power or importance that they can effectively (often without actually or visibly doing anything) limit political discussions and policy making to 'safe' issues; in other words, issues and policies that will not damage their own particular interests (Bachrach and Baratz, 1970: 7. See also Lukes, 1974: Chapter 3). This 'second face' of power offers a key explanation of why certain issues, such as poverty, inequality and 'excessive' boardroom or bankers' pay, have only rarely been defined as problems, because in a capitalist society in which inequalities of wealth are widely deemed natural or necessary, defining these features as problems might then entail policies that would be damaging or detrimental to the material interests of powerful sections of society, such as the business community, corporations and wealthy individuals.

Recognizing that their response to 'punitive' measures to limit their incomes or wealth would almost certainly be yet more tax evasion, or the relocation of their businesses overseas (thus resulting in a substantial loss of jobs and tax revenues in Britain), policy makers have usually shied away from consideration of anything more than the mildest of redistributive policies, a point clearly exemplified by the Blair governments in Britain after 1997, which was loathe to enact any policies which could be construed as anti-business or hostile to those on high salaries.

Indeed, radical policies – such as a statutory 'maximum salary' or a freeze on company directors' pay to counter 'boardroom greed' – are not even placed on the Cabinet's agenda. As such, no decision is actually taken *not* to pursue such policies, they are not seriously considered in the first place. They are automatically deemed 'out of bounds' or 'off message' from the outset; they are 'non-decisions' (Bachrach and Baratz, 1963; Bachrach and Baratz, 1970: 43–6). This means that very often, the choices or alternatives considered by policy makers are confined to a relatively narrow range of 'safe' options, which will not antagonize the interests of powerful sections of society.

Crucially, those possessing such power, by virtue of their economic position or importance (in terms of investment, generating employment or tax contributions), do not necessarily need to take an active or direct part in formal policy making because the official policy makers will usually be acutely aware of the need to avoid taking decisions that would upset those wielding economic power. As a consequence, when ministers meet to decide on a policy *vis-à-vis* a particular issue (especially of an economic character), their range of options is already narrowed considerably, hence the veracity of Schattschneider's (1960: 68) observation that 'the definition of the alternatives is the supreme instrument of power'.

The notion of a 'hidden/second face' of power was developed further by Steven Lukes, who suggested that there existed a 'third face' of power, whereby the most powerful group(s) in society can effectively impose a dominant set of values or beliefs on the rest of society. This helps to ensure that certain social issues are not even recognized – or socially constructed – as being problems, but instead, are simply assumed to be natural and taken for granted. As Lukes rhetorically enquires:

> … is it not the supreme and most insidious use of power to prevent people, to whatever degree, from having grievances by shaping their perceptions, cognitions and preferences in such a way that they accept their role in the existing order of things, either because they can see or imagine no alternative to it, or because they see it as natural and unchangeable, or because they value it as divinely ordained and beneficial?
>
> (Lukes, 1974: 24)

Lukes' model would not only explain why poverty and inequality are rarely subjected to serious attention or discussion by policy makers – that is, they do not normally appear on the policy agenda as acknowledged problems needing to be solved – but might also provide an explanation of why the poor or working class themselves have often seemed fatalistically to accept their relatively low incomes, even while those at the top are being paid millions and the gap between rich and poor is widening. The dominant ideology depicts inequality as natural or necessary, equates wealth with hard work, initiative, risk taking and success, while warning of the dire consequences of introducing higher taxes on the better off as part of a programme of wealth redistribution.

In so doing, it persuades the rest of the population, not least the poor themselves, that 'there is no alternative', and that any attempt at seriously changing the existing economic system or the distribution of earnings and incomes within it would be counter productive, due to the consequent withdrawal of investment by companies and emigration by the rich. In turn, this would result in a loss both of jobs and tax revenues, so that there would be higher unemployment, less money for the government to spend on welfare provision and (even) greater poverty. Through this 'dominant ideology', the poor themselves are subtly but constantly persuaded that any attempt at improving their position through redistributing wealth would actually serve to make them even worse-off. As Conservatives invariably argue: 'You won't make the poor richer by making the rich poorer'.

Whereas Marxists see this as a manifestation of a 'ruling class' or 'bourgeois' ideology, the vast majority of ordinary people and/or the working class seem to accept this scenario as a 'fact of life'; they evince a fatalistic acceptance of their economic hardship. Some of them are also persuaded that their low pay and lack of wealth is a consequence of 'too many immigrants' taking their jobs or undercutting wages, or because ordinary workers have to pay 'too much' tax in order to support social security 'scroungers'. In these ways, the poor are also susceptible to 'divide and rule', so that their impoverishment is not attributed to capitalism itself, profiteering by their employers or the 'greed' of the rich, but is blamed on other, more readily identifiable or visible sections of society, even though these too may be poor.

A literary representation of this working-class fatalism and passivity, coupled with a willingness to blame 'others' for their plight rather than 'the system', is Robert Tressell's classic novel *The Ragged-Trousered Philanthropists*, originally published in 1914, about a group of down trodden, exploited painters and decorators, who accept their ill treatment by employers and poverty-level wages, interspersed with periods of unemployment or pay cuts, as the natural order of things. Indeed, they readily accept that any attempt at improving their situation through political action will probably make things even worse. Consequently, the one painter who tries to persuade his workmates that society could and should be fairer, and that their poverty and ill treatment could be eradicated, is repeatedly ridiculed and condemned by the other painters for being either a utopian dreamer or a trouble maker (Tressell, 2012 [1914]).

This last point highlights another problem invariably encountered by those who are seen to challenge the 'dominant ideology' by criticizing the scale of inequality or poverty in a capitalist society like Britain; they will themselves be denigrated by those who benefit most from the existing system or who support it ideologically. The most common allegation in this context is that those who criticize the scale of inequality and the plight of the poor are promoting 'the politics of envy' or fomenting 'class warfare'. They might also be accused of being 'politically motivated'; citing inequality or poverty in order to promote their own 'extremist' political ideology. Or they might patronizingly be described as 'well meaning', but naïve about human nature or how the 'real world' operates.

In these respects, a dominant ideology not only depicts a state of affairs as being normal, an inevitable and immutable fact of life, but also characterizes those who would challenge it as being personally disreputable or motivated by baser, selfish motives, and therefore as untrustworthy. Hence, radical alternatives to the status quo and those campaigning for them, are routinely criticized or misrepresented to ensure that they do not win support from subordinate sections of society. The existing regime is ideologically portrayed as 'natural', whereas a 'fairer' system is depicted as 'un-natural' – as are those who are campaigning for it.

Meanwhile, the rest of society is readily persuaded that poverty is a consequence of individual failings or moral deficiencies among the poor themselves; they 'choose' to be poor by virtue of their irresponsible behaviour and lifestyle choices, or because social security benefits are too generous. As such, redistributive policies to tackle poverty and reduce inequality would effectively reward the poor for their alleged laziness and indolence, and therefore encourage them to continue with their disreputable or degenerate lifestyles, at the expense of the hard working, decent majority. This perspective has been central to the post-2010 coalition government's determination to reduce welfare provision, as evinced by the previously cited ministerial references to 'workers and shirkers', and 'strivers and skivers'.

Incidentally, this is a classic example of 'divide and rule', whereby subordinate groups or sections of society are encouraged to blame and hate each other (rather than 'the system', in this case, free market capitalism), while dominant groups or elites continue to enjoy their wealth and power unchallenged, and possibly, unnoticed. The rich are, quite literally perhaps, laughing all the way to the bank, while the poor bicker and squabble amongst themselves, and point the finger of blame at anyone and everyone except the rich or capitalism.

SYSTEMIC VS INSTITUTIONAL POLICY AGENDAS

Although we have hitherto referred to 'the policy agenda', as if it was a single entity, some writers have suggested that there are actually two different types of policy agenda, namely a 'systemic' agenda and an 'institutional' agenda. The systemic agenda is based on issues that are 'out there' in the wider political system (hence *systemic*), and which sundry individuals, journalists, academics, think tanks, organized interests or other bodies that are seeking to get acknowledged by policy makers as matters which are worthy of their attention. According to Cobb and Elder, the systemic agenda 'consists of all issues that are commonly perceived by members of the political community as meriting public attention and as involving matters within the legitimate jurisdiction of existing governmental authority' (Cobb and Elder, 1972: 82), and as such, 'is essentially a discussion agenda' (Anderson, 2006: 88).

However, what those involved in the systemic agenda are ultimately seeking to influence is the institutional agenda, which is comprised of those issues and problems which policy makers themselves have accepted need to be addressed. The institutional agenda is therefore a more formal agenda, 'composed of those problems to which public officials give serious and active attention' (Cobb and Elder, 1972: 85). It is 'an action agenda, and will be more specific and concrete than a systemic agenda' (Anderson, 2006: 88). Or as John Kingdon (1984: 205) explains:

A governmental [institutional] agenda is a list of subjects to which officials are paying some serious attention at any given time. Thus an agenda-setting process narrows the set of subjects that could conceivably occupy their attention to the list on which they actually do focus ... [are] seriously considered by governmental officials and those closely associated with them.

The institutional agenda will comprise a combination of ongoing or regularly recurring problems, such as curbing inflation, raising educational standards or tackling social security fraud and new problems – sometimes emerging via the systemic agenda – such as relatively new forms of crime (for example, mobile phone theft, cyber-stalking, human-trafficking/sex slavery, and so on), climate change, internet pornography (especially the ease with which it can be accessed by children), binge drinking or increasing obesity among sections of the population. Of course, many of the 'new' problems will subsequently join the ongoing or recurring problems on the institutional agenda.

While this distinction between systemic and institutional agendas is undoubtedly useful, and reflects how agenda setting and agenda management function on many occasions, it does raise important questions, not only about the ways in which issues become defined or recognized as problems, as discussed above, but how, when and why they move from one agenda to the other. Part of the answer is provided by the concept of 'issue attention cycles', which not only explains how an issue may move from the systemic to the institutional agenda, but how it may then move back off the institutional agenda, thence returning to the systemic agenda.

ISSUE ATTENTION CYCLES

The notion of an 'issue attention cycle' was developed by Anthony Downs (1972) who suggested that many problems tend to progress through five discrete stages, as outlined in Box 1.1.

Box 1.1 Downs' issue attention cycle

1 Pre-problem stage

Policy advocates or professionals might well be aware of, or discover, an issue that they believe constitutes a problem requiring political attention, but at this stage, the nature or scope of the problem has not been recognized by either the public, the media, or policy makers themselves.

2 Alarmed discovery and euphoric enthusiasm

The issue becomes recognized as a problem, whereupon it now receives attention from policy makers. Such recognition might be due to the success of policy advocates (discussed in the next chapter) in persuading the media and/or policy makers of the seriousness or extent of a problem or it might be a consequence of a crisis, which serves to bring the issue dramatically to public attention, thereby obliging policy makers to acknowledge the problem and be seen to act. At this point, the issue moves from the systemic agenda to the institutional agenda.

---

3 Realization of the costs that will be incurred by the solutions

Having acknowledged the problem and considered possible solutions, policy makers and/or the public become aware of the costs that will be incurred in tackling it, and thus lose interest in the problem. At this stage, the problem might consequently be deemed less serious than the 'costs', which are likely to accrue from solving it. These 'costs' might not necessarily be purely financial, but could entail other negative or undesirable consequences, such as higher unemployment or restrictions on individual liberty.

4 Decline in public interest in the issue

When the projected costs of a solution become known, the public is likely to lose interest in the issue, or broadly accepts the problem, possibly on the grounds that it represents the lesser of two (or more) evils. Alternatively, the public's attention might be drawn to a new issue, reflecting the fact that many people have limited attention spans.

5 Issue slips off or back down the policy agenda

The issue effectively disappears or slips back on to the systemic agenda, albeit possibly re-emerging at a later stage. In the meantime, other issues are likely to be moving from the systemic to the institutional policy agenda, and then go through the same cycle themselves.

Downs' 'issue attention cycle' thus provides an explanation of why the placing of an issue on the institutional agenda does not always lead to policy change. However, we would suggest that public interest in an issue also tends to dissipate – stage four – when there *is* a change of policy; once a problem appears to have been solved, or is thought likely to be solved imminently, due to action by policy makers, then the issue is likely to move back down or off the agenda, as the public loses interest and other issues attract their attention. Of course, this might encourage policy makers to enact a superficial measure in order to give the impression that 'something has been done', and thereby assuage public concern, albeit without genuinely tackling the underlying cause(s) of the problem. As such, we would offer a modified version of Downs' issue attention cycle, as illustrated in Figure 1.1.

However, when an issue slips back down or off the institutional policy agenda, in accordance with stage five of Downs' model, it will often re-emerge at a later stage, either when the costs of not addressing the issue originally becomes apparent or because the policy that was adopted has proved ineffective. This illustrates a point to which we referred in the Introduction, namely the circular, rather than linear, character of the policy process. Instead of assuming that policies proceed through stages with a clear beginning and end, they are better understood in terms of an ongoing cycle, whereby the problems they were intended to tackle often re-emerge at some point and thereupon necessitate either a new policy or modification of the original one.

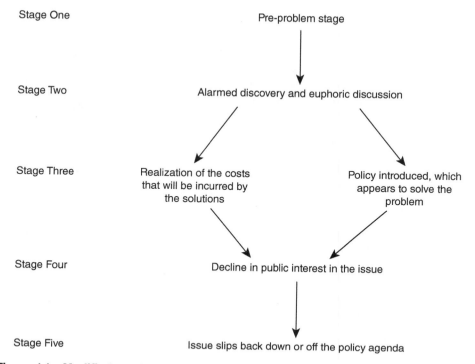

Stage One   Pre-problem stage

Stage Two   Alarmed discovery and euphoric discussion

Stage Three   Realization of the costs that will be incurred by the solutions   Policy introduced, which appears to solve the problem

Stage Four   Decline in public interest in the issue

Stage Five   Issue slips back down or off the policy agenda

Figure 1.1   Modified version of Downs' issue attention cycle

KINGDON'S MODEL OF POLICY CHANGE

Another very useful approach to understanding how and when issues move on to the institutional policy agenda as a prerequisite of introducing new policies is provided by John Kingdon (1984). He suggests that policy change requires the confluence of three 'streams' whose occasional flowing together creates (to switch metaphors) the opening of a 'policy window', as illustrated in Figure 1.2.

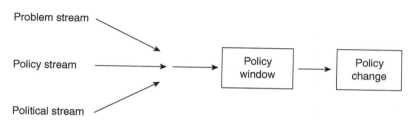

Problem stream

Policy stream

Political stream

Policy window

Policy change

Figure 1.2   John Kingdon's model of policy streams

The problem stream

As previously discussed, due to the manner in which they are ideologically defined or socially constructed, problems are not necessarily obvious or recognized as such. Alternatively, the scale or extent of a problem might not have been acknowledged or realized by policy makers, so that it remains on the systemic agenda. Indeed, the 'problem' might not yet have been recognized or discovered. Whether an issue is defined and acknowledged as a problem by policy makers depends on a range of factors, which we might term the 'four Is'.

- *Indicators* – usually of a quantitative or statistical kind, whereby data reveals that a particular phenomenon is increasing or decreasing in a manner that is deemed undesirable or/and unaffordable. For example, one of the reasons why the Conservative governments decided, during the late 1980s and early 1990s, that single parents were a problem, were figures which showed that their numbers had increased from 840,000 in 1979 to 1.5 million just over a decade later. Furthermore, while many of these were attributable to marital breakdown and divorce, it was also discovered that the number of unmarried mothers had increased from 160,000 in 1981 to 430,000 in 1991, with the total amount of welfare benefits paid annually to single parents having risen from £2.4 billion to £6 billion during the same period. For Conservatives subscribing to a particular view of the family – based on a married man and woman jointly bringing up their children – and also committed to curbing public expenditure (one-third of which was consumed by social security), these statistics were clearly a cause for concern. Consequently, lone parents became defined as a problem that policy makers felt compelled to address, resulting in the establishment of the Child Support Agency in 1993 and John Major's ill-fated 'back to basics' campaign (Dorey, 1998; Dorey, 2000).
- *Interpretation* – whereby policy makers make judgements about whether a particular issue or set of indicators constitutes a problem warranting their attention or action. It has always been axiomatic in the social sciences that, contrary to 'common sense' convention or saloon-bar wisdom, 'the facts' do *not* 'speak for themselves', but have to be interpreted and explained (see Irvine et al., 1979). Interpretation of data or other indicators is itself an important part of defining a problem, and therefore of getting it placed onto the institutional agenda.
- *Ideology* – whereupon the dominant values, norms and beliefs of policy makers will play an important role in defining an issue as a problem requiring political attention. This, to a considerable extent, follows on from the previous point about interpretation, for a particular issue or phenomenon might be deemed a problem according to one ideological perspective, but not according to an alternative ideological stance; poverty being a good example.
- *Instances* – meaning that particular events, when they receive extensive or intensive media coverage, draw attention to an issue or social phenomenon and prompt policy makers to respond accordingly. For example, a major rail or air crash is likely to result in demands for tougher transport safety measures. Alternatively, the media might invoke what sociologists call a 'moral panic', for example a series of reports of horrific attacks on young children by 'dangerous dogs'. Such events, especially when they are graphic and the consequences are clearly visible, alert people's attention to particular issues, serves to define them as problems and thereby leads to demands that 'something must be done' to tackle them.

The policy stream

This second of Kingdon's three streams refers to the manner in which problems, once formally acknowledged, are accompanied by the advocacy of a particular policy, or set of policies, which their proponents claim will provide the solution. Kingdon suggests that at any given juncture, there are a great many policies and policy proposals being devised, developed or drafted by policy makers and other 'policy advocates' (see next chapter).

This plethora of policies is deemed by Kingdon to resemble a 'primeval soup' in which numerous measures are constantly floating around, sometimes bubbling to the surface, in which case they may be extracted and applied to a particular problem or instead be dismissed as inappropriate or impracticable, whereupon they will be discarded and sink back into the 'primeval soup'. He suggests that the various policy actors 'each have their pet ideas or axes to grind; they float their ideas up and the ideas bubble around', whereupon 'some ideas or proposals are taken seriously and others are discarded' (Kingdon, 1984: 87). Kingdon elaborates by explaining that:

> … many ideas are possible in principle and float around in a 'policy soup' in which specialists try out their ideas in a variety of ways … proposals are floated, come into contact with one another, are revised and combined with one another, and floated again … the proposals that survive to the status of serious consideration meet several criteria, including their technical feasibility, their fit with dominant values and the current national mood, their budgetary workability, and the political support or opposition they might experience. Thus the selection system narrows the set of conceivable proposals and selects from that large set a short list of proposals that is actually available for serious consideration.

In this 'primeval soup', therefore, there are (potential) policies that have not yet been successfully attached to a problem and policies that have previously been extracted, only to be thrown back in when they were no longer favoured, perhaps because their likely costs have been realized, in accordance with stage three of Downs' issue attention cycle above.

Crucially, though, the policy stream not only entails policy makers and policy advocates seeking to develop or promote solutions in response to the emergence and identification of particular problems, it also involves policy makers and policy advocates searching for problems to which they can attach or apply a favoured idea or policy. Or as Kingdon himself expresses it, as part of the process of agenda setting, policy advocates 'lie in wait in and around government with their solutions at hand, waiting for problems to float by to which they can attach their solutions' (Kingdon, 1995: 165).

This point has more recently been confirmed by Stephanie Flanders, who became the BBC's economics editor in 2008, having previously worked in the USA's Treasury department and subsequently written lead articles in *The Financial Times*. With regard to economic policy in Britain, she notes that:

> You do often find out from talking to Treasury officials or former Treasury officers that no idea is entirely new. It usually has come from some staffer or official, and the Treasury has been pushing it internally for some time, when they eventually find a Chancellor who's prepared to do it.

(Quoted in Williams, 2012: 30)

Yet even if a proposed policy solution is attached to a problem, this in itself does not guarantee that it will be adopted and enacted. For this to occur requires that the third of Kingdon's streams joins the other two, so that all three are flowing together, at least temporarily.

The political stream

By the 'political stream', Kingdon means wider events or circumstances, such as 'swings of national mood, vagaries of public opinion, election results, changes of administration, shifts in partisan ideological distributions [in Parliament] and interest group pressure campaigns' (Kingdon, 1995: 87), which provide the opportunity and situation in which policy change can be enacted; a new policy introduced. Of course, recognition of a problem and the successful advocacy of a popular solution can themselves often contribute to the political stream, by facilitating a significant shift in public opinion or even the election of a government with a rather different ideological orientation and set of policy preferences. Yet many potential policy solutions to problems are not implemented because they do not encounter favourable political circumstances; the problem stream and policy stream are not joined by the political stream, and so the opportunity for enacting a new policy is lost, at least for the time being.

When these three 'streams' (problem, policy and political) do flow together, Kingdon switches metaphor by suggesting that a 'policy window' opens, providing a unique opportunity for policy change to occur. On such occasions, the recognition of a particular problem, increased support for a proposed solution and the 'right' political circumstances combine to ensure that the issue moves to the top of the (institutional) policy agenda, and provides a major opportunity to introduce a new policy. Kingdon (1995: 20) explains that these 'windows are either opened by the appearance of compelling problems or by happenings in the political stream … The separate streams of problems, policies and politics come together at certain critical times … Solutions become joined to problems, and both of them are joined to favourable political forces'. It is when all three occur simultaneously that a new policy is most likely to be enacted.

Certainly, the prominent free market economist, Milton Friedman (who has been revered by many Conservatives since the 1970s, not least Margaret Thatcher), believed that: 'Only a crisis – actual or perceived – produces real change. When that crisis occurs, the actions that are taken depend on the ideas that are lying around' (Friedman, 2002: xiv). In other words, in such circumstances, policy makers do not necessarily create policies *de novo*; they will often use the crisis as the opportunity to apply policies they have favoured or advocated for many years, long before the crisis occurred.

When it occurs, a crisis often serves to discredit the intellectual or ideological paradigm and concomitant policies that had previously prevailed. This then provides the context in which radical or markedly different policies, based on new ideas (or old ideas given a new lease of life), can be implemented. The crisis therefore provides a justification, or means of legitimation, for policies that would have been widely viewed as extreme or unrealistic prior to the crisis. For example, some Conservatives were viewing the trade unions as a problem back in the 1950s, and in so doing, they proposed various policies, which they believed would solve the 'trade union problem' in Britain. However, these policies, of which secret ballots prior to strikes and weakening the close shop (i.e., compulsory trade union membership in some occupations) were the most frequently advocated, were at odds with the conciliatory approach of the 1951–64 Conservative governments, which wanted to avoid conflict or confrontation with the trade unions (Dorey, 2009a; Dorey, 2009b). Although Edward Heath's 1970–74 Conservative government then attempted to enact some of these measures via the 1971 Industrial Relations Act, he felt obliged to abandon the policy in the face of trade union opposition and 'industrial muscle', as well as anxiety among various ministerial colleagues. In retrospect, there was widespread agreement both among many Conservatives and academic commentators that Heath had attempted too much too soon, and that the time had not quite been right: the problem and policy streams had not yet met the political stream.

Not until 1979 did the political stream appear, and merge with the problem and policy streams to provide the necessary 'policy window' to attack the trade unions, and reduce their role and influence in economic affairs. By 1979, the trade unions were deemed a major problem by many more people and therefore policies such as strike ballots, ballots to elect union leaders, curbing the closed shop and restricting mass picketing during industrial disputes were much more popular, both in the Conservative Party and amongst the electorate. As one senior and highly-respected Conservative, William Whitelaw, remarked: 'It needed further hard experience culminating in the Winter of Discontent in 1978 … before the British people were ready to give continuous backing to a Government for trade union reform' (Whitelaw, 1989: 75–6).

By this time, though, the 'political stream' was reinforced by the ideological shift occurring within the Conservative Party, whereby the One Nation Tories who had largely dominated since the 1940s were steadily being supplanted by Thatcherites. As a consequence, the constructive, partnership approach towards the trade unions, which One Nation Tories had patiently pursued, was enthusiastically discarded in favour of policies fully intended to reduce union power and curb their activities permanently; conciliation was consciously replaced by confrontation. Thus did 1979 provide the 'policy window' that enabled trade union reform to move to the top of the institutional policy agenda.

However, because 'policy windows' are only usually open very briefly, before the three policy streams flow apart again, the opportunities for initiating new policies are often relatively rare or sporadic. If the 'policy window' closes before a policy initiative is enacted, the public and/or policy makers might well lose interest in the issue concerned, particularly if other issues have risen to prominence. In this regard, Kingdon's concept of policy streams should be regarded as complementing Downs' notion of an issue attention cycle, rather than superseding it.

Much more recently and rather more generally, the post-2008 global economic recession, followed by the formation of a Conservative-dominated coalition government in Britain in May 2010, has provided Conservatives with the opportunity to go even further than the Thatcher governments of the 1980s in transferring public services to the private sector and dismantling the welfare state. In so doing, Conservatives have repeatedly cited the dire economic situation, most notably the fiscal deficit, as 'evidence' that public spending on social security, pensions, the NHS and the public sector in general, has been excessive (due in large part to the alleged fiscal recklessness and irresponsibility of the 1997–2010 Labour governments) and is no longer sustainable or even desirable.

Consequently and in spite of serious reservations among many Liberal Democrats, Conservatives have used the post-2008 crisis to enact a series of radical reforms to public services and social provision, including opening-up the NHS, schools and universities to the private sector, increasing student fees to £9,000 per annum, raising the retirement age, and imposing major curbs both on entitlement to social security benefits and the amount that claimants can receive.

It is highly unlikely that such radical and wide-ranging policies would have been enacted or as widely supported by the public without the post-2008 serious economic downturn and large fiscal deficit, because in a period of prosperity and correspondingly higher Treasury tax receipts, most of the expenditure that is being cut by the coalition government would have been (more) affordable. Consequently, such a major programme of cuts would have lacked the degree of justification or legitimacy that they acquire in a period of economic crisis.

This further illustrates Kingdon's crucial point that policy change does not simply require that particular policies are available to be applied to particular problems, but that the political circumstances are also conducive to implementing the new policies or major policy changes. Or as Cortell has observed: 'Every trigger – whether a crisis or non-crisis situation – creates the opportunity for structural change if it discredits existing institutions or raises concerns about the adequacy of current policy-making processes' (Cortell, 1997: 9. See also Cortell and Peterson, 1999).

In this context, we should acknowledge Naomi Klein's (2007) notion of the 'Shock Doctrine', whereby advocates of radical political change, most notably economic neo-liberals, enthusiastically exploit an economic crisis and associated social or political instability to impose the changes necessary to recreate society in accordance with their unique ideological vision or own material interests. The crisis situation facilitates radical change in two discrete ways.

First, justification for such changes is usually easier in a period of crisis; many citizens are likely to be much more readily persuaded of the need for greater labour market flexibility (longer working hours, pay cuts or freezes, less employment protection, fewer workers' rights, hire-and-fire labour laws, lower taxes, privatization and major welfare cuts) in a time of economic crisis.

Furthermore, not only are proponents of radical change able to insist that harsh measures are unavoidable in the circumstances, but also that the previous (social democratic) ideology or (Left-of-centre) government had *caused* the current crisis, and thereby 'proved' that the erstwhile approach was dangerous and unsustainable; there is now 'no alternative' to the new policies. Hence the coalition government's 'narrative' that Britain's post-2008 economic crisis was caused by the financial profligacy and economic incompetence of Gordon Brown and New Labour, regardless of the fact that most Western economies have suffered similarly, not least the USA. By blaming the post-2008 economic crisis on Brown and Labour, public attention can be diverted from the possibility that the crisis is actually a consequence of three decades of increasingly aggressive neo-liberalism and the unregulated international banking system, which many Conservatives worship. Blame is ascribed to a particular individual or government, not to the economic system itself. This has the added advantage that Labour's subsequent criticisms of the coalition's economic policies will often lack credibility, enabling ministers to denigrate and dismiss them with total contempt.

Second, Klein emphasizes how a period of economic crisis means that much of the population is itself in a state of shock, which enables the political drivers of radical change to utilize the citizenry's psychological state to their own advantage. Certainly, such circumstances are ideal for playing divide and rule, whereby one section of society is persuaded to support a particular policy by turning them against another (minority) section of society which is, or can be rendered through propaganda, unpopular and thus undeserving.

Thus has the Conservative-dominated coalition government in Britain since May 2010 repeatedly encouraged workers in the private sector to believe that public sector workers enjoy unfair and unaffordable material advantages in terms of better pay, 'gold-plated' pensions, earlier retirement and jobs for life, all apparently funded by the taxes of the hard-working, wealth-creating, private sector. Such a characterization is deliberately intended to garner support among private sector workers for cuts in the 'unaffordable' and 'over-generous' pay and pensions of public sector workers, as well as a major reduction in the size of the 'bloated' public sector. Ironically, this can also be viewed as promoting 'the politics of envy', something which Conservatives condemn the Left for when it criticizes the rich or the scale of inequality.

At the same time and for the same reason, 'hard-working families' have been encouraged to believe that their taxes are being squandered on social security 'scroungers' who choose to live on 'generous' welfare benefits rather than actively seek employment. In particular, Conservatives and pro-Conservative newspapers have assiduously propagated the view that many welfare claimants live in expensive, quite luxurious, accommodation (which ordinary working people cannot afford themselves) due to the alleged generosity of the Housing Benefit system in paying their rent. Again, the purpose is to win support among the working population for drastic cuts in the social security benefits paid to the unemployed and much tighter eligibility conditions being imposed on the jobless. Hence the afore-mentioned ministerial rhetoric concerning 'workers' versus 'shirkers' and 'strivers' versus 'skivers'.

A similar thesis is advanced by Mirowski (2013) in his book *Never Let a Serious Crisis Go To Waste*. He examines how the international economic crisis of recent years, far from consigning neo-liberalism to the dustbin of history, has actually been seized upon by neo-liberals as 'evidence' of the need to reduce government regulation and welfare provision even further and more vigorously. Mirowski claims that for neo-liberals, no economic calamity or crisis is ever acknowledged as proof of the limits or dysfunctions of the free market, but instead, as proof that the principles and practices of the free market economics merely need to be applied even more rigorously and robustly, and as such, that there is no viable alternative.

In this respect, we would suggest that in spite of being at opposite ends of the ideological spectrum, today's neo-liberals are rather akin to the Communist rulers of the pre-1990 Soviet Union, for neither was able or willing to accept that their ideas were simply erroneous or ultimately unworkable in practice. On the contrary, neo-liberals and Communists alike possessed an unwavering conviction that the academic theories on which their ideologies were based are so intellectually coherent or philosophically logical that they *must* be correct or true; Soviet Communists could cite *ad nauseum* the theories of Karl Marx, Friedrich Engels and Vladimir Lenin to legitimize their policies, while Anglo-American neo-liberals readily quote from Adam Smith, Milton Friedman and Friedrich Hayek to justify more privatization, tax cuts for the rich and big business, coupled with further reductions in welfare provision for the poor and unemployed.

Convinced of the intellectual logic and theoretical rationality of their respective ideologies, communists and neo-liberals automatically assume that any problems that arise from the practical application of their ideas are caused by individuals or institutions failing to act in accordance with the philosophical principles underpinning the respective ideologies. The solution, therefore, is simply to 'deal with' these individuals or institutions and impose the ideology with even greater rigour.

Thus were Soviet Communists convinced that any problems occurring in a state-owned, centrally-planned economy could only be solved by even greater state control and central planning to eradicate them, while today's neo-liberals possess an unshakeable conviction that any and every economic problem signifies the need for an even purer and stronger application of free market economics. In both regimes, the prime beneficiaries are the economic and political elites themselves, while further hardship and increasing misery ensues for the vast majority of the population.

Yet in both regimes, the governing elites and media persuade the citizens that it is the 'other' ideology or regime that is dangerous, unworkable and tyrannical; this serves as a grave warning against seeking regime change and persuades the masses that there really is no (viable) alternative.

THE 'GARBAGE CAN' MODEL

This notion of a primeval soup to which Kingdon alludes can be viewed as an adaptation of another metaphor of the early stages of the policy process, namely the notion of a 'garbage can', as suggested by Cohen et al. (1972). In the context of making choices about which problems to address and which policies to adopt, the garbage can is a repository 'into which various problems and solutions are dumped by participants', but which are then retrieved at a later stage. At any moment, some policy makers will be rummaging in the 'garbage can' for a solution to a problem, while others are sifting through the contents of the garbage can searching for previously discarded 'problems' (one which has perhaps slipped off the 'issue attention cycle') to which they can attach their favoured policy 'solution'.

In advancing the garbage can model or metaphor, Cohen et al. (1972: 2) suggest that 'an organization is a collection of choices looking for problems, issues … looking for decision structures in which they might be aired, solutions looking for issues to which they might be the answer, and decision-makers looking for work.' The 'garbage can' analogy illustrates the often chaotic or disjointed character of much policy making, whereby problems and proposed solutions not only compete for the attention of policy makers, but themselves rise and fall, before re-emerging or being 'rediscovered' and revived by another policy maker (or policy advocate) at a later date.

As with Kingdon's 'policy streams', the 'garbage can' model highlights the manner in which policies are not always devised solely or sequentially in response to a new (or re-emerging) problem, but that advocates of a policy will themselves search for or identify a problem to which their favoured policy purports to provide a solution. These advocates might favour a particular policy because it reflects their ideological beliefs or objectives, or perhaps because it would serve their material interests (of course, ideological beliefs and material interests are not always mutually exclusive; indeed, they might be inextricably linked), but either way, the policy advocates will seek to win support for their preferred policy by presenting it as the most practicable solution to a particular problem. For example, economic liberals who believe, as a matter of principle, in a low tax economy will invariably argue that cutting taxes will solve several problems or achieve numerous valuable objectives, most notably: empowering consumers (by enabling individuals to decide how to spend their money, rather than having it spent on their behalf by the state); boosting economic growth, as people have more disposable income; reducing tax evasion by the rich and big business; providing more incentives and rewards for hard-work; retain employment and investment by firms who would otherwise relocate abroad to escape high taxation; reduce the number of talented individuals emigrating because of 'excessive' taxation.

The 'garbage can' model also reaffirms the point made in our Introduction about the messiness of the policy process, and the extent to which the reality of policy making often diverges markedly from 'stagist' and 'sequential' models of policy making. Policies are not always devised in response to the emergence of a problem, but instead advocates of a policy will often rummage in the 'garbage can' for a problem to which the favoured policy can be presented as the solution, thereby hopefully winning wider support for it, and ultimately resulting in its adoption and enactment by official policy makers. Or as Mucciaroni (1992: 461) notes in his characterization of the 'garbage can' model:

> [Policy] Entrepreneurs decide which problems to dramatize, choose which solutions to push, and formulate political strategies to bring their issues onto the agenda. Actors in the process develop problem definitions and solutions … link them together, and make them congruent with existing political conditions.

We can therefore recognize that the 'garbage can' model depicts a very different vision of policy making than the rational model, because rather than a problem prompting a 'rational' or cost-benefit evaluation of several possible policies, a particular policy option will sometimes be selected prior to the emergence or formal identification of a problem. Yet even when a policy is adopted *after* a problem has been identified or defined as such, it will often derive from ideological goals and values, or perception of material interests, rather than an objective evaluation of the 'pros and cons' of various options, as suggested by the rational model. Besides, even an ostensibly 'objective evaluation' of policy options will invariably be conducted within a government's general ideological perspective or strategic objectives. This is a point to which we return in Chapter 9 when we examine aspects of policy evaluation, including the relatively recent ministerial penchant for 'evidence-based' policies.

HOW GOVERNMENTS SEEK TO MANAGE THE INSTITUTIONAL POLICY AGENDA

So far, we have considered how ideas and issues are defined and developed, and thereby pushed onto or further up the institutional policy agenda. What we now need to consider is how policy makers – particularly governments and their ministers – seek to manage the institutional agenda, in terms of their responses to issues or problems.

Agree and act

Clearly, if ministers accept the existence of a specific problem, are genuinely concerned to tackle it, have an appropriate policy available or readily accessible and the necessary resources are available, then it is highly likely that the relevant measure will be enacted.

If this is the case, and the problem appears to have been solved or looks as if it will be in the very near future (once the policy has started to effect an impact), then the issue is likely to slip back down or off the policy agenda (stages four and five of Downs' 'issue attention cycle'). Policy makers and the public will assume that the problem has been dealt with.

Yet as we will discover in Chapter 8, new policies often fail to achieve their objectives or at least not to the extent originally intended. This is because once a new policy or law has been enacted and is being implemented at sub-national or local level, it might well encounter unforeseen problems that can undermine its effectiveness or practicability. In such instances, the issue or problem is likely to re-emerge or receive renewed attention via the systemic agenda and move back onto the institutional agenda for corrective action.

Acknowledge a problem, but defer action

On other occasions, however, although ministers might acknowledge the emergence or existence of a particular problem, they might not have a policy readily available, or they might not really want to tackle it (perhaps for ideological or partisan reasons, or the envisaged costs that would be incurred). In such circumstances, they are likely to insist on the need for further research into the issue, possibly involving some form of inquiry. Such an investigation might be undertaken by various bodies: a Cabinet committee; an official committee (comprising senior civil servants from the relevant department), a 'working party' (comprising ministers, senior civil servants policy advisers and/or outside experts); a committee of inquiry; a royal commission. A government resorting to such inquiries into a particular issue or problem will usually be guided by one of four motives.

- It will genuinely be seeking a solution to the problem, recognizing the need to ascertain the underlying causes of a problem and/or the efficacy of possible policy solutions, on the basis either of their respective costs and benefits, or their administrative/technical practicability. This will necessitate thorough research, in order to investigate the scale and cause(s) of the problem, prior to devising an appropriate policy.
- Ministers will recognize the need either to introduce a new policy or perhaps modify an existing policy, but will want these to be endorsed by some form of independent and impartial inquiry. This will reflect a desire to imbue the policy with greater justification or credibility in the eyes of the public or even with the government's own backbenchers. By establishing an independent inquiry or Royal Commission chaired by a highly respected 'establishment figure' – a member of the 'great and good' as Peter Hennessy (1986) once expressed it – ministers will hope that the ensuing policy or reform will enjoy greater legitimacy.
- The government will be hoping that the inquiry will provide evidence or arguments, which ministers can then cite as justification for *not* changing existing policy. The inquiry's report might highlight the financial, employment or social costs of a particular policy proposal for example, or perhaps the manner in which implementation would be impracticable or unenforceable. This would correspond to the third, fourth and fifth phases of Downs' 'issue attention cycle' (as outlined above).
- Ministers will be hoping that while the issue is being investigated by an official inquiry, the problem itself will somehow disappear or even resolve itself. At the very least, it will be hoped that public interest will dissipate by the time that any report and its recommendations are published, thereby further obviating the need to introduce a new policy. In this respect,

committees of inquiry or royal commissions might be invoked as stalling mechanisms, enabling ministers to 'buy time' until the issue falls back down or off the policy agenda, or is overtaken by other events.

Whatever the precise motive(s), establishing a formal inquiry into an issue or problem will at least give the impression that policy makers are seriously considering the underlying causes and thus how it can be successfully solved, even when the real motive might be to avoid taking any action.

Place problems in comparative context

Another way in which governments sometimes seek to manage the institutional agenda, in order to remove or downgrade issues that they do not wish to act upon, is to place an alleged problem in comparative perspective, in order to reduce its significance or seriousness. In such instances, comparisons may be historical or international. Placing an alleged problem in historical context will be intended to illustrate that the issue is less prevalent or serious than it was maybe 20, 50 or 100 years ago (or maybe even just last year) and does not therefore warrant action by policy makers. For example, this has often been the response of politicians when faced with calls to tackle poverty, whereupon the position of the poor today is compared favourably to the plight of the poor in Victorian or inter-war Britain.

Crime is another policy issue where governments are inclined to place statistics in historical-comparative context in order to show either that levels of crime overall are falling, or if this is not possible, that particular types of crime have diminished over the last x years. In so doing, they may also seek to show that the likelihood of being a victim of a particular type of crime is statistically much lower today than it was 20 or 40 years ago, for example. Of course, such statistics might not assuage public anxiety about crime and the common perception that crime is increasing, but they are nonetheless often cited by governments uncertain about what else they can do to combat crime, other than persevere with their existing law and order policy.

The other 'comparator' sometimes invoked by policy makers to avoid (further) action on a particular issue is to place it in an international context and show that the alleged problem is less extensive or significant in Britain than in various other countries. For example, when a government is faced by an increase in the number of people officially registered as unemployed, it might claim that Britain's level of unemployment remains lower than that in France/Germany/Italy/Spain or wherever, or that it is increasing at a slower rate in Britain than in other such countries. Alternatively, it might cite figures to show that more jobs have been created in Britain during the last x months or years than in other comparable countries, so that Britain's jobless have a greater chance of finding employment than their foreign counterparts.

Through invoking such comparative 'evidence', governments will seek either to deny the existence of an alleged problem that is being canvassed via the systemic agenda, or deny that it is as serious or extensive as others are claiming. In so doing, ministers will be offering a justification for their intention to persevere with existing policies rather than enact new ones.

Dispute the definitions or data

Sometimes, when faced with demands for action to tackle an alleged problem, governments might query the definition that is being deployed or the accuracy of the statistics being cited by those urging ministerial action. This is particularly true with regard to the issue of poverty, for the definitions of what constitutes poverty are always subject to debate and disagreement. For example, when Left-leaning commentators or politicians talk about poverty in Britain today, they are usually referring to what is known as 'relative' poverty, which compares the poor to the rest of society in terms of how far they are falling behind economically, perhaps in relation to average earnings or their inability to participate in social or cultural activities due to low incomes; they are effectively excluded socially due to their lack of economic resources.

Against this, though, Right-wing commentators and Conservatives usually refer to 'absolute' poverty, whereby people literally do not have enough money to pay for the absolute basics in life, most notably food or domestic fuel. Such poverty, they claim, no longer exists in Britain because the existence of the welfare state means that absolutely no one need go hungry or shiver in winter due to lack of money. This often entails another historical comparator, whereby 'absolute' poverty is deemed a feature of the 19th or early 20th century when lack of welfare provision really did mean that some people risked starvation or hypothermia; such poverty, though, is said to have been eradicated in modern Britain.

Furthermore, those who adopt the 'absolute' definition of poverty in Britain today, in order to deny the problem, would doubtless point out that many of 'the poor' now have smartphones, large wall-mounted plasma TV screens, designer-label trainers (and other fashion accessories) and often drink or smoke. This, it would be claimed, is hardly the destitution and severe hardship redolent of life in the inner-city slums of Victorian Britain or the novels of Charles Dickens. As such, the existence of poverty is either denied or deemed to have been greatly diminished, so that new measures to combat poverty are deemed unnecessary. In this example, ministers are effectively denying claims about the scale of poverty by invoking a different definition or criterion of what constitutes poverty and thereby producing more 'favourable' statistical evidence. This tactic effectively entails: 'Changing the definition of terms in order to create a desired effect' and is often done in order to 'massage' official unemployment figures by narrowing the definition of unemployment (Government Statisticians' Collective, 1979: 148–9).

Question or impugn the motives of policy advocates

One final means by which governments might seek to manage the institutional policy agenda in order to keep off or remove issues they do not want to address is to challenge those individuals or institutions who are citing a problem in order to promote a particular policy. This will often entail querying their motives or asking who they are acting on behalf of – who do they really represent? If they can be discredited and their authenticity or legitimacy undermined, then their policy proposal(s) can similarly be discredited, thereby enabling governments and ministers to avoid enacting particular policies.

Again, the issues of poverty and inequality provide a useful illustration, for when Left-leaning commentators or politicians criticize the immense wealth of the rich, or condemn the 'excessive' pay or bonuses awarded to bankers and the bosses of large companies, the Right invariably accuses such critics of promoting 'the politics of envy'. Certainly, Margaret Thatcher once claimed that there existed in Britain 'a powerful and vocal lobby pressing for greater equality, in some cases even, it would seem, for total equality', but its motives, she alleged, were often 'an undistinguished combination of envy and what might be called "bourgeois guilt". Envy is clearly at work in the case of the egalitarian who resents the gap between himself and those who are better off' (Thatcher, 1975). Similarly,

Chris Patten claimed that 'envy' of the rich and successful was 'often the bed-fellow of egalitarianism' (Patten, 1983: 93. See also Gilmour, 1978: 176). Thus did the Conservatives' 1979 election manifesto accuse the Labour Party of 'practising the politics of envy', whereupon 'they have set one group against another in an often bitter struggle to gain a larger share of a weak economy' (Conservative Party, 1979: 6).

Similarly, when policies purporting to strengthen law and order or national security are introduced, those who criticize them for restricting civil liberties or violating human rights are likely to be accused of being 'on the side' of criminals or terrorists. At the very least, critics will be told that they are naïve in not appreciating how dangerous the world is and how wicked some people really are. Besides, it might be added, if people are innocent, then they have nothing to fear; only those with something to hide or who are a threat (internal or external) to society need to be anxious about such policies.

In a similar context, those who opposed nuclear weapons and the siting of American cruise missile bases in Britain during the 1980s were frequently accused by those on the political Right of being supporters or 'stooges' of the Soviet Union, allies of Moscow and possibly being funded by the KGB (the Soviet secret police). Ironically, nuclear weapons were depicted as essential to defending British democracy and freedom, whereupon anyone who expressed opposition to such weaponry was *ipso facto* opposed to democracy and freedom, and therefore did not deserve to be respected or listened to; they were, in effect, traitors.

Meanwhile, women who campaign against sexism (in its many guises) and male violence – for example, by demanding an end to 'page three' of *The Sun*, curbs on the sale of 'lads' mags', marching to 'reclaim the streets', and so on – are frequently depicted by Conservatives and much of the misogynistic media as 'men-hating feminists'. They are also likely to be told that they are lesbians (as if that is supposed to be an insult), as well as being subject to horrendous abuse and even physical threats by internet 'trolls' typing one-handed in their bedrooms.

CONCLUSION

We can see, therefore, that policy agendas are sites of conflict and contestation, as some policy actors (or would-be policy actors) seek to promote certain issues and push them onto the institutional agenda, while other policy actors seek to keep (or move) certain issues off the institutional agenda, through the various responses delineated above. After all: 'For those who wish to control the dynamics of an issue, the manipulation of the public's perception of it is vital' (Robinson, 2000: 18).

Certainly, in the sphere of policy making, problems are not necessarily self-evident or obvious, but are often subject to definition and interpretation, which in turn may be determined by political perspectives and social values. Only a small proportion of issues become defined or officially recognized as problems at any particular time and thus deemed worthy of attention by policy makers. By focusing on the institutional agenda, policy makers seek to limit the number of problems to be addressed to a (more) manageable level, otherwise they would inevitably face a situation of 'overload'.

We have also seen that it is not normally sufficient to show how a particular policy would solve a particular problem – it is also necessary for the right political circumstances to exist in terms of a sympathetic minister (or Prime Minister) or favourable ideological climate, for example. If the right political circumstances do occur, however, then opportunities may well arise for certain individuals or think tanks to exercise considerable influence on policy makers. On such occasions, moreover, rather than simply devise policies to tackle problems as and when they arise, in a reactive manner, policy makers (or those seeking to influence them) may search for problems to which they can apply a favoured pre-existing policy proposal, and which they may have wanted to implement for some time.

As such, we reiterate just how 'messy' the reality of policy making often is in Britain, and how public policy is developed through the combined impact and interaction of ideas and ideological perspectives, definitions or interpretations of problems, and varying political circumstances. Rather than assuming a neat and logical sequence whereby identification of a problem leads to the adoption of a policy, the reality is often that problems themselves are often disputed or disagreed upon, both in terms of definitions and scale or seriousness.

Yet even when a problem is widely acknowledged, it is still likely to generate different explanations of its causes, with these contrasting or competing accounts reflecting different ideological perspectives or social values. These, in turn, will generate the advocacy of different polices to tackle the problem. Among the institutions that are most closely or regularly involved in policy advocacy are political parties, think tanks and organized interests, and it is these that we examine in the next chapter.

QUESTIONS AND TOPICS FOR DISCUSSION

1. In what ways are 'problems' socially constructed?
2. How does the 'systemic' policy agenda differ from the 'institutional' policy agenda?
3. Why do writers like Bachrach and Baratz criticize the claim that power can be identified and measured when there is a visible conflict between two (or more) policy actors over a particular issue, whereupon one policy actor's preferences or interests prevail over those of the other(s)?
4. Why does 'the environment' provide a good example of the issue attention cycle?
5. Is poverty a problem? Give reasons for your answer?
6. How useful are the metaphors of a 'primeval soup' and 'garbage can' in illustrating the adoption or abandonment of policies?
7. What is the 'political stream' that Kingdon deems essential in creating the conditions for policy change?
8. How might policy makers use statistics to deny the existence or scale of a problem?

RECOMMENDED TEXTS AND FURTHER READING

1. Peter Bachrach and Morton Baratz (1970) *Power and Poverty: Theory and Practice*. Oxford: Oxford University Press.

   Although published back in 1970, this remains a classic political science study of the 'hidden face of power' and the manner in which the political or policy agenda is confined to 'safe' issues, and entails 'non-decisions', thereby militating against radical change.

2. Anthony Downs (1972) 'Up and down with ecology – the issue attention cycle', *The Public Interest*, 28 (Summer): 38–50.

Classic journal article advancing the thesis that issues and problems often proceed through a series of discrete stages before moving back down or off the policy agenda, sometimes without having resulted in any significant change of policy. This is particularly likely when a proposed policy solution is deemed to entail costs or negative consequences of its own. Downs illustrates this by using 'the environment' as a policy case study.

3. Tom Hulley and John Clarke (1991) 'Social problems: Social construction and social causation', in M. Loney, R. Bocock, J. Clarke, A. Cochrane, P. Graham and M. Wilson (eds), *The State or the Market: Politics and Welfare in Contemporary Britain*. London: Sage/Open University.

Good concise chapter explaining how societal values and political ideologies define or shape many 'problems', and in so doing, determine whether policies are introduced to tackle them. Notes that as values and ideologies can change over time, so too do definitions of social problems; what is widely accepted or deemed normal in one era may be deemed unacceptable a few decades later, and conversely, what was previously considered shocking or outrageous a few decades ago might be viewed as acceptable and unproblematic today.

4. Peter John, Anthony Bertelli, Will Jennings and Shaun Bevan (2013) *Policy Agendas in British Politics*. London: Palgrave Macmillan.

Important new analysis of how policy agendas, and thus policy paradigms and specific policies, change in particular circumstances. This study involves case studies of changes in several key areas of public policy in Britain during the last 50 years, in order to ascertain *what* and/or *who* were the drivers of these policy changes, *when* they occurred, and *how* they were enacted.

5. John Kingdon (1984) *Agendas, Alternatives and Public Policies*. London: Longman.

The classic text on the concept of policy streams, examining how and why policy change occurs, through the interaction and confluence of problems, policies and favourable political circumstances.

6. David A. Rochefort and Roger W. Cobb (1994) 'Problem definition: An emerging perspective', in D. A. Rochefort and R. W. Cobb (eds) *The Politics of Problem Definition: Shaping the Policy Agenda*. Kansas: University Press of Kansas.

Introductory chapter outlining why and how problem definition is determined by various factors, most notably cultural values, dominant discourses, ideological outlook, moral panics via the media, political objectives and scientific evidence. Moreover, these criteria not only define problems, but offer accounts of the underlying cause; what or who is responsible? Through these processes, therefore, many problems are 'socially constructed', rather than being obvious or self-evident.

7. Anthony Seldon (1996) 'Ideas are not enough', in D. Marquand and A. Seldon (eds) *The Ideas That Shaped Post-War Britain*. London: Fontana.

One of Britain's most eminent political historians explains how policies and policy change in Britain are shaped not just by ideas, but also by individuals, organized interests and circumstances.

2 Policy Advocates: Political Parties, Think Tanks and Organized Interests

Although a great many institutions seek to influence public policy in Britain, often via the systemic agenda, three of the most significant have been political parties, think tanks and organized interests. Of these, only political parties actively seek election to the House of Commons with the ultimate objective of becoming the government, whereupon they will normally command the political authority and most of the administrative resources necessary to enact legislation and other policies. Although each of the main political parties enshrines discernible ideologies, philosophies or principles, they are also characterized by internal divisions, as different 'wings' or sections either interpret their party's ideology in a particular way or because they believe that particular aspects of its ideology ought to be ascribed greater importance or priority by the leadership.

Traditionally, it has been the Labour Party that was most prone to ideological schisms between its Left and Right 'wings', but since the 1980s, the Conservatives have also been subject to disagreements between Left-leaning, One Nation Tories and Right-wing, Thatcherite Conservatives, although this demarcation has subsequently been overlain by divisions within the party over Britain's membership of the EU.

During the past ten years, the Liberal Democrats have also become slightly more internally divided, due to subtly contrasting visions of liberalism. In essence, the 'Orange Book' tendency has been ascendant, placing greater emphasis on market economics and reducing the role of the state in the provision of public services. By contrast, the party's social liberals generally favour a somewhat stronger or more interventionist role for the state, not least to tackle extremes of wealth and inequality, eradicate poverty and create a fairer society. In terms of public policy, therefore, what matters is not just which political party (or parties!) is in government at any moment, but which 'wing' within each party is dominant or 'hegemonic', and thus broadly shapes the policy agenda within the party and government.

Beyond the main parties, the two key institutional policy advocates have been think tanks and organized interests. Certainly, think tanks have become both more numerous and seemingly more influential since the 1970s, although measuring their actual influence is fraught with methodological difficulties. A think tank might advocate a policy and the government might enact the policy (or a very similar one), but it might have done so in spite of, rather than because of, the think tank's advocacy. Nonetheless, they have undoubtedly become more prominent, and even when professing formal independence, most think tanks have become closely associated with a particular political party or even an ideological 'wing' within it. What has been especially interesting is the number and high profile think tanks on the political Right, and thus associated with the Conservative Party and/or Thatcherism, in spite of (or maybe because of) the Conservatives having traditionally eschewed ideology and ideas based on intellectual theories in favour of moderation and pragmatism. Yet in the Labour Party, the main think tanks seemed to reflect and reinforce the emergence of New Labour, and the explicit repudiation of the Left and Socialism in favour of 'progressive' pragmatism and an often technocratic or 'what works' approach to policy making.

The third institutional policy advocates are organized interests (sometimes referred to as 'pressure groups'), which represent people either on the basis of economic, occupational or professional interests, or in accordance with ethical, moral or social values. Yet our main focus, in terms of policy making, concerns the extent to which some organized interests have enjoyed direct and regular access to policy makers, and thus exercised considerable influence over the institutional agenda and the type of policies enacted, while other groups have mostly been excluded from the corridors of political power. Such exclusion has usually reflected either the incompatibility or 'unreasonable' nature of the groups' policy goals compared to those of the government, or the fact that they lack the resources, such as specialist knowledge, which would render them useful to ministers and civil servants. Consequently, the later type of organized interests generally exert little, or only occasional, influence on policy makers in Britain.

POLITICAL PARTIES

British government is primarily party government, whereby general elections are contested by political parties pledging a package of policies, which they hope will prove more attractive to the electorate than those offered by the other main parties. If and when one party wins a majority of seats in the House of Commons (but *not*, it must be emphasized, a majority of votes cast), then it will duly be declared the government and almost certainly claim that it has been given a 'mandate'[1] by the voters to enact the policies that were in its manifesto. After all, as Blondel (1978: 105) once noted: 'An essential aspect of party activity concerns the elaboration and implementation of policies. In fact, some people see this as the party's main purpose.'

---

[1] The 'mandate' is a controversial political concept. A newly-elected government will often claim that winning the general election means it has been 'given a mandate' by the electorate to implement the policies that were in its manifesto. Yet, governments in Britain are usually elected with between 36 to 44 per cent of votes cast (rather less than half), so their claim that the electorate has given them a mandate is questionable. Besides, few voters actually read the parties' election manifestos, and even if they did, they would be highly unlikely to agree with every single policy pledged within it.

However, during its term of Office, the governing party will also be compelled to devise policies as a response to the crises or other unforeseen problems which all governments face from time to time. Nonetheless, even when unforeseen circumstances or a crisis necessitate a government response, ministers will naturally seek to ensure that, as far as practicably possible, the policies are in accordance with the party's philosophy or ideology – or at least, publicly portrayed as such.

After all, every political party enshrines a discernible set of principles and values, which reflect their 'vision' of a good society and thus shape many of their policies. To understand this crucial factor, we need to look briefly at the core beliefs and general philosophy of Britain's two largest and most electorally successful political parties, namely the Conservatives and Labour, along with those of the Liberal Democrats, the latter having formed a coalition government with the Conservatives following general election in May 2010. We apologize to Scottish and Welsh readers that space precludes a similar overview of the Scottish National Party and Plaid Cymru.

THE CONSERVATIVE PARTY

The Conservatives have usually insisted that they are non-ideological, due to Conservatism's profound scepticism about blueprints or models of a good society that are derived from abstract theories or intellectual visions. As Ian Gilmour argued: 'British Conservatism ... is not an "-ism"... Still less is it a system of ideas. It cannot be formulated in a series of propositions, which can be aggregated into a creed. It is not an ideology or a doctrine' (Gilmour, 1978: 121).

Conservatism has traditionally denounced such schemes and their promise of a new, better society as being 'utopian'. Indeed, Conservatives have usually argued that attempting to create or transform societies on the basis of intellectual ideas or academic theories will not only prove unworkable, due to the complexities of social reality and aspects of human nature, but will almost inevitably lead to tyranny, as proponents of an ideology rely upon coercion in a desperate but futile effort to make the unworkable work; the pre-1990 Soviet Union has frequently been referred to by Conservatives as a prime example of the atrocities accruing from trying to create a society on the basis of an ideological blueprint – in this case, Marxism.

Certainly, prior to the 1980s, most Conservatives prided themselves on their pragmatism and 'common sense', claiming that their policies in government were derived from a judicious blend of practical wisdom, experience, flexibility, circumstances, empiricism, pragmatism, instinct, dealing with the 'here and now' and only enacting 'what works'.

Nonetheless, in spite of Conservatism's claim that it is non-doctrinaire and more a state of mind or instinct, it is certainly possible to identify several principles and beliefs that collectively constitute a Conservative philosophy, and which have strongly shaped and justified very many of the policies pursued by the Conservative Party throughout its long history, as described in Box 2.1.

Box 2.1   Core principles and philosophy of the Conservative Party

- Capitalism is the most effective and efficient economic system that has ever existed. It provides individuals with maximum freedom/liberty and choice. It also generates the wealth that ensures steadily rising living standards.
- A pessimistic – or realistic – view of human nature. People are naturally self-interested and susceptible to selfish behaviour. Hence a 'socialist' society based on altruism, cooperation and sharing would be doomed to fail from the outset.
- Individualism, independence and self-reliance. People should, as far as possible, 'stand on their own two feet' and not expect others (apart from family members) to support or provide for them.
- Liberty and freedom from state control. As long as people are not breaking the law, they should be free to live their lives as they choose – as long as this choice does not entail choosing to live on welfare benefits.
- Private property ownership. This is not only considered to be an inherently good objective, but also provides a strong degree of independence from the state.
- Competition as natural and necessary. Most people are naturally acquisitive and motivated by a ceaseless desire to increase their wealth and material possessions, and in so doing, improve their status. This, of course, links to the precious point about the importance of private property.
- Inequality of incomes and wealth. This reflects differences in ability, effort, skill, success and talent.
- A (free) market economy in which the pursuit of profit is the primary purpose of economic activity, and human endeavour is motivated mainly by expectations of personal gain and material rewards.
- Low taxation. People should be permitted to keep as much as possible of what they earn, rather than having the state take a large proportion of their earnings (as income tax) to spend on 'free' public services. If tax rates were lower, then more people could afford private education, health and pensions, thus reducing reliance on (and indeed the need for) the welfare state.
- The 'traditional' family. This is based on a heterosexual married couple and their children. Hence many Conservatives strongly disapprove both of single parents (especially unmarried mothers) and gay marriage.
- A minimal, but strong, state to ensure defence against foreign threats, maintain internal law and order, enforce contracts and remove obstacles to the efficient operation of the market economy. Individual liberty is only attainable and meaningful if it is under 'the rule of law', otherwise 'anarchy', chaos and disorder would prevail.
- A limited welfare state, which should only assist the 'deserving poor'. It should neither promote equality nor allow a 'dependency culture' to become established.
- Defend and maintain social and political institutions. Any reforms should be intended to strengthen or adapt, but not replace, existing institutions.
- Change should occur gradually, naturally and organically, as society and institutions evolve in an incremental manner. Change should not be introduced on the basis of abstract ideas or intellectual theories. Evolution, not revolution; incrementalism, not insurrection.

However, different Conservatives have interpreted or applied these core principles in differing ways at different times, to the extent that discrete 'tendencies' can be identified within the Conservative Party over time. For example, for much of the period from 1945 until the mid-1970s, 'One Nation' Conservatives towards the Left of the Party exerted a strong influence over many Conservative policies. They were willing to accept a larger or more active role for the state in economic affairs and welfare provision in order to 'humanize' capitalism, keep inequality within civilized limits (albeit these was not clearly defined) and maintain a high degree of social harmony. All of this, they believed, was essential for ensuring popular support – legitimacy – for capitalism in general and ensuring that the working class was not attracted to socialism.

This mode of One Nation Conservatism (or Toryism) often derived from a sense of *noblesse oblige* – the principle that those born into wealth, power or privilege have a Christian or moral duty to show some concern or compassion towards those less fortunate than themselves. Of course, this can also be viewed as a form of 'enlightened self-interest', because by keeping the poor or 'the masses' pacified, the rich can prevent revolution, and thereby ensure their continued enjoyment of wealth and privileges. As Benjamin Disraeli, a Conservative leader and Prime Minister in the latter half of the 19th century expressed it: 'The palace cannot rest if the cottage is not happy' (quoted in Monypenny and Buckle, 1929: 709), while in the late 20th century, Ian Gilmour, a prominent One Nation Conservative, warned that: 'Those who are effectively excluded from the benefits of society cannot be expected to remain passive indefinitely' (Gilmour, 1992: 276).

By contrast, the Conservative Right and most notably those who, since the 1980s, have been associated with Thatcherism (the philosophy and policies associated with former party leader and Prime Minister Margaret Thatcher), have interpreted Conservative principles much more strictly or in a purer form. Whereas the One Nation Conservatives effectively wanted to smooth Capitalism's rougher edges, the Conservative Right believe unequivocally and unashamedly in a much more dynamic and virtually unregulated Capitalism, along with rugged individualism, more competition via the free market and privatization, lower taxes and the desirability or necessity of *greater* inequality. In this context, the philosopher Shirley Letwin characterized Thatcherism as a version of Conservatism which aimed to promote the 'vigorous virtues' (Letwin, 1992: *passim*).

In effect, the Conservative Right believe that the post-1945 era in Britain, up until the election of the first Thatcher government in 1979, had witnessed successive governments relentlessly expanding the role of the state in economic and social affairs, to the extent that: 'the market' could no longer function effectively; private enterprise, wealth creation and competition were grievously hampered by government interference; taxation was excessively high; the trade unions were too powerful (virtually 'running the country'); welfare provision was too generous, and had destroyed self-reliance and the work ethic; 'permissiveness' had led to increases in crime, drug addiction, family breakdown and sexually transmitted diseases (STDs); the pursuit of greater equality or egalitarianism had become an obsession, derived either from 'bourgeois guilt' felt by One Nation Tories, or the 'politics of envy' promoted by Labour and the Left (On the Thatcherite counter-offensive against egalitarianism, see Dorey, 2011a; Dorey, 2011b: 137–63).

Keith Joseph termed the drift of post-1945 politics in Britain the 'ratchet effect', whereby each Labour government took Britain further to the Left, but the subsequent Conservative governments failed to repeal Labour's policies. Conservatives had taken their name too literally; they had merely sought to conserve the status quo as they found it after a Labour government (Joseph, 1976: 20–21. See also Joseph, 1987: 29; Thatcher, 1993: 104). It was now imperative, Joseph argued, that the Conservatives began 'reversing the trend' – the title of a pamphlet that he penned to canvass this critique (Joseph, 1975).

In advancing this argument, Keith Joseph declared that: 'it was only in … 1974 that I was converted to Conservatism. I had thought that I was a Conservative, but I now see that I was not really one at all' (quoted in Kavanagh, 1987: 117). Meanwhile, Margaret Thatcher herself once declared, in a speech to the Conservative Philosophy Group, that: 'We must have an ideology. The other side have got an ideology … we must have one too' (quoted in [Hugo] Young, 1990: 406).

The policies resulting from the ascendancy of this mode of (Right-wing or Thatcherite) Conservatism during the 1980s and 1990s included: extensive privatization of formerly nationalized industries; major cuts in direct taxation (most notably income tax), particularly for high earners; the introduction of market principles and practices into education and the NHS; deregulation of banking, financial services and 'the City'; the emasculation of the trade unions through a combination of prescriptive legislation, unemployment, de-industrialization and the restoration of 'management's right to manage' in the workplace; allowing 'the market' to determine pay, which yielded massive increases for those at the top; a consequent and constant increase in inequality, with an ever-widening gap between rich and poor; a meaner, leaner welfare state with stricter curbs on entitlement to and rates of social security benefits; selling council houses (this extending home ownership and private property); increased spending on policing and defence; disapproval of 'alternative' lifestyles and families (i.e., gays and lesbians, single parents, unmarried mothers).

The ideological stance of the Conservative Party under David Cameron's leadership was initially difficult to discern. In Opposition, Cameron seemed to be determined to move the Conservatives away from Thatcherism, and refashion it as a more progressive or compassionate party, with allusions to One Nation Toryism. This was intended to 'detoxify' the Conservative brand, and persuade moderate or floating voters that it was no longer 'the nasty party'.[2] Various speeches and policy documents emanated from sundry senior Conservatives, which suggested a more conciliatory and constructive approach to the public sector and the poor, for example and a recognition that 'the market' was not always the solution to every problem (for Cameron's 'modernization' project prior to 2010, see Bale, 2010: Chapter 7; Dorey, 2007; Dorey, 2009c; Dorey, 2011c; Dorey et al., 2011; Hayton, 2012).

Yet since becoming Prime Minister and in the context of a serious economic downturn following the 2008 global banking crisis, the Conservative-dominated coalition government has pursued or proposed several measures that are more redolent of Thatcherism:

---

[2] This was the phrase used by Theresa May at the Conservatives' 2002 annual conference to warn delegates that this was the view that many people still held of the party, and why it therefore needed to change or 'modernize'.

targeting the public sector for 'shrinking' and/or privatization, large-scale redundancies, pay curbs and increased pension contributions; constantly berating public sector workers for being inefficient, lazy, overpaid and economically unproductive (not creating wealth), as well as enjoying 'gold-plated pensions' when they retire; further opening up schools and universities to private companies; significantly cutting welfare provision and imposing much more stringent eligibility criteria on social security claimants; reducing corporation tax (on company profits) and lowering the top rate of income tax from 50 per cent to 45 per cent; threatened further 'reform' (weakening) of the trade unions and a reduction in employment rights and protection (to make it easier for employers to sack workers, in the name of 'labour market flexibility' and cutting red tape on businesses).

Alongside these measures, Cameron and his Chancellor, George Osborne, have steadfastly refused to take action against the continued payment of enormous salary increases and bonuses to bankers in 'the City', even though Cameron had himself condemned such greed and profligacy before becoming Prime Minister, when he had claimed (with regard to the recession and the need for restraint or sacrifices) 'we're all in this together'.

THE LABOUR PARTY

Ironically, although Conservatives have often claimed to be non-ideological, it is somewhat easier to identify Conservative principles than those of the Labour Party, precisely because the latter has traditionally been more prone to internal disputes over its principles and policies, and partly because of a disjuncture between what Labour has said in Opposition and what it has actually done (or not done!) when in government. Indeed, right from the time it was formally created (in 1906, although it had existed, since 1900, as the Labour Representation Committee), the Labour Party was characterized by internal ideological uncertainty and inconsistency. The party was the product of several industrial and political bodies, most notably the trade unions, the Independent Labour Party (ILP), the Social Democratic Federation (SDF) and the Fabians. Labour's professed commitment to 'socialism' varied considerably, both in the meaning of socialism subscribed to, and as a consequence, the type of policies promoted, by individuals and 'factions' in the party. For example, in sharp contrast to the Marxism of the SDF, the Fabians firmly believed that 'socialism' would develop gradually and organically as the state, governed by enlightened leaders and expert administrators, enacted policies to eradicate exploitation, inequality and poverty, and also planned economic activity rather than leaving it to the 'anarchy' of the free market.

The trade unions, meanwhile, although often espousing socialist rhetoric via rousing conference speeches denouncing the exploitation of workers by wicked capitalist employers, have mostly been rather more modest (or realistic) in their objectives, namely focusing on improving the terms and conditions of employment of their members, most notably through higher pay. In many respects, though, this has served to weaken or prevent working-class 'solidarity', as trade unions represent workers on the basis of their occupation, which often means that they are actually competing against each other; they are each seeking a marginally larger slice of the cake, or even just a few more crumbs from the rich (wo)man's table, rather than demanding control of the bakery!

With these important caveats in mind, we can identify a number of core features of Labour Party 'ideology', as listed in Box 2.2.

Box 2.2   Core principles of the Labour Party

- Capitalism is divisive, exploitative and unstable – prone to lurch from boom to slump, and from one crisis to another. It generates unacceptable economic and social inequalities; those who actually do the work and create wealth do not receive a fair reward in terms of the wages they are paid.
- Public ownership or state regulation of key industries and sectors of the economy – to ensure that these serve the interests of 'the people', not just 'capitalists'.
- A more optimistic or charitable view of human nature – people have the potential to be altruistic and caring. Bad behaviour and selfishness is deemed to be a consequence of poverty and other forms of social injustice; people's behaviour is strongly shaped by their socio-economic environment. Capitalism does not derive from human nature, it distorts and corrupts it.
- Collectivism – whereby the state acts on behalf of otherwise powerless or disadvantaged individuals to improve their material conditions and standards of living.
- Universal welfare state – to guarantee a minimum income for all citizens and provide protection against the vagaries and injustices of 'the market'. Also, free education and healthcare; these should not be dependent on an individual's income or ability to pay. The welfare state is a means by which (greater) equality can be secured.
- Liberty – defined as freedom based on having sufficient resources to make effective choices; to be able to afford to do things rather than be prevented by poverty. Liberty and freedom therefore require greater equality, otherwise the choices that the poor can make are severely limited. Telling a penniless homeless person that they are 'free' to sleep in a five-star hotel is both meaningless and grossly insulting.
- Cooperation – as more desirable and socially beneficial than the pursuit of self-interest.
- Equality (or rather, less inequality) – redistribution of wealth from rich to poor; comprehensive schools; equality of opportunity; equal treatment regardless of ethnic background, sex/gender or sexual orientation.
- 'Progressive' taxation – those who earn more money should pay more in tax; those who are paid the most money should pay the most tax.

It has been the Labour Left that has subscribed to, or interpreted, these principles and objectives most literally and in their purest form. For example, the Left used to view nationalization (public ownership) as a litmus test of the Labour leadership's commitment to 'socialism', the reasoning being that the greater the number of industries that were nationalized, the less that would remain of a capitalist economy. Consequently, the repeated reluctance or refusal of Labour leaders to pursue extensive nationalization (after the initial tranche of public ownership enacted by the 1945–50 Attlee government) was viewed by the Left as evidence of 'betrayal' by the party's leadership and the latter's lack of commitment to 'true' socialism.

The Left has also been in favour of very high taxation of the richest in society, partly because of strong disapproval that 'bosses' and 'captains of industry' should be paid so much more than the workers who actually perform the physical labour, which creates wealth in the first place, and partly to finance the welfare state, which the Left viewed as a major vehicle for achieving equality through wealth redistribution.

By contrast, Labour's 'revisionists' or 'social democrats' emanating from the Right of the party were always much looser and more flexible in their interpretation of these principles and objectives, and therefore highly pragmatic when in government, insisting (like many Conservatives have traditionally done) on the need to 'govern according to circumstances' rather than pursuing policies for the sake of ideological purity. For example, even when the Attlee government nationalized several key industries, such as coal, gas, iron, steel and the railways, most Labour ministers viewed this as strategically important and desirable, particularly in the context of post-war reconstruction, rather than as vital for ideological reasons.

Thereafter, Labour's revisionists were generally unenthusiastic about further nationalization, unless there was a particular economic or strategic reason for taking an industry into public ownership; in other words, any subsequent nationalization would be enacted on a pragmatic, *ad hoc* basis, not as part of a continuous ideological crusade to 'socialize' the whole economy. Labour's revisionists subscribed to the view that a fairer, more equal society could, and should, be pursued primarily through faster economic growth, creating equality of opportunity, particularly through the reform and expansion of education, and eradicating various forms of discrimination, most notably those deriving from gender, ethnicity and sexual orientation. The expansion and growth of the economy would be attained by utilizing Keynesian techniques of demand management, strategic investment and economic planning, which would in turn foster full employment, increasing prosperity, the eradication of poverty, and deliver the tax revenues that would fund the welfare state (see Crosland, 1956, for the classic advocacy of this type of 'revisionism' and riposte to the Labour Left).

Of course, the most recent manifestation of Labour's revisionism was New Labour and the 'third way' policies closely associated with Tony Blair, and fellow 'modernizers' like Peter Mandelson (Blair, 1996; Blair, 2010: Chapter 3; Mandelson and Liddle, 1996. See also Anderson and Mann, 1997: Chapter 1; Coates, 2005; Driver, 2011: 96–111; Driver and Martell, 2006; Finlayson, 2003; Gould, 1999; Heffernan, 2000; Leach, 2009: Chapter 10; Rawnsley, 2001; Seldon, 2004; Chapters 17 and 19). One of the leading intellectual proponents of this approach was Anthony Giddens, whose book *The Third Way* (1998) was tellingly subtitled *The Renewal of Social Democracy*.

Since losing the May 2010 general election, there has been an ongoing debate in the Labour Party about its future ideological orientation, and thus what kind of policies it ought to promote. Although such intra-party debates are to be expected when a party finds itself back in Opposition after a lengthy term in government, they were lent added resonance in (New) Labour's case by the fact that the May 2010 election defeat precipitated a protracted leadership contest over the summer (for a detailed account of this leadership contest, see Dorey and Denham, 2011). Throughout this campaign, the candidates' speeches were scrutinized for clues about their judgements on New Labour's record in Office and how they viewed the future of the party; did they intend to continue with New Labour or were they aiming to revert to a more Left-wing stance? The result of the leadership contest was eventually announced at the Labour Party's conference in September 2010, with Ed Miliband narrowly defeating his brother David, which many commentators interpreted as presaging a shift to the Left.

Yet even by the summer of 2013, virtually three years on from Miliband's election, it was still not clear what the Labour Party's 'vision' or ideological stance actually was. The party was struggling to oppose the coalition's austerity programme without either being labelled 'deficit deniers' who would thus be financially reckless and profligate again in government, or being accused of 'lurching to the Left' and threatening to take Britain back to the 1970s – an allegation emanating almost as much from embittered Blairites as Conservatives.

THE LIBERAL DEMOCRATS

The Liberal Democrats were created in 1988 through a merger between the Liberal Party, and the Social Democratic Party (SDP), the latter having been formed in 1981 by a group of 'revisionists' who left the Labour Party due to its shift to the Left. Initially, the merged parties called themselves the 'Social and Liberal Democrats', but in 1989, shortened this to the current nomenclature.

The development of a Liberal Democratic ideology was particularly interesting because of the historical evolution of liberalism, which has previously enshrined two discrete strands, namely classical liberalism and social liberalism (Clark, 2012: 86–8. See also: Fisher, 1996: 104–7; Freeden, 1986; Greenleaf, 1983: Chapters 2–5; Hobhouse, 1911; Leach, 2009: Chapter 2; Vincent, 2009: Chapter 2). The 'classical' variant of liberalism emphasized free trade and limited government, and it was this version that prevailed in the Liberal Party during most of the 19th century.

However, from the early 20th century onwards, 'social' liberalism became increasingly prevalent, deriving from a growing recognition that pure *laissez-faire* itself caused or exacerbated many economic and social problems, most notably instability (boom and slump) and excessive inequality, the latter also fuelling sundry social problems. For example, the economist John Maynard Keynes and the 'architect' of Britain's post-1945 'cradle-to-grave' welfare state, William Beveridge, were both liberals of a 'social' or interventionist kind.

When the Liberal Democrats were formed, this 'social' liberalism was still dominant in the Liberal Party and doubtless made merger with the Social Democrats easier because elements of 'social' liberalism are not dissimilar to aspects of social democracy (see, for example, Grayson, 2007; Grayson, 2009; Webb, 2000: 102–3). Yet there remained an underlying problem in crafting a coherent and distinct Liberal Democrat ideology because party members, even at the most senior level, were uncertain about whether their purpose was to challenge Labour as the main alternative to the Conservatives, which would imply that 'social liberalism' should be adhered to, or whether the objective should be to supplant the Conservatives as the chief opposition to Labour, in which case reversion to 'classical liberalism' would be more appropriate.

Of course, it was also conceivable that the Liberal Democrats could seek to attract supporters from both parties, by adopting a centrist stance or policy of equidistance. After all, it is considered axiomatic that general elections in Britain are usually won by occupying the centre ground, and thereby attracting the median, 'middle-of-the-road', voters who dislike ideology or perceived extremism, and thus pride themselves on their political moderation and pragmatism. Yet the danger for the Liberal Democrats in seeking to locate themselves in the ideological centre, on the middle ground of British politics, was that this might result either in a lack of distinctiveness or identity, or in being squeezed by the two major parties themselves converging on the centre ground.

For these reasons, some Liberal Democrats sought to portray themselves as representing the 'radical centre' (ostensibly an oxymoron), or argued that the very discourse of 'Left' versus 'Right' was obsolete on the grounds that the real demarcation between Britain's political parties was that of 'centralization' versus 'decentralization' and devolution of political power, or 'authoritarianism' versus 'libertarianism'. On this basis, many Liberal Democrats have viewed themselves as committed proponents of decentralization, devolution and libertarianism, while depicting both Labour and the Conservatives as being inclined to authoritarianism, and an arrogant top-down approach to policy making. Thus did Nick Clegg, in his speech to the Liberal Democrats' 2011 spring conference, declare that:

> ... we are the inheritors of a century and a half of radical liberal tradition. We're not the heirs to Thatcher. We're not the heirs to Blair. We are the heirs to Mill, Lloyd George, Keynes, Beveridge, Grimond. We are the true radicals of British politics ... For the left, an obsession with the state. For the right, a worship of the market ... Our opponents try to divide us with their outdated labels of left and right. But we are not on the left and we are not on the right. We have our own label: Liberal. We are liberals and we own the freehold to the centre ground of British politics. Our politics is the politics of the radical centre. We are governing from the middle, for the middle.

> (Liberal Democrats, 2011)

The main principles that have characterized the Liberal Democrats since 1989 are listed in Box 2.3.

Box 2.3   Core principles of the Liberal Democrats

- Diversify Britain's economy to reduce reliance on banking and financial services, while also reforming the banking system itself.
- Reduce the tax burden on low-income families while finding new or more effective ways to tax the better off (such as a 'mansion tax'), and clamping down on tax avoidance by wealthy individuals and big businesses.

(Continued)

(Continued)

- Industrial democracy to overcome 'them and us' attitudes in the workplace. Workers to be represented on company boards and cooperatives to be promoted, along with profit-sharing schemes or employee share ownership.
- Equality of opportunity and treatment – opposed to all forms of discrimination on the basis of ethnicity, race, sex or sexual orientation.
- Constitutional reform – devolution of political power to the regions of Britain, a (more) proportional electoral system for general elections, more open government, an elected House of Lords and a codified (written in one document) constitution.
- Localism – local communities and citizens to be empowered through elected health and police authorities; a local income tax to replace the Council Tax.
- Strong emphasis on civil liberties and individual rights, and therefore limits on the power of the state. Opposed to ID cards. Stricter controls on use of CCTV cameras. Support for statutory human rights.
- Tackling crime should place a stronger emphasis on prevention via more police officers 'on the beat'. More emphasis too on rehabilitation, restorative justice (making criminals confront the impact of their crime on their victims) and 'community sentences' rather than custodial sentences, except for the most serious crimes or serial offenders.
- Environmentalism – expand 'clean' or renewable forms of energy and offshore wind turbines, and promote energy-efficiency schemes for homes and workplaces. Impose or increase 'green taxes' on polluters.
- Internationalist in foreign affairs, believing that nation states achieve more through cooperation and partnership than by isolationism and nationalism. Consequently pro-European, albeit critical of the EU's 'democratic deficit'. Opposed to replacing Britain's Trident nuclear weapons system.

Yet within these general core principles, the tension between the two modes of Liberalism previously identified, namely economic and social liberalism, has become clearer during the 2000s. This was largely attributable to the 2004 publication of *The Orange Book*, a series of essays by sundry Liberal Democrats, including several MPs, which sought to re-orientate the party's policies in a much more market-orientated direction (Marshall and Laws, 2004). Indeed, the book was subtitled *Reclaiming Liberalism*, and advocated such policies as greater deregulation of industry, economic liberalization, further reform of, and more competition in, public services in order to foster greater choice and empower individuals, and modernization of Britain's pensions system in order to promote greater individual responsibility. As David Laws explains:

A key question for the Liberal Democrats is to what extent we can draw on our heritage of economic liberalism to address some of the current problems in public service delivery … to ask to what extent we can utilise choice, competition, consumer power and the private sector to deliver a better deal for those on low incomes or otherwise reliant on public services.

(Laws, 2004: 36)

Laws also urged the Liberal Democrats to reduce the state's role in the economy, one manifestation of which would be to consider the privatization of the Post Office. He also called for a 'repatriation' (reclaiming) of some powers previously transferred to the EU (Laws, 2004: 41), a particularly notable demand given that the Liberal Democrats have long been viewed as Britain's most pro-European political party.

Not surprisingly, some Liberal Democrats were deeply unhappy about this advocacy of an ostensibly more Right-wing economic liberalism, whose discourse concerning 'competition' and 'choice' often seemed akin to contemporary Conservatism. Consequently, social liberals in the party sought to provide an intellectual defence and restatement of their position and concomitant policy preferences by publishing their own collection of essays in 2007. Entitled *Reinventing the State: Social Liberalism for the 21st Century* (Brack et al., 2007), this volume generally defended the role of the state in tackling market failure and associated social problems, and insisted that while Liberal Democrats were absolutely concerned with individual liberty, such freedom was only attainable in the context of a more equal distribution of wealth. This too necessitated a more active state than that envisaged by 'classic liberals' and 'Orange Book' Liberal Democrats, albeit in tandem with the *a priori* commitment to the decentralization and devolution of political power, and ensuing empowerment of local communities.

Yet by 2010, Grayson was lamenting that the 'Orange Book' Liberal Democrats seemed to be in the ascendancy in the parliamentary party, to the extent that:

> ... the coalition [government] can ... best be understood as the preferred option of a leadership grouping which since it took over the party has consistently sought policies which will reduce the role of the state and steadily take a centre-left party to the centre-right. The major debates in the past two to three years have seen the small Orange Book tendency steadily whittling away at broadly centre-left policies on, for example, the level of public expenditure, the level of income tax and the role of local government in education. That has given the leadership much common ground with the Conservatives.
>
> (Grayson, 2010: 11)

Indeed, since their party entered into a coalition government with the Conservatives in May 2010, the tensions between the two strands of liberalism have become even more resonant, and the intra-party debates even more rebarbative, exacerbated by the controversial or unpopular decisions that the leadership has consented to in the context of austerity and the concern to cut Britain's fiscal deficit.

THE 'HIDDEN FACE' OF POWER IN POLITICAL PARTIES

Ultimately, the extent to which a political party's philosophy and principles will be translated into actual policies when in government will depend on various factors, most notably which 'faction' or 'tendency' (if any) within the parliamentary party is dominant, the nature of the problems on the institutional agenda at any given moment (which can either be viewed as constraints or as opportunities), the degree of support or opposition emanating from other key individuals or institutions beyond government and the character or style of the party leader in their role as Prime Minister.

Certainly, it is important to emphasize that however much authority and public prominence a party leader or Prime Minister seems to enjoy, they cannot take the support of their backbench MPs for granted too often. This, in turn, means that the role of the political parties, and particularly their backbench MPs, in policy advocacy and development is often subtle or nuanced; even when the party leadership appears to be determining policies, they will usually need to consider the likely response and degree of support on their backbenches – anticipated reactions. As such, some putative policies are not pursued because party leaders are aware (or made aware) that they will not be able to secure sufficient support among their own MPs for them.

Incidentally, this is a manifestation of the 'second face' of power, which we discussed in the previous chapter, whereby some decisions, issues or polices are avoided because the formal policy makers know that they are likely to encounter strong opposition if they proceed. Their power is thus constrained and confined to what are assumed to be 'safe' issues. This contextual and contingent character was emphasized by Jack Brand in his major study of the relationship between British political parties and policy making. He noted that:

> ... party leaders exercise their control over policy within limits maintained by the parliamentary party. They may not know at any time where these exact limits are ... since their location will depend not just on the ethos and philosophy of the party, but also on current events ... The whips' task of reporting on the feeling on the back benches, as well as relaying instructions to them, indicates the importance given to back-bench feeling. If ministers or shadow ministers are agenda-setters, back-bench tolerance sets limits within which these agendas can be set.

> (Brand, 1992: 22)

Another academic expert on British party politics has similarly noted that 'national governmental policy in Britain is still predominantly party rather than prime ministerial or bureaucratic policy' (Webb, 2000: 262), while Norton has argued that a minister's decision on whether to proceed with a policy will often take into account the 'anticipated reactions' of their own party's MPs, for 'ministers do not want to alienate their own supporters', and so 'may thus be influenced ... by anticipation of parliamentary reaction' (Norton, 2005: 78).

One further point remains to be made about the relationship between parties and public policy in Britain. As alluded to above, governments face an increasing number of external pressures and constraints that often limit their policy options, and can compel them to dilute or delay their party's objectives until circumstances are more propitious. However, even when faced with serious constraints or external pressures, a government will usually be able to exercise *some* choices about which polices to enact and thus ensure that these are compatible with the party's philosophy or ideological goals. For example, since 2010, all of Britain's main political parties have fully accepted the vital need to reduce the fiscal deficit, yet this still left some room for manoeuvre or autonomy in deciding precisely how to achieve this agreed and necessary objective. Upon being formed in May 2010, the Conservative-Liberal Democrat government could have opted for a 50:50 ratio between cuts in public expenditure and increases in taxation, or it might have decided to pay off some of the deficit by increasing Treasury revenues through clamping down on tax evasion and avoidance and/or introducing a Tobin (financial transactions) tax. Other potential policies to reduce the fiscal deficit were to increase taxes on the super rich (and call their bluff over their repeated threats to emigrate if they had to pay more in tax), and/or abandon the commitment to replace or upgrade Britain's (Trident) nuclear submarines at an estimated cost of £20 billion.

Yet instead of adopting these policy options to cut Britain's deficit, the coalition government decided to adopt an 80:20 ratio, whereby 80 per cent of deficit reduction would be funded from cuts in public expenditure and 20 per cent from increases in taxation, most notably increasing VAT. The options of imposing higher taxes on the super rich and/or cancelling Trident were rejected, while only the most half-hearted or modest measures were enacted to tackle tax evasion (in stark contrast to the urgency and vigour with which ministers vowed to combat welfare dependency).

In other words, while accepting that ministers had little choice but to cut the fiscal deficit, they did have choices about *how* to reduce it, *where* to impose the cuts and *who* or *which* sections of the population would bear the brunt of the sundry cuts. Ultimately, these were *political* choices; the coalition made a conscious decision that the vast majority of deficit reduction would accrue from cutting public expenditure, which would thus have serious implications for education, the NHS and social security. This can clearly be viewed as a reflection of the priorities of the Conservatives, particularly the neo-liberal strand in the party, although 'Orange Book' Liberal Democrats also wanted to reduce the size and role of the state in order to promote decentralization and localism in the delivery of public services.

Ultimately, therefore, although governing parties face various constraints – both exogenous and endogenous – on which policies they can enact at any given juncture, they are usually able to exercise *some* choice. After all, as Karl Marx (1963: 15) once famously observed: 'Men [*sic*] make their own history, but they do not make it just as they please; they do not make it under circumstances chosen by themselves, but under circumstances directly encountered'. Consequently, governing parties remain vitally important policy actors, even when circumstances impose limits on their degree of choice and room of manoeuvre in deciding which policies to enact. Whatever their own intrinsic limitations, and regardless of the limits that are variously imposed upon them when in government, 'parties continue to provide the most obvious way in which the body politic can generate a range of democratically accountable and distinct policy alternatives' (Webb, 2000: 267).

THINK TANKS

Since the late 1970s, there has been an increase in the number of 'think tanks' in Britain, and an apparent increase in their influence. We say 'apparent' because 'influence' is often difficult to gauge in political science, due to the problem of identifying independent variables, or determining the degree to which (or whether) a particular individual or institution has shaped a political event or policy outcome. Or as one contemporary writer on think tanks has expressed it: 'Establishing direct causal relationships between think tank activity and a party's or a government's policy programme is nearly impossible, as policy processes are complex and involve a multitude of actors. However, we are able to establish congruence between ideas and the content of policy decisions', although 'finding congruence does not establish proof of impact' (Pautz, 2012a: 364. See also Yee, 1996).

Consequently, while it is fairly straightforward to measure the rise of 'think tanks' quantitatively, it is rather less easy to gauge their actual influence on public policy in Britain qualitatively, especially as some such bodies might want to claim credit for certain policies in order to enhance their kudos – and attract new clients and funding – in an increasingly crowded think tank universe (for an overview on the rise and role of think tanks in Britain see: Cockett, 1994; Denham and Garnett, 1998; Denham and Garnett, 1999; Denham and Garnett, 2004; James, 1993; Mulgan, 2006; Stone, 1996).

One commentator has referred to think tanks as 'idea brokers', defining them as formally independent (from government) bodies, which are 'engaged in multi-disciplinary research intended to influence public policy.' In this context, the 'distinctive contribution of think tanks to British politics has been to broaden the repertoire of politicians by offering an extra, unorthodox alternative which makes it easier to question the premises of existing policy' (James, 1993: 492, 505). Or as Geoff Mulgan, the founder of the think tank, Demos, claims:

> At their best, think tanks exist to help organizations, political parties or whole societies to think. Their justification is that large organizations are generally poorly designed for original thought; indeed modern bureaucracies are arguably much better designed for eliminating originality and dissent. Hence the need for specialized organizations that work with ideas, and analyses and arguments, and that do not need to worry too much about discipline, delivery of responsibility ... Think tanks have thrived in part because the traditional civil service monopoly of policy advice has been broken. However, governments continue to need substantial capacities to think, analyse and even imagine ... they have to access a diverse range of different types of knowledge.
>
> (Mulgan, 2006: 147, 150)

Although formally independent of government, the ideological orientation of some think tanks means that two broad types can be identified.

First, there are those that are recognized as being politically neutral, or what Denham and Garnett term as 'traditional' (1996: 49) think tanks, as indicated in Table 2.1.

These aim to provide objective information and evidence on issues, which they hope will influence the ideas of policy makers, irrespective of which political party is in government or regardless of the dominant intellectual framework or paradigm prevalent at any particular time.

Table 2.1 'Traditional' think tanks in contemporary Britain

Name of think tank	Formed	Focus or orientation
Institute of Fiscal Studies	1969	'… to promote effective economic and social policies by understanding better their impact on individuals, families, businesses and the government's finances. Our findings are based on rigorous analysis, detailed empirical evidence and in-depth institutional knowledge. We seek to communicate them effectively, to a wide range of audiences, thereby maximising their impact on policy both directly and by informing public debate' (www.ifs. org.uk/aboutIFS). 'We meet regularly with policymakers across Whitehall, from the Downing Street Strategy Unit to the Department for International Development. We give evidence to parliamentary select committees, we brief MPs ahead of each Budget and we meet annually with the Chancellor of the Exchequer' (www.ifs.org.uk/aboutIFS/engagewith).
National Institute of Economic and Social Research	1938	'… to promote, through quantitative research, a deeper understanding of the interaction of economic and social forces that affect people's lives, so that they may be improved' (www.niesr.ac.uk).
Policy Studies Institute	1978	Aims to conduct 'rigorous and impartial' research and disseminate information – via publications (including a journal), workshops and – which will 'promote economic well-being and improve quality of life' (www.psi.org.uk).

Ideological or partisan think tanks: the New Right

The second category of think tanks are those that, while remaining formally independent of government, have a clear political or ideological orientation, to the extent that they often become identified with a particular ideology, a specific political party or even a particular 'strand' within that party. In this respect, these have been labelled 'advocacy' think tanks (Denham and Garnett, 1998: 49), for they clearly seek to influence policy makers on the basis of a particular ideological orientation or political perspective. Similarly, in his essay on the Adam Smith Institute (ASI), Heffernan adopts the term 'policy advocate', clearly characterizing it as a 'political' rather than an 'independent' think tank' (Heffernan, 1996: 81).

These 'think tanks' are generally either on the political Right (and particularly what became known from the 1970s as the New Right), or towards the centre-Left (often associated with New Labour or the 'third way'), although some of the latter are sceptical about the continued relevance of terms such as Left and Right, and thus prefer to depict themselves as 'progressive' instead. Table 2.2 illustrates, the think tanks associated with the political Right in Britain, and particularly the New Right or Thatcherism.

Table 2.2 The main think tanks associated with the political Right in Britain

Name of think tank	Formed	Focus or orientation
Adam Smith Institute	1977	Leading advocate of ideas concerning private enterprise, the virtues of competition and the need to base economic activity and variables (such as prices, wages and levels of employment) on the 'laws' of supply and demand. Sees itself providing suggestions and concrete proposals about how to put these principles into practice *vis-à-vis* particular policies.
Centre for Policy Studies	1974	Margaret Thatcher and Sir Keith Joseph founded the Centre for Policy Studies (CPS) in order to promote the case for a social market economy and greater freedom (from the State) for individuals. Strong emphasis on the importance of individual choice and responsibility, and the concepts of duty, family respect for the law, national independence, individualism and liberty' (www.cps.org,uk/mission; see also, Harris, 1996).
Institute of Economic Affairs	1955	Has always advocated applying market principles (competition, contracting out, internal markets, private sector involvement or practices, etc.) and consumer choice to the provision of public services and the welfare state, but only from the mid-1970s did the Institute find these ideas being taken seriously and sympathetically by an increasing number of Conservative politicians.
Policy Exchange	2002	Claims to be 'non-partisan', but strongly advocates free-market and local solutions to public policy questions. However, calls for traditional centre-Right themes *vis-à-vis* market forces and individual responsibility to be linked to the pursuit of progressive ends, such as extending opportunities to sections of society that don't usually have them. Policy Exchange has become closely associated with David Cameron's purported modernization of the Conservative Party.
Centre for Social Justice	2004	Launched by former Conservative Party leader, Iain Duncan Smith, but purports to be politically eclectic (some non-Conservatives are on its Advisory Board, including two Labour MPs and a journalist for *The Observer*). Is concerned with examining the causes of poverty in Britain (other than low wages), in terms of lifestyles (alcohol addiction, gambling, long-term unemployment, etc.), and thereby proposing policies to address these issues. Sees itself as a source of ideas and policy proposals that will mend 'broken Britain'.

These think tanks seek to influence public policy and policy makers in various ways, most notably through hosting conferences and seminars, submitting proposals to relevant civil servants and ministers, writing articles in newspapers, and publishing books and pamphlets. Some of them, such as the Institute of Economic Affairs (IEA), even publish their own journal three or four times per year plus occasional supplements on specific topics.

The apparent impact of the IEA and ASI

Although the IEA was formed back in 1955, it was not until the crumbling of Keynesianism and social democracy in the 1970s that it began to attract wider credence and credibility, not least among some senior Conservatives and sympathetic intellectuals or commentators. As Desai notes (1994: 49):

> The IEA's role was crucial in these early years of the emergence of the New Right. It played a part in keeping neo-liberal ideas alive, and attempted with increasing success to demonstrate their relevance, thus preparing the ground for a neo-liberal challenge to the Keynesian consensus.

Similarly, a former official in the Conservative Research Department recalls that Thatcher immersed herself in sundry publications by think tanks such as the IEA in response to the experiences and problems facing Britain in the 1970s, whereupon her growing conversion to economic neo-liberalism was given further impetus and intellectual confidence (Ranelagh, 1992: 194). The IEA is also credited with strongly influencing several of Thatcher's senior ministerial colleagues from the 1970s onwards, including Chancellors Geoffrey Howe and Nigel Lawson, and Leon Brittan, who served as Home Secretary during the mid-1980s (Jones, 2012: 161).

Certainly, the Thatcher-Major governments' education and NHS reforms seemed to bear a strong similarity with many of the 'proposals consistently canvassed by the IEA (Bosanquet, 1983: 75–83), particularly in terms of promoting markets, consumer choice and competition within the public sector. Such policies were intended to weaken the monopolies that these services enshrined, and *inter alia* the alleged power of 'self-serving' professionals or 'producer interests' working in education and health, and instead instil the principles and practices of 'the market' into the public sector.

In tandem with the IEA, the ASI promoted a plethora of policies closely associated with Thatcherism. Indeed, the ASI claims to have published 'over 300 *influential* policy reports' (Adam Smith Institute, 2013, emphasis added) between 1977 (when it was formed) and the end of 2002, while also claiming that the Thatcher governments implemented 200 of the 624 policy proposals listed in the ASI 1985 *Omega File*. For example, the ASI is credited with having influenced various Conservative privatizations during the 1980s, along with the Poll Tax. The ASI itself also claims at least some of the credit for John Major's introduction, in 1991, of a Citizen's Charter, formally intended to empower consumers of public services (Pirie, 2012: *passim*; Heffernan, 1996: 84–5).

Nonetheless, Heffernan suggests that there was a subtle difference between the strategies of the IEA and the ASI, with the former tending to focus mainly on changing elite-level opinion, particularly among academics, media commentators and senior civil servants, and thereby 'win the intellectual battle of ideas'. In contrast, the ASI has been much more concerned with 'seeking to communicate suitable methods ... to enact designated ideas in practice'. In other words, the IEA has broadly presented the intellectual case for long-term market-orientated policies and values, whereas the ASI has focused rather more on short-term or practical means of actually implementing such policies (Heffernan, 1996: 77). Or as Madsen Pirie, a founder and President of the ASI has suggested by way of analogy, some think tanks act as policy 'scientists' providing analyses and prognoses, while others play the role of 'policy engineers' (Pirie 1988: Chapter 4), the clear implication being that the IEA fulfilled the former role and the ASI the latter.

This characterization of the IEA is broadly endorsed by Muller's observation that the think tank 'engaged less in offering practical solutions and means of implementation to government, and rather sought to change the climate in which government thinking was taking place' (Muller, 1996: 95). Similarly, Denham and Garnett have noted that the IEA's main audience 'was (and continues to be) not so much people with day-to-day policy-making responsibilities as those who help to frame the context in which policy-making takes place' (Denham and Garnett, 1998: 93. See also Desai, 1994: 29).

The Centre for Policy Studies

Formed in 1974 by Keith Joseph and Margaret Thatcher, the Centre for Policy Studies was intended to reshape Conservatism, following their disappointments as ministers in the (1970–74) Heath government and thus reverse the 'ratchet effect' towards socialism in Britain since 1945. To this purpose, the Centre for Policy Studies aimed to provide an intellectual case for promoting markets in the economic sphere and traditional morality in the social sphere (for accounts of the CPS, see Denham and Garnett, 1998: Chapter 4; Desai, 1994: 50–59; Harris, 1996).

Far from viewing markets and morality as representing contradictory or conflicting values, namely between economic liberty and social discipline, the Centre for Policy Studies considered them to be complementary and mutually reinforcing. This was because a dynamic market economy was largely predicated on a particular set of moral values, namely independence (from the state), individual responsibility, self improvement, self reliance and self help. In other words, what Margaret Thatcher (1983) famously lauded as 'Victorian values', and Shirley Letwin later termed the 'vigorous virtues' (as we noted above) (Letwin, 1992). These values, the CPS believed, were prerequisites of a market economy characterized by competition, entrepreneurship, hard work and the allocation of rewards in proportion to effort and/or success.

The CPS therefore saw its role as being to advance the intellectual case reversing the post-1945 extension of the state's role in economic and social affairs, because this was deemed simultaneously to have suppressed the operation of 'the market' and private enterprise, while destroying independence and the work ethic due to the expansion of the welfare state, coupled with the veneration of egalitarianism, which allegedly penalized wealth creation. As such, there was considerable congruence between the critique and consequent policy prognosis canvassed by the CPS and what became commonly known as Thatcherism – hardly surprising given that Thatcher herself was one of its founders.

Policy Exchange

Rather more recently, 2002 heralded the formation of Policy Exchange, a think tank that aimed to foster the development of a post-Thatcherite Conservatism, and thereby help the Conservatives to challenge New Labour and Blairism. In this respect, Policy Exchange was an integral part of a process of Conservative 'modernization', which really gathered pace after the election of David Cameron as party leader at the end of 2005. Indeed, Pautz has suggested that Policy Exchange 'could well be the most important think tank for the Conservative modernization discourse' articulated by the Conservative Party under David Cameron's leadership (Pautz, 2012a: 369). Cameron himself once claimed that 'without Policy Exchange, there would be no Conservative revolution' (quoted in Parker, 2008: 4), although this is almost certainly hyperbole.

Formed by Conservative MPs Francis Maude, Archie Norman and Nicholas Boles, Policy Exchange can also boast Michael Gove (appointed Secretary of State for Education when the coalition government was formed in May 2010) as a former Chair. By 2008, one political journalist was describing Policy Exchange as: 'The think tank closest to the government-in-waiting of David Cameron, a hothouse for many of its likely personnel, and the deviser of much of what the Conservatives are likely to do in Office' (Beckett, 2008: 7).

With characteristic modesty, Gove once claimed, via the think tank's website that: 'Policy Exchange were a tiny band of guerrillas, partisans in the hillside fighting a lonely campaign but now, that tiny guerrilla band has turned into the most formidable regular army on the think tank battlefield' (quoted in Williams, 2010: 10). Similarly, having been elected as MP for Grantham (Margaret Thatcher's hometown), Boles deems Policy Exchange to have become 'the largest and most influential policy research institute on the centre right ... Many of our ideas have been adopted by the Conservative Party under David Cameron' (Boles, 2013).

Much of Policy Exchange's focus is on public sector reform, and the alleged need to involve the private and voluntary sectors much more extensively in providing services (see, for example, Worth, 2013). Many of the policy proposals promoted by Policy Exchange appear to have been adopted by Cameron's Conservative Party and *inter alia* the post-May 2010 Conservative-Liberal Democrat coalition, most notably opening up more of the welfare state and public services to the private or voluntary sector, encouraging 'non-state' bodies, individuals and businesses, to create 'free' schools, relaxing planning laws and devolving power to local communities.

The Centre for Social Justice

The Centre for Social Justice (CSJ) was established by the former Conservative leader Iain Duncan Smith in 2004. Its professed objective was to contribute towards the development of a new social policy agenda for the Conservative Party, and to this end, the CSJ focused primarily on the causes of poverty and social disadvantage in contemporary Britain, and thereupon proposed policies to tackle these problems. The CSJ declares itself to be an independent (non-political) think tank, and has included Labour's David Blunkett and Frank Field on its Advisory Board, along with Gaby Hinsliff, a political correspondent on the liberal-Leftish Sunday newspaper *The Observer*.

Yet in spite of its professed political neutrality and the apparent ideological eclecticism of its Advisory Board, much of the CSJ's analyses of social problems and consequent policy proposals have been wholly commensurate with David Cameron's promotion of the 'Big Society' (on which, see Dorey and Garnett, 2012; Edwards, 2012; Norman, 2010). For example, the CSJ has identified five main causes of poverty, namely: family breakdown; educational failure; economic dependency and worklessness; serious personal debt; and addiction to drugs and alcohol.

While these are doubtless serious problems for many people and certainly perpetuate poverty and social exclusion, the CSJ seems to overlook or underestimate the role of low incomes, especially wages, as a major cause of poverty. Moreover, there is an implicit assumption that these five causes of poverty derive from failings by the individuals affected – poverty is pathologized – rather than being attributable to wider structural factors concerning the highly unequal distribution of wealth in Britain and the role of an unregulated free market in fuelling vast disparities of incomes.

Furthermore, the CSJ's proposals for tackling these five causes of poverty, and the consequent social breakdown or civic disorder they often underpin, primarily entail expanding the role and activities of charities, the independent (private) sector and voluntary bodies, while simultaneously reforming the social security system, promoting marriage and invoking tougher sanctions against the unemployed and partially-disabled. This is why we would categorize the Centre for Social Justice as a predominantly Right-wing think tank, perhaps promoting 'compassionate Conservatism', or what some might term 'tough love'.

With regard to the New Right think tanks in general, Cockett's seminal study suggests that they, and various individuals associated with them, 'did as much intellectually to convert a generation of "opinion formers" and politicians to a new set of ideas as the Fabians had done with a former generation at the turn of the century' (Cockett, 1994: 5), while Seldon, although fully acknowledging the difficulties of accurately gauging their precise influence on particular policies, concurs that since the 1970s, think tanks 'have had an influential role in collating the thoughts of like-minded intellectuals and funnelling them into governing circles' (Seldon, 1996: 273. See also Harris, 1996: 57–8; Jones, 2012: 161–73). Desai went further, though, by asserting that:

> ... most of the specific policy initiatives of the Thatcher governments originated as proposals from these think tanks: monetarism, the abolition of exchange controls, the sale of council houses, the contracting out of government services, the curbing of union powers, and the abolition of metropolitan councils are all examples.
>
> (Desai, 1994: 34)

In similar vein, one of Margaret Thatcher's closest ministerial colleagues during the 1980s, Nicholas Ridley (1991: 8), asserted that:

> The CPS became the furnace in which the new economics was forged. Margaret Thatcher and Keith Joseph were also helped by two other think tanks: the Institute of Economic Affairs ... and the Adam Smith Institute ... Nonetheless, it was the CPS which was always closest to Margaret Thatcher and Keith Joseph, and from where many of their most formidable allies were drawn.

Likewise, Kenneth Baker, the Secretary of State for Education who introduced the 1988 Education Reform Act (which established the National Curriculum, regular testing of pupils and facilitated the 'opting out' of schools from Local Education Authority control), averred that:

> ... the Centre for Policy Studies ... together with the Adam Smith Institute and the Institute of Economic Affairs was to become such an influential powerhouse of ideas and policies for 1980s Conservatism. It acted as a focus for talented individuals of the Right, many of whom were to make a significant impact both as policy initiators and as selected politicians.
>
> (Baker, 1993: 162)

Of course, as we have previously intimated, the Thatcher governments would probably have enacted these policies anyway, but the sundry New Right think tanks probably still played a signal role in imbuing such reforms with greater ideological coherence and intellectual credibility, and helped 'spread the message' to a wider audience, at least in parts of academia, the media, among some senior officials in the core executive and also various Policy Advisers serving ministers, including the Prime Minister.

Ideological or partisan think tanks: 'progressive', centre-Left or New Labour

In response to the apparent or perceived influence exercised by New Right think tanks from the mid-1970s onwards, some figures on the centre-Left were prompted to form their own think tanks during the late 1980s and 1990s, or rejuvenate those that already had a long history. The three main centre-Left or self-proclaimed 'progressive' think tanks are outlined in Table 2.3.

The Institute for Public Policy Research, and Demos

Like their Conservative or New Right counterparts, most of the centre-Left or 'progressive' think tanks claim to have exercised at least some influence on the Labour Party since the early 1990s, to the extent of partly fashioning 'New Labour' even before the term was actually invoked. For example, the Institute for Public Policy Research (IPPR) claims to have played a major role in the 1992 establishment, by the Labour leadership, of the (Borrie) Commission on Social Justice, which in turn, provided the basis for such New Labour policies as the New Deal. The IPPR also claims that several of its other policy ideas and initiatives were readily embraced by the Blair governments, including environmental taxation, the Human Rights Act and an expansion of 'social housing'. However, the IPPR might be most remembered for its enthusiastic endorsement of Public–Private Partnerships, whereby public sector infrastructure (such as schools and hospitals) was built and financed 'up front' by private sector companies and consortiums, but thereafter leased back to the public sector, often for 25–30 years. Such was IPPR's perceived influence on various New Labour policies from the mid-1990s onwards that it was once referred to as 'New Labour's civil service' (Rowan, 2003: 17; see also, Bentham, 2006; Ruben, 1996).

Meanwhile, having been founded in 1993, Demos claimed to eschew allegedly outdated ideological notions of Left and Right, and instead purported to signify the shift towards 'new times', a term originally invoked by senior figures formerly associated with the journal *Marxism Today* (Hall and Jacques, 1989).

Table 2.3 Centre-Left or 'progressive' think tanks associated with New Labour

Name of think tank	Formed	Focus or orientation
Demos	1993	Describes itself as 'a greenhouse of new ideas' intended to underpin five main themes, namely democracy, learning, enterprise, global change and quality of life. Strong focus on cultural issues – environmental affairs, drugs, gender relations, political apathy, parenting, and so on. When New Labour was in Office, Demos claimed that its ideas 'regularly influence government policy' (www.demos.co.uk; see also, Bale, 1996).
Fabian Society	1884	Always espoused a gradualist yet progressive approach to social reform to establish a fairer society, but has experienced something of a renaissance, claiming to have made a significant contribution to the Labour Party's process of modernization since 1992, particularly the 1995 rewriting of Clause IV. Viewed itself as the Blair government's 'critical friend' (see Callaghan, 1996, for an overview).
Institute for Public Policy Research	1988	Claims to be 'the leading independent think tank on the centre left', whose 'well-researched and clearly argued policy analysis' makes a significant contribution to 'maintaining the momentum of progressive thought'. Through its ideas and policy proposals, the Institute aims to create 'a fairer, more inclusive and more environmentally sustainable world', deriving from its values of 'social justice, equality, and democratic empowerment' (www.ippr.org.uk).

However, according to one writer on think tanks, whereas the IPPR had been largely concerned with policy advocacy, Demos 'did not have as much interest in proposing concrete policies', but was orientated more towards ideas and debates about post-ideological politics, and perhaps providing a framework in which others developed policy policies (Pautz, 2010: 292. See also Bale, 1996; Pautz, 2012b: 69). This would imply that the relationship between Demos and the IPPR was analogous to that between the IEA and the ASI (as noted above), with the former in each case focusing more on the intellectual framework or battle of ideas and the latter more concerned with actual policy proposals.

Yet as if to confirm the difficulty of gauging think tank influence on party policies, some authors have suggested that Demos published pamphlets on topics that subsequently formed the basis of several policies or priorities of New Labour, most notably welfare into work, joined-up government, parental leave and greater democracy. That said, the authors note that these policy proposals were mostly canvassed before 1997 (that is, before New Labour was elected), but that thereafter, Demos did shift its focus more to ideas and themes – such as democracy, globalization, quality of life – in an attempt at promoting more general political debate over key issues for the early 21st century (Denham and Garnett, 2006: 163).

Individual links between think tanks and governments

A further indication of the apparent affinity between these think tanks and New Labour was that immediately after the party's 1997 election victory, the co-founder of Demos, Geoff Mulgan, was appointed by Tony Blair to serve in the Cabinet Office, his remit being to coordinate the implementation of various policies, thereby assisting the pursuit of 'joined-up government'. This exemplifies an important means by which some of the ideas canvassed by the more political or partisan think tanks can be transmitted to governments, namely through the appointment of some senior think tank staff to key posts within the 'core executive' (discussed in the next two chapters). Some of the most notable of these appointments are listed in Table 2.4.

Certainly, it has been suggested that during the latter half of Margaret Thatcher's premiership, key aspects of education policy were strongly influenced by sundry Right-wing think tanks, which established links with the Prime Minister's Policy Unit. This 'was happy and willing to act as a "conduit" between the various education think tanks', such as the Hillgate Group, along with more general think tanks such as the Centre for Policy Studies and the Institute of Economic Affairs (Chitty, 2009: 133. See also Jones, 2003: 125, 141). Similarly, Peter Riddell observes that by the mid-1980s, there had developed 'growing pressure within the government for more radical action, encouraged by the various free-market think tanks and the Downing Street Policy Unit' (Riddell, 1991: 143).

Table 2.4   Examples of senior think tank staff subsequently appointed to posts in the core executive since 1979

Name	Former think tank membership or post	Subsequent political post
Dan Corry	Institute for Public Policy Research	1. Special Adviser to Margaret Beckett, Peter Mandelson and Stephen Byers, Department of Trade and Industry (1997–2001) 2. Special Adviser to Stephen Byers, Department of Transport, Local Government and the Regions (2001–02) 3. Special Adviser to Gordon Brown in Prime Minister's Policy Unit, 2007–10
Patrick Diamond	Institute for Public Policy Research	Special Adviser to Tony Blair, 10 Downing Street Policy Unit, focusing on public sector reform, 2001–04
Iain Duncan Smith	Founder of the Centre for Social Justice (while still a Conservative MP)	Secretary of State for Work and Pensions (from May 2010)
Beth Egan	Deputy Director of Demos	Special Adviser to Gordon Brown, Chancellor of the Exchequer
Amy Fisher	Policy Exchange	Special Adviser to Caroline Spelman, DEFRA (from May 2010)

(Continued)

Table 2.4   (Continued)

Name	Former think tank membership or post	Subsequent political post
Patricia Hewitt	Deputy Director, Institute of Public Policy Research	Secretary of State for Trade and Industry, 2001–05
Nick Hillman	Policy Exchange	Special Adviser to David Willetts, Minister for Higher Education (from May 2010)
John Hoskyns	Centre for Policy Studies	Head of 10 Downing Street Policy Unit under Margaret Thatcher (1979–82)
Michael Gove	Chair of Policy Exchange	Secretary of State for Education (from May 2010)
Gavin Lockhart	Policy Exchange	Special Adviser to David Cameron (from May 2010)
Francis Maude	Co-Founder of Policy Exchange	Minister for the Cabinet Office (from May 2010)
David Miliband	Institute for Public Policy Research	1. Head of 10 Downing Street Policy Unit under Tony Blair 2. From 2001, a Labour MP and Minister of State for Education
Ferdinand Mount	Director of Centre for Policy Studies	Head of 10 Downing Street Policy Unit under Margaret Thatcher (1982–83)
Geoff Mulgan	Co-Founder and Director of Demos	1. Special Adviser to Tony Blair (with particular reference to tackling social exclusion) 2. Head of Cabinet Office's Strategy Unit
James O'Shaughnessy	Policy Exchange	Special Adviser to David Cameron (from May 2010)
John Redwood	Centre for Policy Studies	1. Head of 10 Downing Street Policy Unit under Margaret Thatcher (1983–85) 2. Minister of State, Department of Trade and Industry, 1990–92 3. Minister of State, Department of Environment, 1992–93 4. Secretary of State for Wales, 1993–95
Richard Reeves	Demos	Special Adviser to Nick Clegg, Deputy Prime Minister (from May 2010)
Sir Alfred Sherman	Director of Studies at the Centre for Policy Studies	10 Downing Street Policy Unit under Margaret Thatcher (Special Adviser)
Norman Strauss	Centre for Policy Studies	10 Downing Street Policy Unit under Margaret Thatcher (Special Adviser)
Philippa Stroud	Co-Founder of Centre for Social Justice	Special Adviser to Iain Duncan Smith, Department of Work and Pensions (from 2010)
Matthew Taylor	Institute for Public Policy Research	Head of (Tony Blair's) 10 Downing Street Policy Directorate (2003–2005)
Sir Alan Walters	Centre for Policy Studies	Special (Economic) Adviser to Margaret Thatcher

Name	Former think tank membership or post	Subsequent political post
David Willetts	Director of Centre for Policy Studies (1987–1992) Board Member of Social Market Foundation after 1992	1. 10 Downing Street Policy Unit under Margaret Thatcher 2. Minister of State for Universities (since 2010)
Giles Wilkes	Centre Forum (Liberal Democrat think tank)	Special Adviser to Vince Cable, Secretary of State for Business, Innovation and Skills (since 2010)

One consequence of these developments was that the 1988 Education Reform Act, presaging the National Curriculum and 'key stage' tests for pupils, was largely 'assembled *in secret* ... There was a determined effort *not* to consult with either the DES [Department of Education and Science] or the civil servants or chief education officers or local politicians' (Maclure, 1988: 166, emphasis in original).

Much more recently, a number of previously senior members of the centre-Right think tanks, Policy Exchange, and the Centre for Social Justice, have been appointed as Special Advisers by ministers – including David Cameron himself – in the coalition government. This is not really surprising, given that the afore-mentioned strong affinity between many of the ideas and polices canvassed by these think tanks, and those associated with Cameron and fellow Conservative modernizers, particularly the promotion of 'free schools' and aspects of the 'Big Society'.

ORGANIZED INTERESTS

The number and range of organized interests (sometimes referred to as 'pressure groups') is enormous; on almost any issue or topic, there is likely to be at least one organization representing those who are involved in it, affected by it, support it or oppose it. Not surprisingly, there have been numerous attempts by political scientists to categorize organized interests in terms of shared characteristics or the role they play (if any) in policy making.

One of the earlier attempts distinguished between 'sectional' and 'promotional' groups, the former referring to those organizations whose membership was based on a particular occupation or profession, and who were arguably concerned primarily with economic issues or the material interests of their members, whereas 'promotional' groups had a looser and more varied membership derived from support for a particular issue or 'cause', often of an ethical, moral or social character (Stewart, 1958; Potter, 1961). Trade unions are prime examples of 'sectional' groups, while the Campaign for Nuclear Disarmament (CND) and the (anti-abortion) Society for the Protection of the Unborn Child (SPUC) are examples of groups 'promoting' a cause, or campaigning for a change in public policy, based on particular beliefs or values.

Membership of a sectional group almost always entails material advantages to the members, meaning that they personally benefit from joining. By contrast, the members of a promotional group rarely gain tangible benefits, but join because they feel strongly about a particular issue, such as abortion, the environment, fox hunting, homophobia or racism. Also, of course, there are promotional groups concerned with the welfare of animals, with the Royal Society for the Protection of Animals (RSPCA) being the most notable example.

'Insider' and 'outsider' groups

This two-fold categorization was then developed further by Wyn Grant, who defined organized interests on the basis of their position in the political system and thus their proximity to, and relationship with, policy makers (Grant, 1989: 14–21; Grant, 2000: 18–35). Groups that enjoyed close and regular access to policy makers, most notably ministers, government departments and senior civil servants, were categorized as 'insiders'.

These groups were deemed important to policy makers, either in terms of their economic or strategic importance (governments can hardly afford to ignore the views of business leaders or 'the City', on whom investment, and thus jobs, economic growth and tax revenues, so strongly depends), or the expertise that they could offer. For example, the British Medical Association (BMA) can offer specialist advice on aspects of health policy, while the National Farmers Union (NFU) can similarly advise policy makers on rather scientific or technical aspects of agricultural affairs and farming methods. In effect, the organized interests that Grant classified as 'insiders' tended to be those previously defined as 'sectional' groups.

By contrast, most 'outsiders' were similar to 'promotional' or 'cause' groups and thus lacked the close or regular contact with senior policy makers in the core executive. Consequently, 'outsider' groups generally had to rely on public campaigns, such as advertisements, marches or rallies in order to raise public or media awareness of an issue, and thereby persuade policy makers to take it seriously – to place it on the institutional agenda. Alternatively, an 'outsider' group might collect signatures on a petition, in an attempt to convince policy makers that there is popular support for the adoption or repeal of a particular policy.

A few 'outsider' pressure groups, however, might deliberately reject such constitutional methods and instead engage in 'direct action' or forms of 'civil disobedience', reflecting their conviction that policy makers who are part of 'the Establishment' will refuse to listen to 'reasoned arguments' or accept 'inconvenient' evidence. Such 'outsiders' include the environmental group Greenpeace, and 'animal welfare' groups such as the Animal Liberation Front and the Hunt Saboteurs Association.

Of course, in most cases, their 'outsider' status is self-perpetuating; policy makers will not talk to such groups because their policy goals and/or tactics are deemed to be too extreme and irresponsible, and such groups will engage in direct action or forms of civil disobedience because policy makers refuse to listen to them. Each 'side' will blame the other for being dogmatic or intransigent and of making compromise impossible.

Although the 'insider' versus 'outsider' distinction provided a useful account of the role of some organized interests at the 'macro' or governmental level, while also explaining why some groups were effectively excluded from the corridors of political power and policy making, some writers subsequently developed a 'meso-level' classification to explain the role of organized interests and their relationships with formal policy makers at the sectoral level or in particular spheres of public policy, such as agriculture, education, health, and so on. This yielded the notion of policy networks, an approach that not only 'emphasises the need to disaggregate policy analysis and stresses that relationships between groups and government vary between policy areas', but also recognizes that 'in most policy areas, a limited number of interests are involved in the policy-making process' (Rhodes and Marsh, 1992: 1, 4).

In particular, the policy networks approach suggested a continuum comprising varying relationships and degrees of contact, interaction and influence between organized interests and formal policy makers. At the respective ends of this policy networks continuum are tightly-knit and relatively closed 'policy communities' and looser, rather more open, 'issue networks'. It is policy communities that have traditionally exerted the greatest influence on policy making in Britain, or as Grant himself expressed it, the concept 'clearly provides a good fit with the available empirical evidence on how decisions are made in British government' (Grant, 2000: 50), so it is to policy communities that we now turn our attention.

Policy communities

Richardson and Jordan once noted that: 'The policy-making map is in reality a series of vertical compartment or segments – each segment inhabited by a different set of organized groups, and generally impenetrable by "unorganized groups" or the general public' (Richardson and Jordan, 1979: 174). Similarly, Grant acknowledges that: 'Policy communities are generally organised around a government Department and its network of client groups', whereby the 'real divisions are between the different policy communities, rather than within the communities themselves' (Grant, 2000: 50).

The political scientists who have done most to popularize the concept of policy communities are Rod Rhodes and David Marsh (Rhodes and Marsh, 1992. See also Rhodes, 1997: 44), the defining characteristics of which are listed in Box 2.4.

Box 2.4   Defining characteristics of policy communities

- Limited membership, comprising a very small number of policy actors, often with just one key organized interest closely involved with senior civil servants, the relevant government department and the appropriate minister(s).
- Functional membership, usually based upon economic function and occupation or profession, which gives the organized interest a strategic importance or possession of valuable expertise.
- Actual membership *vis-à-vis* potential membership is high, meaning that a majority of those who are eligible for membership actually are members and thus enable the group to claim it is 'representative'; the 'voice' of that occupation or profession. This, in turn, can imbue the group with 'legitimacy' in its dealings with policy makers.

(Continued)

(Continued)

- The organized interest has a hierarchical and disciplined structure, thereby ensuring that agreements entered into with policy makers by the group's leadership will subsequently be adhered to by the mass membership. Otherwise, policy makers would have little confidence in jointly developing policies with the group's leadership.
- The leaders of the organized interest enjoy close and regular access to the relevant government department, so that discussions over policies occurs continuously and routinely.
- There are mostly shared values and objectives between the organized interest and the relevant department. This ensures that they tend to focus on management of the institutional policy agenda: 'a policy community exists where there are effective shared "community" views on the problem. *Where there are no such shared views, no community exists*' (Jordan, 1990: 327, original emphasis).
- A symbiotic exchange relationship based on respective resources; governments and relevant departments provide political authority, legislative endorsement, an appropriate policy framework and overall legitimation, while the key organized interest(s) provide specialist knowledge and expertise, technical or professional advice and assistance in implementing agreed policies.
- Relationships usually entail bargaining and negotiation due the existence of exchange relationships. The participants cannot normally *impose* their preferences on each other because of the need to share resources in order to achieve shared objectives and mutually beneficial policy goals. This tends to encourage a more consensual, 'give and take', approach to policy making.

It has therefore been noted that:

> Policy communities are closed networks within which membership is restricted to a limited number of groups and government actors who share a largely consensual perspective on policy in a particular policy area. Only those insider groups with requisite resources gain access to this segmented world of policy-making. Within a community, there is mutual dependency between groups and government ... [derived from] resource exchange.

> (Judge, 2005: 107)

Until the 1980s at least, several policy communities could be identified, as illustrated in Table 2.5.

The attributes of policy communities had a significant impact on many areas of public policy in Britain, at least until the late 1980s. The most important of these was a tendency towards extensive stability and continuity of public policy in their particular policy sub-system. Policy communities are commonly characterized by the durability of existing policies and their resistance to change, especially in the short term. This (small 'c') conservatism is not really surprising, for existing policies in their particular policy sub-system will usually

Table 2.5 Examples of policy communities in Britain until the 1980s

Policy sphere	Key department	Key organized interest(s)
Agriculture	Ministry of Agriculture, Fisheries and Food (replaced by DEFRA in 2001)	National Farmers Union
Crime/Law and order	Home Office	Police Federation Association of Chief Police Officers
Education	Department of Education	National Union of Teachers Local Education Authorities
Health	Department of Health	British Medical Association
Transport	Department of Transport	Road Haulage Association Freight Transport Association Society of Motor Manufacturers and Traders

have been the outcome of previous bargaining and negotiation between the key organized interest(s), senior civil servants inside the relevant government department and the appropriate minister, these negotiations having yielded a compromise or consensus.

Hence Marsh and Rhodes observed that: 'the existence of a policy network/community is a key cause of ... continuity', and that 'the existence of a policy network or community acts as a major constraint upon the degree of policy change ... fosters incremental changes, thereby favouring the status quo or the existing balance of interests in the network.' However, because some changes are inevitable over time, policy networks will normally seek 'to contain, constrain, redirect and ride out such change, thereby materially affecting its speed and direction ... a dynamic conservatism' (Marsh and Rhodes, 1992a: 261–3).

Similarly, Jordan and Richardson observed that the 'logic of negotiation' intrinsic to a policy community tended to ensure that 'policy-makers in both government and groups will share an interest in the avoidance of sudden policy change. Working together, they will learn what kind of change is feasible, and what would so embarrass other members of "the system" as to be unproductive' (Jordan and Richardson, 1982: 93–4).

Consequently, the strength of a policy community has often been such that new ministers keen to promote new ideas and initiatives were met with considerable scepticism and resistance, and persuaded that their proposals were not really feasible or practicable. While some ministers persevered with their initiatives, many were either persuaded of the arguments against a particular policy proposal, or simply accepted that the policy community's resistance was likely to be so pronounced that perseverance would consume too much time and energy: some battles were simply not worth fighting, and (political) life was too short.

Certainly, as noted above, policy communities often played an important role, along with the relevant Department, in disputing or redefining issues emerging from the systemic agenda, which might challenge their interests and thereby result in significant policy change. In this respect, the relationship, between policy communities and institutional agendas corresponds closely to Bachrach and Baratz's 'second' or 'hidden' face of power and their concept of 'non-decision-making', which (as we noted in the previous chapter) is 'exercised by confining the scope of decision-making to relatively safe issues'. This means that 'demands for change in the existing allocation of benefits and privileges in the community can be suffocated before they are even voiced; or kept covert; or killed to prevent access to the relevant decision-making arena' (Bachrach and Baratz, 1970: 7).

Somewhat more recently, Marsh and Smith explained that 'tight policy networks persist, in large part, because they are characterised by a large degree of consensus ... on [the] policy agenda, the boundaries of acceptable policy' (Marsh and Smith, 2000: 6). Similarly, Smith himself observes that:

> If there is a dominant set of beliefs, it protects the institutions by justifying the inclusion of certain interests and preventing the conceptions of alternatives. The institutional structures protect the ideology by preventing the access of groups which could suggest new ideas and policies ... If groups do arise which question the agenda, then the institutional means can be used to keep them out.
>
> (Smith, 1990: 45–6)

With regard to the transport policy community, for example, the close relationship between road haulage companies, road construction firms, the Automobile Association (AA) and the Royal Automobile Club (RAC), and the Department of Transport has been deemed as a prime example of the 'shared professional understanding or economic interest', which underpins policy communities (Glaister et al., 2006: 168).

However, policy communities can and do change, depending on circumstances and conditions. Indeed, many of the factors prompting changes in, or even the destabilization of, a policy community are similar to the drivers of policy change more generally, as identified in the previous chapter.

A 'paradigm shift' in the ideological framework or political climate

In Britain, the early 1980s heralded a paradigm shift to economic neo-liberalism, whereupon many of the social democratic principles and policies pursued since 1945 were explicitly abandoned. The consequent paradigm shift, entailing the increasing hegemony of economic neo-liberalism, and its fetishization of the free market as the solution to all societal problems, was subsequently to have a major impact on the policy process, because many policy communities were attacked or marginalized, as ministers sought to reassert political authority over professionals and 'producer interests'.

This shift was particularly pronounced with regard to the (1979–97) Thatcher-Major governments' pursuit of radical reforms in education and health policies, entailing the promotion of 'markets' and 'managerialism'. The imposition of such reforms often entailed confrontation with the medical and teaching professions and their respective representative bodies or trade unions. Indeed, such clashes were not merely an unfortunate consequence of such reforms, but were often deliberately sought and relished by ministers precisely so that they could display their authority and earn plaudits from those who welcomed their seemingly courageous challenges to allegedly selfish, self-serving vested interests among professionals in the public sector.

Therefore, the changing ideological framework and political approach accruing from a paradigm shift not only results in a significant change in the content and objectives of public policy, but also in the *style* of governing and policy making. In this instance, the previous social democratic emphasis on consensus and partnership, which was clearly conducive to the operation of policy communities, was replaced by 'conviction politics' and an insistence that ministers and markets should determine public policy, not those professionals who were employed as doctors or teachers, for example.

Furthermore, within public sector institutions or organizations, professionals were further weakened by the deliberate promotion of 'managerialism', whereby a new cadre of managers was employed explicitly to impose authority on front-line staff, and ensure their compliance with governmental objectives, albeit couched in the rhetoric of serving their 'customers' more efficiently and courteously.

Ministerial imposition

This occurs when ministers are more proactive, and willing to seize the political initiative by instigating and imposing change in key policy areas. As we will note in the next chapter, since the 1980s, a growing number of ministers have adopted a more adversarial style in order to enact significant reforms or even introduce new policies, which would almost inevitably be opposed by the organized or professional interests in the relevant policy community. Martin J. Smith has referred to this mode of ministerial imposition as a form of 'despotic power' (Smith, 1993: 95–6), as was evident in the Thatcher-Major governments' NHS reforms: 'It was clear that in reforming health policy, and in changing the management structure, the Thatcher governments were preparing to challenge the existing policy community', so that with the introduction of the reforms, 'relations between doctors and the government ... deteriorated' (Smith, 1993: 182–3. See also Wistow, 1992: 71).

Elsewhere, but with similar implications and consequences for hitherto close and (usually) cordial relations between Whitehall and the teaching profession, two of the Education Secretaries in the Thatcher-Major governments, Kenneth Baker and John Patten, made clear their total contempt for the 'education establishment' and its alleged egalitarian/pro-comprehensive schools ideology (Baker, 1993: 168; Patten, 1995: 196–7).

Needless to say, this contempt was fully shared by Thatcher herself, as illustrated by her claim that 'the ethos of the DES was self-righteously socialist ... Equality in education was not only the overriding good, irrespective of the practical effects of egalitarianism on particular schools; it was a stepping stone to achieving equality in society'. Moreover, she was highly critical of the extent to which the DES had 'become as closely connected with its clients as the DES was with the teaching unions, in particular the National Union of Teachers (NUT) ... a large number of DES senior civil servants ... and the NUT leaders were on the closest terms', sharing 'a common sympathy' (Thatcher, 1995: 166).

Such views were shared by one of Margaret Thatcher's closest advisers in the Downing Street Policy Unit. Alfred Sherman (2005: 107, 108), who alleged that in post-1945 Britain: 'The education establishment ... had brought standards steadily down', while also alluding to the pernicious influence of 'Marxoid dons' in shaping higher education policy since the 1960s. Thatcher's successor, John Major, similarly denounced 'the giant left-wing experiment in levelling down' (Major, 1992: 9), 'the failed nostrums of the 1960s and 1970s' (Major, 1993: 31) and 'the fads and fashions that short-changed an entire generation of children … called … progressive education' (Major, 1997: 20).

Crisis/crises

Just as we noted in Chapter 1 how a crisis, or series of crises can precipitate substantive policy change, so too can such phenomena serve to weaken a policy community, by undermining or discrediting the assumptions, norms and shared policy objectives upon which it was based, and through which it had previously controlled the institutional agenda. This in turn can foster the conditions in which other policy actors can gain admittance to the policy process and thereby help to promote a change of policy, as it becomes apparent that the status quo is no longer tenable; indeed, may have become a major part of the problem. For example, the agricultural policy community seems to have been significantly weakened by various crises since the later 1980s, most notably the 'salmonella in egg production' crisis (Smith, 1991), the BSE crisis (Grant, 1997; Greer, 1999) and the 2001 foot-and-mouth epidemic (McConnell and Stark, 2002). These served to raise serious questions about aspects of modern farming methods, food production and animal husbandry.

The emergence of new knowledge or evidence

In the previous chapter, we noted briefly how new evidence and knowledge can exercise an influence on public policy, perhaps pushing an issue onto the institutional agenda and constituting a source of policy change. In such instances, new evidence or knowledge can serve to de-stabilize or disrupt extant policy communities by challenging the core principles or values upon which they, and the institutional policy agenda, have hitherto been based.

Again, the agricultural policy community provides a good example because of the scientific evidence that has posited links between intensive farming methods and health risks among humans, epidemics among cattle, such as the bovine spongiform encephalopathy (BSE) crisis and also the deleterious impact of pesticides (to kill insects which would damage crops).

For example, Martin J. Smith cites a late 1980s study that revealed that out of 426 pesticides approved by the Ministry of Agriculture, Fisheries and Food (MAFF), 124 were suspected of being linked to cancer (Smith, 1991: 249). At the same time, Smith remarks, 'food issues, like heart disease, additives and food poisoning touch people much more directly than agricultural support prices', whereupon farming and food production attracted interest from a wider range of organizations, including medical experts and the British Medical Association, the Department of Health, nutritionists and consumer groups (Smith, 1991: 253, 251).

Concerns have also been raised by some environmentalists and ornithologists about the possible impact of large-scale use of pesticides and other agri-chemicals on wildlife and some birds in Britain's countryside. With regard to the latter, for example, questions have been raised about whether the diminishing numbers of some bird species are a partial consequence of farmers (understandably) seeking to eradicate insects that would otherwise destroy their crop, but in so doing, inadvertently eliminating the natural food supply of many of Britain's birds.

The combined impact of such knowledge has further weakened the former prominence of the NFU, and obliged it to accept that policies pertaining to food production and rural affairs entail rather more than just agriculture and farming interests only. Consequently, 2001 saw the MAFF abolished, and replaced by a new, more broad-ranging, Department of the Environment, Food and Rural Affairs (DEFRA). Although the NFU is still an important and often influential organized interest, it now has to operate alongside various other organizations with an interest in policies pertaining to the countryside, the rural environment and food production, but which might not necessarily be commensurate with the interests of farmers themselves

Similarly, Read's case study shows how the tobacco policy community was forced onto the defensive when, in the 1970s, medical evidence established a clear and incontrovertible correlation between cigarette smoking and various diseases, most notably lung cancer (Read, 1992). Since then, further medical research discovered that 'passive smoking' (inhaling smoke from other people's cigarettes) can itself increase the likelihood of developing cancer. As a result of this scientific and medical evidence, the tobacco policy community has been compelled to accept increasing statutory restrictions on cigarette advertising, and since 2007, a statutory ban on smoking in pubs, restaurants and various other public places. There have since been proposals to place further restrictions on the advertising of cigarettes.

In the context of such examples, Richardson notes that: 'New ideas have a virus-like quality and have an ability to disrupt existing policy systems, power relationships and policies ... knowledge is a powerful change agent (either endogenous or exogenous) for policy communities and networks', and can 'lead to major changes in public policy, and to the power and composition of existing policy communities' (Richardson, 2000: 1017–20).

Since the 1980s, therefore, various policy communities in Britain have been affected by these developments, to the extent that a number of writers, including some who were previously closely associated with the concept, now suggest that policy-making 'is often much more fluid and unpredictable – and less controllable' than policy community theorists previously assumed. Policy communities remain in various policy domains and subsystems, but they are nonetheless more susceptible to 'counter-tendencies which lead to lack of control, policy instability, and unpredictable outcomes' (Richardson, 2000: 1008).

Policy communities seem to have become more vulnerable to various challenges since the 1980s, so those that remain do so in a less stable political and institutional universe, and consequently find it more difficult to retain control over the institutional policy agenda.

Moreover, even if they continue to enjoy regular access to ministers, departments and senior civil servants, they have often had to accept that other organized interests have also been admitted to the corridors of power, along with think tanks and Special Advisers.

Yet the degree to which access by organized interests to core policy makers has been opened up or become more fluid should not be over-exaggerated, for there remain many groups who continue to play a peripheral or sporadic role in the policy process, and who are primarily part of the systemic agenda, namely those groups who constitute 'issue networks'.

Issue networks

If policy communities represent one end of a 'policy networks' continuum, based on close (and closed) relations and regular interaction between policy makers and the leaders of organized interests, then issue networks constitute the other end (Marsh and Rhodes, 1992a; Rhodes, 1997: Daugbjerg, 1998), as indicated in Box 2.5.

Box 2.5   Main characteristics of issue networks

- Open membership, whereby several organized interests (some perhaps only loosely organized) are involved in a sphere of policy, often reflecting the broad-ranging or eclectic character of the issue or problem, for example 'the environment' or 'poverty'. This actually means that the plethora of organized interests in an issue network might lack coherence in their particular policy because they are focusing on a specific aspect of a broad-ranging problem.

- Membership is often based on ethical, moral or social beliefs, rather than material, professional or self-interest.

- Actual membership is often low in relation to potential membership. For example, suppose the Campaign for Nuclear Disarmament (CND) had one million members, this ostensibly large number would still represent only a small proportion of Britain's 60 million population. This often enables policy makers to claim that such groups are 'unrepresentative' because only a very small proportion of British people join them.

- The organization and its membership are often loosely organized, and may also be characterized by high turnover as members develop other interests, face other demands on their leisure time or become disillusioned at the group's lack of success.

- The leaders of the organized interest enjoy only limited or sporadic contact with policy makers. Much, if not most, of the time, ministers and senior civil servants will not seek to establish regular links with such groups. If and when there is any contact, it will tend to be on an *ad hoc* or one-off basis, over a particular issue. Moreover, such contact will be based on consultation, perhaps entailing a polite but inconclusive exchange of views, rather than serious bargaining and negotiation to agree a definite policy.

- There are few, if any, shared values between the organized interests in an issue network and formal policy makers. Very often, groups in an issue network are part of the systemic agenda and trying to highlight issues that are not on the institutional agenda, either because policy makers do not acknowledge that there is a (serious) problem, or because ministers and senior civil servants do not accept that it should be the government's responsibility to solve the problem.

- There is thus no symbiotic exchange relationship because organized interests in an issue network do not normally possess or have access to resources in the form of specialist knowledge and expertise, which are required for policy making. Nor do policy makers require their cooperation in implementing policies; the groups or affected interests are not able to obstruct the enactment of a policy, so are again disregarded.

The relatively large and diverse membership that collectively constitutes an issue network reflects the multi-faceted or multi-causal nature of the issue, which the various organized interests are campaigning on. Or as Glaister et al. (2006: 169) observe: 'The issue is commonly one for which no government department serves as an obvious focal point, either because the problem cuts across departments (which might hold different views on the solutions), or because it is new to the political agenda.' This is a problem that particularly affects organized interests campaigning on issues such as 'the environment' or poverty, for neither issue can be deemed the formal responsibility of just one government department. For example, as Table 2.6 indicates, 'the environment' is an eclectic, broad-ranging issue that requires the involvement of several departments.

Table 2.6 Departments with remits that include an environmental dimension

Department	Environmental policy roles
Department for Business, Innovation and Skills	Pursuing 'sustainable' economic growth
Department for Communities and Local Government	Planning issues; new buildings and 'green belt' development; make homes and offices more 'energy efficient'
Department of Energy and Climate Change	Cutting UK greenhouse gas emissions; promoting renewable energy; cooperating with other countries to tackle global warming
Department of the Environment, Food and Rural Affairs (DEFRA)	Promoting sustainable and environmentally-friendly methods of food production; reducing the amount of waste sent to landfill; protecting areas of parkland and nature reserves; enforcing regulations that keep water and air clean
Department for International Development	Tackling the effects of climate change in developing countries; providing clean water and sanitation in developing countries; promoting and coordinating international action to tackle climate change
Department of Transport	Reduce greenhouse gas emissions from vehicle exhaust pipes; promote low-carbon transport technology; expand the rail network (to reduce car/lorry usage and traffic congestion)

As a consequence, those groups who collectively constitute the 'environmental lobby' will usually be unable to target just one department. Instead, they will often need to lobby several departments, sometimes simultaneously, which might serve to dilute their impact.

It might be assumed that the greater number of groups involved in an issue network would enhance their strength and thus make it easier to lobby relevant departments. Yet instead of enjoying strength in numbers, an issue network is often debilitated by the sheer range of groups and interests involved. This tends to yield a range of policy objectives, some of which might actually be incompatible and which might lead ministers to play divide and rule by playing one group off against the others. Certainly, the range of groups and interests that constitute an issue network usually makes it difficult for a clear and coherent policy to be advocated, and for the groups to speak with a single voice. Or as Ball and Millward (1986: 166) observe, 'environmental groups ... range over such a wide spectrum that it is difficult to generalise about common objectives, ideology and membership.'

Another example of an issue network, but one which illustrates similar problems, is the 'poverty lobby', defined by Whiteley and Winyard (1988: 197) as 'those voluntary organizations which regularly or sporadically attempt to influence the income maintenance policies of government in favour of the poor.' Some of the main bodies that collectively constitute the poverty lobby are listed in Box 2.6.

Box 2.6   Examples of organizations constituting the 'poverty lobby'

Age Concern
Big Issue Foundation
Child Poverty Action Group
Children's Society
Disability Alliance
Gingerbread
Joint Council for the Welfare of Immigrants
National Council for One Parent Families
Salvation Army
Save the Children
Shelter
Tax Justice Network
War on Want
War Widows Association

As is invariably the case with an issue network, the eclectic membership of the poverty lobby reflects the wide-ranging nature of the problem – to the extent that poverty is recognized as being a problem viz. the previous chapter's discussion of problem definition or denial. After all, poverty and low incomes not only have different origins, they also affect different sections of society at different times and in different ways. This makes it difficult to organize a coherent, consistent and focused campaign, not least because bodies such as Age Concern, the Child Poverty Action Group and Gingerbread – representing the elderly, children in low-income families and lone parents respectively – will often feel little affinity or solidarity with each other, even if they are concerned with issues pertaining to poverty.

Furthermore, some of the organizations identified in Box 2.6 are not necessarily *primarily* concerned with eradicating poverty or are only concerned with the issue indirectly because they campaign on a range of issues affecting the elderly, the homeless, disadvantaged or vulnerable children, immigrants, asylum seekers, and so on. Poverty will certainly be one of the problems experienced by many in these sections of society, but there will be other issues of concern too, which will add to the practical problems faced by the poverty lobby, in terms of lack of focus, consistency or coherence of objectives.

Yet even when these groups are focusing on poverty *per se*, they are likely to face debilitating weaknesses, not least because their policy goals will be different for each section of society. For example, Age Concern will variously campaign for improved pensions for the elderly, but is unlikely to feel much affinity or solidarity with a campaign by Gingerbread for more resources for single parents. Of course, such divergent interests and objectives within the poverty lobby again offer considerable opportunities for unsympathetic policy makers to play divide and rule, and thereby foster dissent and mutual resentment among some of the groups in the poverty lobby.

Another problem faced by the poverty lobby is the difficulty of determining which particular policy makers to target, because (as with environmentalism) the multi-faceted nature of the problem means that several departments have *some* responsibility for dealing with *some* aspects, albeit perhaps indirectly, relating to poverty in their policy sub-system. For example, Table 2.7 illustrates the departments that might be deemed to have a role to play in tackling poverty and low incomes, and how or why.

Consequently, the sheer number of groups involved in an issue network like the poverty lobby, coupled with their potentially competing and conflicting demands or objectives, and also the fact that the issues or problems transcend departmental boundaries, militates

Table 2.7   Departments that could be involved in tackling poverty

Department	Potential role in tackling poverty
Department for Business, Innovation and Skills 1. Department for Business, Innovation and Skills 2. The Treasury (HM Revenue and Customs)	Creating the right conditions for economic growth and increasing job opportunities Enforce the statutory minimum wage
Department for Communities and Local Government	1. Expanding supply of 'affordable' housing 2. Help households/families to reduce their fuel bills through energy saving schemes
Department of Education	Improving educational standards and literacy in order to increase 'employability' among the poor
Department of Energy and Climate Change	Tackling 'fuel poverty'
Department of Work and Pensions	1. Reforming the social security system to ensure that people are always better off working than remaining on the dole 2. Reforming the pensions system/increasing old age pensions
Treasury	1. Generally ensure that other Departments have the necessary funds to enact their anti-poverty policies 2. Reform the tax system to advantage those on low incomes – cutting the basic rate of income tax or/and raising the tax threshold)

against the development of permanent and stable relationships, either between the organized interests themselves or between them and the government departments. This instability both reflects and reinforces the absence of a clear consensus in an issue network, both over policy priorities and with regard to *who* should accept responsibility for solving it, quite apart from the question of *how* it should be solved.

As Smith explains: 'In an issue network, it is unlikely that there will be a consensus – the sheer number of groups means that consensus is practically unachievable', while the number of government departments involved further compounds the problem of 'conflict over who is responsible for a policy or issue, who should be involved and what action should be taken' (Smith, 1993: 63; see also Rhodes and Marsh, 1992: 14).

A final reason why the organized interests comprising the poverty lobby are confined to an issue network is that their active involvement is not considered necessary (by policy makers) in policy implementation. Ministers, civil servants and other agencies do not really require the assistance of the elderly in devising and administering pensions policies, or the active involvement of the low paid in determining either social security levels or the rate at which the minimum wage is set.

Furthermore, the poverty lobby, and indeed the poor themselves, lack the ability – either in terms of resources or structural position (in the economy or society) – to obstruct the implementation of policies in order to register discontent, and perhaps, compel ministers to think again. Or to express it another way, the organized interests constituting the poverty lobby 'are unable to deliver their clientele; they do not have sanctions such as non-co-operation with a new government policy' (Whiteley and Winyard, 1987: 133).

Ultimately, therefore, the organized interests in an issue network will usually enjoy only limited or sporadic contact with policy makers, usually in the form of consultation and a polite, possibly rather symbolic, eliciting of their views, rather than serious bargaining and negotiation. Hence, issue networks tend to focus more on attempting to influence the systemic agenda, in the hope of highlighting issues that will subsequently be addressed by those with greater political power and policy influence, or which might even enable the interests concerned to become at least partly incorporated.

CONCLUSION

All three of the policy advocates have experienced changes in the past three decades or so, which have in turn had an impact on policy making in Britain. Each of the three main political parties have experienced internal ideological shifts, the cumulative effect of which has been to extend and entrench neo-liberalism in Britain and foster the belief that 'marketization' or privatization, not more public ownership, are the solution to most problems.

The Conservatives have replaced the pre-1979 One Nation perspective with a Thatcherite approach to problem solving and policy making, while the Labour Party, in response, sought to acclimatize itself to the hegemony of neo-liberalism by becoming New Labour. This entailed a rejection of its former commitment (albeit rarely subscribed to by the leadership) to such policies as public ownership, high taxation of the rich, workers' rights and partnership with the trade unions. In turn, since the mid-2000s, the Liberal Democrats have witnessed the ascendancy of the pro-market 'Orange Book' liberals in the party, and the concomitant downgrading or reduced influence of the more Left-leaning social liberals.

In tandem with these changes, think tanks have become more numerous and prominent, and have advocated many of the policies that the Conservatives and then New Labour enacted when in Office. This does not mean that the parties actually enacted particular polices in direct response to their advocacy by think tanks, but it does strongly suggest that many think tanks have played a significant role in disseminating or legitimizing particular policy proposals, and thereby creating what Denham and Garnett (1998) term a 'climate of opinion'.

Meanwhile, the ideological shift since the early 1980s, and the associated changes both in the style of government and the policy objectives, have resulted in changes in the role of many organized interests. In particular, several policy communities were deliberately destabilized or dismantled during the 1980s and 1990s by governments and ministers determined to enact radical policies and major reform of various public services. This resulted in the explicit abandonment of the former consensual or partnership approach to many spheres of policy making, which policy communities had symbolized.

QUESTIONS AND TOPICS FOR DISCUSSION

1. Why have the Labour Party and the Conservative Party both experienced internal conflicts and disagreements over their respective 'ideologies' from time to time?
2. What are the differences between the Liberal Democrats' 'Orange Book' liberals and the party's 'social' liberals?
3. In rejecting the notion that politics reflects Left–Right divisions, what do Liberal Democrats believe is the main difference between themselves and the other two parties?
4. Why have think tanks become more prolific since the 1980s?
5. In spite of their broadly similar ideological stance, what has been the main difference between the IEA and the ASI?
6. Which of New Labour's policies seemed to reflect those advocated by Demos, and the IPPR?
7. How do policy communities differ from issue networks?
8. Why have policy communities generally been characterized by policy continuity?
9. What problems do both the 'environmental lobby' and the 'poverty lobby' encounter in seeking to influence policy makers?

RECOMMENDED TEXTS AND FURTHER READING

Political Parties

1. Jack Brand (1992) *British Parliamentary Parties*. Oxford: Clarendon Press.

   Important (if slightly dated) case study of policy making within the main political parties at Westminster. Examining six separate policy areas, Brand challenges the common assumption that the Parties' policies are developed in a simple, top-down, manner by the parliamentary leadership and then imposed on their respective backbench MPs. Instead, he argues that backbench MPs, particularly those in the governing party, play a much more important and influential role than is usually assumed, albeit in subtle ways.

2. Stephen Driver (2011) *Understanding British Party Politics*. Cambridge: Polity.

   Clearly and concisely written contemporary account of Britain's political parties across the ideological spectrum. Of particular interest for this chapter are the chapters on the Conservative Party after Thatcher, the linkages between the Labour Party and New Labour, and how the Liberal Democrats (increasingly divided between 'Orange Book' and 'social democratic' liberals) have been affected by entering into coalition with the Conservatives.

3. Simon Griffiths and Kevin Hickson (eds) (2010) *British Party Politics and Ideology after New Labour*. Basingstoke: Palgrave Macmillan.

   Comprising chapters written by leading academic experts, this volume superbly discusses the ideological debates and developments in the three main political parties at Westminster since 1997, and how these have impacted upon their respective policies. Indeed, there are several chapters on the Labour Party (since Tony Blair), the Conservatives (under David Cameron) and the Liberal Democrats (under Nick Clegg).

4. Robert Leach (2009) *Political Ideology in Britain*, second edition. Basingstoke: Palgrave Macmillan.

   Marvellous book whose well-organized examination of ideologies is applied to the policies of, and debates or divisions within, the political parties. In particular, there are three extremely useful chapters on different strands of Liberalism, the links (and tensions) between Labour, socialism, social democracy and New Labour, and Conservatism, Thatcherism and post-Thatcherism. Each of these helps to contextualize and explain the different policies promoted or enacted by the parties at different times.

Organized Interests

1. Wyn Grant (2000) *Pressure Groups and British Politics*. Basingstoke: Macmillan.

   Good overview of the types and activities of organized interests, and the various ways in which they seek to influence politics and policy making in Britain.

2. David Marsh and R. A. W. Rhodes (eds) (1992) *Policy Networks in British Government*. Oxford: Clarendon Press.

   Seminal text on this topic, commencing with a conceptual overview before providing a series of case studies, written by appropriate experts, spanning a range of policy areas and sub-systems.

3. Jeremy. J. Richardson (2000) 'Government, interest groups and policy change', *Political Studies*, 48 (5): 1006–25.

   Excellent article examining how various policy communities were destabilized during the 1980s and 1990s. Notes, though, that many organized interests responded by seeking new arenas and channels of influence, with the EU especially offering new opportunities for involvement in the policy process.

4. Martin J. Smith (1993) *Pressure, Power and Policy: State Autonomy and Policy Networks in Britain and the United States*. Hemel Hempstead: Harvester Wheatsheaf.

   Highly informative and well-written discussion about the concept of policy networks, illustrated by good use of empirical examples, and noting the implications for policy making. Also considers how policy networks (and hence policies) change.

Think Tanks

1. Justin Bentham (2006) 'The IPPR and Demos: Think tanks of the new social Democracy', *The Political Quarterly*, 77 (2): 166–74.

   A rather rare, and thus much needed, article on the two think tanks most closely associated with New Labour, and its purported aim of charting a 'third way' between the Old Left and the New Right.

2. Andrew Denham and Mark Garnett (1998) *British Think Tanks and the Climate of Opinion*. London: UCL Press.

   One of the first major surveys of the rise of think tanks in Britain, paying particular attention to those which became prominent in the 1980s, and were thus mainly associated with Thatcherism. Examines the ways in which they sought to shape public policy, as well as evaluating their success in so doing.

3. Michael Kandiah and Anthony Seldon (eds) (1996) *Ideas and Think Tanks in Contemporary Britain: Volume 1*. London: Routledge.

   Comprehensive collection of essays on the key ideas and think tanks in post-war Britain, and the manner in which these have helped shape aspects of public policy. The ideas examined include Collectivism, Classical Liberalism/Monetarism, and the influences on economic policy, while the think tanks studied include the Adam Smith Institute and the Institute of Economic Affairs.

4. Michael Kandiah and Anthony Seldon (eds) (1996) *Ideas and Think Tanks in Contemporary Britain: Volume 2*. London: Routledge.

   Companion text to the previous volume, this time examining the ideas which have shaped defence policy, social policy and foreign affairs, as well as the role of science in shaping aspects of public policy. The think tanks examined are the Centre for Policy Studies, Demos, the Fabian Society and the Institute for Public Policy Research.

5. Hartwig Pautz (2012) 'The Think Tanks behind "Cameronism"', *British Journal of Politics and International Relations*, 14 (2): 362–77.

   Much needed article on the extent to which David Cameron's mode of Conservatism has been influenced by think tanks such as Policy Exchange and the Centre for Social Justice.

3

The Core Executive, Part One: The Individuals and their Policy Roles

The concept of the core executive was developed from the late 1980s onwards, primarily by political scientists dissatisfied with the limitations of the 'Prime Minister versus Cabinet' debate, which had been rehearsed and rehashed for at least the previous two decades (see, for example, Dunleavy and Rhodes, 1990; Rhodes, 1995). This debate implied that the possession and exercise of political power in British government could be understood in 'either/or' terms, as a zero-sum phenomenon, whereby more power for the Prime Minister automatically meant less power for the Cabinet and its ministers, and vice versa. Furthermore, this debate tended to overlook or undervalue the increasingly important role of other individuals and institutions in central government, surrounding and supporting the Prime Minister, the Cabinet and individual ministers.

What the emergence of 'core executive studies' sought to illustrate, therefore, was not only the range of individuals and institutions involved in central policy making in Britain, but also their respective sources of power, which ensured that many decisions entailed bargaining and negotiation between individuals or institutions. Each policy actor possesses (or has access to) particular resources and can pursue various strategies to achieve their policy goals. Consequently, core executive studies emphatically reject any notion of policies being routinely imposed by one central individual or institution; political reality and policy making are usually rather more complex, subtle and nuanced.

The classic definition of the core executive was provided by Rhodes, when he identified it as:

… all those organizations and procedures which co-ordinate central government policies, and act as final arbiters of conflict between different parts of the government machine … the 'core executive' is the heart of the machine, covering the complex web of institutions, networks and practices surrounding the prime minister, cabinet, Cabinet committees and their official counterparts, less formalised ministerial 'clubs' or meetings, bilateral negotiations and interdepartmental committees. It also includes co-ordinating departments, chiefly the Cabinet Office, the Treasury [and] the Foreign Office.

(Rhodes, 1995: 12, original emphasis)

To this list, Smith adds government departments in general, not only because these are 'the core policy-making units within central government', but also because they are headed by ministers, who themselves are 'key actors within the institutions of the core executive' (Smith, 1999: 5).

The central importance of the core executive to the policy process in Britain is clearly confirmed by the opening words of Smith's book on the topic, namely that:

> The core executive is at the heart of British government. It contains the key institutions and actors concerned with developing policy, co-ordinating government activity and providing the necessary resources for delivering public goods.
>
> (Smith, 1999: 1)

In similar vein, Holliday notes that: 'The heart of the UK state, and the key driving force in UK politics, is the core executive' (Holliday, 2000: 8).

Indeed, the importance of the core executive to policy making in Britain is such that we are devoting two chapters to it. This chapter examines the policy roles and political relationships of the individuals who collectively comprise the core executive, and how these impact upon policy making in Britain. The next chapter will analyze the institutions of the core executive that provide many of the resources and much of the support, which individuals utilize in policy making, while also facilitating coordination between them.

THE PRIME MINISTER

Since the 1960s, discussions about the role of the Prime Minister in British politics have almost invariably focused on his/her apparently increased powers, to the extent that a number of commentators – some of them former ministers, no less – have asserted that parliamentary government and Cabinet government have been supplanted by the establishment of 'Prime Ministerial government' (Benn, 1980: *passim*; Crossman, 1963: 51; Mackintosh, 1977: 629).

According to this perspective, the increased role of government in 20th century Britain, the corresponding expansion of the core executive and the emergence of the 'career politician' dependent on prime ministerial patronage to further their political careers, have all imbued the Prime Minister with ever greater power. Indeed, Tony Blair's premiership heard this line of argument taken further, to the extent that some commentators spoke of a new 'Presidentialism' (Foley, 2000; see also Foley, 1992; Pryce, 1997), with Blair variously accused of adopting a 'Napoleonic' style of leadership and control.

In response to the allegations about the rise of 'prime ministerial government' or 'British Presidentialism', there have been three alternative – but not necessarily mutually exclusive – counter perspectives, emphasizing either the constraints that impinge upon contemporary British Prime Ministers, or the manner in which their authority is contingent and contextual.

The relational character of prime ministerial power

One of the first writers to refute the 'prime ministerial government' thesis was G.W. Jones (1965), who argued that the power of the post-war British premier was exaggerated because a Prime Minister is dependent upon the support of their Cabinet colleagues (and ultimately, one might add, their backbench MPs too). As such, Prime Ministers are only as powerful as their senior ministers allow them to be. Or as another commentator expressed it in the mid-1990s, 'Prime Ministers are, in effect, captains of their teams, but they owe their position (and its very real powers) ... to the team itself' (Hodder-Williams, 1995: 232).

For such commentators, what has been most notable about prime ministerial 'power' in Britain is precisely its contingent and contextual character, and the practical limitations that British Premiers invariably encounter, irrespective of their formal or constitutional powers. The very complexity of contemporary British society, which has arguably served to downgrade the role of Parliament in policy making (as discussed in Chapter 5) and yielded a corresponding centralization of power in the core executive, can equally be cited as evidence of the constraints facing any modern Prime Minister in Britain. No British Prime Minister can seriously expect to grasp the intricacies of more than a couple of policies at any one time. Indeed, even focusing on just one particular sphere of public policy will almost certainly mean neglecting many others, or at most, giving them only cursory consideration.

Certainly, beyond the realms of economic affairs and international relations, prime ministerial involvement in domestic policy initiatives has generally been sporadic and *ad hoc*, varying from one premiership to another (Barber, 1991: Chapters 9 and 10). For example, during her first two years as Prime Minister, Margaret Thatcher took a keen interest in trade union reform, while towards the end of her premiership, she became actively interested in the reform of education and also local government finance *pace* the Poll Tax.

Tony Blair, meanwhile, initially sought to involve himself closely in the pursuit of peace in Northern Ireland (as had his Conservative predecessor, John Major) before focusing on the pursuit of war in Iraq. As a consequence of the latter, from 2003 onwards, Blair's attention was diverted from some of his domestic policy objectives, such as public sector reform and tackling anti-social behaviour. More recently, Conservative leader and Prime Minister, David Cameron, initially focused strongly on promoting the 'Big Society' as an integral part of his professed determination to mend 'broken Britain', while also curbing public expenditure and 'rolling back' the welfare state.

Clearly, the more time or energy that any Prime Minister devotes to one particular policy, the less time and energy this leaves them to pursue other policies. Consequently: 'Management by exception is the only way to find time to deal with high priority matters' (Rose, 2001: 155). Even 'activist' or 'innovator' Prime Ministers – as personified by Margaret Thatcher and Tony Blair – cannot involve themselves in more than a very small number of policy issues at any one time; they lack 'the time, resources and the inclination to occupy, on a significant and continuous basis, policy space outside that of high policy' (Norton, 2000: 105–6) – 'high policy' referring to economic and foreign affairs.

If Prime Ministers do attempt to intervene and involve themselves more widely, they are likely to deal only superficially with each policy issue or problem, while also potentially antagonizing more ministerial colleagues, each of whom may well resent what they consider to be ill-judged or half-hearted 'interference' by 10 Downing Street in their departmental policy domain (Donoughue, 1987: 6; Pym, 1984: 16).

Indeed, while most Prime Ministers have sought to concern themselves with a few specific policies, it has been suggested that: 'Few post-war Prime Ministers ... have left much of an intended and enduring legacy on public policy' (with Margaret Thatcher as the obvious exception), reflecting the fact that while the precise origins of any individual policy are often difficult to pinpoint accurately, 'most derive not from Number Ten, but from the parties' work in Opposition or friendly think tanks, or from within the Departments, which then go on to shape them and in so doing can change them beyond all recognition' (Kavanagh and Seldon, 2000: 316–17). Not dissimilarly, Smith et al. (2000: 161–2) argue that: 'The impact of a prime minister on a department is highly variable, depending on the policy, the departmental minister and the particular circumstances'.

This should not be too surprising, because lack of time, energy and expertise, coupled with a necessary focus on the broader picture and strategic objectives or oversight, means that Prime Ministers are obliged to leave many, if not most, domestic policies to their ministerial colleagues. This reaffirms the crucial point that in many respects, a Prime Minister is as dependent upon his/her senior ministers for policy success as they are on him/her (see, for example, Smith, 2011: 167–8).

In fact, it has been suggested that the contemporary British premiership is subject to a perennial paradox of politics, which has serious implications for prime ministerial power, and also governmental policy outputs and outcomes, namely that:

> ... the higher an institution is placed within an organizational hierarchy, the more distant it tends to be from the outcomes it seeks to bring about; and the more dependent it is upon the cooperation of others. The principle applies to central government in general, since decisions taken at the highest level in Whitehall can be implemented only elsewhere, either down the chain of command or relevant departments, or by hived-off agencies or bodies such as local government. Within the central executive, this tendency is exceptionally relevant to the premiership.
>
> (Blick and Jones, 2010: 171–2)

Blick and Jones' observations are especially relevant in the era of governance, as discussed in Chapter 6.

The Prime Minister and resource dependency

A second rebuttal of the 'prime ministerial government' thesis, therefore, is that the Prime Minister is but one of several individuals and institutions at the centre of the British political system. In this respect, as noted at the beginning of this chapter, 'core executive studies' emphasizes the interdependency of policy actors in the higher echelons of the British political system, this deriving from the different resources that each policy actor possesses or has access to, as illustrated in Table 3.1.

Table 3.1 **Resources of key policy actors in the core executive**

Prime Minister	Ministers	Senior civil servants
Patronage (appointing ministers)	Political/party support	Permanence/longevity
Authority	Authority	Knowledge
Political/Party support	Department	Time
Popular/Electoral support	Knowledge	Whitehall network
Prime Minister's Office	Policy networks	Control over information (gatekeeper function)
Bilateral policy making	Policy success	Defenders of the constitution

Source: Adapted from Smith, 1999: 32.

However, Smith is quick to emphasize that this quantitative 'measurement' of resources must also recognize the qualitative aspect, because even when a policy actor possesses particular political resources, s/he needs to utilize them effectively and their success in this regard will depend on their own personality and judgement, as well as their relationships with their colleagues and wider circumstances: 'capabilities in deploying resources and the strategic settings are critical to understanding who influences outcomes', because 'power is rarely, if ever, based directly on command. Power depends on how resources are exchanged, and hence it is about dependence not control' (Smith, 1999: 31).

Consequently, against those who talk of increasing prime ministerial power, apparently assuming that power entails a 'zero sum' relationship between political or policy actors (whereby more power for one means correspondingly less power for another), 'core executive studies' emphasize the extent to which policy actors are invariably dependent on each other, and therefore need to cooperate in order to achieve their policy goals. A Prime Minister can only achieve his/her policy objectives if they have a clear vision of what they want to achieve, the necessary resources are available and their ministerial colleagues share this vision. It also requires that the relevant minister(s) and department(s) are competent in pursuing it.

Yet even then, the Prime Minister's policy objectives might not be fully realized or successfully enacted, perhaps because of resistance or misinterpretation during implementation, when sub-national policy actors and 'street-level bureaucrats' might not apply the policy in the manner that was originally intended, or the sections of society to whom the policy was supposed to apply do not respond as envisaged (issues that we will examine in Chapter 8).

The Prime Minister in a 'shrinking world'

The third critique of the 'prime ministerial government' thesis has been advanced by Richard Rose, who locates the contemporary British Prime Minister 'in a shrinking world' (Rose, 2001). Analyzing the British Premiership in the context of Europeanization and globalization (both of which are discussed in Chapter 7), Rose argues that although British Prime Ministers now enjoy a higher profile than ever before, due both to modern 24/7 mass media and the frequency of international summits, the power that these imply is largely illusory because in the world beyond Westminster – where important policy decisions are increasingly taken – the Prime Minister is often constrained by external or global factors; omnipresence does not mean omnipotence.

On the contrary, the extent to which contemporary British Prime Ministers seem to be involved in an almost constant series of high-profile international conferences and prestigious summits with their overseas counterparts can actually be interpreted as a two-fold limitation on their power. First, because the increasing amount of time and energy expended in intergovernmental and supranational forums is time and energy not being expended at home on domestic affairs, although, of course, many international summits and their subsequent decisions will have an impact on domestic policies, particularly in the era of globalization (discussed in Chapter 7).

Prime Ministers therefore increasingly have to delegate policy issues to their ministerial colleagues and other senior officials in the Downing Street Policy Unit and Cabinet Office (these two institutions are discussed in the next chapter).

Second, the increasing number of international meetings and summits, which Prime Ministers are obliged to attend, is itself an indication of the extent to which public policy is being 'Europeanized' and 'globalized', and thus subject to international agreement and coordination. Or as Rose expresses it: 'National policies are no longer national' (Rose, 2001: 45, Chapters 3 and 10).

The contingent and contextual character of prime ministerial power

Meanwhile, to return to what still remains of domestic British politics and policy making, two other factors must be noted when considering the policy role of the Prime Minister in the core executive. First, irrespective of their formal or constitutional powers, the actual authority and influence of a Prime Minister cannot be isolated from the economic and political circumstances of their premiership (Elgie, 1995: 40–50). Prime ministerial 'power' will often ebb and flow according to such variables as the state of the economy, levels of (un)employment, the degree (or perceptions) of prosperity, the size of the government's parliamentary majority, the degree of party unity or backbench support, opinion poll ratings, and so on.

These are all subject to fluctuations: an apparently buoyant economy can be hit by a major economic crisis, whereupon unemployment increases, previously rising prosperity stalls, consumer confidence declines and plummeting opinion poll ratings or heavy by-election defeats cause growing anxiety among government backbenchers, quite possibly resulting in debilitating or demoralizing rumours of an imminent leadership challenge. In such circumstances, Prime Ministers will often be (or certainly appear to be) weaker than s/he or their immediate predecessor was in more propitious circumstances, and thus constrained in their policy options or room for manoeuvre.

Consequently, Martin J. Smith has argued that 'Prime Ministerial authority is largely relational' (Smith, 2003: 65). Similarly, when giving evidence to the House of Commons select committee on public administration, Sir Richard Wilson, a former Cabinet Secretary, explained that:

> His or her power varies from time to time according to the extent their Cabinet colleagues permit them to have that power, depending on whether the Cabinet is split, depending also on the strength of the government majority in the House of Commons and also popular opinion in the electorate and attitudes in the party.

> (House of Commons Public Administration Committee, 2002a: Q. 209)

Sir Richard reiterated this crucial observation towards the end of the 2000s (and in so doing, echoed G.W. Jones' 1965 argument), when he emphasized that:

> Prime Ministers are only as powerful as their colleagues allow them to be. You may have times, we have had times, when Prime Ministers have been so strong that their colleagues accepted anything that they wanted to do … but that does not alter the fundamental fact that if circumstances are different and a Prime Minister is in a weak position … it is not possible for the Prime Minister to have his way.

> (House of Lords Constitution Committee, 2010: 57, Q. 110)

Similarly, Sir Michael Barber, formerly Head of Tony Blair's [Downing Street] Delivery Unit, has emphasized that:

> … the power of a given Prime Minister is very contingent on the moment. I remember in 2003 that one of the things Tony Blair was considering was ring-fencing funding for schools … but he chose not to take it to the Cabinet because he was exhausted. It was immediately after the Iraq War and he did not think he had the political capital to take it through … you get an ebb and flow in prime ministerial power.

> (House of Lords Constitution Committee, 2010: 101, Q. 220)

The second factor to be borne in mind concerning the policy role of the Prime Minister is their personality and style. Prime Ministers will adopt different approaches to political leadership, deriving from their own personality, style of leadership and temperament (see, for example, Barber, 1991: *passim*; Hennessy, 2001: *passim*; James, 1999: 98–100; King, 1985: Chapter 4; Rose, 2001: 59–61). As such, the formal constitutional powers vested in the office of Prime Minister will actually be exercised in different ways, by different Premiers. For example, Sir Gus O'Donnell, a former Cabinet Secretary, has explained how 'John Major … had a very collegiate style', whereas 'Tony Blair, when he came in 1997 … had a strong emphasis on stock takes and delivery … There is a personality element' (House of Lords Constitution Committee, 2010: 12). Professor Peter Hennessy, meanwhile, suggests that Margaret Thatcher and Tony Blair could both be viewed as Prime Ministers who saw a 'destiny', which meant that their style was very much different to Prime Ministers 'more attuned to a collective style, such as James Callaghan and John Major' (House of Lords Constitution Committee, 2010: 12).

SENIOR CABINET MINISTERS

Apart from the Prime Minister, most of the senior ministers in Britain's core executive ('senior' here referring to those of Cabinet rank) have the official title of Secretary of State (although a few will have alternative appellations, such as Chancellor of the Exchequer), and most of these will be political heads of a key government department or ministry. In addition, two or three senior ministers will be appointed as 'Ministers without Portfolio' – usually free of any departmental responsibilities – with quaint, usually archaic, titles such as Lord President of the Council, Lord Privy Seal, and Chancellor of the Duchy of Lancaster.

It is these Secretaries of State and 'Ministers without Portfolio', who, along with the Prime Minister, and the government's Chief Whip, collectively constitute the Cabinet (whose policy role is examined in the next chapter). The senior ministers in the Conservative-Liberal Democrat coalition government (in August 2013) are listed in Table 3.2.

Table 3.2 Senior Ministers in the Conservative-Liberal Democrat coalition government in August 2013

C = Conservative

LD = Liberal Democrat

Post	Name of post holder (party in brackets)
Prime Minister	David Cameron (C)
Deputy Prime Minister and Lord President of the Council	Nick Clegg (LD)
Chancellor of the Exchequer	George Osborne (C)
Chief Secretary to the Treasury	Danny Alexander (LD)
Foreign Secretary	William Hague (C)
Home Secretary	Theresa May (C)
Secretary of State for Business, Innovation and Skills	Vince Cable (LD)
Secretary of State for Education	Michael Gove (C)
Secretary of State for Health	Jeremy Hunt (C)
Secretary of State for Defence	Philip Hammond (C)
Secretary of State for Work and Pensions	Iain Duncan Smith (C)
Secretary of State for Justice	Chris Grayling (C)
Secretary of State for Transport	Patrick McLoughlin (C)
Secretary of State for Communities and Local Government	Eric Pickles (C)
Secretary of State for Environment, Food and Rural Affairs	Owen Paterson (C)
Secretary of State for Energy and Climate Change	Edward Davey (LD)
Secretary of State for International Development	Justine Greening (C)
Secretary of State for Culture, Olympics, Media and Sport	Maria Miller (C)
Secretary of State for Northern Ireland	Theresa Villiers (C)
Secretary of State for Scotland	Michael Moore (LD)
Secretary of State for Wales	David Jones (C)

The precise role that any Secretary of State plays in policy making will vary from minister to minister, and depend upon a range of variables, most notably:

- the extent to which the minister has a clear policy objective that they are determined to pursue
- the extent to which there is a strongly entrenched departmental philosophy, which the minister becomes persuaded by. Gerald Kaufman (1997: Chapter 2), a Labour minister in the 1970s, warns of the danger of contracting the disease of 'departmentalitis', whereby a minister increasingly views issues primarily from their department's perspective and interests, and pursues policy objectives accordingly (the notion of 'departmental philosophies' is discussed in the next chapter)
- the degree of support that a minister receives from the Prime Minister. If a Cabinet Minister is known to enjoy the full support of the Prime Minister, they are much more likely to pursue a policy initiative successfully because prime ministerial backing will usually incentivize departmental officials or other policy actors who the minister partly depends upon for policy development and implementation
- the nature of the issues or problems with which a Cabinet Minister is faced during his/her tenure at a particular department. A crisis, for example, is both an opportunity and a threat: if successfully overcome, then the minister's political stature and authority are likely to increase accordingly, whereas failure to tackle the problem satisfactorily – even if it is unfair or unrealistic to expect them to have done so, given its nature or scale – is likely to prove detrimental to their political stature and authority
- the Cabinet Minister's own style and personality: just as Prime Ministers vary in their approach to leadership, so do Cabinet Ministers have different styles of departmental leadership and policy making.

With regard to the last of these factors, Norton has identified five main types of minister in Britain (Norton, 2000: 109–10):

> *Commanders*, who pursue policy goals based on personal experience or motivation of what they believe ought to be done.
> *Ideologues*, who are concerned primarily to pursue policies based on a clear political philosophy or doctrine.
> *Managers*, these being ministers who are essentially pragmatic decision takers, and who are generally more concerned with the efficient administration of their department.
> *Agents*, namely ministers who effectively act on behalf of others, such as the Prime Minister or departmental civil servants.
> *Team players*, being those ministers who believe in collective decision taking and seek to secure the agreement of as many Cabinet colleagues as possible.

Norton suggests that the two most common types of ministerial role are commander or manager, although we would argue that since the 1980s, an increasing number of senior ministers have adopted a 'commander' role, this reflecting a general transformation in the roles and styles of many ministers since the 1980s. While there have always been some Cabinet Ministers adopting such a proactive and agenda-setting role in their departments – such as Roy

Jenkins' socially liberal or 'permissive' reforms at the Home Office in the mid-1960s – their numbers have increased since the 1980s (Campbell and Wilson, 1995; Foster and Plowden, 1996; Marsh et al., 2001: Chapter 6; Richards, 1997).

Initially, this shift in ministerial style was largely attributable to the ideological objectives of the Thatcher governments, and their determination to break with the post-war consensus in British politics. To achieve this, several Cabinet Ministers in the 1980s and 1990s deemed it essential to challenge and confront the long-established departmental philosophies and policy communities, which militated against policy change and innovation. Hence the proactive, innovative or agenda-setting policy role adopted by senior ministers such as Nigel Lawson at the Department of Energy in the early 1980s, Lord (David) Young at the DTI in the late 1980s, Michael Howard at the Home Office in the 1990s, and Peter Lilley at the Department of Social Security during the same decade (Marsh et al., 2001: Chapter 6).

This trend towards more proactive, agenda-setting Cabinet Ministers subsequently continued during the Blair premiership, as evinced by Gordon Brown's tenure as Chancellor of the Exchequer, David Blunkett at the Home Office and Charles Clarke at the Department of Education and Skills. Brown sought to be actively involved in the development of policies beyond the Treasury's traditional remit, such as welfare reform, on which the Chancellor regarded himself as 'the overlord' (Rawnsley, 2001: 111). Indeed, it has been argued that:

> … the real architect of Labour's welfare strategy was the Chancellor, Gordon Brown … unlike previous Chancellors, Brown was not simply concerned with scrutinising expenditure, but also played a much greater role in directing social policy … policy units were established in the Treasury for health, education, transport and social security.
>
> (Bochel and Defty, 2007: 37. See also, Connell, 2011: *passim*; Naughtie, 2001: 339)

Meanwhile, Blunkett and Clarke became strongly identified with controversial policies – albeit polices that Tony Blair was known strongly to support – such as advocacy of ID cards in Blunkett's case, and the introduction of university top-up fees in the case of Clarke.

A similar ministerial style has also been evident in the post-2010 Conservative-Liberal Democrat coalition government, with former Secretary of State for Health, Andrew Lansley, pursuing a major (and controversial) reorganization of the NHS in spite of widespread opposition, and Education Secretary Michael Gove actively pursuing several radical initiatives to transform secondary education in Britain. Indeed, during much of 2013, it seemed as if Gove was announcing a new policy or additional targets for England's schools and their teachers every week!

The increasing trend towards more proactive or 'commander' Cabinet Ministers has been both reflected and reinforced by such factors as: the increased use of Special (Policy) Advisers as a source of original – or more partisan – ideas (see below); the modified role of senior civil servants, who are now expected to focus somewhat more on policy 'delivery' and management; the weakening or restructuring of particular policy communities (discussed in the previous chapter); the general increase both in policy transfer and of 'evidence-based' policy.

Of course, the extent to which an individual Cabinet Minister will adopt a proactive or agenda-setting role will depend on various factors, including the minister's own personality and style, the nature of the issue they are seeking to address, the wider economic, social or political context and circumstances, the degree of prime ministerial support, and the degree of cooperation (or acquiescence) provided by other policy actors in their field. Yet it remains the case that more Cabinet Ministers are adopting a more proactive or agenda-setting role in their departments.

As a consequence, the erstwhile image of senior ministers being content merely to act as reactive or steady-as-she-goes managers of their department, who only responded to problems as and when they occurred and looked primarily to their senior civil servants for policy initiatives, looks increasingly outdated.

Meanwhile, the Ministers without Portfolio will often be allocated specific tasks or policy roles by the Prime Minister, these usually *not* corresponding to particular departmental responsibilities. For example, a Minister without Portfolio might be tasked with helping to coordinate the work of several government departments, thereby helping the Prime Minister – and the Cabinet Office – to achieve 'joined-up government' and supervise policy 'delivery' (for a fuller discussion of the roles generally ascribed to Ministers without Portfolio, see Lee et al., 1998: Chapter 11).

Certainly, Tony Blair tended to appoint a Minister without Portfolio to act as a 'Cabinet enforcer', whose role was to chase up and monitor the extent to which departments and their ministers were actively pursuing agreed policies. More recently, David Cameron appointed Oliver Letwin as Minister for Government Policy, based in the Cabinet Office, to assist in the coordination and enforcement of policies agreed by the Cabinet.

Perennial problems faced by many Cabinet Ministers

In pursuing their departmental responsibilities, numerous Secretaries of State have encountered various problems, which have either hindered their ability to pursue policy change, or threatened the overall cohesion of the government of which they are the most senior members.

Short-termism and reactive policy making

One notable problem that many Cabinet Ministers encounter in pursuing their departmental responsibilities, and which also has implications for the achievement of long-term policy innovation or reform, is the pressure of short-term decisions and events. These can seriously distract ministers from adopting a broader or more strategic perspective, or from devising a new policy. A newly-appointed Secretary of State does not arrive at their department with a clear desk, an empty in-tray, a blank sheet of paper or a clear computer screen into or onto which they can immediately draft a new strategy or policy for immediate enactment. Instead, they will invariably be presented with a range of ongoing issues, problems and cases requiring an instant decision, quite apart from the new issues and problems that occur during their tenure at the department, and which may similarly require an immediate response.

A minister in the Blair governments emphasized that:

Ministers do not work in a vacuum, and policies do not come out of thin air. It is rare to start with a clean sheet. Rather, policies are formulated … within the context of great complexity. And also against the backcloth of history … Economics and finance, administrative realities, existing legislation and the courts, party policy and public opinion, science and research, sectional interests, pressure groups, the media, and so much more, all play their part.

(Wicks, 2012: 593)

This is part of the wider phenomenon of 'policy inheritance' (Rose and Davies, 1994), which impacts upon all new governments and ministers, and often limits their room for manoeuvre and constrains their choices, at least in the short term. As a consequence, immediate or major policy changes when a new government is elected or a new minister is appointed, are often difficult to achieve. They frequently have too many immediate issues and unresolved problems, bequeathed by their predecessor(s), which they need to tackle before they can start working on their own policy objectives.

Many of these 'inherited' issues or new problems might be rather technical or administrative or politically 'low-level' in which case they might well be delegated to the department's civil servants, but a variety of issues and problems will still require ministerial consideration and authorization, and demand the minister's repeated attention. This immersion in day-to-day decision taking and problem solving, coupled with the need to respond to new problems that suddenly arise, almost inevitably means that a new policy initiative will either have to be pursued alongside these other issues and cases, therefore limiting the time that the Secretary of State can devote to it, or that the minister will defer pursuit of a new policy until his/her desk or in-tray 'clears' – which it might never do.

As Lord Croham, a former Head of the Civil Service once explained, 'in general, the Minister is so captivated … by the day-to-day affairs of being a Minister … that he finds the long-term issue is something he'll do tomorrow – and tomorrow never comes' (quoted in Hennessy, 1990: 492).

Lack of time spent in the department

A Secretary of State will only spend a limited amount of time each week actually in their department, because their other departmental and political responsibilities oblige them to be elsewhere: attending Cabinet committees; holding meetings with another minister – a bilateral – over a shared (interdepartmental) policy or problem; sundry appearances in the House of Commons for Question Time, the 'Readings' or committee stage of a Bill they are 'sponsoring'; and giving evidence to select committee inquiries. Secretaries of State will also need to attend meetings of the Council of the European Union (previously called the Council of Ministers) when their particular sphere of policy is under discussion, as well as other occasional international summits or intergovernmental conferences (for recent detailed accounts of ministers' weekly workloads, see Rhodes, 2011: 77–85, 90–8; Wicks, 2012).

It would seem that many ministers spend less than 40 per cent of their time physically in their department each week, due to these other activities and attendance. Indeed, in a recent study of day-to-day life inside government, Rod Rhodes 'shadowed' several ministers to observe directly the demands on their time and the relentless pressure they faced. It transpires that for many of them, a 15-hour day is normal, but with only about three hours devoted to dealing directly with departmental policy issues (Rhodes, 2011: 102–3).

Departmentalism

As mentioned above, another problem faced by many Cabinet Ministers and which can have serious implications for their, or even the government's, policy objectives, is 'departmentalitis'. This is something that many Cabinet Ministers have become afflicted with, meaning that they 'go native' by adopting the views and values of their particular department (see next chapter). Certainly, during the 1970s and 1980s especially, several memoirs and diaries published by former Cabinet Ministers testified to the extent to which they – or some of their ministerial colleagues – became pre-occupied with their department's interests and objectives, and therefore paid insufficient attention to policies pursued by their ministerial colleagues (see, for examples: Barnett, 1982: 81–2; Castle, 1993: 341; Crossman, 1975: 201, diary entry for 18 April 1965; Dell, 1980: 25; Healey, 1990: 326–7; Marsh, 1978: 87).

This tendency was also noted by Sir Douglas Wass, another former Head of the Civil Service, when he observed that 'for each minister, the test of success in office lies in his ability to deliver his departmental goals … No minister I know of has won political distinction by his performance in the Cabinet or by his contribution to collective decision-taking' (Wass, 1983: 25). Similarly, when an inquiry was conducted into the mid-1990s BSE crisis, which affected British farming and the meat industry, a Special Adviser to one of John Major's senior ministers confessed that:

> The BSE report confirms everything we have been saying about Whitehall as a whole. Whenever there is a potential conflict between different departments, or an awkward problem, they do not search for the right answers. Their priority is to defend their own departmental position. They do not share knowledge, but keep information to themselves. They judge the quality of their work purely on the basis of how well they defend their own department.
>
> (Quoted in Richards, 2000: 13; see also, Greer, 1999)

Certainly, within months of New Labour's May 1997 election victory, Tony Blair was bemoaning the already evident trend towards departmentalism among his ministerial colleagues: 'One of the things we have lost from Opposition is that shared sense of purpose and strategy. Ministers have become preoccupied by their departmental brief and we need to draw them back more' (Quoted in Wintour, 1997: 1–2). This tendency clearly places a premium on Ministers without Portfolio and the Prime Minister, along with institutions such as the Cabinet Office and the [Downing Street] Policy Unit, to facilitate policy coordination within the core executive, and thereby pursue joined-up government.

Interdepartmental policy conflicts

One manifestation of 'departmentalism' is the phenomenon whereby the policy preferences or proposals of one minister (or their department) impinge on those of another department. For example, in the post-May 2010 coalition government, there were public disagreements between the Home Secretary, Theresa May, and the former Justice Secretary, Kenneth Clarke (both of them Conservatives), over aspects of penal policy, as well as asylum/immigration and the Human Rights Act.

These public spats have partly reflected different personal or ideological views over policies themselves, but have also occurred because of the potential or actual overlap of responsibilities between the Home Office and the Department of Justice. One such clash was between Clarke's preference for a stronger emphasis on the rehabilitation of offenders, whereas May has strongly defended the role and importance of custodial sentences in combating crime and making communities safer (Travis, 2010; Williamson and Sparrow, 2010; Morris, 2011; Ford, 2012). The coalition government has also witnessed interministerial disagreements due to perennial tensions between the twin goals of fostering economic growth and promoting environmental protection. In this instance, public disagreements have sometimes occurred between two senior Liberal Democrat ministers because the Business Secretary, Vince Cable, has favoured (along with Conservative Chancellor, George Osborne) reducing some of the regulations and red tape on businesses in order to boost economic growth and employment, while the former Climate and Energy Secretary, Chris Huhne, wanted to ensure that companies adhered to various 'green' policies and targets commensurate with (environmentally) sustainable economic development (Stratton, 2011). Huhne was also unhappy at reports, in Spring 2011, that the Department of Transport was seriously considering an increase in the motorway speed limit from 70 to 80 mph; Huhne's concern deriving from the fact that faster driving would increase carbon emissions (McGee and Ungoed-Thomas, 2011).

Another form of interministerial tension, which has been evident in the coalition government (but has also occurred in many previous governments) is that between the Chancellor George Osborne's insistence on the need for significant cuts in public expenditure, and thus in departmental budgets, and the insistence by many other senior ministers either that they cannot find the savings being asked of them, or that the cuts being sought by the Treasury will impede their own departmental (and, *inter alia*, coalition) policy objectives. For example, Theresa May has been anxious that swingeing cuts to her Home Office budget would mean far fewer front-line police officers to tackle crime and anti-social behaviour.

Similarly, Liam Fox, while he was Defence Secretary, also clashed with the Chancellor and the Treasury because of his concern that major cuts in his ministry's budget might make the renewal of Britain's Trident nuclear submarines unaffordable. In this context, one senior civil servant in the Ministry of Defence complained that: 'Treasury officials are running amok. The Treasury needs to understand that it is a dangerous world out there' (quoted in Oliver, 2010: 1).

There were also intra-Cabinet disagreements in autumn 2012, over plans (subsequently abandoned in summer 2013) to introduce minimum prices for alcohol, in order both to reduce binge drinking and drink-related crime, and improve public health. The proposal emanated from Theresa May's Home Office, with the support of David Cameron and Jeremy Hunt (the Health Secretary), but encountered Treasury objections over the potential loss of revenue from alcohol duty (approximately £9.5 billion) if the 'minimum' price was set 'too high' and sales of alcoholic drinks fell significantly (Hennessy and Donnelly, 2012; Morris, 2012).

Ideological tensions between senior ministers

Although membership of a political party obviously reflects general support for its philosophy, principles and policy goals (as noted in the previous chapter), these are still open to slightly different emphases and interpretation. Consequently, even the most senior members of the governing party, namely its Cabinet Ministers and the Prime Minister, will sometimes be prone to differences of opinion or disagreements over whether, or how far, a particular policy (or series of policies) should be pursued.

Until the advent of New Labour and the subsequent marginalization of the Left, ideological tensions were most commonly associated with the Labour Party, so that pre-1979 Labour Cabinets were particularly prone to Left versus Right disagreements. These had derived from tensions between those on the Left (seeing themselves as the party's true socialists), who favoured more public ownership (nationalization) of industry and more vigorous efforts at redistributing wealth from rich to poor, whereas those on the (revisionist) Right or social democratic 'wing' of the Labour party had been rather more cautious or conservative in their approach to achieving 'socialism'; indeed, they were more inclined to reform capitalism in order to make it fairer or more humane, rather than replace it completely.

These ideological divisions between Labour's 'fundamentalist' Left and 'revisionist' Right inevitably underpinned many of the disagreements, which ensued over particular policies, and reflected differing interpretations of the Labour Party's principles, as discussed in the previous chapter. This in turn did much to foster the image of a deeply divided Labour Party, which could not be trusted to govern the country effectively because it would be preoccupied with its own internal arguments and associated disputes over policies.

During the 1980s and 1990s, though, it was Conservative Cabinets that evinced ideological tensions and disagreements over the general orientation of policy, as ministers on the party's Right or Thatcherite wing battled for supremacy against representatives of the party's 'One Nation' tradition on the party's Left. These tensions were particularly prominent with regard to economic and social policies during the early 1980s, when monetarists and economic neo-liberals on the Conservative Right insisted that the recession and rising unemployment rendered it essential that stricter control was exercised over the money supply, primarily through curbing public expenditure. For these Conservatives, a major cause of high public expenditure was the cost of the welfare state, so it seemed logical, indeed unavoidable, that reducing government spending necessitated extensive cuts in welfare provision.

By contrast, One Nation Conservatives believed that the recession was not only being exacerbated by their government's economic strategy, but that this was precisely the time to relax monetary policy and carefully boost public expenditure in order to reflate the economy and thereby get Britain out of recession. These One Nation Conservatives similarly reasoned that a period of high unemployment was exactly the time when the welfare state was most needed, in order to assist those who, due to economic circumstances beyond their control, were without jobs. To curb welfare entitlement at such a time was deemed both politically insensitive and potentially socially destabilizing.

This ideological demarcation was also replicated with regard to issues such as industrial relations reform, for while the Thatcherites were keen to emasculate the trade unions permanently, some 'One Nation' ministers believed that beyond a few modest reforms to 'clip the wings' of the trade unions, the Conservative governments ought to resume the pursuit of partnership and regular dialogue with the unions, which had been pursued by pre-Thatcher Conservative administrations throughout the 1950s and 1960s (Dorey, 2002a).

This was, of course, anathema to the Thatcherite Conservatives, who not only believed that trade union power had contributed to many of Britain's economic and industrial problems, but who reasoned that if the trade unions could be permanently emasculated, then there would be no need for a return to dialogue and partnership; the unions could simply be ignored (Dorey, 2002b; Dorey, 2003).

Since the 1990s, ideological divisions within Conservative Cabinets (and Shadow Cabinets when the party was in Opposition) have been most apparent over the issue of Britain's relationship with, or membership of, the EU. After Margaret Thatcher's replacement by John Major as Conservative leader and Prime Minster in November 1990 (her downfall partly caused by her increasingly strident anti-European views and speeches), Thatcherite ministers adopted an increasingly sceptical, if not openly hostile, stance towards the EU and Britain's membership of it.

This was particularly evident in their stance on such issues as European integration, the Maastricht Treaty's avowed objective of Economic and Monetary Union and the EU's social dimension, including employment protection and workers' rights. Indeed, some of these Cabinet Ministers made life so difficult for John Major that on one notorious occasion, when he mistakenly thought that the recording of a television interview had come to an end, he complained to the interviewer about the three 'bastards' in his Cabinet; unfortunately for Major, his microphone was still on and his comments were soon 'leaked'.

In sharp contrast, prominent ministers on the Left or One Nation wing of the Conservative Party, most notably Kenneth Clarke and Michael Heseltine, made no attempt to conceal their strong pro-European views. Instead of viewing European integration as a threat to Britain, and particularly to parliamentary sovereignty, Left-ish Conservatives adopted a more positive view of the EU. They were convinced (and still are today) that desirable policy goals, beneficial to Britain, could far more readily be attained through working in partnership with other member states than by 'splendid isolation' and self-imposed exclusion from EU policy making. As such, they rejected the 'zero sum' conception of EU power, which their Thatcherite colleagues seemed to adopt, whereby any additional power or influence for the EU *ipso facto* meant less power and influence for Britain.

Meanwhile, the general marginalization of the Left in New Labour ensured that open ideological divisions were relatively rare in Tony Blair's 1997–2007 Cabinets, with 'Old Labour' figures such as John Prescott proving reliable allies on most policy issues. When the Blair Cabinets did disagree over policy issues, the differences were not usually derived from Labour's traditional intra-party ideological divisions, although some of the oft-reported tensions between Tony Blair and Gordon Brown were partly explicable in terms of Brown ostensibly being just a little nearer to the remnants of 'Old Labour' than Blair. Instead, most political disagreements were over policy priorities and details, rather than objectives; over means rather than ends.

For example, on various occasions, there were disagreements over the allocation of increased public expenditure with some ministers, most notably Brown himself as Chancellor, favouring raising social security benefits and extending tax credits for the low paid in order to tackle poverty, while others in the Cabinet – including Blair – preferred to target any public expenditure increases on services, most notable health and education. The reasoning underpinning the latter approach was that increasing welfare benefits might be seen as merely providing 'hand outs' and increasing welfare dependency amongst the poor, whereas 'investing' in public services would be viewed by more voters – particularly Middle England – as a worthwhile and justified way of spending their tax contributions, especially as they themselves would benefit from an improved NHS and 'better' schools. Besides, Blair was inclined to emphasize that poorer people would also be beneficiaries of better schools and hospitals (Reeves and Wintour, 1999; Ward, 2001).

Rather more recently, and not surprisingly, the Conservative-Liberal Democrat coalition, formed in May 2010, has yielded some discernible tensions deriving partly from differences in philosophy and concomitant policy preferences between the two parties. For example, there have been clear disagreements over reform of Britain's banking system (in response to the 2008 financial crash), with Liberal Democrats urging significant reform and restructuring of 'the City' and the financial services sector. By contrast, senior Conservatives, particularly Chancellor George Osborne, have proved reluctant to act, seemingly accepting the City's argument that the middle of an economic downturn is precisely the wrong time to create further uncertainty by reorganizing and imposing regulations, on Britain's banking industry.

Following on from this issue, Conservative and Liberal Democrat ministers have also disagreed over how – or whether – to respond to the continued payment of large bonuses to senior bankers, these reflecting the 'bonus culture' in the City. Senior Conservatives, particularly the Chancellor, George Osborne, have proved totally unwilling to take any action over bankers' pay or bonuses, much to the annoyance and frustration of senior Liberal Democrats. The Liberal Democrats' Business Secretary, Vince Cable, has made his irritation clear on numerous occasions (Grice, 2010; Savage, 2011; Wintour, 2012; Treanor, 2013), while in February 2011, the Liberal Democrats' Lord Oakeshott resigned as a Treasury Junior Minister in February because of his clear frustration at the continued failure to take action to curb bankers' pay.

There have also been disagreements over employment law, with some Conservatives favouring new curbs on trade unions and strikes, coupled with a weakening of statutory employment protection or workers' rights ('labour market deregulation'), particularly with regard to 'unfair dismissal' and maternity leave – their argument being that if employers can sack staff more easily, they will be correspondingly more likely to recruit workers in the first place and thereby reduce unemployment. Such calls and arguments have been strongly condemned by the Liberal Democrats' Vince Cable, who pointedly suggested that those Conservatives urging such measures were 'descendants of those who sent children up chimneys' (quoted in Wintour, 2011: 11).

At the same time, ideological tensions have been increasingly evident *within* the Conservative Party itself, where some on the Right have been deeply sceptical about David Cameron's leadership and strategy. His efforts to 'modernize' the party and 'detoxify' it in order to make the Conservatives attractive to voters again (following its three successive defeats in 1997, 2001 and 2005), have consistently been viewed with suspicion and derision on the party's Right – many of them unreconstructed Thatcherites.

Indeed, many of Cameron's critics on the Conservative Right felt vindicated by his failure to lead the party to a clear victory in the May 2010 general election. They were convinced that this failure was largely due to Cameron's refusal to pursue a more populist Right-wing approach, entailing pledges on tax cuts, much tougher curbs on immigration and a rather more robust stance against the EU (Dorey, 2010b. See also the post-election analysis published by the 'conservativehome' blog, Montgomerie/conservativehome, 2010).

The ensuing frustration on the Conservative Right has manifested itself most clearly on the issue of the EU, particularly as Cameron (in 2009) abandoned an erstwhile pledge to hold a referendum on ratification of the Lisbon Treaty. That Cameron subsequently entered into a coalition with the pro-EU Liberal Democrats merely exacerbated the seething frustration and resentment on the Conservative Right. This culminated in a major rebellion in the House of Commons in October 2011 when 81 Conservative MPs voted in favour of a motion calling for a referendum on whether the UK should remain in the EU, leave it or renegotiate its membership. In so doing, they flagrantly defied a three-line whip imposed by the party's leadership, instructing Conservative MPs to vote *against* the motion.

Another issue that has highlighted ideological divisions within the Conservative Party is that of gay marriage, which many 'traditionalists' on the Right are bitterly opposed to, due to their conviction that same-sex relationships are unnatural or morally wrong anyway, and that a 'proper' marriage entails a man and woman becoming husband and wife, a primary purpose of which is to have children. For such Conservatives, the notion of two men or two women getting married to each other is both nonsensical and morally repugnant, and a debasement of the true meaning of marriage. Such is the hostility of many Conservative MPs to same-sex relationships that 134 of them (more than half of the parliamentary party) voted against the Second Reading of the 2013 Marriage (Same Sex Couples) Bill, which Cameron himself strongly supported. It eventually reached the statute book by virtue of support proffered by Labour and Liberal Democrat MPs.

What has compounded the hostility of many Right-wing/Thatcherite Conservative MPs towards Cameron is their belief that since the formation of the coalition government at the May 2010 election, he has conceded too much to the Liberal Democrats, thereby permitting them to have an excessive influence over the Coalition's policies, out of all proportion to their number of MPs (Helm, 2011: 22. See also Bagehot, 2011; Helm, 2011; Richards, 2011).

Yet some Liberal Democrats believe that they (or their parliamentary leaders) have sometimes yielded too much to the Conservative Right, hence Nick Clegg's promise of a 'more muscular liberalism' (quoted in Mulholland and Wintour, 2011), and Chris Huhne's demand that David Cameron should keep the Conservative Party's 'Tea Party tendency' under control (Grice, 2011).

JUNIOR MINISTERS

Once largely unsung and almost unseen, Junior Ministers have increased both in number and importance since the 1970s. While the precise role ascribed to Junior Ministers varies from department to department, and is also heavily dependent on who their Secretary of State is, there is no doubt that Junior Ministers generally play a much more extensive policy role in the core executive than they did in the 1950s and 1960s. Indeed, Britain's foremost academic expert on Junior Ministers, Kevin Theakston, informed a recent parliamentary inquiry that because 'Cabinet Ministers are already overloaded; without the support of Junior Ministers their jobs would be impossible', as reflected by the fact that Junior Ministers' departmental and policy-making roles have grown more important in recent years (House of Commons Public Administration Select Committee, 2011). In effect, if Junior Ministers did not already exist, they would have to be invented.

The increased importance of Junior Ministers is partly reflected by the growth in their numbers during the past century, from 15 Junior Ministers in 1914 to 66 in 1998 (Theakston, 1999a: 230–1). Prior to the 2010 general election, Gordon Brown's government contained 77 Junior Ministers, although in the post-May 2010 Coalition, the number initially fell back to 66. That Junior Ministers have increased overall since the early 20th century, both in number and importance, is itself indicative of the greatly expanded roles and responsibilities of British governments during the past century, as well as the greater complexity of governing.

There are actually two categories of Junior Minister, the higher-ranking of these being the Minister of State, with the second category comprising Parliamentary Under-Secretaries of State. Junior Ministers are normally selected by the Prime Minister, rather than by the Secretary of State under whom they serve and to whom they are constitutionally accountable, although the Prime Minister may choose to consult the Secretary of State over proposed appointments.

Most of the key government departments now have two or three Ministers of State, each of whom is usually given responsibility for a particular area of policy within their department. In many cases, the Minister of State's full title will clearly indicate their primary policy responsibility in the department – Minister of State for Higher Education, Minister of State for Immigration, Minister of State for Prisons, and so on.

Meanwhile, a Parliamentary Under-Secretary of State is the most junior in the ministerial hierarchy, these usually being allocated very specific tasks, often technically specialized or concerned with administrative minutiae (but still important nonetheless). Again, their precise title usually reflects the nature of their precise remit, such as Parliamentary Under-Secretary of State for Public Health.

Tables 3.3, 3.4 and 3.5 each illustrate the allocation of responsibilities between Secretaries of State, Ministers of State and Parliamentary Under-Secretaries in three government

Table 3.3   Allocation of responsibilities between ministers in the Home Office

Ministerial post	Name of Minister
Home Secretary	Theresa May
Minister of State for Immigration	Mark Harper
Minister of State for Policing and Criminal Justice	Damian Green
Minister of State for Crime Prevention	Jeremy Browne
Parliamentary Under-Secretary of State (Minister for Crime and Security)	James Brokenshire
Parliamentary Under-Secretary of State for Criminal Information	Lord Taylor of Holbeach

Table 3.4   Allocation of responsibilities between ministers in the Department for Work and Pensions

Ministerial post	Name of Minister
Secretary of State for Work and Pensions	Iain Duncan Smith
Minister of State for Employment	Mark Hoban
Minister of State for Pensions	Steve Webb
Parliamentary Under-Secretary of State for Disabled People	Esther McVey
Parliamentary Under-Secretary of State for Welfare Reform	Lord Freud

Table 3.5   Allocation of responsibilities between ministers in the Department of Business, Innovation and Skills

Ministerial post	Name of Minister
Secretary of State for Business, Innovation and Skills	Vince Cable
Minister of State for Universities and Science	David Willetts
Minister of State for Business and Enterprise	Michael Fallon
Minister of State for Trade and Investment	Lord Green of Hurstpierpoint
Parliamentary Under-Secretary of State for Employment Relations and Consumer Affairs	Jo Swinson
Parliamentary Under-Secretary of State for Skills	Matthew Hancock
Parliamentary Under-Secretary of State for Intellectual Property	Viscount Younger of Leckie

departments in August 2013. Although ministerial reshuffles mean that the actual individuals will be moved periodically, the titles and division of departmental responsibilities will remain broadly similar in most cases.

Junior Ministers do not ordinarily attend meetings of the full Cabinet, although they will occasionally be invited if the particular policy issue for which they are directly responsible is on the agenda. Yet on these relatively rare occasions, they will only attend for the duration of the relevant item on the Cabinet agenda, and leave immediately after this is concluded.

The infrequency with which Junior Ministers attend the full Cabinet is not surprising, given that this body does not usually engage in detailed discussion of policies (for reasons which we will explain in the next chapter). Furthermore, even if the Cabinet did conduct such a discussion, the Secretary of State would normally be able to provide sufficient information about any policies emanating from their department. That said, Junior Ministers do regularly serve on Cabinet committees, precisely because these are often concerned with the more detailed aspects of policy development (as will also be examined in the next chapter).

In his seminal study of Junior Ministers, Kevin Theakston noted that their precise role and the authority they enjoy in a department are 'essentially informal and indeterminate, depending upon personal and political, not statutory, factors'. Consequently, the precise policy role of a Junior Minister will depend very much upon their relationship with the Secretary of State heading their department; where there is a good professional relationship or personal rapport between a Junior Minister and his/her Secretary of State, it is likely that the former will be trusted to play a more extensive policy role in the department. Where the relationship is less cordial, however, the Junior Minister is likely to be given a very limited role in policy development, to the extent that they may be confined to administrative tasks or replying to correspondence sent to the department by MPs from outside bodies or members of the public (Theakston, 1987: 93–4. See also Kakabadse and Kakabadse, 2011: 355–6, 365–6; Theakston, 1999a: 235–6; Theakston et al., forthcoming).

Theakston reiterated this important observation about the variable and contingent character of Junior Ministers' roles and relationships in his written evidence to the House of Commons Public Administration Committee's (2011: Ev w7, para. 1) inquiry into ministerial activities and functions. He emphasized that 'what the job of a Junior Minister has amounted to in practice has usually varied between one department and another, and has depended greatly on the style of the Cabinet Minister involved and his or her relations with the Junior Minister(s)', a point reiterated by two Junior Ministers in the Blair governments, Chris Mullin (2011: 2) and Lord [Jeff] Rooker (House of Commons Public Administration Committee, 2011: Ev 9, Q. 47).

A further factor that influences the precise role of Junior Ministers will be the size and jurisdiction of the department in which they work. The larger the Ministry and the broader its range of responsibilities, the more likely it is that a Junior Minister will be granted a more significant policy role, for the Secretary of State would otherwise be overwhelmed (Theakston, 1987: 95).

Meanwhile, with regard to the relationship between Junior Ministers and senior civil servants, the Cabinet Office's *Ministerial Code* decrees that while 'the Permanent Secretary [the most senior civil servant in a department] is not subject to the direction of Junior Ministers', it is also the case that 'Junior Ministers are not subject to the directions of the Permanent Secretary.' As such: 'Any conflict of view between the two can be resolved only by reference to the Minister [Secretary of State] in charge of the department' (Cabinet Office, 2010a: 10). Ordinarily: 'Civil Servants observe the balance of forces and operate accordingly. They gauge whether the junior Minister has his boss's confidence' (James, 1999: 20–1. See also, Riddell et al., 2011: 18).

SENIOR CIVIL SERVANTS

Although the British civil service overall comprises more than 500,000 people, those who are classified as 'senior civil servants' constitute just 0.1 per cent of this tally. It is these senior civil servants who have traditionally played a substantial role in the detailed, day-to-day formulation and administration of public policy within departments. Certainly, it has often been their formal role in helping ministers to devise or draft policies that has attracted most academic attention, often in the context of concerns about the degree of influence that senior civil servants have traditionally exercised.

The constitutional convention has been that 'advisers advise, ministers decide' (advisers in this context meaning senior civil servants – 'Special Advisers' will be treated separately, below), yet this has often begged the question of what advice senior civil servants were giving their ministers and the extent to which this was pre-determining the latter's policy decisions.

Undoubtedly, a major role of senior civil servants has been to provide empirical evidence and policy advice to ministers, this being proffered in a variety of guises, such as statistical data, the viewpoints elicited from consultations with organized interests, the predicted 'pros and cons' or 'costs and benefits' of particular policy options, and so on. In so doing, senior civil servants could present their advice in such a way as to 'steer' the minister towards a particular policy decision, one that the departmental officials themselves preferred rather than one that the minister favoured.

This is certainly one of the criticisms traditionally levelled against some senior civil servants, namely that as 'gatekeepers' controlling the flow of information reaching their minister, they can exercise discretion or be selective in what they allow him/her to see and thereby subtly influence the minister's policy decision. In describing the presentation of policy options by senior civil servants to ministers, former Labour minister, Gerald Kaufman (1997: 30) recalls that:

> Most submissions consist of three or four pages containing a concise summary of a problem with possible courses of action completing the document. Some officials will just suggest one course of action, for you to take or leave. Others, more cunning, will attempt to confuse you with a choice, while carefully steering you in the direction they want you to go.

Yet for many Cabinet Ministers, a heavy reliance on departmental officials has been virtually unavoidable on key issues, partly because of the amount of time that senior ministers will normally spend outside of their department (as noted above) and partly because of the greater expertise that civil servants often possess, having perhaps worked in the department for many years or even decades. Consequently, Cabinet Ministers have previously had to rely heavily on delegation to, and thus discretion by, the senior civil servants in their department.

Meanwhile, detailed or administrative policy work is often conducted deep within the department, often by Grade 6 or 7 civil servants, with the most senior civil servants focusing more on strategic leadership and management in their department. For example, the most senior civil servant in a department is the Permanent Secretary, while immediately below them in the hierarchy will be senior civil servants occupying Grades 2–5, these usually being Directors and Deputy Directors who tend to focus on a particular policy area division or unit within the department (Drewry and Butcher, 1991: *passim*; McClory, 2010: 8; Stanley, 2000: 28–30).

However, since the 1980s, there has been a partial downgrading or diminution of the traditional policy-advising and policy-making role of senior civil servants. This is partly because the machinery of government reforms – the 'Next Steps' programme – of the Thatcher-Major governments sought to steer the civil service more towards a stronger focus on policy implementation and 'delivery' (Richards, 1997; Theakston, 1999b). However, this shift has also been compounded by the increased role of Special Advisers as a source of 'independent' or alternative policy advice for many Cabinet Ministers, as discussed below.

Yet it is important not to exaggerate the reduced role of senior civil servants, for while there has certainly been an overall trend towards more proactive or agenda-setting Cabinet Ministers, and a consequent shift in the role of many senior civil servants towards policy management or 'delivery' (rather than policy advice and formulation), it is very much a matter of degree. Certainly, not all Cabinet Ministers since the 1980s have adopted a proactive or agenda-setting role, and as such, there will remain instances where some senior civil servants continue to play a traditional role in advising their Secretary of State and presenting a range of policy options, accompanied by recommendations as to the most appropriate or practicable one to choose.

As with other relationships in the core executive, much will depend on the context, in terms of specific issues, circumstances, resources, and the minister's own style or personality. According to one senior civil servant interviewed towards the end of the 1990s:

> Your experience around Whitehall depends very much on who your Minister is, and what his/her attitude is. Some Ministers think they are there to run the Department, and others think that the Permanent Secretary is there to do that and they are only there to give broad instructions. I think that will continue to vary depending on the personality and predilection of Ministers.
>
> (Quoted in Marsh et al., 2001: 167)

In other words, although there has undoubtedly been a trend towards more proactive or agenda-setting Cabinet Ministers since the 1980s, and a parallel reorientation of senior civil servants towards policy management and delivery, there remains a close professional relationship between many senior civil servants and Secretaries of State. Nonetheless, it is true that many Cabinet Ministers are less dependent than they used to be on senior civil servants for policy ideas and advice partly because of the increased employment, especially since the 1980s, of Special Advisers.

SPECIAL ADVISERS

In recent decades, senior ministers (including the Prime Minister) have appointed their own Special Advisers in order to secure an additional or independent (of the civil service) source of policy advice and research, and perhaps to engage in 'blue skies' or longer-term, strategic thinking. Certainly, the policy work of Special Advisers is often more ideological or partisan than that of politically impartial senior civil servants. As the 2011 *Cabinet Manual* explains:

> Special advisers are employed as temporary civil servants to help ministers on matters where the work of government and the work of the party, or parties, of government overlap and where it would be inappropriate for permanent civil servants to become involved. They are an additional resource for the minister, providing assistance from a standpoint that is more politically committed and politically aware than would be available to a minister from the permanent Civil Service ... The employment of special advisers adds a political dimension to the advice and assistance available to ministers, while reinforcing the political impartiality of the permanent Civil Service by distinguishing the source of political advice and support.
>
> (Cabinet Office, 2011a: 58)

The precise role of Special Advisers, often referred to as 'SPADs', will vary slightly according to the remit stipulated by each Secretary of State who employs them, but according to the Cabinet Office's *Code of Conduct for Special Advisers*, they can perform 12 main roles for their minister, as listed in Box 3.1.

Box 3.1   Roles and functions of Special Advisers

- Reviewing papers that are going to the minister, drawing attention to any aspect that they think has party political implications and ensuring that sensitive political points are handled properly. They may give assistance on any aspect of departmental business and give advice to their minister when the latter is taking part in party political activities.
- Checking facts and research findings from a party political viewpoint.
- Preparing speculative policy papers, which can generate long-term policy thinking within the department.
- Contributing to policy planning within the department, including ideas that extend the existing range of options available to the minister with a political viewpoint in mind.
- Liaising with the minister's party to ensure that the department's own policy reviews and analysis take full advantage of ideas from the party, and encouraging presentational activities by the party that contribute to the government's and department's objectives.

(Continued)

(Continued)

- Briefing the party's MPs and officials on aspects of government policy.
- Liaising with outside interest groups, including groups with a political allegiance to assist the minister's access to their contribution.
- Speechwriting and related research, including adding party political content to material prepared by permanent civil servants.
- Representing the views of their minister to the media, including a party viewpoint where they have been authorized by the minister to do so.
- Providing expert advice as a specialist in a particular field.
- Attending party functions (although they may not speak publicly at the party conference) and maintaining contact with party members.
- Taking part in policy reviews organized by the party or officially in conjunction with it for the purpose of ensuring that those undertaking the review are fully aware of the government's views and their minister's thinking and policy.

(Cabinet Office, 2010b: paragraph 3. See also McClory, 2010: 3–4)

Most Secretaries of State are permitted to employ two Special Advisers, although a few Cabinet Ministers are allowed to employ more, for example the Foreign Office employs three SPADs while the Chancellor employs four.

The Prime Minister employs a much larger number of Special Advisers than each Secretary of State, but this reflects the fact that a Prime Minister does not have the administrative support and sources of policy advice that a department (via its senior civil servants) provides to his/her Cabinet colleagues. For example, Tony Blair employed up to 27 Special Advisers, approximately two each for most policy areas or issues, but a few more for foreign affairs, while David Cameron (in 2013) employed 19, and Deputy Prime Minister, Nick Clegg, had 14 Special Advisers.

Most Special Advisers will mainly be involved either in dealing with the media in the presentation of policies (the so-called 'spin doctors'), liaising with the minister's political party or in providing their minister with new or innovative policy ideas and proposals. In the latter role, Special Advisers can, in contrast to senior civil servants perhaps, 'bring a more adventurous cast of mind … able to suggest things that officials might dismiss as outlandish.' Ultimately, a Special Policy Adviser 'acts as counsellor, confidant and political ally to a minister surrounded by officials who are – quite correctly – non-political' (James, 1999: 223, 224. See also Gruhn and Slater, 2012: 7; Stanley, 2000: 22–3).

According to Pat McFadden, who was formerly a Special Adviser in Tony Blair's Policy Unit:

… the term 'Special Adviser' covers several different kinds of job. Sometimes it is policy expertise … general speech writing … contact with the media. It is quite difficult in government and in politics to put people into separate boxes and say that the person who deals with the media does not have policy expertise, because they might have both.

(Quoted in Blick, 2004: 260)

This important point has been reiterated in a more recent study of the role of Special Advisers (LSE GV314 Group, 2012: 718–19), which identifies 'two broad, but not mutually exclusive' roles, namely 'the *political commissar* role, where advisers serve as the eyes, ears and mouth of the politician who appoints them' (emphasis in original), and the role of 'political fixer': the person who does the political jobs for the politician that civil servants could not do – dealing directly with party colleagues, legislators and writing political speeches.' However, the same study notes that the role of *political commissar* itself enshrines two aspects, namely 'policy wonk' and 'policy enforcer', although these too are not mutually exclusive (LSE GV314 Group, 2012: 720).

The 'policy wonk' primarily focuses on policy advice and development, while the 'policy enforcer' is mainly concerned to ensure that these policies are then implemented or, in modern political parlance, 'delivered'. Meanwhile, the 'political fixer' role included that of communicating the government's or minister's policies and objectives; in effect, acting as 'spin doctor'.

What is particularly notable about many Special Advisers is the extent to which they tend to emanate from sundry think tanks. Several of the Special Advisers serving ministers in the coalition government have previously worked for think tanks such as the Centre for Social Justice and Policy Exchange. For example, two of David Cameron's Special Advisers, James O'Shaughnessy and Gavin Lockhart, previously worked for Policy Exchange. Yet this link between think tanks and Special Advisers is certainly not unique to the coalition government, for several Special Advisers in the (1979–1990) Thatcher governments originated from New Right think tanks like the Centre for Policy Studies, while the post-1997 Blair governments witnessed a proliferation of SPADs from various 'progressive' or Left-leaning think tanks such as Demos and the IPPR.

Of course, the fact that some Special Advisers emanate from think tanks compounds the methodological difficulty, noted in the previous chapter, of gauging the actual influence of think tanks on public policy, because the advice proffered to a minister by a SPAD might reflect the ideological perspective of the think tank they previously worked for, or it might be totally independent of it and derive from other influences or objectives.

From Special Adviser to senior politician

Serving as a Special Adviser has become 'an important mainstream path to senior political office', and certainly, according to the 2012 study cited above, the vast majority – 79 per cent – of SPADs (or of those who responded to the study's questionnaire) 'had been party members for five years or more before they were appointed', where 'only 6 per cent were not members of the party' (LSE GV314 Group, 2012: 720).

Several Cabinet Ministers since the 1980s previously served as Special Advisers. For example, David Young was a Special Adviser to Sir Keith Joseph at the Department of Trade and Industry in the early 1980s, and was subsequently appointed Secretary of State at the department following the 1987 election (having been awarded a peerage and a seat in the House of Lords three years earlier) (Blick, 2004: 193–4). Other notable examples of Special Advisers in the 1980s who subsequently became (Conservative) ministers include Damian Green, Oliver Letwin, John Redwood and David Willetts, the latter serving as Minister of State for Universities in the coalition government formed in May 2010. Meanwhile, in the early 1990s, David Cameron himself was a Special Adviser to the Chancellor of the Exchequer, Norman Lamont, and then to Michael Howard at the Home Office, before being elected as a Conservative MP in 2001.

Similar career trajectories were followed by several ministers in the 1997–2010 Blair governments. For example, Jack Straw, Foreign Secretary during the second (2001–05) Blair government had been a Policy Adviser to Ministers in the 1974–79 Labour government. Meanwhile, Hilary Benn (son of veteran Labour Left-winger, Tony Benn) worked as Special Adviser to David Blunkett at the Department of Education from 1997 to 1999, before successfully contesting a 1999 by-election in the Leeds Central Constituency. Following the 2001 election, Benn was appointed a Minister of State in the Department for International Development. Elsewhere, Ed Balls (Shadow Chancellor under Ed Miliband), having previously served as one of Gordon Brown's Special Advisers in the Treasury, was elected as a Labour MP in 2005.

Three other notable examples of (New Labour) Special Advisers subsequently entering Parliament and then attaining ministerial office are David Miliband, Ed Miliband and Andrew Adonis. David Miliband was appointed Head of (Blair's) Downing Street Policy Directorate when New Labour won the 1997 general election, having previously worked at the Institute for Public Policy Research. Miliband then became a Labour MP in 2001, thereafter serving in a succession of ministerial posts, culminating in his appointment as Foreign Secretary in 2008, a post he held until Labour's defeat in the May 2010 election.

Following David Miliband's election as an MP, Blair appointed Andrew Adonis, previously a senior journalist for *The Observer* newspaper, as Head of the 10 Downing Street Policy Directorate, but with a special remit also for advising the Prime Minister on education policy. Adonis was subsequently awarded a peerage, whereupon he sat on the Labour benches and held several ministerial posts, initially in the Department of Education and Skills, and then in the Department of Transport.

Finally, Ed Miliband served as a Special Adviser at the Treasury (alongside Ed Balls) prior to being elected as a Labour MP in 2005. He then swiftly ascended the ministerial hierarchy to become Secretary of State for Energy and Climate Change from 2008 until Labour's defeat in May 2010, following which he was elected leader of the Labour Party.

In the context of such examples, it has been suggested that the experience acquired from serving as Special Advisers 'is clearly a big advantage if they become Ministers', for they will be 'more familiar with the workings of Whitehall than most of their new ministerial colleagues'. As such, working as a Special Adviser 'is in many ways a useful apprenticeship for becoming a minister', although one particular criticism is that those ministers who have previously served as Special Advisers will often 'lack a detailed knowledge and understanding of the outside world' (Riddell et al., 2011: 28).

Apparent policy influence of Special Advisers

Although it is difficult to attribute particular policies to specific individuals, because many policies emanate from a variety of sources, and are invariably 'processed' by various individuals and institutions, some policies since the 1980s do seem to have been closely associated with, or strongly influenced by, particular Special Advisers.

With regard to Special Advisers appointed by the Prime Minister (and based in the Downing Street Policy Unit – discussed in the next chapter), Ferdinand Mount, who served briefly as head of Margaret Thatcher's Policy Unit during 1982–3 (for his wry recollection of this short tenure, see Mount, 2009: 281–349), has been credited with having 'contributed to her philosophical and moral approach', for he too was 'a firm advocate of the renewal of discipline and responsibility'. Consequently: 'A number of policy proposals flowed form Mount's philosophy', including tax changes beneficial to married couples, education vouchers, stronger policing and more generous discounts for those wishing to buy their council house (Blick, 2004: 200; Thatcher, 1993: 278–9), although education vouchers were not subsequently pursued. Mount's successor as Head of the Policy Unit, Brian Griffiths, also provided Thatcher with 'a moral basis for her ideological convictions' (Brown, 1990).

Meanwhile, in the early 1980s, during the first of his two spells as Margaret Thatcher's Special (Economic) Adviser, Alan Walters, apparently played a significant role in influencing or emboldening her stance on aspects of economic policy, particularly curbing public expenditure and reducing the Public Sector Borrowing Recruitment (PSBR). Indeed, Walters' influence on such issues reportedly caused some concern to various of Thatcher's Cabinet colleagues, including, on occasions, her then Chancellor Geoffrey Howe (Blick, 2004: 215; Hennessy, 2001: 410–11; Hoskyns, 2000: 273; Thatcher, 1993: 133–6).

During Walters' second spell as Thatcher's Special (Economic) Adviser, Chancellor Nigel Lawson actually resigned following increasing tensions between himself and Walters, and Thatcher's refusal to remove Walters from his post, in spite of requests from Lawson to do so (Lawson, 1992: 957–9). Ironically, Lawson's shock resignation prompted Walter's own resignation later the same day. To paraphrase Oscar Wilde, to lose one close colleague might be regarded as a misfortune; to lose two in the same day looks like carelessness!

More specifically, following his recruitment to the Policy Unit after the Conservative's 1983 election victory, John Redwood played a significant role in 'setting up a government mechanism for implementing the privatization agenda, which he'd been trying to persuade Thatcher to pursue since the early years of her leadership in the mid-1970s' (Blick, 2004: 201). Meanwhile, John Hoskyns, who was appointed Thatcher's first head of the Policy Unit in 1979 – but with the title 'Senior Policy Adviser to the Prime Minister' – seemingly played a significant role in shaping and making much tougher the Conservative governments' programme of trade union reform (Hoskyns, 2000: 157, 168, 170–1, 186. See also Blick, 2004: 205–6; Ranelagh, 1992: 218–22), much to the dismay of the emollient Secretary of State for Employment, James Prior, who wanted to pursue a more cautious and conciliatory approach to curbing the power of the unions (Prior, 1986: Chapter 9).

In John Major's 1990–97 Conservative governments, Nick True, one of the Prime Minister's early appointments as a Special Adviser in the Policy Unit, played a notable role in developing the 'Citizen's Charter', an initiative that it was hoped would make public sector employees provide a more efficient and courteous service to their public sector 'clients' or 'customers' (Hogg and Hill, 1995: 95–6; Blick, 2004: 240).

During Tony Blair's first term as Prime Minister, David Miliband, as head of the Downing Street Policy Unit, 'helped develop Blair's ideological approach … [as] an advocate of what came to be labelled as the "Third Way"' (Blick, 2004: 273). Miliband also, along with Geoff Mulgan (another of Blair's Special Advisers in the Policy Unit during the first term of Office), played a significant role in the development of New Labour's policies for tackling social exclusion and poverty (Riddell, 2001: 33).

Elsewhere, Andrew Adonis was widely believed to have played a significant role in persuading Blair to proceed with the proposals for university top-up fees. Indeed, it has been claimed that Andrew Adonis 'wielded enormous power and influence in the formulation of New Labour's education policy' in general, to the extent that 'education policy was determined by Tony Blair and Andrew [now Lord] Adonis' (Chitty, 2009: 138. See also Chitty, 2002: 45). That said, another of Blair's Special Advisers, Michael Barber, is also deemed to have exercised a strong influence on aspects of New Labour's education policy, albeit in tandem with Adonis (Barber, 2007: 54; Rhodes, 2011: 216).

On another occasion, Matthew Taylor, hitherto Director of the IPPR, was appointed as the head of Blair's Policy Unit (Rowan, 2003: 17). Taylor was a keen advocate of Public–Private Partnerships (PPPs), the policy initiative much favoured by Tony Blair, but bitterly opposed by many Labour MPs as 'creeping privatization' of the public sector.

More recently, David Cameron has attributed his vision of the 'Big Society' to Steve Hilton, his chief strategist and Policy Adviser from 2005 to early 2012.

With regard to the possible policy influence of Special Advisers on Cabinet Ministers, it has been suggested that David Young, when he served as a Special Adviser to Sir Keith Joseph at the Department of Trade and Industry in the 1980s, played a key role in promoting and preparing the privatization of British Telecom, while in the early 1990s, Christopher Foster, a Special Adviser to John MacGregor, Secretary of State for Transport, played 'an important role in the privatization of British Rail' (Blick, 2004: 193, 231).

Similarly, Michael Portillo, while a Special Adviser at the Department of Energy in the early 1980s, played an important role – in tandem with the Prime Minister's Policy Unit – in supervising the stock piling of coal reserves, which subsequently helped the Thatcher government to defeat the 1984–85 miners' strike (Blick, 2004: 208).

In the mid-1990s, Ed Balls (prior to becoming an MP himself) was deemed to be 'the brains behind' much of Gordon Brown's economic strategy and the decision to grant independence to the Bank of England immediately following the 1997 election (Ashley, 2002: 15), while Michael Jacobs was apparently instrumental in persuading Brown to increase National Insurance (NI) contributions by 1 per cent and spend the extra revenue solely on the NHS (Grice, 2004: 2); an example of 'hypothecated taxation'.

The increasing use of Special Advisers both reflects and reinforces the *partial* downgrading of the traditional role of senior civil servants in proffering advice and developing policy, although this role is still often important: it is a question of degree and will depend, to some extent, on both the issues concerned and the minister involved. However, with civil servants increasingly expected to focus on policy management and 'delivery', Special Advisers have acquired much greater opportunities and scope for initiating or developing policies with senior ministers and even of influencing Prime Ministers.

CONCLUSION

In identifying the individuals who collectively comprise the core executive, we have drawn particular attention to the variability of roles that they each play, as shaped by a combination of personal style, the extent to which each has clearly-defined policy objectives and the particular circumstances that prevail at any given juncture. Yet we have also noted some general trends that have occurred since the 1980s, most notably greater ministerial 'activism' in agenda setting and policy initiation, a greater emphasis on policy management and delivery by senior civil servants, and the increasing use, by Cabinet Ministers, of Special Advisers and Junior Ministers in policy making.

The more activist role adopted by many Cabinet Ministers and the consequent willingness to impose policy change in spite of opposition from outside the core executive is part of a more general shift from the consensual mode of policy making that prevailed for much of the 1945–79 period. This had partly derived from a broadly social democratic ethos during this era, which, among other values, had enshrined notions of partnership between governments and the governed. However, it also reflected the role of key organized interests in many policy spheres, as evinced by the existence of several policy communities.

Since the 1980s, though, the superseding of social democracy by neo-liberalism has naturally entailed a change in the governing style and mode of policy making. Many ministers have sought to pursue, and if necessary, impose change derived from conviction rather than being based on consensus, and this in turn, has led both to a downgrading or dismantling of policy communities (as discussed in the previous chapter), and a reduced policy-making role for senior civil servants – the latter now expected to focus more on policy management and 'delivery'. In this context, Cabinet Ministers have increasingly turned to Special Advisers for ideas and policy initiatives, and many of these SPADs have themselves subsequently become ministers.

Meanwhile, the increasingly specialized or technical nature of many policy issues, coupled with the demands on senior ministers' time (much of it spent away from their department), has yielded an increase both in the numbers and the importance of Junior Ministers. These play a vital role inside departments, focusing on a specific aspect of policy, such as immigration, pensions or public health. In so doing, Junior Ministers complement the more strategic leadership role played by the Cabinet Minister who heads the department and also illustrate the interdependency of individuals within the core executive.

QUESTIONS AND TOPICS FOR DISCUSSION

1. What constraints exist on the ability of British Prime Ministers to introduce new policies?
2. In what ways is the power of a British Prime Minister contingent and contextual?
3. How has the policy role and style of (many) Cabinet Ministers changed since the 1980s?
4. What is 'departmentalitis' and what are its main symptoms?
5. How does the role of a Junior Minister differ to that of a Secretary of State?
6. Why do Junior Ministers serve on Cabinet committees, but not sit in the Cabinet?
7. How might senior civil servants steer a minister towards a particular decision or policy?
8. Why has the use of Special Advisers increased since the 1980s?
9. What roles do 'SPADs' perform?
10. In what ways are the individuals in the core executive linked by resource dependency and exchange relationships?

RECOMMENDED TEXTS AND FURTHER READING

1. Andrew Blick (2004) *People Who Live in the Dark: The History of the Special Adviser in British Politics*. London: Politico's.

    The first major study of the role of Special Advisers in British politics and policy making. Examines the manner in which they have increased, both in number, and apparent influence, particularly since the 1980s.

2. House of Commons Public Administration Committee (2011) *Smaller Government: What do Ministers do? Seventh Report of Session 2010–11, Volume 1*, HC 530. Available from: www.publications.parliament.uk/pa/cm201011/cmselect/cmpubadm/530/530.pdf

    In the context of David Cameron's call for smaller government, and for greater efficiency by public servants in an era of fewer resources, the House of Commons' highly-respected public administration committee examines what this might mean for the core executive itself. The report claims both that there are too many Ministers in British government, and that too much time and energy are expended on relatively minor or mundane issues and activities, and often with limited discernible impact. Instead, there should be fewer Ministers overall, and they should operate more strategically, by concentrating on a smaller range of more important policy issues, or on problems where they could actually have a more meaningful impact; achieving more with less.

3. Gerald Kaufman (1997) *How to be a Minister*. London: Faber.

    Wry, often anecdotal, but always highly-informative and enjoyable, account of life as a Minister, based on the author's own experiences, and full of useful, often amusing anecdotes. Offers advice on such issues as how a Minister should: operate in Cabinet committees; work with organized interests; deal with 10 Downing Street; and 'how to make policy.'

4. LSE GV314 Group (2012) 'New life at the top: Special advisers in British Government', *Parliamentary Affairs*, 65 (4): 715–32.

    A welcome and much needed addition to the otherwise limited academic literature on Special Advisers. This article presents the findings of a recent case study (involving interviews and questionnaires) which analyses the different roles performed by SPADs, and their relationships with other policy makers in the core executive. It emphasizes that the precise role(s) undertaken by each Special Adviser, and their degree of authority or policy influence, is heavily dependent on their political and professional relationship with their Minister. This, in turn, will have an impact on how much respect they are accorded, and how seriously they are listened to, by others in the core executive, particularly civil servants in the Department.

5. David Marsh, David Richards and Martin J. Smith (2001) *Changing Patterns of Governance in the United Kingdom: Reinventing Whitehall?* Basingstoke: Palgrave (Chapters 6 and 7).

    Chapter 6 summarizes the changing role of Cabinet Ministers in Britain since the 1980s, noting the extent to which they have acquired a more active role in policy making, to the extent of increasingly challenging traditional Departmental 'philosophies'. Chapter 7 notes how this, in turn, has had an impact on Cabinet Ministers' relationships with senior civil servants, as the latter have increasingly been steered towards a policy management role. However, there remains a significant degree of reciprocity and mutual dependence.

6. R. A. W. Rhodes (2011) *Everyday Life in British Government*. Oxford: Oxford University Press.

Absolutely scintillating account of the day-to-day work of Ministers and senior civil servants in three Departments. In writing this book, Rhodes 'shadowed' the Ministers and their officials for several days while they conducted their daily business; he also conducted several in-depth interviews. This book thus provides a wealth of fascinating insights and anecdotes about daily life inside the core executive.

7. Martin J. Smith (2000) 'Prime Ministers, Ministers and Civil Servants in the Core Executive', in R. A. W. Rhodes (ed.) *Transforming British Government, Volume One: Changing Institutions*. London: Palgrave.

Examines the interaction between Prime Ministers, Cabinet Ministers and senior civil servants with particular reference to notions of mutual dependence and exchange relationships. Thus rejects a zero-sum conception of political power, and emphasizes, instead, the manner and extent to which power is shared between the actors, albeit varying according to personalities, leadership styles, external circumstances and specific policy issues.

8. Kevin Theakston (1987) *Junior Ministers in British Government*. Oxford: Blackwell.

Still the definitive text on this previously under-researched topic. Examines how and why Junior Ministers have increased in both number and importance, in tandem with the expansion and increased policy responsibilities of British governments during most of the 20th century. The increased number of Junior Ministers also reflects the increasing complexity of governing a modern society, and the consequent need for greater specialization among policy makers, even within individual Departments. As a consequence, many Junior Ministers have acquired a significant policy-making role within each Department.

The Core Executive, Part Two: The Institutions and their Policy Roles

4

The individuals whose policy roles and responsibilities were discussed in the previous chapter are themselves part of a network of institutions that also constitute the core executive. Those individuals both shape and are themselves influenced by these institutions, although much will depend on who the individuals and institutions are. Other factors will also determine the relationships, most notably the degree of support (or opposition) from elsewhere in the core executive, and external circumstances that might constrain policy options, or alternatively, compel the adoption of policies that would not otherwise have been chosen.

What can safely be asserted here is that just as the individuals who form part of the core executive are mutually dependent, by virtue of each possessing resources that various of their colleagues require in order to successfully pursue policy objectives, so are the institutions of the core executive also resource-rich in various ways, ensuring that they too are characterized by considerable interdependence. Furthermore, of course, these institutions provide many, if not most, of the resources that the individual policy actors are reliant upon in successfully pursuing policy goals. Once again, therefore, we emphasize that power in the core executive is *not* of a zero-sum character.

GOVERNMENT DEPARTMENTS

There has long been a widespread recognition among political scientists that government departments are the primary *loci* of most decision taking and policy making within the core executive (Burch and Holliday, 1996: 71; Headey, 1974: 60; Hogwood and Mackie, 1985: 47, 58; James, 1999: 12, 172; Judge, 2005: 128–9; Madgwick, 1991: 169; Richardson and Jordan, 1979: 25–34; Smith, 1999: 109; Smith, 2003: 79; Smith et al., 1995). In spite of the reforms of the senior civil service enacted by the Thatcher-Major governments in the 1980s and 1990s, and the penchant for turning to Special Advisers for policy advice and ideas, Marsh, Richards and Smith (following a series of in-depth interviews with senior officials in the 1990s) remain convinced that:

> … departments are both the *key actors and institutions at the centre of the policy-making process*. They continue to provide the foci in which policy is made. Thus, although we

acknowledge that changes brought about by governance have altered both the actors and the distribution of resources in the policy-making arena, most resources remain concentrated within Whitehall Departments. So, it is important to recognise that Departments continue to provide the key terrain in which power can be located within the British political system.

(Marsh et al., 2001: 249, emphasis in original)

A similar perspective was expressed by Geoff Mulgan, former Director of Tony Blair's Strategy Unit, when he informed the House of Commons' public administration committee that: 'Most of the work of government is done in departments, it has to be done in departments and can only be done in departments' (House of Commons Public Administration Select Committee, 2002b: Q. 316).

Certainly, even when broad policy objectives and strategy have been determined via the Cabinet and/or the Prime Minister, the subsequent development of most policies occurs inside individual departments, involving interaction between ministers, Junior Ministers, Special Advisers and civil servants, for 'Departments … are where concentrations of political and bureaucratic resources are located and, as such, they both influence the development of policy, and structure the behaviour of other actors within the core executive' (Smith et al., 2000: 163).

Due to the increasing complexity of governing contemporary Britain, and therefore the degree of administrative or technical expertise required, coupled with the development of new issues or problems on the institutional policy agenda and the particular policy priorities that different governments might adopt, the range, structure and nomenclature of many departments have undergone considerable change since the 1960s. For example, Table 4.1 illustrates how education has experienced significant departmental restructuring and name changes in recent decades.

Table 4.1   Changing departmental responsibility and title for education policy

Year created	Party in government	Name of department
1964	Conservative	Education and Science
1992	Conservative	Education
1995	Conservative	Education and Employment
2001	(New) Labour	Education and Skills (Former employment remit transferred to a new Department of Work and Pensions)
2007	(New) Labour	Children, Schools and Families – primary and secondary education Department for Innovation, Universities and Skills – higher education
2009	(New) Labour	Business, Innovation and Skills – higher education
2010	Conservative	Education (schools)

Another policy sphere that has evinced extensive departmental restructuring is that of employment, as shown in Table 4.2.

Table 4.2   Changing departmental responsibility and title for employment

Year created	Party in government	Name of department(s)
1916	Conservative-Liberal coalition	Ministry of Labour
1968	Labour	Employment and Productivity
1969	Labour	Employment
1995	Conservative	Education and Employment
2001	(New) Labour	Work and Pensions

Finally, trade and industrial policy has undergone extensive departmental changes since the 1970s, as show in Table 4.3.

Table 4.3   Changing departmental responsibility and title for trade and industrial policy

Year created	Party in government	Name of department(s)
1970	Conservative	Trade and Industry
1974	Labour	Department of Trade
		Department of Industry
		Department of Prices and Consumer Protection
1983	Conservative	Trade and Industry
2007	(New) Labour	Business, Enterprise and Regulatory Reform
2009	(New) Labour	Business, Innovation and Skills

Although most government departments are concerned with one particular policy area (education, health, transport, and so on), these are invariably highly detailed or specialized and so the departments invariably contain several directorates, units or sections, each focusing on a particular sphere of policy. This tendency towards intra-departmental sub-division reflects and reinforces the extent to which much policy making is administrative, specialized and technical. For example, Table 4.4 shows that the Home Office is divided into seven offices or units, clearly corresponding to the specific or specialist areas of policy for which it is responsible.

Table 4.4   Divisions and units within the Home Office

Offices and units	Roles and responsibilities
Alcohol and Drugs	Licensing of premises selling alcohol; tackling crime and disorder arising from excessive alcohol consumption; enforcing the Misuse of Drugs Act; tackling drug abuse and addiction; licensing the sale or prescription of 'controlled' (lawful, medicinal) drugs.
Counter Terrorism	Preventing terrorist activity in Britain; identifying and investigating those suspected of posing a terrorist threat; ensuring that the emergency services can respond effectively if a terrorist attack does occur; constantly monitoring the level of risk from terrorist activity.
Crime	Tackling anti-social behaviour; tackling disorder and violence at/near football matches; monitoring the whereabouts of child sex offenders (paedophiles); combating crime; tackling 'human trafficking'; promoting crime prevention measures; combating violence (physical/sexual) against girls and women.
Equalities	Tackling discrimination and disadvantage of all kinds; promoting opportunities and social mobility.
Immigration and Passports	Controlling immigration especially from outside the EU; issuing passports to British citizens; issuing visas to overseas visitors to regulate the conditions or length of their stay; extradition.
Police	Police powers; regulating police use of firearms; police–community partnerships.
Science, Research and Statistics	Forensics; DNA analysis; police technology; animal testing (for medical or scientific purposes); research and statistical evidence or analysis.

Elsewhere, as Table 4.5 shows, the Department of the Environment, Food and Rural Affairs (DEFRA) is divided into four sections or units, each focusing on a particular aspect of the department's remit, although even these seem to be rather broad ranging and could conceivably be further sub-divided.

Such degrees of specialization and sub-division mean that much detailed policy work is conducted deep within government departments with senior ministers often seeking to provide strategic leadership and direction based on their and/or the Cabinet's overall objectives, and only occasionally immersing themselves in the administrative minutiae of specific policies. Instead, as explained in the previous chapter, it is usually the Junior Ministers and civil servants rather than the Secretary of State who focus on more detailed or specific aspects of departmental policy, and these will often correspond closely to the internal departmental directorates, sections or units.

Table 4.5 Sections and units within DEFRA

Sections/Units	Roles and responsibilities
Environment	Natural environment; biodiversity; green economy and green businesses; climate change; flooding and coastal erosion/defence; marine environment; pollution; waste and recycling.
Food and farming	Food composition and labelling; food industry and supply chain; regulating personal food imports (especially dairy and meat products); health, transportation and welfare of farm animals; sustainable crop production; organic farming; GM crops; agricultural management; stewardship of the countryside; fishing industry; conserving fish stocks; EU's Common Agricultural Policy (CAP).
Rural and countryside	Rural communities; rural economies and businesses; rural grants and funding schemes; forestry, national parks; areas of outstanding natural beauty; hunting with dogs; public access to countryside and 'rights of way'; inland waterways.
Wildlife and pets	Animal welfare and preventing cruelty to pets; quarantine arrangements when travelling with pets; dangerous dogs; protecting wildlife; illegal trade in animals; zoos.

The degree of specialization, which characterizes the policy work of many government departments, is a major reason why senior ministers have often found it difficult to make a significant impact, at least in the short term. Traditionally, much of the detailed or specialist work within the sub-divisions of government departments has been undertaken by senior, or even middle-ranking, civil servants, with a relatively high degree of autonomy and discretion. Ministers generally lack the time, expertise or inclination to immerse themselves in technical policy detail or day-to-day issues, and had they attempted to do so, they would very quickly have become overwhelmed.

However, as we noted in the previous chapter, many ministers have adopted a much more proactive policy role since the 1980s (as 'commanders' or ideologues), aided by Junior Ministers (who have themselves acquired more extensive and specialized policy responsibilities in recent years) and Special Advisers.

Departmental cultures

One of the most significant features of many government departments is the extent to which they previously embodied a prevalent 'philosophy' or in-house ideology; what Marsh et al. (2001: Chapter 4) characterize as 'departmental cultures'. These departmental philosophies or cultures have significantly shaped many departments' overall policy perspectives and approaches to problems, including how problems are defined (or denied) in the first place, thereby serving to shape the institutional agenda. As Richards and Smith have noted, 'Departments are organizations with institutionalised policy preferences and cultures which privilege certain policy outcomes' (1997: 62–3; see also Hennessy et al., 1997).

Table 4.6   Dominant ethos in various government departments pre-1980

Department	Philosophy or dominant policy paradigm
Agriculture, Fisheries and Food	Protecting British farmers through the defence of farm subsidies
Education and Science	1. Comprehensive schools
	2. Granting considerable autonomy to local education authorities, schools and universities
Home Office	1. Social liberalism on moral issues
	2. Emphasis on rehabilitation and non-custodial sentences where possible, *vis-à-vis* penal policy
Social Security	Committed to 'universalist' principles of welfare entitlement, as enshrined in the 1942 Beveridge Report
Trade and Industry	1. Trade division; international free trade
	2. Industry division; intervention and regulation to protect/ promote British industry

Source: Adapted from Smith et al., 2001: Chapter 4.

The erstwhile dominant ethos of various departments is summarized in Table 4.6. It can be seen, for example, that the former Department of Trade and Industry evinced a form of political schizophrenia, for according to one of its former permanent secretaries, the Trade side, enshrined 'a strong Cobdenite free trading ethos' (quoted in Smith, 1999: 132), while the Industry side tended to be rather more interventionist (Rhodes, 2011: 67; Sewill, 1975: 44; Young [David], 1990: 244), although both 'sides' would claim that their particular perspectives, international free trade and domestic economic intervention/industrial subsidies, were intended to promote or protect British manufacturing industry and jobs.

However, during the 1980s, a series of Thatcherite Secretaries of State began to steer the department's industrial side away from its *dirigiste* ethos (Marsh et al., 2001: 82–4). It has also been suggested that the interventionist ethos of the department's Industry 'side' was not derived from a commitment to intervention *per se*, 'but rather in the view that a close relationship between government and industry was crucial (Middlemas, 1979), which in practical terms, manifested itself in the pursuit of sponsorship and advocacy of the interests of industry (Richards and Smith, 1997: 67).

Elsewhere, the Home Office, from the 1960s until the 1980s, was widely viewed (often disapprovingly) as a source of social liberalism, largely due to the fact that the latter half of the 1960s witnessed the abolition of the death penalty, the end of theatre censorship, the liberalization of abortion and divorce, and the legalization of homosexuality, while both the 1960s and 1970s heralded various laws to outlaw racial and sexual discrimination. Even during the Thatcher years, successive Conservative Home Secretaries had little discernible success in bringing about significant or permanent change in the 'social liberalism' of the Home Office with regard to criminal justice and penal matters (Marsh et al., 2001: 72–7). Certainly, the Home Office's conservative critics have consistently viewed it as being too concerned with the rehabilitation and rights of criminals and offenders, rather than retribution through harsher punishment and longer prison sentences.

Meanwhile, what is now the Department of Education has often been accused by its Conservative critics of previously being preoccupied with promoting comprehensive schools (and of therefore being hostile to private schooling and parental choice) and diluting academic standards in order to enable more pupils to obtain qualifications, as part of an apparent concern with pursuing egalitarianism and equality of opportunity. Thus did a former Conservative Secretary of State for Education, Kenneth Baker, once claim that:

> Of all the Whitehall Departments, the DES [Department of Education and Science] was among those with the strongest in-house ideology. There was a clear 1960s ethos and a very clear agenda which permeated virtually all civil servants ... It was devoutly anti-excellence, anti-selection, and anti-market.
>
> (Baker, 1993: 168. See also Patten, 1995: 196–7)

On an earlier occasion, Bernard Donoughue (1987: 109–10), who was head of the Downing Street Policy Unit from 1974 until 1976 (serving the Labour Prime Minister Harold Wilson), observed that:

> The problem for all of them [Ministers of Education] was that their department had little power. Education policy was conducted by the local education authorities and the teachers' unions, with the Department of Education, as Harold Wilson once commented to me, being little more than a post box between the two.

Explaining departmental philosophies

The existence of a 'departmental philosophy' can be explained by reference to two inter-related factors. First, there is the notion of 'custom and practice', whereby a particular way of approaching issues or problems becomes the operational norm within a department; 'how we do things here'. This operational norm is internalized by the senior civil servants within a department, so that they too adopt a particular set of principles and practices when dealing with policies. Those in the highest echelons of the civil service or department are likely to have spent their whole careers – 30 years or more – in Whitehall, and therefore internalized a specific set of norms and values that strongly influences how they approach policy making and problem solving in their department: 'each bureaucracy reflects the historical development and institutional context of its administrative setting' (Judge, 2005: 127. See also Rhodes, 2011: 60). Younger civil servants, meanwhile, will be socialized through their career development into adopting these values also, thereby contributing to the continuity of the departmental philosophy, irrespective, to a considerable degree, of the political complexion of the governing party at any particular juncture.

Crucially, the departmental philosophy can sometimes become so pronounced or ingrained that a new minister, intent on pursuing a significant change of policy, will find him/herself being 'persuaded' by their officials that the proposed policy is either unrealistic, requires more consideration, needs to be moderated, or ought be deferred until circumstances are more propitious. In the past at least, many would-be radical or reform-minded ministers have 'gone native' by increasingly adopting their department's perspective, so that relative continuity of policy, rather than radical change, often prevailed. This, of course, is a manifestation of the 'departmentalitis' that we noted in the previous chapter.

Second, as we noted in Chapter 2, many government departments have previously had close links with particular organized interests, thereby facilitating the establishment of 'policy communities'. These erstwhile linkages reflected and reinforced the departmental philosophy or in-house ideology because senior civil servants and the leaders of the relevant organized interests often adopted a broadly similar approach to issues. In so doing, they sought to manage the institutional agenda, which often entailed defining what was, and what was not, a problem.

Indeed, with senior departmental officials and leaders of a department's 'client' group often engaged in a continual process of bargaining and negotiation, the scope for radical departures from existing policies was often greatly reduced or restricted. Consequently, when and where such 'departmental philosophies' prevailed, there was often broad continuity of most policies, and when change did occur, it was predominantly incremental. Rapid or dramatic policy change was the exception rather than the norm. A department's 'in-house ideology' often meant that when faced with a problem, only a relatively narrow range of options and policy proposals were considered, with senior officials insisting on the importance of practicability and what was deemed realistic. There was also a concern to ensure that policy proposals were broadly acceptable to the organized interest(s) which a department had a close relationship with. This further reflected and reinforced the generally conservative impact of policy communities.

Such considerations and criteria usually militated against (at least in the short term) the wholesale abandonment or repeal of existing policies, or the adoption of radical new initiatives, which would depart significantly from the status quo. As such, pursuing policy change has often been compared to steering an oil tanker – it needs to be done carefully and slowly over a relatively long distance or period of time; departments and oil tankers 'both take time to turn around' (Richards and Smith, 1997: 63).

Yet this often posed a serious dilemma for reform-minded ministers; either their tenure would be too short to instigate any significant and lasting change, or they enjoyed longevity at a department, but with the increased risk of 'going native' or at least being worn down by civil service resistance to major reforms.

Challenging and changing departmental 'philosophies'

Since the 1980s, though, several ministers have succeeded in changing a department's prevalent philosophy and thereby successfully effected a change in policy orientation. A minister's success in effecting what Smith et al. term 'a paradigm shift' (2000: 151), and thus a change of policy orientation in a department will not only depend on his/her own objectives and ministerial style (vitally important though these are), but also on propitious circumstances in the wider economic or political environment, in accordance with the third of Kingdon's three policy streams, that of the 'political stream', as discussed in Chapter 1.

The requisite combination of a minister committed to policy change and propitious circumstances provide what Richards and Smith (1997: *passim*) have termed 'critical junctures', whereupon significant and lasting changes in a department's philosophy, objectives and policies can be secured. Similarly, Cortell and Peterson (with explicit acknowledgement of John Kingdon) argue that: 'international and domestic events, including both crises and gradual pressures, open windows of opportunity that provide policy officials with the potential to transform existing institutions' (Cortell and Peterson, 1999: 179).

Yet it is also the case that while individual ministers can seek to change a department's prevailing philosophy or policy perspective, it is usually necessary for a subsequent minister to maintain the momentum in order for the initial change to become more permanent. Otherwise, when a Cabinet reshuffle moves the reforming minister to another department (or s/he returns to the backbenches), the momentum of their reform is likely to dissipate, thereby enabling the department to revert back to its traditional policy perspective. For example, Richards and Smith (1997: 67–9. See also Smith et al., 2000: 150–2; Smith 1999: 133–6; Marsh et al., 2001: 83–4) suggest that it was David Young, during the late 1980s, rather than Sir Keith Joseph, at the beginning of the decade, who enjoyed greater success in steering the Industry 'half' of the Department of Trade and Industry away from its interventionist ethos, towards a rather more neo-liberal stance; Young explicitly promoted it as 'the Department for Enterprise'.

Changing the ethos of the Department of Social Security

Similarly, it was Peter Lilley, during the early 1990s, rather than Norman Fowler, in the mid-1980s, who 'successfully altered the policy bias' (Smith et al., 2000: 152. See also Marsh et al., 2001: 87–94; Richards and Smith, 1997: 73–5) of the Department of Social Security away from universalist welfare provision to selectivity, targeting and tougher eligibility criteria for claimants and recipients of social security benefits.

As Secretary of State for Social Security during the mid-1980s, Fowler had instigated a comprehensive review of social security, precisely in order to effect a shift away from the universal system of welfare provision 'from cradle to grave', previously established as a consequence of the 1942 (William) Beveridge Report. Although the ensuing 1986 Social Security Act did introduce a variety of reforms pertaining to the criteria and eligibility for welfare support, these were not as extensive or far-reaching as many Conservatives had envisaged, and as such, they were 'not radical enough to mark a clear point of departure from the welfare settlement' (Richards and Smith, 1997: 74), even though the reforms were doubtless significant for individual claimants who found themselves worse-off, and attracted considerable criticism from welfare charities and anti-poverty pressure groups.

However, Fowler's reforms did instigate a shift in thinking within the Department of Social Security, which heralded a re-orientation away from the principle of universalism, although it was to be several years until this manifested itself in more radical reform and a much more explicit policy emphasis on selectivity and targeting, along with major initiatives such as the 1993 Child Support Agency.

Richards and Smith consider Peter Lilley's 1992–97 tenure at the Department of Social Security to be decisive in yielding a 'paradigm shift', even though the basis had been laid by Fowler, because not only was Lilley more ideologically committed to welfare reform than his immediate predecessors, but the early 1990s witnessed another economic recession, which lent an added impetus to the search for cuts in the social security budget.

Moreover, during this period, the Chief Secretary to the Treasury – the minister mainly responsible for public expenditure *per se* – was Michael Portillo, who was keen to cut the costs of welfare provision in order to reduce government spending.

Whereas 'spending' ministers have traditionally sought to resist or scale down the Treasury's demands for cuts in their departmental budgets, Lilley seemed happy to accede to Portillo's insistence on cuts to the social security budget, this amenability doubtless informed by the fact that, ideologically, they were both viewed as Thatcherites during the early 1990s. In short, Richards and Smith (1997: 75) assert that:

> the culmination of exogenous pressure for change from the Treasury, an endogenous shift in attitudes within the department dating back to Fowler, and the appointment of a hard-liner, Peter Lilley, created a window of opportunity from which a critical juncture of change arose.

This shift towards greater selectivity and targeting in social security provision, coupled with an increasingly direct link between welfare entitlement and a verifiably active search for work among the unemployed, was subsequently maintained by the 1997–2010 Blair–Brown governments. Although, New Labour professed much more concern about poverty and 'social exclusion' than the Conservatives, the solution was deemed to reside in getting people off benefits into work, rather than merely increasing social security payments to the unemployed. After all, New Labour held that the main cause of poverty was unemployment itself (rather than low pay) and hence the objective of the welfare state should be to move people off social security benefits into work, albeit with a statutory minimum wage to ensure that they were genuinely better off financially than if they remained 'on the dole'.

Thus was the Department of Social Security abolished in 2001 and a new Department of Work and Pensions established whose remit actually included all social security bene-fits, not just pensions; welfare and work were inextricably and explicitly yoked together.

Changing the ethos of the Home Office

Elsewhere, the apparently socially liberal ethos of the Home Office was successfully chal-lenged, not so much by Thatcher's early Home Secretaries, such as Leon Brittan, but by David Waddington who was appointed Home Secretary in 1989. His appointment doubt-less reflecting Thatcher's own frustration that her government's law and order policies had not matched the authoritarian rhetoric and punitive measures previously pledged by the Conservative leadership, and routinely demanded by delegates attending the party's annual conference.

That said, it required the appointment of Michael Howard as Home Secretary, in 1993, to ensure that the 'paradigm shift' initiated by Waddington was effectively maintained, rather than dissipating due to loss of momentum when Waddington was moved from the Home Office in a Cabinet reshuffle. According to Richards and Smith, 'Howard nurtured the seeds planted during the Waddington era and used the still open window of opportunity in order to give priority to civic order over individual liberty', and his insistence that 'prison works' (Richards and Smith 1997: 72. See also Marsh et al., 2001: 72–7).

To some extent, the shift towards a more authoritarian stance at the Home Office was sustained during the 1997–2007 Blair governments when figures such as David Blunkett and John Reid served as Home Secretary. Both were viewed as being 'tough' characters in touch with the party's working-class supporters, who often harboured authoritarian attitudes on issues such as crime and immigration (as opposed to the more liberal stance of many middle-class Labour voters).

Blair himself had famously pledged to be 'tough on crime and tough on the causes of crime' – Old Labour having had a reputation for focusing primarily on the apparent socio-economic causes of criminality, which enabled Conservatives to deride Labour for being 'soft' on crime and this being 'the criminal's friend'. Certainly, Blair was strongly in favour of 'zero tolerance policing' and a clamp down on anti-social behaviour. Indeed, controversial Anti-Social Behaviour Orders (ASBOs) were subsequently enshrined in the 1998 Crime and Disorder Act, introduced by Blair's first Home Secretary, Jack Straw.

His successor at the Home Office, David Blunkett, then introduced tough security measures in response to the 9/11 terrorist attacks in the USA. When these attracted criticism for being authoritarian and inimical to civil liberties, Blunkett scornfully referred to 'a world which is airy fairy, libertarian, where everybody does precisely what they like' (quoted in Wintour, 2001). Moreover, when the Labour MP Kevin Hughes expressed his support in the House of Commons for the anti-terrorist clampdown by referring contemptuously to 'the yoghurt and muesli-eating, *Guardian*-reading fraternity [who] are only too happy to protect the human rights of people engaged in terrorist acts, but never once … talk about the human rights of those who are affected by them', Blunkett readily concurred, emphasizing that 'I do not suffer fools gladly' (House of Commons Debates, 2001: vol. 375, col. 30).

Blunkett's successor, Charles Clarke, similarly attracted criticism for some of his tough law and order or national security policies, not least the 2006 Identity Cards Act (subsequently repealed by the Conservative-Liberal Democrat coalition government in 2010).

Changing the ethos of the Department of Education

Meanwhile, at the Department of Education, it was Kenneth Baker at the end of the 1980s, rather than Keith Joseph during the first half of the decade who successfully secured a decisive shift away from the predominance of teaching unions and Local Education Authorities (LEAs) in determining education policy, and towards empowering parents and promoting competition between schools. Keith Joseph, although widely viewed as a staunch Thatcherite, nonetheless failed to impose significant changes during his (unusually long) tenure as Secretary of State for Education between 1981 and 1986, apparently due to the strength of the education 'establishment' or policy community, whereupon Joseph was prone to 'lapsing into passivity in the face of officialdom' (Sherman, 2005: 102).

Baker's introduction of the National Curriculum and 'key stage' tests of pupils soon led, almost inevitably, to the publication of school league tables, which were depicted as a vital means of providing parents (as 'customers') with the information they needed to make an informed decision about which was the best school for their children. Crucially, in securing this 'paradigm shift', Baker ensured that the education policy community (as we noted in Chapter 2) was condemned, confronted and weakened, whereupon teachers, teaching unions and local education authorities all lost their dominant position and role in education policy making (Bochel and Bochel, 2003: 51–2; Dorey, 1999; Dorey, 2014).

Indeed, Ball (1990: 18) invoked the term 'discourse of derision' to characterize the constant criticism and contempt to which teachers were increasingly subjected to in the 1980s (and which continues unabated today). This has served to legitimize both the need for radical reform of education from the late 1980s onwards, and the parallel exclusion of teachers and their unions from the formulation of education policy.

Certainly, what was particularly notable about education policy making during the latter half of the 1980s and beyond was the deliberate exclusion of the 'education establishment' and the soliciting instead of policy advice from sundry New Right think tanks, most notably the Centre for Policy Studies, the Hillgate Group and the Institute of Economic Affairs. These groups then found a receptive ear in the Downing Street Policy Unit, particularly after Sir Brian Griffiths had been appointed its head in late 1985, whereupon 'it was happy and willing to act as a "conduit" between the various … think tanks and the Prime Minister herself' (Chitty, 2009: 133).

Indeed, it has been claimed that much education policy during the latter half of the Thatcher premiership 'was assembled *in secret* … There was a determined effort *not* to consult either the DES [Department of Education and Science] or the civil servants or chief education officers or local politicians' (Maclure, 1988: 166, emphasis in original). The education policy community was thus eviscerated.

Baker's changes were subsequently entrenched or extended by subsequent Education Secretaries, such as Kenneth Clarke and John Patten, who enthusiastically embraced the new philosophy or strategic orientation of the department. Clarke especially was also renowned for his pugnacious style, which ensured that he would be unsympathetic to any complaints or opposition from the teaching profession.

The trajectory of education policy instigated by Baker was resolutely adhered to, and even extended, when New Labour replaced the Conservatives in government in 1997 and 'Blairites' proved as determined to 'take on' public sector professionals, particularly teachers, as their Conservative predecessors. The mantra of parental choice and inter-school competition was maintained, the role of local education authorities continued to be downgraded and teachers routinely denigrated.

Furthermore, Blair and most of his Education Secretaries proved just as willing as their Conservative predecessors to confront or challenge the teaching profession if and when it sought to resist reforms or pointed out the problems engendered by them. For example, in 2002, Blair appointed Charles Clarke as Secretary of State for Education, evidently impressed by the fact that 'he was tough, and could be rough' (Blair, 2010: 483), presumably the qualities that Blair had discerned in David Blunkett when the latter had been appointed Education Secretary in 1997.

Meanwhile, the very purpose of education was explicitly linked to the perceived requirements of employers and the economy, rather than having any intrinsic social purpose or cultural value. Schools, and increasingly universities too, were expected to impart 'transferable skills' to their pupils and students in order to maximize their 'employability' when they graduated. Education as an intellectual pursuit in itself and learning as an inherently worthwhile activity were derided as unaffordable and outdated indulgences; education was only meaningful if it could be proved to benefit the economy and serve the needs of employers.

In each of these cases, the main challenge to a departmental philosophy (and *inter alia* the cognate policy community) emanated from a minister who, aided by favourable economic or political circumstances, and enjoying explicit prime ministerial support, was able to build on the work initiated by their predecessors and thereby resolutely 'push through' reforms that the department would probably have previously resisted. These reforms were subsequently consolidated or extended by their successors.

In this respect, there is a parallel here with an observation that Richard Rose (1984) made about governments and policy change. He argued that a new government was unlikely to make a lasting impact if it only enjoyed one term of Office, for at least two terms were generally required in order to impose and embed lasting changes of policy. The first term was largely exploratory and preparatory, with new ministers also having to react to problems inherited from the defeated government (and which may well have largely caused that government's defeat in the recent election). In the second (and third or fourth) term, however, more substantive policy changes can be enacted, for by this time a momentum may have gathered, coupled with greater ministerial confidence about what can be achieved.

After all, the radical policies most associated with Thatcherism – the major privatizations, education and NHS reform, the Poll Tax, and so on – were implemented during the Thatcher governments' second and third terms.

We would suggest that a similar principle applies to significant changes in departmental philosophies or 'paradigm shifts', whereby a single minister in post for an average of 18 months or so is usually unlikely to introduce significant or lasting change in the policy perspective of a department. Such change usually requires that s/he is immediately succeeded by a minister who fully shares his/her vision and objectives and can therefore build on the momentum they initiated. The succeeding Minister will also be able to learn from any mistakes made by his/her predecessor, or identify where obstacles or opposition emanated from. Subsequent ministers can then sustain or consolidate the shift in departmental objectives and policy, thereby ensuring that it becomes further embedded and entrenched.

THE CABINET

Comprising 21–23 ministers (including the Prime Minister), the Cabinet was, for much of the 20th century, regarded as the most important arena of decision taking and policy making. However, it is now widely accepted that the policy-making role of the Cabinet has diminished, especially since the 1970s, partly through the transfer of certain powers to the EU, but more importantly because an increasing volume of government business has effectively been delegated down to other policy arenas and modes of ministerial interaction, most notably Cabinet committees, as discussed below.

Apart from the Prime Minister, the vast majority of ministers belonging to the Cabinet are heads of key government departments, namely the Secretaries of State and the Chancellor. In addition to these, one or two of the non-departmental Ministers/Ministers without

Portfolio are usually appointed to the Cabinet. While most Cabinet Ministers are recruited from the government's MPs in the House of Commons, a couple or so will be selected from peers in the House of Lords. Also in regular attendance at meetings of the Cabinet is the government's Chief Whip, who acts as an important conduit of communication between ministers and their backbench colleagues.

It is now widely acknowledged that the traditional textbook or constitutional model of the Cabinet acting as a forum for systematic decision taking and detailed discussions concerning government policies is no longer accurate, and has probably not been for quite some time (Burch, 1988a: 30–2; James, 1999: 81–7). The complexities of governing Britain have increased since 1945, with a consequent expansion of governmental responsibilities and a corresponding increase in both the volume and complexity of legislation.

As a consequence, the Cabinet has virtually ceased to be the political arena in which detailed discussion or careful deliberation occurs on most policy issues, prior to a collective ministerial decision being taken. As Smith et al. observe, 'Ministers are too overloaded and cabinet meetings are too short and ill-informed for the cabinet to be a significant decision-making body' (Smith et al., 1995: 55. See also, Kakabadse and Kakabadse, 2011: 368).

The diminished role of the Cabinet in detailed decision taking and policy making is reflected in and reinforced by the decline in both the number and duration of its meetings. Until the 1960s, the Cabinet often met twice each week, on Tuesday and Thursday mornings, with the standard length of these meetings being three hours (particularly for the Thursday meetings). By the 1980s and early 1990s, however, the Tuesday meetings of the Cabinet had largely been dispensed with, leaving just the Thursday meeting, starting at 10.00am, but still usually lasting for about three hours. Under Tony Blair's premiership, though, the weekly Cabinet meeting became shorter in duration, often lasting an hour and a half at most (Hennessy, 2000; Holliday, 2000: 89; Riddell, 2001: 32).

This partly reflected prime ministerial style, for Blair, like Thatcher, recognized the limitations of the Cabinet as an effective policy-making forum and therefore viewed lengthy or discursive meetings as a waste of his and his ministerial colleagues' time. Indeed, Blair himself once referred contemptuously to 'the old days of Labour governments where meetings occasionally went on for two days and you had a show of hands at the end' (quoted in Rawnsley, 2001: 52). However, Blair's downgrading of the Cabinet prompted Lord (Robin) Butler, the former Cabinet Secretary, to refer – somewhat disparagingly and disapprovingly – to the 'sofa style' of decision taking (Hurst, 2004).

Blair's successor, Gordon Brown, did revert to the traditional three-hour meetings of the Cabinet and this has been maintained by David Cameron since May 2010, but the fact remains that these full-length Cabinet meetings do not ordinarily 'make' detailed policies. Instead, the Cabinet is now widely recognized as having four main functions (Burch, 1988a; Burch, 1988b: 3–4; Burch and Holliday, 1996: 42), namely ratification, coordination, arbitration and information.

Ratification

The primary policy role of the contemporary Cabinet is to provide formal approval of policies and legislative proposals presented to it, but which have normally been determined or drafted elsewhere in the core executive. In this respect, it is hardly an exaggeration to claim that with regard to the majority of policy proposals, the Cabinet acts as a 'rubber stamp', endorsing measures already developed by individual ministers, departments and/or Cabinet committees.

As Giddings has argued, 'the Cabinet has increasingly become the forum for registering and promulgating policy decisions which have been initiated and prepared elsewhere in the government machine, notably Cabinet committees and other meetings of Ministers'. In other words, he suggests, the Cabinet 'receives reports and approves decisions; it is … the place to register rather than formulate decisions' (Giddings, 1995: 41).

With regard to measures proposed by Cabinet committees especially, a senior minister in the Blair governments, Tessa Jowell, explained how:

> … important decisions from Cabinet committees will come as recommendations before the whole Cabinet, but with a degree of confidence that the arguments and the complexity of the difficulties will have been addressed in the discussion in Cabinet committee and will be reflected in the recommended conclusion.
>
> (House of Lords Constitution Committee, 2010: 130, Q. 289)

As such, it is extremely rare for the Cabinet to reject policy proposals if they have already been agreed elsewhere in the core executive. Furthermore, on most issues, ministers will have little direct interest in the policies of their colleagues around the Cabinet table. As a former Chancellor of the Exchequer explains: 'Most Cabinet Ministers, particularly after a longish period in government, tend to be preoccupied with fighting their own battles, and pursuing the issues in their own bailiwick, and lose interest in the wider picture' (Lawson, 1992: 129). Or as Charles Powell, a former Chief of Staff to Tony Blair, expressed in a memorandum to the aforementioned parliamentary inquiry into the machinery of government:

> … the Cabinet is not the right body in which to attempt to make difficult decisions. It has too many members for a proper debate. Many of those who are there will not necessarily be well-briefed on the subjects under discussion unless they come directly within the remit of their departments … It is for that reason that *since at least the late 1970s the Cabinet has been used to ratify decisions rather than to take them*.
>
> (House of Lords Constitution Committee, 2010: 180, emphasis added)

This perspective is further endorsed by a recent academic survey of the roles and activities of Cabinet Ministers, in which one (unnamed) Secretary of State confessed that: 'Each Cabinet member is so concerned with his or her own area of work, which is enormous, they just turn off listening to what's going on' (quoted in Kakabadse and Kakabadse, 2011: 368).

This also reflects the prevalence of departmentalism at senior ministerial level, with most ministers usually so immersed in the affairs of their own departments that the activities of other departments and ministers will not generally concern them, unless a particular policy proposal impinges upon their department's jurisdiction or objectives. Yet if this was the case, then any potential conflicts would normally have been resolved via *ad hoc* meetings of ministers from the affected departments or in a Cabinet committee. Also, the Cabinet Office (discussed below) would probably have identified a potential or actual conflict between departments or ministers over a policy and thus arranged for meetings or a committee to deal with it. In most cases, therefore, potential or actual disputes over policy will not normally reach the full Cabinet, thereby further ensuring that most policy proposals are 'nodded through' by this stage.

Coordination

Given the prevalence of departmentalism and the concomitant risk that the policies of one department might detrimentally impact upon those of another, or even prove incompatible with the government's own objectives, the full Cabinet also plays a crucial role – increasingly assisted by the Cabinet Office (discussed below) – in ensuring that individual ministers are aware of the policy goals and measures being pursued by their ministerial colleagues.

The inclusion in the Cabinet of a couple of Ministers without Portfolio can also prove valuable in facilitating coordination, for by virtue of not having departmental responsibilities, they can assist the Prime Minister in adopting a broader or strategic view of policy issues, thereby providing a corrective to the narrower departmental perspective adopted by some of the other ministers around the Cabinet table; they *can* see the wood for the trees.

Arbitration

In principle, the full Cabinet might be appealed to by a minister feeling aggrieved with a Cabinet committee decision, whereupon the minister concerned would hope to persuade his/her Cabinet colleagues to 'adjudicate' in their favour, effectively overriding or reversing the previous policy decision. However, if a minister wishes to take a Cabinet committee decision to the full Cabinet, with a view to having it reviewed or reversed, s/he needs the permission of the minister who chaired the committee. Perhaps understandably, such permission is rarely likely to be granted (and as such, is rarely sought), otherwise one of the key purposes of establishing Cabinet committees in the first place would be undermined, namely the alleviation of the Cabinet's workload and the minimization of ministerial time that needs to be taken up attending meetings of the full Cabinet.

Even if such permission was granted, though, recourse to such action might make the minister concerned, or their preferred policy option, appear somewhat weak, for they will effectively be admitting to the full Cabinet that they had 'lost the argument' when and where it really mattered, in the committee. Besides, if the policy does not directly affect their own department and its policy responsibilities, other ministers are highly unlikely to be particularly interested in the issue – another manifestation of 'departmentalism' – and therefore disinclined to get involved in it for the sake of pacifying one disgruntled ministerial colleague. For these reasons, aggrieved ministers rarely appeal to the full Cabinet in an attempt at having a Cabinet committee policy decision overturned or reversed.

Information

The Cabinet is undoubtedly a vitally important forum through which senior ministers are kept informed of the government's programme, including forthcoming legislation and parliamentary business for the next week. Cabinet meetings also include reports on international affairs by the Foreign Secretary, particularly those that have diplomatic, military or security implications for Britain. Of course, the provision of information also facilitates coordination, by keeping all Cabinet Ministers aware of the context in which they are collectively operating in, and what their individual colleagues and other departments are doing or planning to do.

Occasionally, the Cabinet might engage in a more general or informal discussion over governmental objectives, policies or strategy, or about how the government ought to respond either to an ongoing and unresolved problem or to an issue that has just risen to the top of the institutional policy agenda. According to a former Chancellor of the Exchequer, Nigel Lawson:

> The Cabinet's customary role was to rubber stamp decisions that had already been taken, to keep all colleagues reasonably informed about what was going on, *and to provide a forum for general political discussion if time permitted*.

> (Lawson, 1992: 125, emphasis added)

However, only occasionally does time and the Prime Minster permit the Cabinet 'to provide a forum for general political discussion', particularly in view of the reduced frequency and length of Cabinet meetings, as noted above.

CABINET COMMITTEES

It has long been the case that much of the detailed decision taking and policy making in the core executive is delegated to Cabinet committees, particularly when an issue affects or involves more than one department. The vital role of Cabinet committees not only reflects the increased responsibilities of British governments in industrial, economic and social affairs, especially since 1945, but also the growing political and administrative complexities of governing contemporary Britain. As a consequence, many policies are both administratively complex or specialized, and often require the contribution and cooperation of more than one department.

As Tony Blair himself once explained in a parliamentary answer: 'The business of Government is by nature cross-departmental and the main way of agreeing policy and driving reform across departmental responsibilities is through Cabinet Committees and sub-Committees' (House of Commons Debates, 2006). The same point was made by some of the (former) ministers and senior civil servants who gave evidence to the House of Lords' Constitution Committee inquiry into the machinery of government in 2009–10. For example, both Lord (Richard) Wilson and Sir Gus O'Donnell acknowledged that Cabinet committees had largely replaced the Cabinet as the place where formal deliberation of crosscutting or potentially conflicting interdepartmental issues are debated and resolved (House of Lords Constitution Committee, 2010: 60). Indeed, Jonathan Powell was rather more trenchant, asserting, via a memorandum, that:

> [Cabinet committees] are an essential instrument of government decision making: all the relevant people can be there (and not the irrelevant), they are focussed on particular decisions, properly prepared and they have as much time as they need to reach a decision. In my view, therefore, rather than arguing about the death of Cabinet government, when it in fact died a long time ago, we should spend more effort reinforcing the

Cabinet committees and their supporting infrastructure as a key part of government decision making.

(House of Lords Constitution Committee, 2010: 180)

This view was broadly echoed by former Labour minister, Tessa Jowell, who observed that Cabinet committees 'are very much the engine of so much government policy development and policy recommendation, which is then taken to Cabinet' (House of Lords Constitution Committee, 2010: 124, Q. 260).

The actual number of Cabinet committees will vary from government to government, depending on such factors as the nature of the problems and policy issues that are on the institutional agenda, the range and remit of government departments, and the Prime Minister's own objectives, strategy and style of leadership. For example, following New Labour's re-election in 2005, there were 44 Cabinet committees, including committees on issues such as:

- Britain's ageing population
- anti-social behaviour
- asylum and immigration
- housing and planning
- local and regional government
- NHS reform
- Post Office network
- schools policy
- serious organized crime and drugs.

By contrast, during his first year as Prime Minister, David Cameron established a mere nine Cabinet committees (although a few of these then established a sub-committee to deal with more detailed aspects of their policy remit), these addressing broader or more thematic problems and policy priorities, namely the:

- Coalition Committee
- National Security Council
- European Affairs Committee
- Social Justice Committee
- Home Affairs Committee
- Economic Affairs Committee
- Banking Reform Committee
- Parliamentary Business and Legislation Committee
- Public Expenditure Committee.

In effect, Cameron opted for fewer, but broader ranging, Cabinet committees, perhaps reflecting his professed commitment to reducing the state intervention and 'micro-management', which he attributes to New Labour's style of governing.

Although the members of a Cabinet committee are usually formally selected by the Prime Minister, membership is usually functional. This means that the ministers appointed will normally be those whose departments are most involved in, or affected by, a particular issue or policy, and thus have a direct interest in it. In such cases, membership is virtually automatic or self-selecting (Catterall and Brady, 1998: 74; James, 1999: 67).

However, one or two other ministers will sometimes be included too, possibly Ministers without Portfolio or other senior ministers particularly trusted by the Prime Minister, who will normally provide a somewhat broader perspective by virtue of not being departmentally involved in the policy under discussion.

Junior Ministers also serve on relevant Cabinet committees, even though they do not usually attend the full Cabinet. Their involvement with Cabinet committees, though, reflects the specialist nature of their particular responsibilities in the department, which will then enable them to make a contribution to the more detailed work of Cabinet committees.

These characteristics are evident, for example, in the membership of the coalition government's Cabinet committee on social justice (as at August 2013):

- Secretary of State for Work and Pensions (Iain Duncan Smith) – Chair
- Chief Secretary to the Treasury (Danny Alexander) – Deputy Chair
- Secretary of State for the Home Department, and Minister for Women and Equalities (Theresa May)
- Secretary of State for Communities and Local Government (Eric Pickles)
- Minister without Portfolio (Baroness Warsi)
- Minister for Cabinet Office, Paymaster General (Francis Maude)
- Minister of State – Cabinet Office (Oliver Letwin)
- Minister of State for Higher Education (David Willetts)
- Parliamentary Under Secretary of State for Justice and Minister for Equalities (Helen Grant MP)
- Parliamentary Under Secretary of State for Business, Innovation and Skills, Minister for Equalities (Jo Swinson MP)
- Parliamentary Under Secretary of State for Health (Anna Soubry MP)
- Parliamentary Under Secretary of State for Education (Elizabeth Truss MP).

Several Cabinet committees will establish a sub-committee to address a specific issue or problem, this further reflecting the highly-specialized or administratively-detailed nature of much policy making in contemporary Britain. For example, the aforementioned Cabinet committee on social justice also presides over a Child Poverty Sub-Committee whose ministerial membership (August 2013) comprised:

- Minister of State for Education in the Cabinet Office (David Laws) – Chair
- Parliamentary Under Secretary of State for Work and Pensions (Esther McVeigh)
- Minister of State for Communities and Local Government (Mark Prisk)
- Economic Secretary to the Treasury (Sajid Javid MP)
- Parliamentary Under Secretary of State for Business, Innovation and Skills (Matthew Hancock)
- Parliamentary Under Secretary of State for Justice/Minister for Equalities (Helen Grant)
- Parliamentary Under Secretary of State for Business, Innovation and Skills, Minister For Equalities (Jo Swinson)
- Parliamentary Under Secretary of State – Health (Anna Soubry).

Meanwhile, the broad-ranging remits of the Economic Affairs Cabinet Committee, the Public Expenditure Cabinet Committee and the National Security Council mean that each of them has four sub-committees, as illustrated in Figures 4.1, 4.2 and 4.3 respectively.

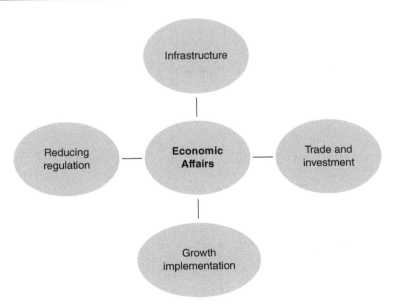

Figure 4.1   Sub-committees of the Cabinet Committee on Economic Affairs

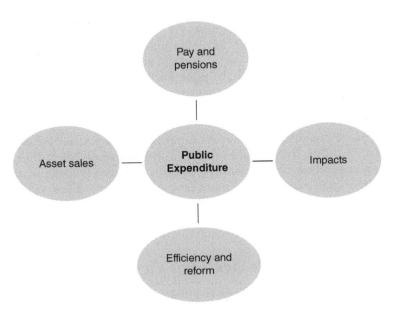

Figure 4.2   Sub-committees of the Cabinet Committee on Public Expenditure

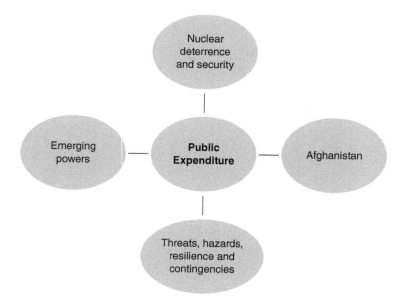

Figure 4.3 Sub-committees of the National Security Council

Most Cabinet committees, especially those not being chaired by the Chancellor, will include a Treasury Minister, to ensure that the policy being considered does not entail unauthorized increases in public expenditure.

Cabinet committees normally enjoy full policy-making authority, to the extent that their decisions subsequently reported to the full Cabinet are usually ratified as a formality, as noted above. This is hardly surprisingly, given the earlier observation about the lack of detailed discussion, which occurs in the Cabinet. As such, once a Cabinet committee comprising the most relevant or affected ministers has agreed on a policy, it is highly unlikely that other ministers will raise objections in the full Cabinet, particularly if the committee was chaired by the Prime Minister or another trusted senior ministerial colleague.

We can see, therefore, how Cabinet committees, rather than the full Cabinet, are one of the most important arenas of policy making in British government, with policies usually determined by a small number of ministers, most of whom serve on a committee due to their department's involvement or direct interest in a particular policy. Cabinet committees therefore constitute key 'institutional mechanisms for melding departmental autonomy with collective government' (Smith, 1999: 168).

THE PRIME MINISTER'S POLICY UNIT

In order to fulfil his/her myriad functions and responsibilities, while simultaneously supervising the implementation of the government's policies and overall strategy, the Prime Minister is aided by a Prime Minister's Office, which actually comprises several discrete units, although many of these vary from one Premier to another. For example, whereas the pre-1997 Prime Minister's Office comprised four discrete sections, namely the Private Office, the Political Office, the Press Office and the Policy Unit (renamed Policy Directorate by Tony Blair), Blair then added a Delivery Unit and a Strategy Unit in 2001 and 2002 respectively – although these straddled Downing Street and the Cabinet Office. For the purpose of our study, though, it is the Downing Street Policy Unit that is of most interest and relevance.

Originally established by Harold Wilson in 1974, the Policy Unit has become a major source of advice for Prime Ministers. Indeed, the Policy Unit has played a dual role by simultaneously keeping the Prime Minister informed of policy developments in government departments (thereby aiding coordination from the centre of the core executive and supplementing the role of the Cabinet Office), while also assisting the Prime Minister in developing their own policy ideas and initiatives (Rhodes, 2011: 24; Willetts, 1987). The often blurred distinction between the Policy Unit's role in policy oversight and policy development is reflected and reinforced by the fact that although it 'belongs' to 10 Downing Street, organizationally it is linked to the Cabinet Office.

This blurring was reinforced by Blair's establishment of the aforementioned Strategy Unit and Delivery Unit, as pointedly emphasized by some of the witnesses, including former senior civil servants and Cabinet Secretaries, who gave evidence to a 2009–10 inquiry on the machinery of government, undertaken by the House of Lords Constitution Select Committee (House of Lords Constitution Committee, 2010: 9, paras. 13–14). Certainly, the Labour MP and chair of the Public Administration Committee, Tony Wright, observed that 'if you went through the last ten years and just drew up a list of all these different named units ... it is utterly bewildering' (House of Lords Constitution Committee, 2010: 18, para. 65).

Or as a senior civil servant explained to the same inquiry:

> Number 10 has a discrete role and a discrete identity within the Cabinet Office [but] the border between the two is very porous. Many of the Prime Minister's top advisers are located in the Cabinet Office ... the apparently clear distinction between the Prime Minister supported by Number 10 staff and the Cabinet Office supporting the Cabinet ... just does not capture the reality of the situation.
>
> (House of Lords Constitution Committee, 2010: 10, para. 18)

Ambiguity over the precise roles and responsibilities both of the Policy Unit itself, and its relationship with the Cabinet Office, are compounded by the fact that the former 'is both reactive and proactive' (Smith, 1999: 174). Burch and Holliday similarly note that the Policy Unit is 'sometimes engaging in forward thinking and policy initiative, sometimes in evaluation of initiatives taken by government Departments' (Burch and Holliday, 1999: 35). Likewise, Lee et al. (1998: 119) observe that staff in the Policy Unit 'both react to departmental proposals and initiate their own for departments to turn their attention to, study and work on'.

According to two former Policy Unit 'insiders' during John Major's premiership:

> The Policy Unit's job is to keep the Prime Minister in touch with outside thinking, to work on his own ideas and to act as a sounding board for ministers, advising on the flow of proposals and counter-proposals that pour in continually from all around Whitehall. The Prime Minister can use his unit as storm troops, invading the complacent hinterland of Whitehall, or as peacemakers, building bridges between warring departments and ministers. In practice, the Unit tried to do a bit of both: to be both grit and oil in the government machine.
>
> (Hogg and Hill, 1995: 24. See also Lee et al., 1998: Chapter 7; Willetts, 1987)

During Margaret Thatcher's premiership in the 1980s, for example, the Policy Unit participated in her 'famous "judge and jury" sessions, in which ministers would be called to No. 10 and interrogated on their policies and performance, and by the mid-1980s had become a feared and hated part of their lives' (Hennessy, 2001: 424). Later, while Tony Blair was Prime Minister:

> the Policy Unit became central to Blair's style of leadership … was systematically involved in the development of departmental proposals from a very early stage, representing the Prime Minister's preferences in central areas.
>
> (Blick, 2004: 276)

As such, an eminent contemporary political historian has noted that: 'The Policy Directorate made Number 10 into more of a policy-making powerhouse for the Prime Minister' (Seldon, 2004: 631), and 'sought to develop and promote the Prime Minister's agenda in Whitehall' (Kavanagh and Seldon, 2000: 221. See also Smith, 2011: 173–74). Or as Blair himself recalls, it 'handled the day-to-day, and focused on managing the departments to produce the policies and their implementation' (Blair, 2010: 339).

When he became Prime Minister in May 2010, David Cameron embarked on a rationalization of the Downing Street Policy Unit, both by reducing the number of Special Advisers (as noted in the last chapter) and by streamlining the structure of the Policy Unit; for example, the Strategy Unit's functions were hived-off to units within the Cabinet Office in November 2010.

The degree of institutional support provided by the Prime Minister's Policy Unit might seem to provide further evidence of prime ministerial power at the centre or apex of government and dominance *vis-à-vis* their ministerial colleagues. However, it can just as readily be interpreted as an indication of relative weakness, for Prime Ministers are effectively seeking to match some of the support and resources that Cabinet colleagues derive from their departmental officials, Special Advisers and 'client' groups. After all, as Kavanagh and Seldon note:

> Compared with most Departmental Ministers, a Prime Minister has a tiny budget, a small staff, and few formal powers. He has to work through Secretaries of State, in whom statutory powers are vested. Viewed from Number Ten, Whitehall Departments can look at times like a series of baronial fiefdoms, to which it can only react. Departmental Ministers

have large staffs, budgets, policy networks, information and expertise ... The strength of most Departments is such that it requires enormous willpower, obstinacy, political authority, and excellent briefing for the Prime Minister to prevail ...

(Kavanagh and Seldon, 2000: 318)

This perspective was effectively endorsed by one of Tony Blair's closest advisers, Philip Gould, when he asserted that:

The centre actually has far less power than is typically ascribed to it. Anyone who spends time at Number 10 quickly realises that it is a tiny corner of a huge government machine, staffed with talented people, but lacking the resources necessary to be a commanding and dominating nerve centre. The idea that officials at Number 10 headquarters are smoothly pulling strings and levers, and effortlessly controlling events, is ridiculous.

(Gould, 1999: xxiii)

Furthermore, Prime Ministers also encounter the paradox that the more staff and resources they employ in order to underpin or bolster their authority, the greater can be: the problem of coordination of such staff and resources; the possibility of conflict, either between these staff themselves or with others in the core executive; the potential for 'information overload'.

According to one academic expert on the core executive, 'whilst institutional resources have increased, the power of the Prime Minister to achieve his or her goals has not' (Smith, 2003: 62). With regard to the last point, for example, Richard Rose refers to Tony Blair's reported appointment of over 300 task forces during his first term of Office, a tally that sounds highly impressive, Rose observes, before enquiring rhetorically: 'How much time does he have to give to their reports?' (Rose, 2001: 154). With particular reference to Tony Blair's enhanced and expanded Policy Unit/Directorate, for example, one writer highlighted the risk of 'overburdening an already fully stretched Number 10' (Seldon, 2004: 631).

THE CABINET OFFICE

The Cabinet Office plays a crucial role in the coordination of public policy in Britain, both by fostering cooperation and communication between departments and ministers, and also by providing a conduit between the Prime Minister, the Downing Street Policy Unit and government departments. Located primarily at 70 Whitehall – but with a connecting corridor to 10 Downing Street – and a few offices in nearby streets, a former Cabinet Secretary, Sir Robert Armstrong (1986), observed that:

Throughout its history ... there has been a clear thread: the Cabinet Office has seen itself, and has been seen as, the servant of the Cabinet and of the government collectively, its purpose being to promote and assist the discussion and resolution of issues that transcend departmental boundaries, and the reaching and disseminating of conclusions and decisions commanding the collective assent of ministers.

It has since been suggested that the Cabinet Office 'has responsibility for the co-ordination of Cabinet business' (Judge, 2005: 152), and as such, it is 'something of a corporate head-quarters overseeing government strategy' (Kavanagh and Seldon, 2000: 70. See also Rhodes, 2011: 219–21). Or as Whitehall expert, Peter Hennessy once remarked, the Cabinet Office 'is *the* crucial junction box of the central government system' (Hennessy, 1990: 390, emphasis in original).

The 2011 *Cabinet Manual* decrees that:

> The Cabinet Secretariat exists to support the Prime Minister, and currently the Deputy Prime Minister, and the chairs of Cabinet committees in ensuring that government business is conducted in an effective and timely way and that proper collective consideration takes place ... The Cabinet Secretariat reports to the Prime Minister, the Deputy Prime Minister and other ministers who chair Cabinet committees. The Cabinet Secretariat prepares the agenda of Cabinet committee meetings, with the agreement of the chair; it also provides them with advice and support in their functions as chair; and issues the minutes of the committees.

> (Cabinet Office, 2011a: 36)

In fact, much of the coordinating and liaison work of the Cabinet Office is performed by its constituent Secretariats, as well as various *ad hoc* units. The precise number and nomenclature of the Secretariats varies from government to government, or even from Prime Minister to Prime Minister, but they are usually organized thematically, so that each is responsible for the coordination of a particular range of interrelated or cross-cutting policies and liaising with the relevant departments, as illustrated by Table 4.7. In this respect, the Cabinet Office is crucial to the pursuit of 'joined-up government'.

Table 4.7   Cabinet Office Secretariats under Thatcher, Blair and Cameron

Thatcher	Blair	Cameron
Economic	Economic and Domestic	Economic and Domestic Affairs
Home Affairs	Defence and Overseas	European and Global Issues
Overseas and Defence	European	National Security
European	Civil Contingencies	
Science and Technology	Machinery of Government	
Joint Intelligence	Ceremonial	
	Joint Intelligence and Security	

In the final year of Margaret Thatcher's premiership, there were six Secretariats in the Cabinet Office, these increasing to seven under Tony Blair. However, upon becoming Prime Minister in May 2010, David Cameron reduced the number of Cabinet Office Secretariats to just three. Regardless of their name or number, the role of these Secretariats is:

... to provide an effective, efficient and impartial service to the Cabinet and its committees, and co-ordinating departmental contributions to the government's work ... The Office ensures that decisions are consistent with overall government policy and where appropriate, co-ordinates effective follow-up policy decisions.

(Cabinet Office, 1997: 5, 15)

More specifically, this entails the Secretariats:

- Preparing Cabinet committee meetings, setting their agendas (as requested by the Chair) and circulating the relevant papers to the relevant ministers in advance of the meetings.
- Recording the minutes, conclusions and policy decisions, and distributing these to the relevant ministers monitoring the subsequent progress of interdepartmental policy issues.
- Facilitating the coordination between departments when they are affected by, or involved in, a particular policy initiative.

Through its sundry Secretariats, therefore, the Cabinet Office seeks to counter the innate trend towards departmentalism, and thereby facilitate coherence and coordination between ministers and their departments at all 'stages' of the policy process.

Presiding over the Cabinet Office is the Cabinet Secretary, a post which one of its former occupants, Sir Robin (now Lord) Butler, likened to being 'the chief engineer in the engine room of government' (quoted on BBC Four, 2011).

Alongside the various Secretariats, the Cabinet Office also enshrines sundry Units, these reflecting governmental or prime ministerial priorities. For example, whereas there was a Social Exclusion Unit during Tony Blair's premiership, reflecting New Labour's professed concern to tackle poverty and re-integrate marginalized or disadvantaged sections of society, under David Cameron, there is an Office for Civil Society, which is specifically devoted to promoting the 'Big Society'.

Cameron envisages that this will facilitate the tackling of social problems through a 'mixed economy' of public, private and voluntary organizations, along with philanthropic individuals and 'active citizens', all of which are intended to reduce dependency on (and thus the costs of) the welfare state. Clearly, the range of organizations expected to participate in the 'Big Society' places a premium on the Cabinet Office's role in interdepartmental policy coordination.

CONCLUSION

It is evident that the individuals in the core executive, identified in the previous chapter, are both supported, and to some extent, constrained, by the institutions of the core executive; they are simultaneously empowered and enmeshed by it. The institutions of the core executive enshrine a vital array of resources necessary for the formulation, development and implementation of public policy in Britain, but as with individual actors in the core executive, their interaction should be comprehended in terms of resource dependency and exchange relationships, rather than attempting to identify the 'most important/powerful' institution.

Even though one particular policy actor might appear to be prominent with regard to one particular issue at one particular moment in time, they might be considerably weaker when dealing with a different policy, or operating in a different set of circumstances.

Hence the vital point that power in the core executive is neither fixed nor of a zero-sum character. Instead, it is contingent and contextual, and depends on a range of economic and political circumstances, as well as on the personalities, leadership styles and interrelationships of the individuals and institutions who collectively comprise the core executive.

Meanwhile, the core executive enshrines a permanent tension between tendencies, which can cause fragmentation and interdepartmental rivalry, and counter trends that seek to prevent interministerial or intra-Cabinet conflicts and ensuing policy paralysis. In this respect, the Policy Directorate in the Prime Minister's Office and the Cabinet Office both play an absolutely vital coordinating role, aiming to provide strategic oversight and brokering agreements between conflicting or competing departments, or even scanning the horizon to pre-empt such conflicts in the first place. Yet the Cabinet Office and Policy Directorate are themselves heavily dependent on departments, either for policy advice and expertise or for compliance in the pursuit of policies.

Ultimately, therefore, on most issues at least, the institutions of the core executive, just like the individual policy actors identified in the previous chapter, are obliged to work together, if only for reasons of enlightened self-interest. Different institutions in the core executive possess, or enjoy ready access to, particular resources, such as expertise, the 'right contacts', political authority, the support of 'client' groups, and so on, and as such, much policy making necessarily entails a constant process of mutually beneficial bargaining and brokering of deals to achieve shared policy goals.

QUESTIONS AND TOPICS FOR DISCUSSION

1. Why does the Cabinet rarely discuss policies in detail?
2. What are the main roles of the Cabinet?
3. In what way is the membership of a Cabinet committee functional?
4. What are the main roles of a Cabinet committee?
5. Why do some departments develop their own culture or in-house ideology?
6. What might the consequences of a departmental culture or in-house ideology be for ministers at the department?
7. How might a department's culture be changed?
8. What is the purpose of the Prime Minister's Policy Unit?
9. What are the roles of the Cabinet Office?

RECOMMENDED TEXTS AND FURTHER READING

1. Peter Hennessy (2001) *Whitehall*. London: Pimlico.

   Voluminous, but highly-readable, text, incorporating a wealth of empirical evidence, examples and anecdotes. What could all too easily be a rather 'dry' academic topic is rendered rich, vibrant and thoroughly engaging because of Hennessy's inimitable style of writing and delightful phrasing.

2. House of Lords Constitution Committee (2010) *The Cabinet Office and the Centre of Government*, Fourth Report of Session 2009–10, HL Paper 30. Available from: www.publications.parliament.uk/pa/ld200910/ldselect/ldconst/30/30.pdf

Having taken evidence from a range of distinguished (current and former) Ministers, Special Advisers, senior civil servants and academic experts, the House of Lords' Constitution Committee reports on the roles of the various institutions of the core executive, namely the Cabinet, Cabinet committees, Departments, the Cabinet Office and the Prime Minister's Office. Emphasizes the vital importance of ensuring coordination between the constituent institutions, while still upholding the principles of Ministerial responsibility and parliamentary scrutiny of the executive.

3. Simon James (1999) *British Cabinet Government*, second edition. London: Routledge.

Well-written and informative overview of the role and structure of the contemporary Cabinet, including chapters on the role of Cabinet Ministers, the Prime Minister, and collective decision making, as well as coverage of the individuals and bodies which support or serve Ministers and/or the Cabinet.

4. J. M. Lee, G. W. Jones and June Burnham (1998) *At the Centre of Whitehall: Advising the Prime Minister and the Cabinet*. Basingstoke: Palgrave.

A superb in-depth and very detailed study of the bodies which service and support the Prime Minister and the Cabinet, particularly the Prime Minister's Policy Unit (Directorate), and the Cabinet Office (and its various Secretariats).

5. Dennis Kavanagh and Anthony Seldon (1999) *The Powers Behind the Prime Minister: The Hidden Influence of Number Ten*. London: HarperCollins.

A very incisive and informative analysis of the support network – especially the Prime Minister's Office, and its constituent units – which serve British Prime Ministers. Highlights how the different personalities and leadership styles of each Prime Minister shapes the manner in which they utilize the (potential and actual) support of staff in the PM's Office. Also examines the relationship between the Prime Minister's Office and other elements of the core executive, such as the Cabinet Office, and the Cabinet itself.

6. David Richards and Martin J. Smith (1997) 'How departments change: Windows of opportunity and critical junctures in three departments', *Public Policy & Administration*, 12 (2): 62–79.

An important article detailing how, why and when Departmental philosophies and established approaches to policy are challenged, thereby enabling policy change to be introduced. Emphasizes that Ministerial intentions or objectives alone are rarely enough; circumstance and conditions need to be conducive to effective change, thereby creating a 'critical juncture' or paradigm shift in a Department's history and policy trajectory.

7. Martin Smith (2011) 'The paradoxes of Britain's strong centre: Delegating decisions and reclaiming control' in C. Dahlström, B. G. Peters and J. Pierre (eds) *Steering from the Centre: Strengthening Political Control in Western Democracies*. Toronto, Canada: University of Toronto Press.

Explores a major dialectic of British politics and governance since the 1980s, namely the perennial tension between devolving and decentralizing power and policy implementation on the one hand, and Ministerial concern to retain or regain control on the other; an oscillation between delegation and dirigisme. Smith lucidly explains how this has placed a premium on central coordination and the pursuit of 'joined-up government', via the expansion and increased authority both of the Prime Minister's Policy Unit (Directorate under Tony Blair) and the Cabinet Office.

8. Martin J. Smith, David Marsh and David Richards (1995) 'Central Government departments and the policy process', in R. A. W. Rhodes and P. Dunleavy (eds) *Prime Minister, Cabinet and Core Executive*. Basingstoke: Macmillan.

Valuable essay emphasizing the extent to which much detailed policy making is conducted within Departments, thereby placing a premium on coordination to ensure that Departmental interests do not undermine the government's overall goals and strategy.

5 Parliament and Public Policy

With a few notable exceptions, most political scientists have downplayed the role of Parliament in the policy process, reasoning that since the late 19th century, policy making has increasingly been conducted elsewhere, away from the House of Commons and the House of Lords. Initially, following the establishment of well-organized, highly-disciplined, political parties (see Norton, 1979), power accrued with the governing party and was then further concentrated in the expanding core executive. Alongside this, as we noted in Chapter 2, the emergence of organized interests led, in some spheres, to the establishment of policy communities, which reflected and reinforced a trend towards sectorization and specialization within the core executive.

These policy communities also seemed to signify the continued marginalization of Parliament as a significant policy actor, as major decisions were increasingly determined by ministers and a small number of powerful organized or professional interests, with little regard or respect for Parliament itself.

Indeed, writing on the eve of the October 1974 general election, Ray Pahl and Jack Winkler (1974: 72–6) portentously declared that whichever party won, key policy decisions would increasingly be taken, behind closed doors in Whitehall, by a coterie of key organized interests and their leaders, senior civil servants and government ministers, thus completing the transformation of Britain from a parliamentary democracy to a corporatist state. Meanwhile, Richardson and Jordan's (1979) book on the British policy process, *Governing Under Pressure*, was pointedly subtitled *The Policy Process in a Post-Parliamentary Democracy*.

This 'declinist thesis', concerning the seemingly relentlessly diminishing power and policy-making role of Parliament, was lent considerable credence in 1973 when Britain joined the then European Communities (EC) and which eventually became the EU. As the EC/EU has subsequently acquired greater power over an increasing range of policies, and increasingly pursued policy harmonization between member states, there has been a corresponding increase in 'Euro-scepticism' – most notably on the Right-wing of the Conservative party, but also on the Labour Left – attacking the seemingly inexorable loss of parliamentary sovereignty and policy autonomy to Brussels.

One further, rather more recent, development that seemed to confirm the apparent decline of Parliament was devolution in 1999, which established a Scottish Parliament and a National Assembly for Wales. As we discuss in the next chapter, this ensured that Scotland acquired legislative autonomy over a wide range of policy areas and issues, while Wales was granted much greater administrative or 'executive' power, but with the promise of greater legislative power and autonomy at a later stage – as subsequently confirmed both by the 2006 Government of Wales Act and the result of the ensuing Welsh referendum.

Clearly, then, this 'declinist thesis' depicts a relentlessly emasculated Parliament, one whose power and authority have been consistently diminished by the aforementioned developments, to the extent that it has been rendered little more than a 'rubber stamp' for policies and legislation drafted and determined elsewhere, or a mere 'talking shop' that has long since ceased to exercise much influence on public policy in Britain.

Such a conclusion, though, seriously overlooks or underestimates the important roles that Parliament does play in debating, scrutinizing and subsequently evaluating legislation and other measures of public policy (on which, see the voluminous output by Britain's foremost academic expert on Parliament, Philip Norton, including: Norton, 1981; Norton, 1985; Norton, 1990; Norton, 1991; Norton, 1993a; Norton, 1998; Norton, 2005; Norton, 2013). Parliament still plays an important role in aspects of the policy process; if it did not exist, some comparable institution would need to be established to perform the valuable functions that are conducted by Parliament with regard to legislation and other aspects of public policy in Britain.

Norton has consistently argued that Parliament's primary roles should be understood as those of policy modification and policy legitimation, rather than actual policy making *per se*. For example, Norton has suggested that: 'The importance of Parliament lies in the fact that it is the body *through* which power is exercised, and concomitantly in the fact that its giving of consent is accepted as legitimate and binding' (Norton, 1981: 219, emphasis in original. See also Norton 1990).

This perspective is clearly echoed by Kalitowski (2008: 707) when she notes that: 'Parliament … makes a difference to legislation, sometimes in major ways, and more frequently through many minor but significant changes'. Similarly, Cowley observes that 'MPs may not make policy, but they do constrain and occasionally prod government. All but the most technical of decisions are affected by some consideration of party management' (Cowley, 2005: 9. See also Judge, 1993: 124–5; Richards, 1988: 14, 15).

However, before we examine the specific ways in which Parliament fulfils its role in the policy process, we need to briefly explain the relationship between the House of Commons and the House of Lords, and how they interact.

THE RELATIONSHIP BETWEEN THE HOUSE OF COMMONS AND HOUSE OF LORDS

Once the franchise was steadily extended via the 1832, 1867 and 1884 Reform/Representation of the People Acts, so the balance of political power and popular legitimacy shifted steadily towards the House of Commons, for this alone was elected. In stark contrast, the House of Lords remained almost wholly comprised of hereditary peers, and the few peers who had not inherited their titles sat in the Second Chamber as *ex-officio* members, such as the archbishops. However, in spite of the increasingly democratic basis of the House of Commons, the House of Lords still retained legal supremacy in the sense that it retained the right to veto legislation approved by the elected Chamber.

Furthermore, in terms of party affiliation, the Conservatives enjoyed a numerical preponderance in the Second Chamber, due to the fact that the vast majority of (pre-1999) hereditary peers – often descended from the aristocracy or landed gentry – sat on the

Conservative benches. The House of Lords was thus doubly undemocratic; it remained totally unelected and one particular political party enjoyed unrivalled dominance. It was virtually inevitable that, sooner or later, clashes would occur between the elected House of Commons and the (overwhelmingly) hereditary and Conservative House of Lords, particularly when the Liberals were in government.

Indeed, the 1906–11 Liberal government encountered repeated opposition from the House of Lords over a wide variety of economic and social policies, and this culminated in the 1911 Parliament Act, which removed the House of Lords' veto over 'Money Bills' (viz. the Budget), while also limiting its veto over other legislation to two years (for the background to the 1911 Act, and the struggle to get it onto the statute book, see Dorey and Kelso, 2011: Chapter 1).

The 1911 Parliament Act ensured that the House of Lords was finally subordinate to the House of Commons. As the preamble to a 2001 White Paper (on House of Lords reform) asserted: 'The House of Commons has … long since been established as the pre-eminent constitutional authority within the UK … This constitutional framework, founded on the pre-eminence of the House of Commons, has provided Britain with effective democratic government and accountability for more than a century, and few would wish to change it' (Stationery Office, 2001: paras. 9–10, 13–18. See also, Straw, 2007: 42, para. 135). One could quibble over the claim *vis-à-vis* 'more than a century' – from 1911 to 2001 was actually 90 years – but the substance of the declaration was undeniable.

The House of Lords' veto or power of delay was then halved by the 1949 Parliament Act, and to this day, it can only delay Bills for one year, although some Labour MPs have sporadically urged a further reduction, to six months. This call, however, has gone unheeded, not least because of concern by the party's senior parliamentarians that if the House of Lords' power of delay was only six months, it would almost inevitably be inclined to invoke such a veto more frequently against a Labour government's legislation – certainly far more often than the one-year delay – and thereby cause a legislative 'pile up' or backlog of Bills at the end of each (annual) Session.

In other words, as has often been the case with the issue of reform of the House of Lords, more prescient Labour MPs and ministers have strongly suspected that further reducing the Second Chamber's veto and/or making it a democratically-elected body, would almost certainly render it a more 'active' institution, whereupon it would probably cause more problems, more frequently, for Labour governments. Consequently, beyond removing all but 92 of the hereditary peers, via the 1999 House of Lords Act, the Labour Party, especially when in government, has often proved to be rather conservative in its approach to House of Lords reform, fearful that more substantial reforms would actually enhance the legitimacy of the Second Chamber, and thus revitalize it, whereupon it would play a more active and 'obstructive' role (Dorey, 2006b; Dorey, 2008a: Chapter 3; Dorey, 2008b; Dorey and Kelso, 2011: Chapters 2, 5 and 6).

Apart from the 1911 and 1949 Parliament Acts and the 1999 removal of most of the hereditary peers, the most significant and far-reaching reform of the House of Lords in the 20th century occurred via the 1958 Life Peerages Act. This was actually introduced by a Conservative government, reflecting recognition among some senior Conservatives (not least in the Second Chamber itself) that the House of Lords' legitimacy was seriously weakened because of the overwhelmingly hereditary character of its membership. This, in turn, rendered it vulnerable to radical reform or even abolition by a future Labour government (not withstanding our preceding observation about Labour's conservatism on this issue).

Keen to imbue the House of Lords with renewed legitimacy and 'relevance' to contemporary British society, but loathe to attack the hereditary principle and membership (not surprising, given the preponderance of Conservatives among the hereditary peers), the 1955–59 Conservative government enacted the 1958 reform, which created a new type of peer, one whose title and membership of the House of Lords would be for the duration of their lifetime only and so not passed down the family line (Dorey, 2009d).

However, what was really innovative about this new category of peer was not simply that it would be awarded to people who had made an important and distinguished contribution to public life, but that it would inject much greater and wider expertise into the House of Lords, as peers were increasingly appointed by virtue of their successful role or achievements in such professions as academia, broadcasting, business, journalism, medicine, science, and so on. True, Life Peerages have routinely been awarded to many former MPs and/or ministers, but in spite of this, the period since 1958 has witnessed a significant change in the social composition of the House of Lords and this has made it somewhat more representative of British society; or at least, more so than it was prior to 1958, as illustrated in Table 5.1.

The 1958 Life Peerages Act thus effectively poured new wine into an old bottle or injected new blood into the body politic. This imbued the House of Lords with a wider range of expertise than hitherto, and thus facilitated more authoritative and well-informed

Table 5.1 Occupational background of Life Peers, 1958–2008*

(Occupation/Profession and number (in brackets, as percentage) of all Life Peers**)

Academia 89 (7)

Arts (inc actors and musicians)13 (1)

Civil Service 60 (5)

Engineering (inc architect, surveyor) 10 (1)

Finance (banking, insurance) 34 (3)

Industry 133 (11)

Journalism 16 (1)

Land (landowner, farmer) 7 (1)

Law (judge, solicitor, barrister) 55 (5)

Local government 50 (4)

Medical 31 (3)

Media 43 (4)

Military 18 (2)

Politics (former MP, Minister) 470 (39)

Public sector 32 (3)

Teaching 8 (1)

Trade union 45 (4)

Voluntary 40 (3)

Other 36 (3)

* Extrapolated from Brocklehurst, 2008: 20–1.

** May add up to more than 100% because of individual percentages being rounded up.

debates on legislation and other aspects of public policy (Baldwin, 1985: 103–8; Judge, 2005: 76; Norton, 2005: 110–11; Russell, 2013: *passim*; Shell, 2007: 112–19). For example, when (in April 2004) the House of Lords held its second reading (concerned with the general principles) of the Blair government's Higher Education Bill, to introduce top-up fees for university students, over half of the 45 Peers who participated were, or had been, directly involved with universities, mostly in a professorial or vice-chancellor role (Dorey, 2009e: 239–40).

Furthermore, while most Life Peers adopt a party affiliation (sitting as Conservative, Labour, Liberal Democrats, peers, for example), there is generally less partisanship and political point scoring in speeches in the House of Lords than in House of Commons. Indeed, it has been suggested that 'members of the House of Lords are rather more unpredictable in their allegiance and voting than MPs ... with marked consequences for legislation' (Rogers and Walters, 2004: 11). Furthermore, a sizeable minority of peers sit as Crossbenchers, meaning that they are 'Independents' who do not align with or belong to a political party; in the 2012–13 parliamentary session, 182 peers (out of 753 peers in total) sat as Crossbenchers.

As a combined consequence of its post-1958 composition, greater expertise and less pronounced partisanship: 'The capacity of the Lords to stage impressive debates across the range of public policy issues is undoubted – and probably equalled by few other assemblies', for the background of its membership 'equips it for insightful deliberation on virtually any matter' (Adonis 1990: 144). Similarly, Donald Shell has observed that speeches and debates in the House of Lords 'tend to be less concerned with asserting party advantage, more concerned with well-informed argument – more cerebral and less populist' (Shell, 2007: 114), while another academic expert on Parliament, Michael Rush, notes that: 'The membership of the Lords covers a remarkable range of expertise, and legislation is often discussed more thoroughly in the Upper House than in the Commons' (Rush, 2001: 114).

These favourable judgements clearly echo Baldwin's assertion that as a consequence of the wider social composition and greater expertise yielded by the creation of Life Peers, 'the House [of Lords] has members with very considerable knowledge of almost every aspect of life', and because of this, 'it has become the custom for only experts, or at least people with considerable knowledge, to speak on specialised subjects. This leads to a very high level of debate' (Baldwin, 1985: 104–5).

Another manifestation of the House of Lords' broader, more expert, membership and slightly weaker partisanship has been its increasing willingness to challenge aspects of governmental legislation emanating from the House of Commons. One manifestation of this, as illustrated in Table 5.2, has been the increased number of defeats inflicted on successive governments' legislation by the House of Lords, notwithstanding our earlier observation about the post-1911 constitutional supremacy of the House of Commons.

Clearly, Labour governments have been particularly affected by defeats in the House of Lords, although two caveats should be borne in mind. First, the 1974–79 Labour governments lacked an overall majority in the House of Commons for much of this period and so the House of Lords – especially the Conservative peers – was more willing to challenge the legitimacy or 'mandate' for Labour's more radical legislative measures, particularly those aiming to extend nationalization and strengthen trade unionism.

Table 5.2   Government defeats in the House of Lords since 1970

Government	No. of defeats
Conservative 1970–74	26
Labour 1974–79	355
Conservative 1979–83	45
Conservative 1983–87	62
Conservative 1987–92	72
Conservative 1992–97	63
Labour 1997–2001	108
Labour 2001–05	245
Labour 2005–2010	175
Conservative-Liberal Democrats 2010–13	75

Source: Figures up to 1983 from Shell, 1985: 17; figures from 1983 to 2000–01 from Strickland and Cracknell, 2001:14; figures from 2001–02 to 2005–13 from House of Lords annual reports.

Second, the 245 defeats suffered by the second (2001–05) Blair government came after the removal of all but 92 hereditary peers; Labour could not simply blame these defeats on Conservative 'bias' in the Second Chamber. On the contrary, it seems that with the majority of hereditary peers now abolished and somewhat greater parity of numbers between Conservative, Labour and Crossbench peers, the House of Lords considered itself to have acquired much greater legitimacy, and therefore felt less reticent about defeating controversial or unpopular measures from a government that nonetheless enjoyed a large majority in the House of Commons.

However, it should not be assumed that the relationship between the House of Commons and House of Lords is normally an adversarial one. The vast majority of legislation emanating from the House of Commons is endorsed by the House of Lords, and on those occasions when the Second Chamber does initially inflict a defeat on the government, perhaps over a specific clause in a Bill, a compromise is usually reached, either by virtue of the House of Lords conceding (i.e., abandoning its opposition) if ministers insist on pursuing it, or because ministers agree to remove, rewrite or otherwise amend it to the satisfaction of the Second Chamber.

In other words, although clashes and stand-offs between the two Houses make good headlines and stories for journalists, the normal relationship is more prosaic, usually entailing a close and constructive partnership over the conduct of parliamentary business. The routine work of the House of Lords is remarkably similar to that of the House of Commons, and in this respect, the Second Chamber generally complements the business of the Commons. Indeed, in many respects, the House of Lords alleviates some of the pressure on the House of Commons; if a Second Chamber did not exist, then (quite apart from a diminution of parliamentary checks and balances) either MPs would become completely overwhelmed and/or a second chamber of some kind would have to be invented *de novo*.

It is to the roles and functions that the House of Commons and House of Lords play in the policy process that we now turn our attention.

LEGISLATION

As Parliament is a legislature, detailed consideration of proposed laws (Bills) is naturally a major function both of the House of Commons and the House of Lords. There are three types of Bill variously considered by Parliament (especially the House of Commons), namely Public Bills, Private Bills and Private Members' Bills, each of which will be briefly discussed.

Public Bills

These are Bills that are introduced by the government, via a senior minister (deemed to be 'sponsoring the Bill'), to enact legislation that is applicable to all citizens or institutions in Britain – in effect, general law – unless explicitly specified otherwise. These Public Bills follow a clear sequence when proceeding through Parliament, as indicated in Figure 5.1.

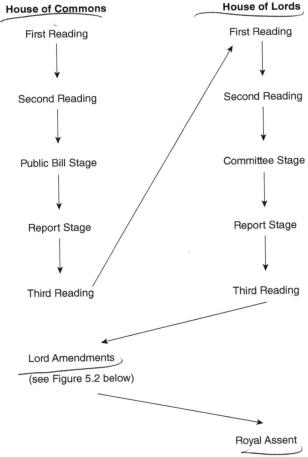

Figure 5.1   Parliamentary stages of a Public (Government) Bill starting in the House of Commons

Although this illustrates the stages of a Public Bill introduced in the House of Commons before proceeding to the House of Lords, such Bills can be launched in the House of Lords, and then proceed to the House of Commons. In either case, the stages that a Bill passes through are identical. In general, the Public Bills that commence in the House of Lords are often less partisan or politically controversial, or perhaps more 'technical' in character or content.

Each stage of a Bill's passage through Parliament serves a different purpose.

- First Reading – This simply entails the title of the Bill being read to the House of Commons (or Lords) by the Clerk, and a 'dummy' copy of the Bill being presented.
- Second Reading – This stage is concerned with the principles and purpose of a Bill, and usually entails a parliamentary debate lasting just a few hours (and thus completed on the same day), although very occasionally, in the case of a particularly major or controversial Bill, the Second Reading Debate may take place over 2–3 days. At the end of the Debate, there is a Division (vote) on the Bill, and if is supported by a majority of MPs, then the Bill is said to have been given its Second Reading.
- Public Bill Stage (previously called the (standing) committee stage) – This is where a Bill is examined in detail, line-by-line, clause-by-clause, usually by a relatively small group of MPs. The work of a Public Bill committee is discussed below, in the section on scrutiny.
- Report Stage – Having been through standing committee, an amended Bill is 'reported back' to the House, whereupon further debate on the revised Bill takes place and additional amendments may be proposed.
- Third Reading – This represents a final debate on the Bill before it goes to the House of Lords (or to the House of Commons if the Bill was first introduced in the Second Chamber). At this stage, no further amendments are usually made and Third Readings are usually a formality, dispensed with fairly swiftly, sometimes in less than an hour.
- The 'other' House – When a Bill has completed these stages in the House of Commons, it is then sent to the House of Lords (usually referred to by MPs in parliamentary parlance as 'another place') where it proceeds through exactly the same stages as in the Commons. Alternatively, if a Bill has first been introduced in the House of Lords, it will subsequently be debated and scrutinized in the House of Commons, proceeding through exactly the same stages and procedures.
- Lords' amendments – After a Bill has completed its stages in the House of Lords, it is returned to the House of Commons, where MPs debate whether to accept the amendments made by peers in the Second Chamber. If they are willing to accept these amendments, then it can finally receive its Royal Assent.
- Royal Assent – Once a Bill has been approved by both the House of Commons and the House of Lords, it then receives the Royal Assent. This reflects the fact that strictly speaking, Parliament comprises not only the two Houses, but also the Monarch ('the Queen in Parliament'), so that only after the Royal Assent has been given can it constitutionally be claimed that Parliament has consented to a particular Bill. However, the Royal Assent is a formality – no Monarch has refused to grant it since 1707.

However, if ministers are not happy about the amendments proposed by the House of Lords, then one of four options are available to them, as illustrated by Figure 5.2.

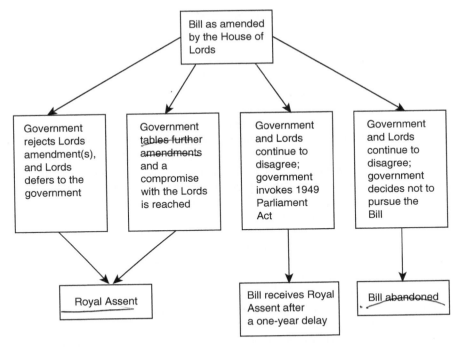

Figure 5.2   Options when a government is unhappy with House of Lords amendments to a Bill

The overwhelming majority of Public Bills do reach the statute book, and the fact that governments are so rarely defeated over their legislative proposals strongly underpins the common view that Parliament is a weak body, largely subordinate to the (core) executive. For example, only three Public Bills failed to secure their Second Reading during the 20th century, namely the 1924 Rent Restrictions Bill, the 1977 Reduction of Redundancy Rebates Bill, and the 1986 Shops Bill, although in the case of the 1924 and 1977 defeats, the government lacked a clear parliamentary majority and was therefore much more vulnerable to defeat.

Meanwhile, of the 26 government (Public) Bills introduced in the 2008–09 Parliamentary Session, 22 received the Royal Assent, three were 'carried over' to the next Session, and one was withdrawn by the government itself. However, the rarity of governmental defeats does not necessarily constitute incontrovertible evidence that Parliament is a weak institution that lacks influence over government legislation or other forms of public policy. It is reasonable to assume that governments will normally only introduce Bills that they are confident will be supported by the majority of their backbench MPs, thereby minimizing the likelihood of defeat at Second Reading stage.

Ministers will either make judgements about 'anticipated reactions' before deciding to proceed with the introduction of a Bill, or they will elicit the views of their backbench colleagues before introducing legislation, perhaps by addressing one of their party's various backbench committees, or by asking the party whips to 'sound out' backbench opinion on a particular proposal or issue. Ministers might also, time permitting, 'mingle' with their backbench colleagues in the House of Commons tea room or bars and ascertain their views on a possible Bill.

If any of these channels of communication reveal that a proposed policy is strongly opposed by the government's own backbench MPs, then the relevant minister or the Cabinet might decide quietly to abandon it rather than risk a public (and morale-sapping) defeat on the Floor of the House of Commons.

Viewed from this perspective, the rarity of government defeats in the House of Commons suggests not so much the seemingly invincible and irrevocable power of the (core) executive over Parliament, but the latent power of governmental backbenchers. If governments invariably secure parliamentary approval for their legislative proposals, it is likely to be because they usually pursue legislative proposals that they are confident will be endorsed.

Another reason why so few Public Bills are defeated at Second Reading stage is that even if government backbenchers do harbour reservations about specific details or clauses, the minister 'sponsoring' the Bill is likely to promise that the government will accept the tabling of appropriate amendments during the Public Bill stage. Such a ministerial pledge will usually be sufficient to pacify the government's backbenchers, and so persuade them to give the Bill its Second Reading, thereby endorsing the broad principles or objectives in lieu of specific revisions to follow.

A more general reason for the degree of success enjoyed by Public Bills, though, is simply that the government has overall control over, and consequently enjoys the lion's share of, the allocation of time in the House of Commons: 'the government dominates the timetable' (Norton, 1993a: 54). For example, in the 2010–12 Parliamentary Session, out of the total 2,344 hours of business conducted in the House of Commons, 652 hours were consumed by government (Public) Bills, whereas Private Members' Bills took up less than 76 hours.

Private Members' Bills

Private Members' Bills are legislation introduced by backbench MPs and represent one of the few opportunities available to backbenchers to initiate laws (rather than responding to the government's legislative initiatives). Each year, at the beginning of the new Parliamentary Session, a ballot is conducted in the House of Commons, in which the first 20 backbench MPs to be drawn are entitled to introduce a Bill. In practice, though, only the first 12 MPs, at most, are likely to be granted sufficient parliamentary time, due mainly to the fact that Private Members' Bills are usually debated on Fridays, with the rest of the week being consumed by Public and Private Bills, debates, various other government business and the 'Opposition Days', when the Opposition parties are entitled to select a topic for debate.

Subject to the proviso that their proposed legislation does not involve additional public expenditure – unless the Treasury has costed and approved any such increase beforehand – Private Members' Bills can be used by MPs to introduce legislation on almost any issue they wish. An MP may opt to introduce a Bill on a policy issue which s/he feels strongly about, or on behalf of a section of British society which they believe is disadvantaged or discriminated against.

Private Members' Bills also attract considerable attention from numerous organized interests, for such legislation is seen as a valuable means by which 'outsider' pressure groups especially can seek to influence public policy in Britain and promote an issue from the systemic agenda. Consequently, the interest displayed by such groups tends to be both 'intense' and 'broad' (Norton, 1990: 201. See also Brazier et al., 2008: 161–3; Judge, 1990; Norton, 2005: 72), as evinced by the fact that following the ballot of MPs conducted at the beginning of the Parliamentary Session, the 20 successful backbenchers will often be inundated by suggestions or even draft proposals for legislation by various organized interests, particularly those who neither enjoy close or regular contact with the core executive nor form part of a policy community.

An oft-cited example is that of the Labour MP, Austin Mitchell, who came sixth in the ballot for the 1983/4 Parliamentary Session, whereupon: 'Letters, draft Bills, ideas and invitations poured in'. Before too long, Mitchell 'had fifty suggestions, twenty possible Bills (three in draft) and five front runners' (Mitchell, 1986: 2). Similarly, when introducing the Second Reading of her Female Genital Mutilation Bill (to prohibit parents from sending or taking their daughters abroad for such operations, most notably female circumcision; these operations having been outlawed *in* the UK since 1985), Ann Clwyd explained that she had chosen to introduce this particular Bill 'over the many hundreds of others that were suggested to me' (House of Commons Debates, 2003: vol. 401 col. 1190).

An indication of the eclecticism of Private Members' Bills is indicated by Table 5.3, which lists the 20 MPs who were successful in the (16 May 2013) ballot for Private Members' Bills for the 2013–14 Parliamentary Session and the title of their Bill.

MPs who have not been successful in the ballot at the start of the Parliamentary Session may subsequently seek to introduce a Private Members' Bill via Standing Order Number 23, more commonly known as the 'Ten Minute Rule'. This permits an MP – subject to them having given prior notification of their intention – to ask the House of Commons for permission to introduce a Bill on a particular topic or issue. If the House consents to this request (a Division is not always necessary at this stage), then the Bill is deemed to have been granted a First Reading and a date will be set for its Second Reading.

The parliamentary stages for a Private Members' Bill, irrespective of whether it is a 'Ballot' or a Ten Minute Rule Bill, are similar to those for a Public (government) Bill (for a more detailed overview, see: Blackburn and Kennon, 2003: 539–62; Marsh and Read: 1988: Chapter 1). However, most Private Members' Bills fail to complete all the necessary stages in the congested, government-dominated, parliamentary timetable and so are often unlikely to reach the statute book unless sympathetic ministers make time available (Marsh and Read, 1988: 54–61). For example, in the 2010–12 Parliamentary Session, only six of the 20 Private Members' Bills tabled reached the statute book.

In spite of the difficulties that Private Members' Bills often face, some landmark legal changes and social reforms have been secured as a consequence of such legislation since the 1960s, as listed in Table 5.4.

Private Bills

Private Bills are concerned with a request by private or public organizations (often local authorities) or occasionally an individual, for certain, specified statutory powers: they may wish to pursue a course of action that they are not otherwise legally empowered to undertake and for which special legislative provision has to be enacted. Private legislation is

Table 5.3 MPs successful in the ballot for Private Members' Bills in the 2013–14 Parliament, and title of their Bill

Name of MP	Party	Title
James Wharton	Conservative	European Union (Referendum) Bill
Paul Blomfield	Labour	High Cost Credit Bill
Jonathan Lord	Conservative	Citizenship (Armed Forces) Bill
Sheryll Murray	Conservative	Deep Sea Mining Bill
Dan Byles	Conservative	House of Lords Reform (No. 2) Bill
Sir Alan Meale	Labour	Private Landlords and Letting and Managing Agents (Regulation) Bill
Andrew Gwynne	Labour	Apprenticeships and Skills (Public Procurement Contracts) Bill
Karl McCartney	Conservative	Freedom of Information Requests (Disclosure of Identity of Applicants)
Sir Robert Smith	Lib Dem	Delivery Surcharges (Transparency for Consumers) Bill
Graham Evans	Conservative	Drug Driving (Assessment of Drug Misuse) Bill
Mike Crockart	Lib Dem	Communications (Unsolicited Telephone Calls and Texts) Bill
Justin Tomlinson	Conservative	Graduated Driving Licence Scheme Bill
Mark Williams	Lib Dem	Child Maltreatment Bill
Sir Malcom Bruce	Lib Dem	Communication Support (Deafness) Bill
Caroline Spelman	Conservative	Property Blight Compensation Bill
Andrew Selous	Conservative	Education (Information Sharing) Bill
Margot James	Conservative	Prisons (Drug Testing) Bill
William Cash	Conservative	Gender Equality (International Development) Bill
Michael Meacher	Labour	United Kingdom Corporate and Individual Tax and Financial Transparency Bill
Dr Matthew Offord	Conservative	Local Government (Religious etc. Observances) Bill

Source: Parliament, 2013a.

Table 5.4 Notable Private Members' Bills since the 1960s, and the resultant change in public policy

Year enacted	Name of Bill/Act	Change in public policy
1965	Murder (Abolition of the Death Penalty)	Death penalty abolished for those found guilty of murder; life imprisonment to be imposed instead
1967	Abortion	Legalized abortion up until the 28th week of pregnancy
1967	Sexual Offences	Legalized homosexuality

Year enacted	Name of Bill/Act	Change in public policy
1967	The National Health Service (Family Planning)	Permitted local health authorities to give contraceptive advice, regardless of marital status, and on social as well as medical grounds
1968	Theatres	Abolished censorship of plays and other public performances in theatres
1969	Divorce Reform	Permitted divorce on the grounds of 'irretrievable breakdown of marriage'
1972	Sunday Cinemas	Permitted cinemas to open on Sundays
1972	Sunday Theatre	Allowed theatres to open on Sundays
1973	Employment of Children	Imposed limits on the employment of children below the school-leaving age
1975	Guard Dogs	Regulate the circumstances and conditions in which, and by who, guard dogs can be kept and used
1978	Protection of Children	Outlawed the taking, distribution or display of indecent photos of children
1984	Cycle Tracks	Enabled a local or highway authority to designate a footpath (or part of it) as a cycle track, shared with pedestrians
1985	Prohibition of Female Circumcision	Outlawed surgery on the female genitalia (or female circumcision) unless performed solely for essential medical – as opposed to cultural/religious – reasons
1985	Sexual Offences	Outlawed 'kerb crawling' (driving slowly, or sitting, in a vehicle, in order to proposition women for the purpose of prostitution)
1986	Protection of Children (Tobacco)	Made it an offence to sell tobacco to anyone under 16 years of age
1987	Access to Personal Files	Gave individuals the right to see files (or other information) on them, held and used by various public authorities
1987	Motorcycle Noise	Made it an offence to sell or supply motorcycle exhaust systems that were likely to produce excessive noise
1988	Access to Medical Records	Gave individuals the right to see their medical record before their GP supplied a copy in response to a request by an employer or insurance company

(Continued)

Table 5.4 (Continued)

Year enacted	Name of Bill/Act	Change in public policy
1990	Computer Misuse	Outlawed unauthorized access to another person's computer and the files or data contained on it ('computer hacking')
1991	Football (Offences)	Prohibited both the throwing of objects and the chanting of indecent or racist language
1991	Smoke Detectors	All new residential properties to have smoke detectors installed, with at least one on each level or storey
1994	Marriage	Allowed marriages to be conducted in 'approved premises', other than churches and register offices
1996	Dogs (Fouling of Land)	Obliged dog owners to clear up and dispose of their dog's faeces from 'designated land'
1999	Protection of Children	Established an official list of people deemed unsuitable to work with children, and required 'child care organizations' to check the list prior to appointing staff. Other bodies working with children expected to check as part of their recruitment procedure
2003	Female Genital Mutilation	Made it illegal to take or send a girl abroad to undergo female circumcision or any other form of genital 'surgery'
2004	Christmas Day (Trading)	Prohibited large shops (supermarkets and chain stores) from opening on Christmas day
2006	Emergency Workers (Obstruction)	Made it unlawful to obstruct or hinder an emergency worker while they were dealing with an emergency situation
2007	Forced Marriage (Civil Protection)	Provided legal protection and redress for individuals threatened or coerced into a marriage without their free and full consent
2010	Sunbeds (Regulation)	Sunbed use prohibited for individuals under 18 years of age

Source: House of Commons Information Office, 2010: *passim*.

most commonly concerned with providing local authorities or public bodies with specific statutory powers to undertake a specific course of action. For example, in recent years, several city or borough councils have had Private Bills enacted, in order to increase their powers with regard to the regulation of street trading and stall holders. Meanwhile, the (Norfolk) Broads Authority Act 2009 originated as a Private Bill to grant the Authority greater powers with regard to enhancing the safety of boating on the Norfolk Broads.

SCRUTINY

Subjecting proposed laws and other measures of public policy to scrutiny is a major function of Parliament. This ensures that policies requiring parliamentary approval are usually subject to debate in at least one of the Houses (and usually both), whereupon the relevant minister(s) will be expected to explain or justify a Bill or other policy proposal. Alternatively or additionally, a policy proposal will be subject to examination by a committee of MPs, either before being enacted, or afterwards, the latter being a means of evaluating and reviewing government policies. Furthermore, ministers routinely appear on the Floor of the House for Question Time, on which occasions they will face questions from MPs about the activities and policies of their departments, or face demands to introduce new policies.

All of these activities are integral both to facilitating parliamentary scrutiny of the (core) executive and subjecting public policy to detailed examination or probing questions, either of which compels ministers (at least constitutionally) to defend, explain and justify their policies, and *inter alia* those of the government, in front of MPs and/or peers.

Draft Bills and pre-legislative scrutiny

A relatively recent innovation in the process of parliamentary scrutiny has been the use of pre-legislative committees to examine proposed legislation. The principle of pre-legislative scrutiny has long been advocated by proponents of parliamentary reform, for example various Labour politicians proposed such committees back in the 1920s and 1930s (Hanson, 1956; Toye, forthcoming), and similar calls have sporadically emanated both from academics specializing in the study of parliament and also from sundry parliamentary committees concerned with reviewing or modernizing the House of Commons' procedures.

Yet it is only since the latter half of the 1990s that pre-legislative scrutiny has become a somewhat more regular component of the parliamentary policy process, although the scale and scope of such committees should not be exaggerated; by no means all Draft Bills are subjected to pre-legislative scrutiny prior to being enacted. Indeed, the publication of Draft Bills has itself been somewhat sporadic and *ad hoc*, very much at the initiative of the government itself. Consequently, there have been repeated calls, not least from within Parliament itself, for Draft Bills and pre-legislative committees to be deployed more frequently and consistently.

In response, governments have generally responded that while they readily accept, in principle, the desirability of publishing more Draft Bills and submitting them to pre-legislative committees, this is not always feasible or practicable, due to the nature of the legislation, time constraints and/or the existing volume of parliamentary business already being conducted.

Nonetheless, several Draft Bills are now published each year, usually by Easter at the latest, in order to provide pre-legislative committees with adequate time, usually 3–4 months (prior to the summer recess), to undertake their inquiries and publish a report. This then enables the relevant minister and department to consider their response prior to introducing the full or final version of the Bill, usually in the late autumn. Examples of Draft Bills published from 1998 to 2009 are provided in Table 5.5, along with the committee(s) that conducted pre-legislative scrutiny and the legislation that was subsequently enacted. Table 5.6 lists the Draft Bills published by the coalition government during its first two years in Office and the Departmental Select Committee(s) that undertook pre-legislative scrutiny.

Table 5.5   Examples of Draft Bills subject to pre-legislative scrutiny 1998–2009

SC = select committee

Draft Bill	Pre-legislative scrutiny committee	Subsequent legislation
Pension Sharing on Divorce 1998	Social Security (SC)	Included in the Welfare Reform and Pensions Act 1999
Freedom of Information 1999	Public Administration (SC)	Freedom of Information Act 2000
Extradition Bill 2002	Home Affairs Committee (SC)	Extradition Act 2003
National Health Service (Wales) Bill 2002	Welsh Affairs Committee (SC)	Health (Wales) Act 2003
Extradition 2002	Home Affairs (SC) and Joint Committee on Human Rights	Extradition Act 2003
Civil Contingencies Bill 2003	Defence Committee (SC)	Civil Contingencies Act 2004
Animal Welfare Bill 2004	Environment, Food and Rural Affairs Committee (SC)	Animal Welfare Act 2006
School Transport Bill 2004	Education and Skills Committee (SC)	Incorporated into Education and Inspections Act 2006
Children (Contact) and Adoption Bill 2005	A Joint Committee of both Houses	Children and Adoption Act 2006
Terrorism Bill 2006	Home Affairs Committee (SC)	Terrorism Act 2006
Human Tissues and Embryos Bill 2007	A Joint Committee of both Houses	Human Fertilisation and Embryology Act 2008
Local Transport Bill 2007	Transport Committee (SC)	Local Transport Act 2008
Climate Change Bill 2007	Environment, Food and Rural Affairs (SC) and Joint Committee of both Houses	Climate Change Act 2008
Marine Bill 2008	Environment, Food and Rural Affairs (SC) and Joint Committee of both Houses	Marine and Coastal Access Act 2009
Bribery Bill 2009	A Joint Committee of both Houses	Bribery Act 2010

Source: Kelly, 2010: *passim*.

Table 5.6 Draft Bills published by the coalition government, 2010–12, and their pre-legislative scrutiny

(SC = select committee)

Draft Bill	Pre-legislative scrutiny committee
Enhanced Terrorism Prevention and Investigation Measures Bill 2011	Joint Committee
Civil Aviation Bill 2011	Transport (SC)
Recall of MPs Bill 2011	Political and Constitutional Reform Committee
Defamation Bill 2011	Justice (SC)
Groceries Code Adjudicator Bill 2011	Business, Innovation and Skills (SC)
House of Lords Reform Bill 2011	Joint Committee
Financial Services (Banking Reform) Bill 2012	(Joint) Parliamentary Commission on Banking Standards
Energy Bill 2012	Energy and Climate Change (SC)
Communications Data Bill 2012	Joint Committee, and Intelligence and Security Committee
Care and Support Bill 2012	Joint Committee
Children and Families Bill 2012	Justice (SC)
Local Audit Bill 2012	*Ad hoc* House of Commons Committee
Water Bill 2012	Environment, Food and Rural Affairs (SC)
Anti-Social Behaviour Bill 2012	Home Affairs (SC)
Pensions Bill 2012	Work and Pensions (SC)
Voting Eligibility (Prisoners) Draft Bill 2012	Joint Committee
Dangerous Dogs (Amendment) Bill 2013	Environment, Food and Rural Affairs (SC)

Source: House of Commons Liaison Committee, 2012: 16–17, para. 37; Parliament, 2013b.

Part of the rationale for publishing Draft Bills and subjecting them to pre-legislative scrutiny is that it is usually easier to make changes at this early stage than it is during later stages, when the Bill has been 'firmed up'. Indeed, this is a more general feature of the policy process, for in most cases, the further a Bill or other public policy proceeds through its various stages from initial formulation to enactment, the more it becomes 'set', thereby making it increasingly difficult to introduce significant changes.

The pre-legislative committee examining a Draft Bill will usually be either the relevant Departmental Select Committee or a joint committee (i.e. comprising members from both Houses), the latter possibly established specifically to examine the Draft Bill and thereafter dissolved – an *ad hoc* committee. In either case, the method of scrutiny is similar to that ordinarily undertaken by Departmental Select Committees (discussed below), whereby oral and written evidence is elicited from relevant or interested policy actors and 'stakeholders'.

Having obtained oral and written evidence, the pre-legislative committee will produce a report on the draft Bill. Although such committees are not expected to challenge the overall objective or purpose of a draft Bill, they are likely to make recommendations about how the proposed legislation could be improved or highlight specific aspects that would benefit from further consideration by the relevant minister or department, prior to proceeding with the official version of the Bill.

Crucially, though, governments are under no obligation to accept the recommendations enshrined in a pre-legislative committee's report, although ministers will usually issue a formal response to such reports within two months. Often, though, governments do accept some of the changes recommended in such reports, thereby ensuring that the legislation which is subsequently presented for its First Reading is a modified version of the draft Bill, to a lesser or greater degree.

Certainly, a senior member of Parliamentary Counsel (responsible for the drafting of Bills) informed a House of Lords inquiry into the legislative process that 'Bills that have gone through pre-legislative scrutiny … end up as better Bills and better Acts … I think it does lead to fewer amendments in the House', although the official noted that pre-legislative scrutiny also added to the workload of parliamentarians (House of Lords Constitution Committee, 2004: 106, Q. 354. See also Hansard Society, 2004; House of Commons Modernisation Committee, 2006: paras.16–29).

This concern about the potential overload of MPs, deriving from the additional work generated and time consumed by pre-legislative scrutiny, has also been noted by senior Conservative MP and former minister, Ann Widdecombe (2005: 81). Indeed, it is worth noting, in passing, that virtually any institutional or procedural innovation to enhance the role of MPs, and enable them to play a more active part in scrutinizing the executive, adds to their workload and risks further overloading them. This is a perennial parliamentary paradox.

Nonetheless, a 2012 report by the Liaison Committee (comprising the chairs of the Departmental Select Committees) expressed its 'regret that more bills have not been published in draft', and that even when they were, sometimes 'the time available for pre-legislative scrutiny has been unreasonably short'. The Liaison Committee also complained that:

> … the Government has on occasion sought to establish a joint committee even when the relevant departmental select committee wished to scrutinise the draft bill. We appreciate that the House of Lords may also have a legitimate interest in pre-legislative scrutiny, and that members of that House may bring valuable expertise to this work; but – as we have made clear in correspondence with the Leader of the House of Commons – we feel strongly that there should be no departure from the principle that Commons select committees should have a first right of refusal.

> (House of Commons Liaison Committee, 2012: 17, para. 38; 18, para. 39)

Meanwhile, even if and when a government declines to modify a Draft Bill in response to recommendations from a pre-legislative committee, the recommendations might re-appear as amendments tabled at the Public Bill (committee) stage, for as a former clerk in the House of Lords has noted, MPs and peers 'can use pre-legislative scrutiny to inform and lend credence to their own means of seeking changes to a bill' at this stage of the legislative process. This is particularly true of those parliamentarians who served on the Bill's pre-legislative committee (Smookler, 2006: 532–3).

Subsequent legislative scrutiny

Once a Bill has been given its Second Reading (i.e., its principles have been formally approved), it then proceeds to a committee for detailed scrutiny. Until 2006, this was conducted via 'standing committees', but in 2006 these were reconstituted as Public Bill committees. Although these perform exactly the same functions as the erstwhile standing committees, namely subjecting Bills to detailed, line-by-line, clause-by-clause, examination and proposing various amendments – ostensibly to improve the legislation – they differ in that they are also entitled to call for written evidence and/or invite witnesses to answer questions, just like pre-legislative and Departmental Select Committees (the latter discussed below).

Such evidence-taking sessions are conducted at the beginning of a Public Bill committee's examination of legislation, before it proceeds to scrutinize the Bill in detail. The information gleaned from 'interested parties', relevant bodies or experts should enable the Public Bill committee to conduct more informed or meaningful scrutiny of legislation and identify potential problems or inconsistencies well before the Bill is enacted (for a brief overview of their *modus operandi*, see Levy, 2009: 23–5).

In this important regard, Public Bill committees have the potential to play a valuable role both in enhancing the quality of legislation, and by enabling the MPs serving on them to scrutinize Bills with a greater degree of expertise or intelligence due to the evidence obtained at the outset. It could also be argued that the submission of written and/or oral evidence from outside organizations and individuals constitutes a means of bringing Parliament a little closer to 'the people'. Certainly, Philip Cowley, a highly-respected academic expert on Parliament, has adjudged the Public Bill committees to offer 'the potential to do more to improve the quality of the parliamentary scrutiny of bills than any other Commons' reform in the last twenty ... years' (Cowley, 2007: 22. See also Norton, 2013: 82–4; Thompson, 2013).

A similarly favourable view has been expressed by the author of a detailed study of Public Bill committees during their first two years:

> As a result of the introduction of evidence-gathering legislative committees, the [House of] Commons committee stage has become more informed, more transparent and characterised by improved debate ... The availability of more information has engaged MPs and empowered backbench members of these committees, who are becoming more confident to take part in both questioning and debate ... Public Bill Committees have proved more efficient than their standing committee predecessors. (Levy, 2009: 49)

As a result of these parliamentary innovations, there are now two stages at which MPs can elicit information and evidence from interested individuals and organizations beyond Parliament when examining legislation: pre-legislative scrutiny committees; and (post-Second Reading) Public Bill Committees.

Ministers' Question Time

Questions addressed to ministers by backbench MPs have long been a major means by which Parliament seeks to scrutinize the (core) executive and hold ministers to account for their decisions and the work of their department. In so doing, they contribute to a key aspect of the doctrine of individual ministerial responsibility, whereby ministers have to defend their policies in Parliament.

Ministers' Question Time is organized on a four-weekly rota, so that the Secretary of State and relevant Junior Ministers from each government department answer questions on a specific day each month, usually for 30–60 minutes, depending on their department and range of responsibilities. However, while these oral questions are the most visible manifestation of such ministerial scrutiny and can provide good images for the media, the overwhelming majority of questions submitted to ministers are written and themselves receive a written reply, these then being published at the back of *Hansard* (the official daily record of parliamentary proceedings and votes). For example, in the 2010–12 Parliamentary Session, a total of 9,484 questions were submitted for an oral answer, of which 4,710 – about half – actually received a reply in the Chamber (there are always more questions submitted for an oral answer than there is time to answer them in Ministers' Question time). By contrast, no less than 97,753 written questions were submitted.

Although Ministers' Question Time is often an opportunity for political point scoring, it nonetheless performs a vital function in ensuring that ministers regularly appear before MPs to explain and justify the policies of their departments and *inter alia* the policies of the government itself. In this respect, Ministers' Question Time is a crucial means by which the legislature seeks to hold the (core) executive to account and ensure that public policy is subject to scrutiny beyond the legislative process. This in turn can help to ensure that ministers themselves are made aware of particular problems concerning a policy, thereby possibly persuading them of the need to modify it. As John MacGregor, a former Conservative minister and leader of the House (of Commons) has acknowledged:

> … questions sometimes draw to the attention of a minister an aspect of policy, or of the working of his department with which he was not familiar, and through the briefing that he gets, to pursue issues on that particular aspect of policy, and that does sometimes lead to changes. (quoted in Giddings, 1993: 134–5. See also, Norton, 1993b: 198)

In this respect, Ministers' Question Time can play a role in parliamentary agenda-setting (Norton, 2013: 77), with MPs alerting a minister's attention to an issue or problem and potentially persuading him/her to review an existing policy or law, or even, albeit rarely, repeal it.

This is also an illustration of the circular character of the policy process, whereby problems manifest themselves during the implementation 'stage' (discussed in Chapter 8) and so result in the policy moving back onto the institutional agenda for modification or occasionally replacement. In this regard, Ministers' Question Time constitutes part of a 'feedback loop' whereby MPs, acting on behalf of their constituents, make ministers aware of the deficiencies or problem associated with particular policies, and *inter alia* contribute to (possible) policy review and subsequent revision.

However, while these parliamentary mechanisms and procedures are very important means of scrutiny, and of holding ministers and governments to account for their laws and policies, Matt Korris, a research fellow at the highly prestigious Hansard Society, has noted that 'the torrent of legislation parliamentarians face each session, and the increasingly complex and technical nature of many statutes, today mean that there is currently a mismatch between the scrutiny mission of Parliament and its capacity to carry out that mission' (2011: 565).

To some extent, the purpose of the pre-legislative scrutiny committees discussed above was to tackle this imbalance, by ensuring that an additional means of parliamentary scrutiny was enshrined beyond that afforded by the Public Bill stage of the legislative process and Ministers' Question Time.

EVALUATION

Closely related to the scrutiny function of Parliament is that of evaluation, whereby legislation and policies are subject to critical examination *after* they have been enacted or implemented. In this respect, Parliament plays an important role in gauging the outputs and outcomes of laws and policies, in order to determine their degree of success (or lack of) and to identify possible means of improvement.

As evaluation invariably entails detailed examination of the impact and consequences of laws and policies, this aspect of parliamentary activity is mostly conducted via various committees explicitly established for this purpose. Through various parliamentary committees, a small group of backbench MPs will undertake in-depth inquiries into a particular law or policy, often summoning the relevant ministers to appear before a committee to answer detailed questions on a specific issue or topic.

Departmental Select Committees

Undoubtedly the most important, and potentially influential, of these parliamentary committees are the House of Commons' Departmental Select Committees, most of which were established in 1979. Indeed, Philip Norton has claimed that the creation of the Departmental Select Committees 'constitute the most important parliamentary reform of the [20th] century' (1998: 34; 2005: 28).

Previously, select committees had been established on an *ad hoc* basis, with a view to examining a particular policy area or topic. This was the case in the latter half of the 1960s, for example when the 1966–70 Labour government, encouraged by one of its Cabinet Ministers, Richard Crossman (Dorey and Honeyman, 2010), experimented with the creation of a small number of select committees to investigate specific issues on a generally 'one-off' basis. Although the experiment was viewed as something of a mixed success, it certainly whetted the appetite of those backbench MPs who favoured a more systematic means of investigating public policies, and of holding departments and their ministers more fully to account.

For such MPs, if the experiment had proved only partly successful, the answer was not to abandon the principle of select committees, but to devise a more coherent and rigorous system, whereby such committees could play a more regular and meaningful role in the parliamentary scrutiny of public policy.

Thus it was that in 1979 – the time lag itself indicative of the often slow or incremental character of many new policy initiatives in Britain, even in Parliament itself – a new system of select committees was established, each of which corresponded to a particular government department. Originally, it had been intended that 12 such select committees would be created, but following the failure of the outgoing Labour government's devolution measures, two further select committees were established – one on Scottish Affairs, and the other on Welsh Affairs – thereby yielding a total of 14 (for an overview of their introduction and early operation, see: Drewry, 1989; Englefield, 1984; Johnson, 1988; Rush, 1990).

Since then, sporadic restructuring of the core executive by successive governments has resulted in the abolition or merger of some government departments, as well as the occasional creation of new ministries, which has in turn yielded corresponding changes to the Departmental Select Committees during this period, to the extent that by 2013 there were 18 such bodies, as listed in Table 5.7.

Most of these Departmental Select Committees comprise 11 MPs, in which case the government is allocated six MPs, while the other five MPs are drawn from the Opposition parties, although most of these will be recruited from the largest Opposition party (currently Labour). Since the formation of the coalition government in May 2010, most Departmental Select Committees have comprised five Conservative MPs and one Liberal Democrat (reflecting their respective numerical size in the House of Commons) and five Labour MPs, although a few might have four Labour MPs and one from a smaller party. For example, on the Environment, Food and Rural Affairs Select Committee, the Opposition is

Table 5.7   Departmental Select Committees operating in 2013

Name	Number of MPs
Business, Innovation and Skills Committee	11
Communities and Local Government Committee	11
Culture, Media and Sport Committee	11
Defence Committee	12
Education Committee	11
Energy and Climate Change Committee	11
Environment, Food and Rural Affairs Committee	11
Foreign Affairs Committee	11
Health Committee	11
Home Affairs	11
International Development Committee	11
Justice Committee	12
Northern Ireland Affairs Committee	14
Scottish Affairs Committee	11
Transport Committee	11
Treasury Committee	13
Welsh Affairs Committee	12
Work and Pensions Committee	11

represented by four Labour MPs, and an MP from Northern Ireland's Social Democratic and Labour Party.

However, five of the Departmental Select Committees have more than 11 MPs serving on them, with the Northern Ireland Affairs Committee being the largest, with a membership of 14. The Treasury Committee, meanwhile, comprises 13 MPs.

The work of Departmental Select Committees in scrutinizing the core executive, of enhancing the accountability of departments, ministers and senior officials to Parliament, and evaluating the outcomes or effectiveness of governmental policies, comprises ten core roles or tasks, as defined by the House of Commons Liaison Committee (2003: 9, para. 13. See also Brazier and Fox, 2011), which itself is comprised of the chairs of the select committees:

- To examine policy proposals from the UK government and the European Commission in Green Papers, White Papers, draft guidance and so on, and to inquire further where the committee considers it appropriate.
- To identify and examine areas of emerging policy, or where existing policy is deficient, and make proposals.
- To conduct scrutiny of any published Draft Bill within the committee's responsibilities.
- To examine specific output from the department expressed in documents or other decisions.
- To examine the expenditure plans and out turn of the department, its agencies and principal non-departmental public bodies (NDPBs).
- To examine the department's public service agreements, the associated targets and the statistical measurements employed, and report if appropriate.
- To monitor the work of the department's executive agencies, NDPBs, regulators and other associated public bodies.
- To scrutinize major appointments made by the department.
- To examine the implementation of legislation and major policy initiatives.
- To produce reports that are suitable for debate in the House, including Westminster Hall or debating committees.

In pursuing these roles, Departmental Select Committees are entitled (according to the Standing Orders of the House) to 'send for persons, papers and records ... and adjourn from place to place' (House of Commons, 2011: 134, para. 135; 136, para 137a). The last aspect refers to the occasional practice of conducting visits to other parts of the country or overseas to conduct interviews or obtain further evidence in connection with a particular inquiry.

The Departmental Select Committees enjoy considerable autonomy and discretion in determining their topics of inquiry. They are entitled to choose which aspect of 'their' department's expenditure, administration or policies to investigate, and in so doing, can decide between a rather general inquiry or a very specific one, perhaps examining a particular aspect of a policy in detail. Table 5.8 lists six examples of inquiries undertaken by each of the main Departmental Select Committees since 2008.

These examples indicate both the breadth and depth, or the generality and specificity, of topics that Departmental Select Committees choose to investigate.

Table 5.8   Examples of inquiries conducted by Departmental Select Committees, 2008–13

Select Committee	Title/Topics of inquiry
Business, Innovation and Skills	1. Post offices: securing their future 2. Energy policy: future challenges 3. Future of higher education 4. Government assistance to industry 5. Rebalancing the economy – trade and investment 6. Pub companies
Communities and Local Government	1. Financing of new housing supply 2. Localism 3. Regeneration (of communities) 4. Audit and inspection of local authorities 5. Localization issues in welfare reform 6. Financing new housing
Culture, Media and Sport	1. Tourism 2. Harmful content on the internet and in video games 3. Football governance 4. 2018 World Cup bid 5. BBC licence fee 6. News International and phone hacking
Defence	1. Helicopter capability 2. Russia: a new confrontation? 3. Operations in Afghanistan 4. Operations in Libya 5. Recruiting and retaining armed forces personnel 6. The Strategic Defence and Security Review
Education (and Skills)	1. Behaviour and discipline in schools 2. The role and performance of Ofsted 3. English Baccalaureate 4. Attracting, training and retraining the best teachers 5. Chief regulator of qualifications and examinations 6. Participation by 16–19 year olds in education and training
Energy and Climate Change	1. Fuel poverty 2. Electricity market reform 3. EU emissions trading system 4. Effect on energy usage of extending British Summer Time 5. Shale gas
Environment, Food and Rural Affairs	1. Food contamination 2. The English pig industry 3. Energy efficiency and fuel poverty 4. The National Forest 5. Rural communities 6. The Welfare of Laying Hens Directive – implications for the egg industry

Select Committee	Title/Topics of inquiry
Foreign Affairs	1. The Role of the Foreign and Commonwealth Office in UK government 2. The UK's foreign policy approach to Afghanistan and Pakistan 3. Piracy off the coast of Somalia 4. The implications of cuts to the BBC World Service 5. UK–Brazil relations 6. The FCO's human rights work 2010–11
Health	1. Alcohol (use and abuse) 2. Health inequalities. 3. Social care 4. Revalidation of doctors 5. Public health 6. Breast implants and regulation of cosmetic surgery
Home Affairs	1. Policing large-scale disorder (the August 2011 riots) 2. Immigration cap 3. Roots of violent radicalization 4. Forced marriages 5. Police use of Tasers 6. Visas for overseas students
International Development	1. The World Bank 2. Working effectively in fragile and conflict-affected states: Democratic Republic of Congo, Rwanda and Burundi 3. Financial crime and development 4. Humanitarian response to the Pakistan floods 5. The future of the department's programme in India 6. The department's role in building infrastructure in developing countries
Justice	1. Role of the Prison Officer 2. The Crown Prosecution Service 3. Draft sentencing guideline: drug offences and burglary 4. Youth justice 5. The role of the probation service 6. The government's proposed reform of legal aid
Northern Ireland Affairs	1. Corporation Tax in Northern Ireland 2. Fuel laundering and smuggling (across the border) 3. Cross-border cooperation between the governments of the United Kingdom and the Republic of Ireland 4. Policing and justice 5. The 'Bloody Sunday' inquiry 6. Political developments in Northern Ireland

(Continued)

Table 5.8 (Continued)

Select Committee	Title/Topics of inquiry
Scottish Affairs	1. Postal services in Scotland. 2. Scotland and the UK: cooperation and communication between governments 3. Banking in Scotland. 4. Enforcement of the national minimum wage in Scotland. 5. The student immigration system in Scotland 6. The referendum on separation for Scotland
Transport	1. Priorities for investment in the railways 2. The future of aviation 3. Licensing of taxis and private hire vehicles 4. Cost of motor insurance 5. Reducing congestion on Britain's roads 6. High speed rail
Treasury	1. Banking crisis 2. Women in the City 3. The private finance initiative 4. Future of cheques 5. Principles of tax policy 6. Competition and choice in retail banking
Welsh Affairs	1. S4C (the Welsh language broadcaster) 2. Inward investment in Wales 3. Broadband in Wales 4. The future of the Newport Passport Office 5. The Severn Crossings toll 6. Representation of consumer interests in Wales
Work and Pensions	1. The government's proposed child maintenance reforms 2. The government's plans for pension reform 3. Impact of the changes to Housing Benefit announced in the June 2010 Budget 4. Tackling pensioner poverty 5. The role of incapacity benefit reassessment in helping claimants into employment 6. Automatic enrolment in workplace pensions and the National Employment Savings Trust

Having decided on its topic of inquiry, a Departmental Select Committee will normally invite written evidence from 'interested parties', that is, individuals or organizations that are either directly affected by, or professionally knowledgeable about, the particular policy or problem chosen for investigation. Needless to say, the volume and range of written submissions can be considerable. For example, when the Health Select Committee (HSC) launched its 2008–09 inquiry into the use and abuse of alcohol, it received over 50 written submissions from an extremely wide range of organizations, an indication of which is provided in Table 5.9.

Table 5.9 Organizations and people that submitted written evidence to the HSC's 2008–09 inquiry into alcohol (use and abuse)

Department of Health	Professor Eileen Kaner
Professor David Foxcroft	Royal College of Nursing
Royal Pharmaceutical Society of Great Britain	Breakthrough Breast Cancer
	Children in Scotland
Alcohol Education and Research Council	Children in Northern Ireland
	Scotch Whisky Association
Sovio Wines Ltd	Gin and Vodka Association
British Medical Association	Local Government Association
Professor Neil McIntosh	Our Life (North West)
The College of Emergency Medicine	Portman Group
Royal College of Midwives	Nuffield Council on Bioethics
National Association for the Children of Alcoholics	Barnardo's UK
	Scottish and Newcastle UK
British Liver Trust	Morrison Supermarkets Ltd
Professor Sir John Marsh	Association of Convenience Stores
Alcohol Concern	NHS Confederation
National Society for the Prevention of Cruelty to Children (NSPCC)	Advertising Standards Association
	National Organisation for Fetal Alcohol Syndrome – UK
National Association of Cider Makers	
Socialist Health Association	Business in Sport and Leisure Limited
Royal College of General Practitioners	Royal College of Physicians
Diegeo	Wine and Spirit Trade Association
Family Planning Association	Alcohol Focus Scotland
J. Sainsbury Ltd	Royal College Psychiatrists
ASDA	Dr Noel Olsen
Professor Forrester Cockburn, Dr John McClure, and Dr Margaret Watts	Alcohol Health Alliance
	SABMillar
British Retail Consortium	British Society of Gastroenterology and the British Association for the Study of the Liver
Institute of Alcohol Studies	
Scottish Health Action on Alcohol Problems (SHAAP)	

Among these were trade associations representing the alcohol industry and super-markets, health and medical associations, and various charities that support people affected by alcohol abuse (such as the children of heavy drinkers or alcoholics). It can also be seen that several senior academics submitted evidence, such as Professor Eileen Kaner, Professor of Public Health at Newcastle University, and Professor David

Foxcroft, Professor of Community Psychology and Public Health at Oxford Brookes University.

When the written submissions have been received, the Departmental Select Committee will then invite some of the respondents to appear in person and give oral evidence, although many other individuals will also be invited to answer questions in front of the committee, even though they might not have submitted written evidence. The oral evidence is elicited through questioning by the MPs on the select committee, with a view to obtaining further or more in-depth information. The aforementioned Health Select Committee into alcohol consumption and associated problems devoted seven sessions to obtaining oral evidence from experts and interested parties.

In addition to hearing oral evidence presented by some of those who had previously submitted written evidence, the committee also heard oral evidence from a variety of other individuals either representing relevant organizations or with professional expertise of alcohol issues, including the chief executive of the Campaign for Real Ale (CAMRA), the Chief Constable of Northumbria (representing the Association of Chief Police Officers), the Director of Communications and Public Policy at the (football) Premier League and a Professor of Addiction Studies at the University of the West of England.

Ministers themselves, and also senior civil servants, will often be invited to give oral evidence when a select committee is investigating a policy or issue for which their department is responsible. Such ministerial appearances are another important means by which they are rendered accountable to Parliament for their department's policies, while simultaneously enabling Departmental Select Committees to scrutinize the executive. Ministers may well be asked to explain or justify a policy initiative or decision, particularly if the policy has engendered problems, or perhaps, apparently failed. Similarly, senior civil servants from the relevant department will also routinely be invited to provide oral evidence, as well as officials from the executive agencies formally responsible for the day-to-day administration and 'delivery' of many government policies.

Table 5.10 illustrates the number of appearances by ministers, civil servants and senior officials from relevant public or non-departmental government bodies, such as executive agencies (discussed in the next chapter) as well as sundry individuals, to give oral evidence to Departmental Select Committees during the 2010–12 Parliamentary Session.

Upon completion of its inquiry, a Departmental Select Committee will publish its report, often in the hope that this will prompt at least some modification of existing policy or legislation, although Norton has suggested that: 'Most of the recommendations contained in [select] committee reports may be termed humdrum rather than major in policy terms' (Norton, 1993a: 65). Yet it may be precisely because they tend to be 'humdrum' (i.e., administrative or technical in nature) that ministers might feel more inclined to accept various select committee recommendations, whereas they would probably be rather reluctant to accept recommendations that were 'major in policy terms'.

In the above example of the HSC's inquiry into alcohol use and abuse, its report, published in January 2010, comprised 40 general observations, criticisms of specific

Table 5.10   Number of appearances to provide oral evidence to Departmental Select Committees in the 2010–12 session

Select Committee	Total number of meetings	Number of Cabinet Ministers/ Junior Ministers	Number of departmental civil servants	Number of agencies, public or non-departmental bodies	Number of other witnesses
Business, Innovation and Skills	79	7/12	8	24	182
Communities and Local Government	63	5/23	6	57	179
Culture, Media and Sport	83	4/9	8	16	113
Defence	76	8/7	35	0	67
Education	76	5/12	5	12	263
Energy and Climate Change	79	6/16	5	13	200
Environment, Food and Rural Affairs	88	6/14	22	19	109
Foreign Affairs	67	6/7	16	10	55
Health	76	6/4	23	32	148
Home Affairs	70	5/16	21	18	244
International Development	59	8/7	11	43	33
Justice*	65	3/10	17	29	142
Northern Ireland Affairs	42	3/4	11	13	31
Scottish Affairs	63	16/7	9	35	109
Transport	60	7/18	7	18	302
Treasury	102	9/3	14	43	169
Welsh Affairs	55	5/9	5	15**	74
Work and Pensions	67	3/10	13	3	75

* In addition to the categories listed here, the Justice Committee also took oral evidence from the Attorney-General and six members of the Judiciary.

** Includes appearances by two Welsh Assembly Members and three Welsh Assembly Government Ministers.

Source: House of Commons, 2012: *passim*.

aspects of government policy and several recommendations, the most notable being listed in Box 5.1.

Box 5.1 Main recommendations of the HSC's 2010 report into alcohol (use and abuse)

- Government policies are much closer to, and too influenced by, that of the drinks industry and the supermarkets, than those of expert health professionals.
- Government has given greatest emphasis to the least effective policies, such as education and information, and too little emphasis to the most effective policies, namely pricing, availability and marketing controls.
- Universities should exercise their moral 'duty of care' to their students much more seriously than they have done hitherto, by discouraging irresponsible drinking among students and ensuring that students are not subjected to marketing activity that promotes dangerous binge drinking.
- Information and education policies should be improved by giving more emphasis to the number of units in drinks and the desirability of having a couple of days per week without alcohol.
- All containers of alcoholic drinks should have labels, which should warn about the health risks, indicate the number of units in the drink (for example, nine units in a bottle of wine) and the recommended weekly limits. As a voluntary agreement would probably not be adequate, the government should introduce a mandatory labelling scheme.
- Restrict alcohol advertising and promotion in places where children are likely to see it, for example no billboards and posters promoting alcohol within 100 metres of any school, no TV adverts for alcoholic drinks before 9pm, cinema adverts for alcohol to be restricted to films classified as '18' and no alcohol advertising on social networking sites.
- For every five television adverts it broadcasts, an alcohol company should be required to fund one public health advertisement.
- The police should enforce, more rigorously and consistently, section 141 of the Licensing Act 2003, which makes it an offence to serve alcohol to someone who is already drunk.
- More stringent controls on the number and activities of off-licences, particularly in areas where there is a large number in relatively close proximity.
- Government should introduce a statutory minimum price for alcohol. Indeed, this would constitute 'the most powerful tool at the disposal of a government', for it would simultaneously make binge drinking and heavy drinking prohibitively much more expensive, and prevent supermarkets from selling alcohol at excessively low prices (which they justify on the grounds of intense competition with each other in a free market, resulting in them seeking to undercut each other).
- Tax on alcohol should be reformed, so that a higher duty is imposed on strong alcoholic drinks, but with a lower rate on wines and beers with a lower alcoholic content.

(House of Commons Health Committee, 2010: 121–9)

Government departments are expected to reply, within 60 days, to each report published by 'their' departmental select committee. At the very least, if no modification of policy is envisaged, the department will be expected to explain why it does not intend to act upon the recommendations of the select committee and is thus intent on continuing with the existing policy without modifying it. In such instances, the fact that a department and its minister are obliged to justify their continued adherence to a particular policy is an important means of ensuring accountability to Parliament. Furthermore, a few select committee reports will be debated on the Floor of the House of Commons each Session, providing other MPs with opportunities to question aspects of public policy and thereby compel ministers to provide a further justification for their policy stance.

A recent in-depth case study of the policy impact of six Departmental Select Committees, plus the Public Administration Select Committee, notes that government responses to individual proposals or recommendations naturally range from full acceptance to outright rejection. The various intermediate responses include: partial or implied acceptance; assertion that the government was already pursuing the recommended action or policy; partial or implied rejection of a select committee proposal; a claim that further research or evidence was needed before finally reaching a decision. In this particular study, it was found that about 40 per cent of select committee recommendations were fully or partly accepted, whereas 33 per cent were fully or partly rejected (Russell and Benton, 2011; 47).

The House of Commons Liaison Committee, comprising the chairs of Departmental Select Committees, has also recently conducted an inquiry into their role and effectiveness, and reported that: 'The consensus of those who gave us evidence is that committees are successful in influencing government', although it was readily acknowledged that there was room for improvement, both by select committees themselves and by some government departments in terms of the seriousness with which they responded to criticisms and recommendations by such committees (House of Commons Liaison Committee, 2012: 25).

A government department's response to a select committee report will usually 'block highlight' the main recommendations and then give the government's responses below each one in the order that they appeared in the select committee's report. For example, Box 5.2 reproduces a few short verbatim extracts from the Department of Health's 2010 response to the Health Select Committee's inquiry into the use and abuse of alcohol.

Box 5.2   Examples of Department of Health's responses to the HSC's inquiry into alcohol (use and abuse)

HSC Recommendation 15

We also recommend that all containers of alcoholic drinks should have labels, which should warn about the health risks, indicate the number of units in the drink and the recommended weekly limits, including the desirability of having two days drink-free each week.

　78. We agree that Government should provide the public with consistent unit and health information, and providing consumers with this information is crucial to our alcohol strategy. Including this information on the labels of alcoholic products ... is an

(Continued)

(Continued)

integral part of our campaign to raise consumer awareness and understanding. Labels are a key vehicle for unit and health information ... Government wishes the vast majority (at least 75 per cent by 2014) of labels to have unit and health information in order for consumers to be better informed.

HSC Recommendation 16

We doubt whether a voluntary agreement would be adequate. The Government should introduce a mandatory labelling scheme.

84. The Government's general approach to legislation in the alcohol industry is first to seek commitments to self-regulation, wherever this may be effective and feasible, and it is right that we continue to do so. We will work with the alcohol industry where we can, but where it does not act responsibly, we will act in a proportionate way to protect the consumer, young people and local communities.

HSC Recommendation 22

There is a pressing need to restrict alcohol advertising and promotion in places where children are likely to be affected by it. Billboards and posters should not be located within 100 metres of any school

130. The Government recognises that the appropriate regulatory systems already exist to address concerns about this form of advertising. However, we will continue to monitor the regulatory regimes to ensure that suitable protections are put in place for children and young people.

HSC Recommendation 32

We note the concerns of the ACPO [Association of Chief Police Officers] and other witnesses about the difficulties local authorities have in restricting and revoking licences. The Government has made some improvements in the Policing and Crime Act 2009, but must take additional measures.

167. The Government accepts that it should be easier for local authorities to tackle groups of very late licensed premises, and has brought forward proposals in the Crime and Security Bill currently before Parliament. However ... licence reviews are far from being the only means of regulating the sector. Much enforcement on the ground is done through effective partnerships and, where necessary, securing improvements through the threat of formal action.

HSC Recommendation 33

It is of concern that section 141 of the Licensing Act 2003, which creates the offence of selling alcohol to a person who is drunk, is not enforced. We note the police and

Home Office's preference for partnerships and training, but do not consider these actions should be an excuse for not enforcing a law which could make a significant difference to alcohol-related crime and disorder. We call on the police to enforce section 141 of the Licensing Act more effectively.

168. Whilst we agree in principle that the offence of selling alcohol to a person who is drunk should be enforced, there are a number of practical difficulties in doing so. A successful prosecution needs the sale to be witnessed and to prove beyond reasonable doubt that the person was drunk ... Successful prosecutions have proved very resource intensive and require surveillance by undercover officers ... the police feel that their resources for tackling alcohol-related crime and disorder can achieve greater results elsewhere.

169. [However] where the condition of people leaving a premises suggests that sales to drunks are likely, this may be grounds for seeking review of the licence and for appropriate measures to be put in place to ensure that such sales are not being made.

(Secreatry of State for Health, 2010: *passim*)

Another recent case study (Hindmoor et al., 2009: 36–7), this time of the Education Select Committee, concluded that it:

... appeared to have an impact on policy. Successive secretaries of state all identified areas where a committee inquiry changed existing policy or caused new policy to be made, and there are more recent cases outside the timeframe of this study, such as the Education and Inspections Bill 2007, where the committee's role in the development of the legislation was highly visible.

However, the authors point out that 'demonstrating broader patterns of influence on policy is difficult. In comparing committee reports with government legislation there are certainly instances of correlation, but causation is much harder to establish'.

This last point is echoed by three senior researchers in the House of Commons Library, who emphasize that: 'A mere checklist of committee recommendations against the government response will not pick up instances where the government took on select committee ideas in later months or even years' (Maer et al., 2009: 36). Besides, a government might enact a policy recommended in a select committee report, not directly because of that recommendation, but because it was planning such a policy already, quite independent of the select committee.

Departmental Select Committees and their impact on MPs

It is likely that serving on a select committee enables MPs to acquire considerable expertise in a particular sphere of public policy. As MPs usually serve on a select committee for the lifetime of a Parliament (and often have their membership renewed for a further five years following a general election), they are able to immerse themselves in a specific area of public policy and become highly knowledgeable about it.

This might enable them to ask more probing or searching questions of those appearing before a select committee inquiry and subsequently of the relevant minister(s) at Question

Time on the Floor of the House of Commons. In other words, the expertise acquired through serving on a select committee for several years is likely to enhance MPs' ability or effectiveness in terms of scrutinizing the executive and its policy decisions via other parliamentary activities.

This could also be viewed as another aspect of the 'professionalization' of MPs in Britain and the rise of the 'career politician'. Indeed, some MPs seem to view service on a Departmental Select Committee as an alternative career to seeking ministerial office, for it enables backbench MPs to play a more active role in Parliament and offers the potential for exercising some influence on public policy, at least occasionally.

Gerald Kaufman, for example, having been a minister in the 1974–79 Labour governments, was a formidable and respected chair of the culture, media and sport select committee from 1992 until 2005, while Tony Wright, a prominent Labour 'modernizer' (and previously a politics lecturer at Birmingham University), served as a highly-respected chair of the renowned Public Administration Select Committee (see below) from 1999 until leaving the House of Commons in 2010.

Indeed, since 2003, the chairs of select committees have received an additional salary, in addition to the standard salary paid to MPs, in recognition of the responsibilities and additional workload associated with chairing these important parliamentary bodies.

Another advantage variously attributed to the longevity of MPs serving on most select committees, along with the degree of expertise they acquire, is that the adversarial and partisan stance that characterizes many other aspects of parliamentary business is often superseded by a strong sense of teamwork and shared purpose among the committee members. Instead of a division between government and Opposition MPs serving on a select committee, the demarcation is generally between the select committee and minister or department whose policies or conduct are being investigated. This is clearly reflected in the physical layout of a select committee inquiry, as illustrated by Figure 5.3, which show that the MPs sit at a semi-circular or horseshoe shaped table facing the person giving oral evidence.

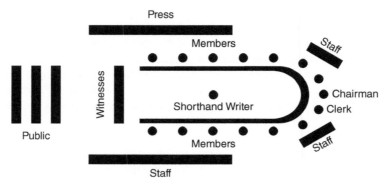

Figure 5.3   The layout of a select committee inquiry

Source: House of Commons, 2013: 11.

Consequently, government backbenchers serving on a select committee are just as likely as Opposition MPs to ask critical or searching questions of 'their' minister if and when s/he appears before them. As Andrew Tyrie MP, explains, length of service by MPs 'helps develop a committee memory and a sense of collegiality, modifying tribalism. The balance between committee loyalty and party loyalty has certainly been altered, and in subtle ways' (Tyrie, 2011: 11).

Indeed, Tyrie suggests that Departmental Select Committees are developing a more proactive or agenda-setting role in the policy process, by virtue of selecting topics for investigation and highlighting policy issues or problems, which they then urge ministers to address. In other words, rather than just investigating policies retrospectively (as was traditionally the case), or waiting for ministers to present them with a draft Bill to examine in the guise of pre-legislative scrutiny, select committees are now increasingly acquiring the confidence and credibility to take the lead by conducting inquiries into issues or problems that they feel are not being acknowledged or adequately addressed by ministers (Tyrie, 2011: 19).

Various trends and evidence therefore seem to suggest that the importance and impact of Departmental Select Committees are likely to increase. Certainly, one academic expert on Parliament has argued that 'the longer term impact on policy and administration is likely to be significant, especially as committees increasingly review earlier inquiries and return to particular policy areas' (Rush, 2000: 127).

Public Administration Committee

While the Departmental Select Committees are probably the most well-known of Parliament's investigatory or 'evaluation' committees, there are two others that are also of considerable importance in contributing towards the scrutiny and evaluation of governmental administration, expenditure and policy, even though they do not 'shadow' a specific department. These are the House of Commons' Public Administration Committee, and the House of Commons' Public Accounts Committee.

The Public Administration Committee was established in July 1997, having previously been the Committee for the Parliamentary Commissioner for Administration (more commonly known as the Ombudsman). In this earlier guise, it was primarily concerned with examining the reports published by the Ombudsman, paying close attention to policy issues that had acquired particular prominence in these reports. Having become the Public Administration Committee, its remit has been widened to include matters concerning the civil service and governmental administration more generally. In its relatively short life to date, the Public Administration Committee has acquired considerable prominence and a formidable reputation.

As Table 5.11 illustrates, the Public Administration Committee has conducted a wide range of inquiries in recent years, reflecting its broadened remit. Furthermore, in 2002, it was announced that Tony Blair had agreed to be questioned, on a twice-yearly basis, by the Public Administration Committee. Prime Ministers had previously been spared appearances in front of select committees, due to their lack of direct departmental responsibilities.

Table 5.11   Examples of inquiries undertaken by the Public Administration Committee since 2008

Topic/Title of inquiry
Smaller Government: Bigger Society?
Leaks and Whistleblowing in Whitehall
The Publication of Political Memoirs
Top Pay in the Public Sector
Role of the Head of the Civil Service
Funding of the Voluntary Sector
Work of the Cabinet Office
Lobbying: Access and Influence in Whitehall
External Appointments to the Senior Civil Service
Public Services: Putting People First
Smaller Government: Shrinking the Quango State
Public Services: Putting People First
The Big Society

Furthermore, the Public Administration Committee often elicits oral evidence from a somewhat wider range of ministers and senior civil servants than the Departmental Select Committees, due to the much more eclectic choice of topics it investigates. Similarly, the Public Administration Committee will tend to invite appearances from a wider variety of agencies, non-governmental bodies and other public organizations. Table 5.12 illustrates the range of people and bodies that appeared before the Public Administration Committee during its 82 meetings in the 2010–12 parliamentary session.

Table 5.12   Appearances (by category) before the Public Administration Committee, 2010–12

Cabinet Ministers	1
Junior Ministers	19
Backbench MPs	1
Members of the House of Lords	17
Number of appearances by officials from, or representatives of:	
Cabinet Office	10
Department for Culture, Media and Sport	1
Ministry of Defence	2
Foreign and Commonwealth Office	1
HM Revenue and Customs	1
Home Office	1
Ministry of Justice	2
Department for Work and Pensions	1

Number of appearances by officials from or representatives of public bodies and non-ministerial departments comprising:

Administrative Justice and Tribunals Council	1
Advisory Committee on Business Appointments	2
Appointments Commission	1
Charity Commission	1
Committee on Standards in Public Life	1
National Policing Improvement Agency	1
Office of the Civil Service Commissioners	2
Office of the Commissioner for Public Appointments	2
Parliamentary and Health Service Ombudsman	3
Sport England	1
Youth Justice Board for England and Wales	1
United Kingdom Statistics Authority	1
Appearances by other witnesses	99

Source: House of Commons, 2012: 334.

Public Accounts Committee

The other main investigative committee is the Public Accounts Committee, which was established back in 1861, and as such, is the oldest of the select committees. The 16 MPs on the Public Accounts Committee examine the expenditure of government departments and agencies – thereby supplementing the examination of expenditure occasionally performed by the Departmental Select Committees – but have increasingly, since the 1980s at least, paid particular attention to the criteria of cost-effectiveness and 'value for money' in scrutinizing the way that departments have spent public funds and what has been achieved by their expenditure. In performing this function of financial scrutiny, the Public Accounts Committee works very closely with the National Audit Office, and its chief, the Comptroller and Auditor General.

The Public Accounts Committee has a formidable – even feared – reputation in Westminster and Whitehall, and reports that are critical of the way that public monies have been (mis)spent are normally taken very seriously. Table 5.13 gives a sample of the topics and issues, which have been investigated by the Public Accounts Committee since 2008.

The broad-ranging, cross-departmental nature of its remit also means that (like the Public Administration Committee) the Public Accounts Committee obtains evidence from a wider range of departments and their senior civil servants than the Departmental Select Committees, as well as from a wide variety of agencies and other public bodies. This eclecticism is illustrated in Table 5.14.

As with Departmental Select Committee reports, the reports of the Public Accounts Committee sometimes receive prominent media coverage, as was the case in December 2011, for example, when it published a scathing report concerning the Inland Revenue's failure to secure up to £25 billion in unpaid tax from large companies. The report listed eight significant failings or criticisms, as illustrated in Box 5.3.

Table 5.13   Selection of topics investigated by the Public Accounts Committee since 2008

Topic or issue investigated
Building the capacity of the third sector
NHS pay modernization in England: agenda for change
Widening participation in higher education
Progress in improving adult literacy and numeracy
HM Revenue and Customs: Tax Credits and Income Tax
Independent Police Complaints Commission
Financial Management in the Home Office
Department for Work and Pensions: management of benefit overpayment debt
Regenerating the English coalfields
Scrutiny of value for money at the BBC
Transforming NHS ambulance services
Immigration: the Points Based System
Getting value for money from the education of 16- to 18-year-olds
Lessons from PFI and other projects
Flood risk management in England
Cost reduction in central government: summary of progress

Table 5.14   Appearances (by category) before the Public Accounts Committee, 2010–12

Number of appearances by officials from, or representatives of:	
Cabinet Office	22
Department for Business, Innovation and Skills	6
Department for Communities and Local Government	9
Department for Culture, Media and Sport	3
Department for Education	9
Department of Energy and Climate Change	4
Department for Environment, Food and Rural Affairs	2
Department of Health	27
Department for International Development	5
Department for Transport	10
Department for Work and Pensions	13
Foreign and Commonwealth Office	3
HM Treasury	28
Home Office	6
Ministry of Defence	27
Ministry of Justice	5

Executive Agencies, comprising:	
Highways Agency	4
HM Courts Service	3
Rural Payments Agency	1
UK Border Agency	1
Number of appearances by officials from or representatives of public bodies and non-ministerial departments comprising:	
BBC	3
BBC Trust	2
Children and Family Court Advisory and Support Service	1
Environment Agency	1
Higher Education Funding Council for England	1
HM Revenue and Customs	14
Independent Review Service	1
National Audit Office	2
Network Rail	1
Ofcom	1
Office of Rail Regulation	2
Student Loans Company	1
Youth Justice Board	1
Members of the House of Commons	3
Appearances by other witnesses:	94

Source: House of Commons, 2012: 320–1.

Box 5.3   Public Accounts Committee's 2011 criticisms of the Inland Revenue's failure to recoup up to £25 billion in unpaid tax from big businesses

- The department's refusal to disclose taxpayer information prevents proper scrutiny of the process for reaching tax settlements with large companies.
- The evidence of the department's senior officials fails to give us any confidence in the way large settlements are reached.
- The department chose to depart from normal governance procedures in several cases, which allowed Commissioners to sign off on settlements that they themselves negotiated.
- Governance procedures have lacked the independence and transparency needed to provide sufficient assurance to Parliament.
- The department's failure to comply with its own processes resulted in a substantial amount of money being lost to the Exchequer.

(Continued)

(Continued)

- Those at the top of the department have not taken personal responsibility for serious errors.
- The department has left itself open to suspicion that its relationships with large companies are too cosy.
- The department is not being even handed in its treatment of taxpayers.

Source: House of Commons Public Accounts Committee, 2011: 5–17.

What attracted so much media attention and criticism was not simply the enormous sum of money involved, but the wider context, in which the coalition government was cutting billions from public expenditure in order to eradicate Britain's fiscal deficit. Critics were not slow to suggest a gross inequity, whereby teachers, nurses and police officers were being made redundant or having their pay frozen for several years, social security benefits were being cut and university students were about to be charged £9,000 per year to study for a degree (while the universities', arts' and humanities' teaching budgets from the government were virtually being scrapped), but big business and large companies were apparently being allowed to avoid or defer paying £25 billion in taxes.

The House of Commons European Scrutiny Committee

One other House of Commons select committee that should be mentioned is the European Scrutiny Committee. Consisting of 16 MPs, its remit is to assess the legal and/or political importance of each EU document (more than 1,000 per annum) and decide which of them should be debated by MPs. Most documents are technical or administrative in character, so that only a few are politically controversial. The committee also monitors the work of UK ministers *vis-à-vis* the Council of the European Union (formerly the Council of Ministers), and keeps EU developments – institutional, legal and procedural – under review.

Given the often highly specialized or technical character of many EU policies, the European Scrutiny Committee is served by three European Committees, each of which focuses on a specific range of policy areas, albeit corresponding to the main departments and ministries, as illustrated by Table 5.15.

Table 5.15 Policy areas covered by the House of Commons' European Committees

European Standing Committee A	European Standing Committee B	European Standing Committee C
Communities and Local Government	Foreign and Commonwealth Office	Business, Innovation and Skills
Energy and Climate Change	Home Office	
Environment, Food and Rural Affairs	International Development	Culture, Media and Sport
Transport	Justice	Education
	Treasury	Health
	Work and Pensions	

Each of these committees comprises 13 MPs who serve for the duration of a Parliament (five years), although other MPs may also attend sittings, but not cast a vote. In conducting their scrutiny of EU documents – allocated to them by the European Scrutiny Committee – the committees might invite the relevant minister(s) to give evidence or answer a series of questions in order to provide clarification, similar to the Departmental Select Committees.

It should be emphasized, though, that this European scrutiny system 'supplements, but does not replace, the usual opportunities Members [of Parliament] have to examine and question government policies, such as parliamentary questions and select committee inquiries' (Department of the Clerk of the House of Commons, 2010: 4).

A House of Commons' resolution passed in 1990 decreed that a British minister should not give their approval to a policy proposal in the Council unless it had already been debated and endorsed by one of these European Committees. If such approval or support is offered, the minister is expected to provide an explanation to the European Legislation Committee.

Through such means, therefore, the House of Commons can seek to ensure at least a modicum of ministerial responsibility to Parliament for EU legislation, even though qualified majority voting means that a British minister will be unable to prevent the Council of the European Union from adopting a particular policy if it is proffered sufficient support by ministers from other member states.

The House of Lords' select committees

There is also a wide range of select committees in the House of Lords, but instead of directly shadowing departments, these focus on somewhat broader, more thematic spheres of public policy. For example, whereas in the House of Commons, fiscal or monetary policy would normally be a suitable subject for the Treasury Select Committee, in the House of Lords, these would be investigated by the Economic Affairs (Select) Committee, which was established in 2001.

Apart from this organizational difference, the operation and purpose of the House of Lords' select committees are similar to those in the House of Commons, namely to conduct inquiries, invariably involving calls for evidence and the questioning of 'witnesses' (i.e., key individuals involved in, or affected by, the law or policy that is being investigated) in order to evaluate the effectiveness and impact of governmental legislation and policies, and *inter alia* hold policy makers to account for decisions (for more on House of Lords' select committees, see Blackburn and Kennon, 2003: 696–705; Grantham and Moore Hodgson, 1985; Shell, 2007: 115–24).

In so doing, these committees have also enhanced the attractiveness of the House of Lords to many organized interests (Baldwin, 1990), for these bodies can now submit evidence, written or oral, to the relevant committee in the Second Chamber, in addition to targeting Departmental Select Committees in the House of Commons.

The two most renowned House of Lords select committees are the science and technology committee, and the European Union Committee. The former was established in 1979, and soon acquired a reputation as a formidable and prestigious investigative body due the expertise of its members – many of them former scientists and engineers who had been awarded Life Peerages – and the often highly technical nature of the topics that it investigates, as illustrated in Box 5.4.

Box 5.4 Examples of inquiries pursued by the House of Lords Science and Technology (Select) Committee since 2010

Behaviour Change

Higher education in science, technology, engineering and mathematics (STEM) subjects

Nuclear research and development capabilities

Regenerative medicine

Scientific infrastructure

Sports and exercise science and medicine: building on the Olympic legacy to improve the nation's health

The role and functions of departmental Chief Scientific Advisers

---

As Shell has observed, the House of Lords Science and Technology Select Committee has 'earned a reputation … for the authority of its reports based on the expertise within its membership', which has ensured that 'Ministers and civil servants … have been made aware that they are dealing with some of the most eminent scientists in the country' (Shell, 2007: 118–19. See also Norton, 2013: 135; Russell, 2013: 213–14).

Meanwhile, the House of Lords' Select Committee on the European Union has responsibility for examining proposals emanating from the European Commission, with particular reference to their potential or likely impact on public policy in Britain. It comprises 19 peers, and is serviced by both a clerk and a legal adviser. Various academic experts on Parliament have deemed the European Union Committee to be one of the House of Lords' (indeed Parliament's) most respected select committees (see, for example, Kelso, 2009: 151; Russell, 2013: 212–13; Shell, 2007: 116–17), and Norton claims that its work 'is seen as particularly good at contributing to debate, both within government and in the institutions of the EU' (Norton, 2005: 153).

The breadth of its remit, coupled with the legal or technical complexity of many EU documents and other matters, means that much of the committee's work is undertaken by six sub-committees, each specializing in specific areas of policy, as illustrated by Figure 5.4. These sub-committees each have 11–12 members and a clerk, with sub-committee E (justice, institutions and consumer protection) also having its own legal adviser.

Each member of the European Union Committee (except for the chair) also serves on one of these sub-committees, which also co-opts other peers in the House of Lords to provide expertise relevant to a particular inquiry. As such, a total of about 70 peers are involved in the European Union Committee and its six sub-committees, this number representing about 10 per cent of the total (post-1999) membership of the House of Lords.

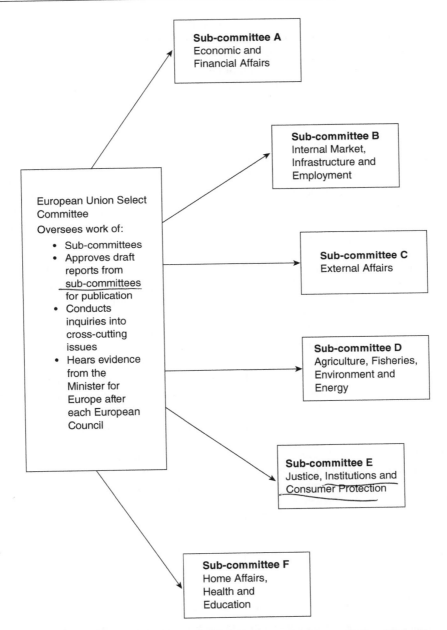

Sub-committee A
Economic and
Financial Affairs

Sub-committee B
Internal Market,
Infrastructure and
Employment

European Union Select
Committee
Oversees work of:

- Sub-committees
- Approves draft
  reports from
  sub-committees
  for publication
- Conducts
  inquiries into
  cross-cutting
  issues
- Hears evidence
  from the
  Minister for
  Europe after
  each European
  Council

Sub-committee C
External Affairs

Sub-committee D
Agriculture, Fisheries,
Environment and
Energy

Sub-committee E
Justice, Institutions and
Consumer Protection

Sub-committee F
Home Affairs,
Health and
Education

Figure 5.4   Sub-committees of the House of Lords' European Union (Select) Committee

As we noted above, the influx of Life Peers since 1958 has imbued the House of Lords with a wealth of expertise, and this, along with its less tribal or partisan conduct, has enabled its work to acquire considerable respect, to the extent that it is often viewed as highly authoritative. As Norton notes: 'The committees are designed to play to the strengths of the House [of Lords], with members appointed because of their expertise in the field' (Norton, 2005: 125. See also, Judge, 2005: 76; Shell, 2007: 118–19).

CONCLUSION

Although it is widely recognized that Parliament is not normally a policy-making institution *per se*, it still performs a number of very important roles in the policy process. Indeed, those critics who refer to the 'decline' of Parliament fail to appreciate that it has almost always been a body *reacting to* policy initiatives from above or beyond, so that executive dominance is not really a new phenomenon or recent trend. As noted at the outset, experts such as Norton categorize Parliament as a policy-modifying body, rather than a policy-making one.

Once it is understood that parliamentary activity entails so much more than just the formal passage of governmental legislation, it can be appreciated that Parliament provides several opportunities and procedures for influencing and scrutinizing public policy in Britain. Even when such activities as Ministerial Question Time or Departmental Select Committee inquiries do not directly result in policy changes, they do compel ministers to offer a public defence of their policies to MPs, thereby fulfilling the vital function of scrutiny of the executive.

Ultimately, Parliament's various Debates (including those pertaining to the passage of Bills), investigative committees and other forms of scrutiny, are vital means of imbuing public policies with legitimacy, both 'manifest' and 'latent': 'As the body accepted by both mass and elites for legitimating measures of public policy, Parliament is a powerful body' (Norton, 1993a: 131–46. See also, Norton, 2005: 9–12, 250; Judge, 1993: *passim*; Judge, 2005: 52).

Admittedly, the British electorate has become more cynical about politicians, and indeed, much of the political process in general, but Parliament remains the main institutional forum in which government measures and public policies are regularly debated and examined by elected representatives, and which ultimately confers legitimacy on these policy outputs. For these reasons, and various others of a more normative nature beyond the remit of this study, as we noted at the outset, if Parliament did not exist, it would almost certainly have to be invented.

QUESTIONS AND TOPICS FOR DISCUSSION

1. What is the relationship between the House of Commons and the House of Lords in the parliamentary policy process?
2. What are the main stages of the legislative process and what does each one entail?
3. What are Private Members' Bills and how have they sometimes proved highly significant?
4. What roles are played by Departmental Select Committees?

5. Apart from Departmental Select Committees, in what other ways does Parliament subject a government's policies to scrutiny?
6. Why should a 100 per cent success rate for a government in getting its Bills passed *not* be viewed as evidence that Parliament is weak and ineffective?
7. In what ways can a government minister keep in touch with his/her party's back-bench MPs in order to gauge their support for, or opposition to, a proposed policy?
8. Why are debates and scrutiny in the House of Lords often deemed to be of a higher quality than those in the House of Commons?
9. Why do some academic experts (most notably Philip Norton) suggest that Parliament's main role should be seen as policy legitimation, rather than policy-making *per se*?

RECOMMENDED TEXTS AND FURTHER READING

1. Alex Brazier, Susanna Kalitowski and Gemma Rosenblatt with Matt Korris (2008) *Law in the Making: Influence and Change in the Legislative Process*. London: The Hansard Society.

   Valuable examination of the law-making process in Parliament, from policy proposal through to enactment, based on five case studies of laws introduced between 2002 and 2007. Utilizes interviews with Ministers, MPs and senior civil servants to explain how and why these five policies were adopted in the first place, and then examines how they were debated, scrutinized and amended in Parliament before receiving the Royal Assent.

2. Ruth Fox and Matt Korris (2010) *Making Better Law: Reform of the Legislative Process from Policy to Act*. London: The Hansard Society.

   Rich and incisive account of the legislative process in Parliament, with a strong focus on the factors which determine the quality of the legislation in Britain. In so doing, the authors identify how and why 'bad' Bills are sometimes enacted, and offer numerous recommendations for improving the law-making process to ensure better legislation.

3. House of Commons Liaison Committee (2012) *Second Report of Session 2012–13; Select Committee Effectiveness, Resources and Powers, Volume I,* HC 697. Available from: www.publications.parliament.uk/pa/cm201213/cmselect/cmliaisn/697/697.pdf

   Report from an inquiry into the functioning and activities of the House of Commons' select committees during the 2010–12 parliamentary session, and recommendations for enhancing their influence and impact on public policy. Includes an examination of the different types of scrutiny undertaken by these committees, and the ensuing responses of Government Departments.

4. Philip Norton (2013) *Parliament in British Politics*, second edition. Basingstoke: Palgrave Macmillan.

   Characteristically lucid account by Britain's leading academic expert on Parliament (who is also a peer in the House of Lords). Clearly explains the various roles played by Parliament in the policy process, such as approving (and amending) legislation and the scrutiny of policies. Norton also provides a wealth of empirical examples and evidence.

5. Meg Russell (2013) *The Contemporary House of Lords: Westminster Bicameralism Revisited*. Oxford: Oxford University Press.

In-depth and scholarly analysis of the activities and functions of the House of Lords, paying particular attention to such aspects as legislative scrutiny, legislative debates, the nature and impact of defeats inflicted on governmental legislation, and scrutiny of public policy other than legislation. The analysis is supported and illustrated with very useful empirical examples and small case studies.

6. Meg Russell and Meghan Benton (2011) *Selective Influence: The Policy Impact of House of Commons Select Committees*. London: The Constitution Unit.

Very detailed and systematic study focusing on seven Departmental select committees, the main objective being to ascertain their degree of influence or impact on public policy. This entailed both examining the type of recommendations enshrined in the reports of the seven select committees, and evaluating the extent to which the relevant Department/Minister responded positively to policy proposals in a committee's report. The authors conclude that the select committees studied did exercise considerable, albeit variable or indirect, influence on Departmental policies, notwithstanding the perennial problem in political science of identifying and measuring influence.

6 From Government to Governance

The concept of governance has become increasingly popular among political scientists and policy analysts since the 1980s, for it represents an intellectual innovation that aims to characterize key changes in the structure of the British polity, and the impact that these changes have had on the development and 'delivery' of public policy in Britain. Previously, textbooks tended to refer to 'government', which implied the existence of a unitary state, in which central government or the 'core executive' – Cabinet, ministers, departments and senior civil servants – administered policies in a top-down manner. This notion of 'government', both as a noun and a verb (viz. 'to govern'), was both implicit and extensive in most political science and policy studies literature.

Since the late 1980s, however, the character and structure of government in Britain has changed considerably, as has the manner in which many policies are implemented or administered. The scale of these changes have been such that many political scientists no longer consider the term 'government' to be adequate or appropriate when delineating how public policy is formulated and delivered. The British polity has undergone a process (albeit uneven) of fragmentation and decentralization since the late 1980s, which has affected administrative units, political institutions and the policy process itself.

Whereas older, traditional depictions of British government invariably depicted ministers, deriving their political authority and legitimacy from Parliament, announcing policies and piloting legislation through the House of Commons and the House of Lords, which were then expected to be faithfully implemented at sub-national level by 'street-level bureaucrats', the concept of governance highlights the absence of a clear chain of command, and instead draws attention to the vital importance of cooperation and coordination between a plethora of policy actors and agencies at various levels; central, regional and local.

Furthermore, just like individuals and institutions in the core executive, the policy actors involved in governance are invariably enmeshed in a web of exchange relationships, reflecting and reinforcing resource dependency and the need to cooperate to achieve shared policy objectives. Hence the tendency towards voluntary or self-organized networks and partnerships at local and regional (sub-national) level, as policy actors seek to establish priorities, develop common strategies, share intelligence, exchange resources, and determine mutual roles and responsibilities in the development or administration of policies and services.

In this context, the main role of central government or the core executive is increasingly to establish overall policy objectives and stipulate targets or other performance indicators, but with the policy actors themselves developing the strategies and collaborative mechanisms through which the goals can best be achieved, although their choices or degree of discretion might still be constrained by the nature of the goals prescribed by national-level policy makers. For example, following an unusually severe winter in 2010–11, a 'Cold Weather Plan' was developed by the Meteorological Office, the Department of Health, and the Health Protection Agency, but also supported by the charity for the elderly, Age UK (which had been formed in 2009 by a merger between Age Concern and Help the Aged). This 'Cold Weather Plan' was intended to highlight the health risks associated with cold weather, particularly for the elderly, and thereby both encourage preventative action in lieu of cold weather and protective measures when such weather occurred.

To this end, from 1 November to 31 March each year, the Met Office, the Department of Health, and the Health Protection Agency, issue warnings of imminent cold weather, not just to the general public, but directly to a range of social and healthcare services serving the elderly and other at-risk sections of society, such as:

- NHS Trusts
- Community and District Nursing Associations
- Royal College of General Practitioners
- Royal College of Nursing
- Community and District Nursing Association
- Community Practitioners and Health Visitors Association
- Directors of Social Services
- Relevant voluntary organizations and charities
- Housing authorities/associations
- National Care Association
- English Community Care Association
- Department of Communities and Local Government (Resilience and Emergencies Division)
- Cabinet Office Civil Contingencies Secretariat.

The inclusion of the Department of Communities and Local Government, and also the Cabinet Office, in this list further illustrates the crucial point that the transition to governance has obliged the core executive both to work in partnership with an array of sub-national or non-state bodies to achieve shared policy objectives, and to place a stronger emphasis on coordination of those organizations more directly involved in policy 'delivery'. The coordinating role of central government or the core executive in an era of governance has been characterized as that of 'steering, not rowing' (Osborn and Gaebler, 1992: 34).

THE MEANING OF GOVERNANCE

The political scientist who has probably done the most to popularize the concept of governance is Rod Rhodes (1996; 1997), and while he identifies a number of potential meanings and applications of the term, he ultimately opts for a definition that emphasizes (Rhodes, 1997: 53):

- Interdependence between organizations, which includes not only traditional state actors and political institutions, but also private sector and voluntary bodies. The boundaries between these actors have become 'shifting and opaque.'
- Interaction between the various policy actors, derived from resource dependencies and exchange relationships, and their mutual need to develop common objectives or agreed strategies. These interactions also entail the development of trust and acceptance of the 'rules of the game' between the various policy actors.
- Relative autonomy from the state, with the policy actors often establishing their own processes and practices to pursue objectives, strategies or targets, even though the latter might have been decreed by the state itself.
- A 'coordinating', rather than 'commanding', or 'steering', not 'rowing', role for the state or central government. The range of policy actors now involved at all levels of British society means that while the 'core executive' is still a vitally important institutional entity – as illustrated in Chapters 2 and 3 – its ability to play a directive role has been somewhat curtailed.

Similarly, Kooiman and Van Vliet (1993: 66) emphasize that the role of central government in a system of governance entails a number of discrete, but clearly interlinked, obligations and objectives, namely:

- Coordination, which involved identifying the key actors or 'stakeholders' with regard to a particular policy issue or objective and then promoting linkages between them.
- Collaboration and steering, which logically follows on from the above, and entails central government seeking to ensure that these policy actors work effectively together in the pursuit of 'desired outcomes'.
- Integration and regulation, entailing the development of institutional mechanisms and procedures for ensuring that these 'desired outcomes' are actually achieved.

Rhodes therefore emphasizes how governance 'blurs the distinction between state and civil society' (Rhodes, 1997: 57), while Flinders (2008: 1) similarly observes that:

> Government [in Britain] now takes place within a broader context of governance in which governmental actors operate within an increasingly fragmented, complex and delegated administrative environment, involving private, voluntary and parastatal organizations.

This transition from government to governance has not only blurred the boundary or distinction between policy making and policy implementation (delivery) – which was never as clear-cut as older textbooks and British constitutional theory seemed to imply – it has also yielded inconsistencies by actors in the core executive itself, as ministers and governments have oscillated between delegating power to sub-national policy actors (albeit in the context of responding to market pressures or the wishes of those who use public services), and attempting to re-assert control from the centre to ensure that the central government's policy objectives are more closely adhered to; what Lee (2000) has termed 'the centralization of policy and the devolution of administration'.

Certainly, Tony Blair's early leadership of 'New Labour' heard sundry speeches in which he extolled the virtues of a more constructive, collaborative and partnership-based approach to public sector reform and service delivery. However, once he became Prime Minister, Blair's speeches concerning the public sector often entailed considerable criticism of professionals and other front-line staff in such services as education and the NHS, who were routinely condemned not only for being conservative and thus resistant to change and modernization, but also for comprising self-serving producer interests who had little regard or respect for the preferences of their 'customers'. Blair and his closest colleagues also berated public sector staff for being afraid of accountability.

David Cameron's leadership of the Conservative Party since December 2005 has followed an identical pattern. In his early years as Conservative leader, Cameron (and several other purported 'modernizers') waxed lyrical about the need to move away from Thatcherism's ideological opposition to, and condemnation of, the public sector, and instead to work *with* professionals, rather *against* them. This would entail both listening to front-line staff in the public sector when reforms were being mooted, and also granting those staff much greater professional discretion and autonomy to do their jobs properly without being micro-managed or constrained by New Labour's obsession with targets and box ticking. For example, in one particular speech, Cameron promised public sector staff a new mode of decentralized service delivery, which 'will not only get rid of the targets and bureaucracy that drives you so mad', and makes you feel 'demoralised, disrespected and unrecognised', but would empower front-line staff by enabling them to 'offer the public a better service the way you think it should be done, not the way some bureaucrat thinks it should be done' (quoted in Watson, 2010. See also Cameron 2007; Perry and Dorrell, 2006: 4). Meanwhile, David Willetts declared that: 'We want to raise standards by working with the professions, not beating up on them' (quoted in Woodward, 2006).

Yet since becoming Prime Minister, Cameron (and other Conservative Cabinet Ministers) has ditched this conciliatory and empowering approach, so that his speeches pertaining to public services and their front-line professionals have generally echoed the criticisms canvassed by Blair. Certainly, when public sector staff or their representative bodies articulate any criticism of governmental reforms, Cameron is inclined to denounce them for being 'vested interests', just as Blair was wont to do.

As a consequence, the promise of a partnership-based approach to public sector reform, in which the views and grievances of professionals would be listened to, has largely been abandoned in favour of an often authoritarian, top-down approach, with many Conservative ministers adopting the 'commander' or ideologically-driven roles and style discussed in Chapter 3. This has been most evident in education and health policies, with Michael Gove simultaneously pursuing 'free schools', proposing changes to the way that history is taught (more 'facts' and key dates), suggesting significant changes to the school calendar, which would affect teachers' working hours and holidays, and stipulating new targets for schools and/or teachers.

Meanwhile, Andrew Lansley pushed through a major reform and restructuring of the NHS – in spite of Cameron's assurances, before becoming Prime Minister, that he would refrain from enacting yet another major reorganization on a health service already punch-drunk with change, and which he had deemed symptomatic of New Labour's constant meddling.

Education and health policies have therefore exemplified some of the key tensions arising from the transition to governance, with ministers often oscillating between rhetoric extolling the virtues of decentralization and delegation to sub-national policy actors, albeit operating in the context of 'the market' or responding directly to the preferences of service 'users', and attempts at re-asserting ministerial command and control from the centre deriving from annoyance or impatience that their policy objectives are not being enacted with sufficient competence, enthusiasm or speed (Smith, 2011: 169; Moran, 2007: *passim*).

The transition from government to governance has been driven primarily by four key developments since the late 1980s, namely: 'agencification'; the rise of the 'regulatory state'; devolution to Scotland and Wales; and an increasing role for non-state actors (particularly from the private sector) in the policy process, particularly with regard to the implementation or 'delivery' of various public services. All of these phenomena are discussed below. Other aspects of the transition to governance are primarily concerned with the importance of securing coordination and cooperation between the range of policy actors, as well as routinely measuring and monitoring the implementation or delivery of policies (and their success). The latter has primarily been pursued through the application of 'new public management', and the increased role of 'audit' in the public sector, which this has spawned; these will be discussed separately, in Chapters 8 and 9 respectively.

AGENCIFICATION

Since the late 1980s, there has been a major reform of the core executive *vis-à-vis* the organization and operation of government departments and the civil service. In 1987, Sir Robin Ibbs, the then Head of the Efficiency Unit in the Cabinet Office, wrote *Improving Management in Government: The Next Steps* (but commonly referred to merely as *The Next Steps*), although this major report into the future structure and operation of the civil service was not actually published, via the Prime Minister's Efficiency Unit, until early 1988 (Efficiency Unit, 1988). The report reflected Margaret Thatcher's desire to reform the civil service, as part of her wider desire to cut costs, reduce red tape and 'roll back the state'. Whether these objectives were really achieved is beyond the scope of this particular study; our concern is with the implications for the policy process which accrued from the implementation of *The Next Steps*.

The Next Steps proposed a much clearer demarcation in each department between those responsible for policy advice and formulation on the one hand, and policy implementation or delivery on the other. To secure this division of responsibility, *The Next Steps* proposed that the sections and staff responsible for administering a department's policies and services should be made semi-autonomous, in the form of 'Executive agencies' that would have responsibility and considerable freedom over day-to-day operational matters, management of their budgets and staffing levels, albeit within a 'framework agreement' laid down by the 'parent department'. Ministers would remain constitutionally responsible for the formulation of public policies, while the administration and implementation of those policies would henceforth be the responsibility of the agencies (Drewry and Butcher, 1991: 222–38; Flynn et al., 1990: 159–78; Hennessy, 1990: 619–27; Jordan, 1994: Chapter 5; Judge, 2005: 135–8).

It was envisaged that a smaller, leaner, core of policy advisers and policy makers would remain at the heart of the core executive, while civil servants focused much more extensively on policy implementation and the delivery of public services at sub-national level. Consequently, the traditional civil service hierarchy 'has been replaced by an almost federal system of core and periphery, with the periphery not being directly controlled by the centre' (Smith, 1999: 194).

By the time the first 'New Labour' government was elected in May 1997, more than 110 agencies had been established, these employing 400,000 civil servants. Indeed, as Table 6.1 indicates, individual departments will often preside over several agencies. The Blair governments, far from halting or reversing the process of agencification, extended it further, so that by 2009, there were 192 agencies, although, again, the actual word 'agency' did not always appear in the official name of such bodies.

Table 6.1   Examples of executive agencies and other related public bodies operating under the aegis of various government departments

Department of Business, Innovation and Skills	Department of Education	Department of Environment, Food and Rural Affairs
Advisory, Conciliation and Arbitration Service (ACAS)	Education Funding Agency	Animal Health and Veterinary Laboratories Agency
Companies House	Office of Qualifications and Examinations Regulation (Ofqual)	Environment Agency
Met Office	The Office for Standards in Education, Children's Services and Skills (Ofsted)	Food and Environment Research Agency (Fera)
Skills Funding Agency	Standards and Testing Agency	Forestry Commission
UK Space Agency	National College for Teaching and Leadership	Rural Payments Agency
Department of Health	**Department for Transport**	**Home Office**
Care Quality Commission	Driver and Vehicle Licensing Agency	HM Passport Office
Food Standards Agency	Highways Agency	National Fraud Authority
Medicines and Healthcare Products Regulatory Agency	Maritime and Coastguard Agency	Office of the Immigration Services Commissioner
National Institute for Health and Care Excellence	Office of Rail Regulation	Serious Organised Crime Agency
The NHS Business Services Authority	Trinity House	UK Border Agency

Source: Gov.UK (2013a).

Following the formation of the Conservative-Liberal Democrat coalition government in May 2010, the Cabinet announced plans to reduce the number of government quangos and similar bodies. This reduction was to be pursued for three main reasons, the first of which was to contribute to the wider objective of cutting public expenditure in order to eradicate Britain's fiscal deficit.

Second, cutting the number of quangos was intended to have a populist appeal by convincing the British public that ministers were determined to rein in state bureaucracy, Labour's legacy of 'big government' and the 'bloated' public sector that consumed (and allegedly wasted) so much of taxpayers' money.

Third, by culling quangos and *inter alia* 'shrinking' the state, it was envisaged that a much wider range of non-state bodies could become an integral part of the policy process, particularly with regard to the implementation and delivery of public services. This was inextricably linked to David Cameron's much-vaunted advocacy of the 'Big Society', for it was envisaged that as the state and its burgeoning bureaucracy were 'rolled back', so a 'mixed economy' of private, voluntary and not-for-profit organizations would flourish, and thereby play a major role in the provision or management of sundry social policies.

Thus did the coalition government launch a review of 901 quangos and similar bodies during the summer of 2010, the result of which was announced in October 2010. This declared that 192 of these would cease operating as public bodies, with some of them becoming 'committees of experts' instead. A further 171 would be substantially reformed, while 118 would be merged with, or into, existing public bodies. Another 40 organizations were to be kept 'under consideration', and thus face possible reform or abolition in the near or medium-term future (Maer, 2011: 6. For the full list of decisions, see Directgov, 2010).

Yet it has been noted that in addition to this planned reduction and rationalization of Britain's agencies and similar bodies, the coalition was committed to establishing at least 17 new ones, including an Office of Tax Simplification, and the Office of Budget Responsibility. Like previous governments, the coalition government has apparently discovered that even if some quangos are scrapped or slimmed down, new issues or Cabinet priorities can necessitate the creation of additional executive bodies and agencies, especially if it is judged that existing institutions are ill-suited to dealing with them. After all, as the Treasury noted in March 2010: 'It can be easier to set up a new arm's length body, rather than fit functions into existing bodies' (HM Treasury, 2010: 11. See also Gash et al., 2010: 52). It has also been suggested that merely 'abolishing quangos without abolishing functions does not save money and may in fact incur unexpected costs' (Flinders and Skelcher, 2012: 332).

Meanwhile, the trend towards agencification, as part of the wider transition to governance in Britain since the early 1990s, has variously raised serious issues about accountability, and *inter alia* the constitutional convention of individual ministerial responsibility, issues which we return to later in this chapter.

THE 'REGULATORY STATE'

The privatization programme pursued by the 1979–97 Thatcher-Major governments was imbued with several objectives: extending competition, increasing efficiency, empowering the consumer, fostering an enterprise culture, and so on – but it was also frequently linked to the professed objective of 'rolling back the state'.

Thatcherism viewed the state and its allegedly self-serving, anti-enterprise, non-wealth creating, economically unproductive bureaucracy as a major impediment to the operation of private enterprise and the market economy. By removing the 'dead hand' of state intervention and control, privatization was heralded as a major means of unleashing entrepreneurial talent and innovation, and allowing the consumer-responsive private sector to provide the goods and services that the British public wanted, rather than what the 'gentleman in Whitehall' assumed they wanted, needed, or ought to have.

Even in areas of the public sector where privatization was not considered feasible or appropriate, certain 'market' principles and private sector practices were to be introduced. Privatization and 'marketization' would therefore usher in a new era of limited government, less political interference and freedom from bureaucratic meddling. Or so neo-liberal Thatcherite ideologues purported to believe and were wont to claim. In fact, since the 1980s, the state has not so much been 'rolled back' as restructured and re-orientated, and intervention has taken new forms. Consequently, a number of writers have identified the emergence of a new 'regulatory state' (Hood et al., 1999; Loughlin and Scott, 1997; Majone, 1994; Moran, 2001). This, in turn, has fostered the establishment of the 'audit society' (Power, 1997).

The most obvious manifestation of the manner in which privatization has yielded a new mode of regulation is through the plethora of regulatory bodies that have been established since the 1980s. Calculating the precise number of such bodies is problematic, due to the different definitions deployed as to what actually constitutes a 'regulatory body' in an era of agencification and sundry other semi-autonomous commissions and councils. In 1997, for example, Rhodes believed that there were at least 32 regulatory bodies in post-privatization Britain (Rhodes, 1997: 91–2), some of which are listed in Box 6.1.

Box 6.1   Examples of regulatory bodies in contemporary Britain

Advertising Standards Authority
Consumers' Association
Financial Services Authority
Funding Agency for Schools
Higher Education Funding Council for England
Higher Education Funding Council for Wales
National Consumer Council
Office of Communications (Ofcom)
Office of Gas and Electricity Markets (Ofgem)
Office of Rail Regulation
Office for Standards in Education, Children's Services and Skills (Ofsted)
Police Complaints Authority
Postal Services Commission

Postwatch Press Complaints Commission
Quality Assurance Agency (Higher Education)
Social Services Inspectorate
Strategic Rail Authority
Teacher Training Agency
Trading Standards Institute
Water Services Regulation Authority (Ofwat)
Welsh Consumer Council

Many of these are commonly known by their acronyms, which have entered the lexicon of ordinary conversation and news reportage, such as the Office for Standards in Education, Children's Services and Skills, commonly known as 'Ofsted', and the Higher Education Funding Council for England, usually referred to as HEFCE (pronounced 'hef-kee').

With regard to the privatized industries, regulatory bodies such as Ofcom, Ofgem and Ofwat are supposed to ensure some degree of protection for consumers, either by restricting price increases, or imposing financial penalties for poor service. As such, Feigenbaum et al. have noted that these regulatory bodies 'possess considerable power over the operation, service standards and pricing structure of the privatized utilities' (1998: 80).

They also reflect the fact that in spite of the Thatcherite discourse of competition and consumer choice, many of the privatized industries and services remained near-monopolies, albeit no longer in the public sector. Consequently, it was recognized that the consumer still required some form of 'protection' against excessive price increases, unfair practices or poor service. Thus it was that privatization heralded the development of a new tranche of bodies to regulate the practices and activities of the privatized industries, so that government effectively 'substituted regulation for ownership' (Rhodes, 1997: 91).

However, it is certainly not just privatized utilities that are subject to such regulation. Virtually all public services and bodies today are subject to forms of regulation by various semi-autonomous bodies or funding agencies and councils that impose targets, establish performance indicators, conduct regular 'audits' to measure the extent to which these targets and indicators have been met, and often allocate (or withhold) funding accordingly. For example, universities are closely regulated, with both their teaching and research quality subject to regular audit and inspection by bodies such as the Quality Assurance Agency (for Higher Education).

As such, through its relentless drive to improve public sector/public service performance and ensure compliance with governmental objectives, the regulatory state inaugurates new modes of intervention and surveillance from, or at the behest of, the core executive. This particular paradox has been well-noted by Moran, who observes that while the new governance is characterized by central government's relinquishing of direct control, and a fragmentation of administrative processes and institutions at sub-national level, it has nonetheless been accompanied by new attempts at exercising control and direction from the centre. He explains that: 'The regulatory state has replaced nationalization with regulation' so that although 'privatization removed a large area of command from the British economy ... it did so at the cost of creating huge new areas of intervention and institution building' (Moran, 2000: 6–8).

In this respect, Moran suggests that 'the supposed rise of governance has been accompanied by something that looks like its very antithesis', namely new forms of command, control, regulation and surveillance, either from, or at the behest of, the centre. The ultimate irony, therefore, is that the rhetoric of deregulation, which pervaded the 1980s and 1990s, has belied a parallel trend towards increased regulation: 'the social world of 2000 is infinitely more tightly controlled than the world of 1950' (Moran, 2000: 6–8. See also Moran, 2001; Moran 2007; Smith, 2011) – as doctors, nurses, police officers, probation officers, social workers, teachers and university lecturers would doubtless confirm.

In similar vein, Gamble observes that: 'One of the consequences of the rise of the regulatory state may therefore be an increase rather than a decrease in government' (Gamble, 1997: 370), while Majone notes how privatization and 'de-regulation' have actually 'created the conditions for the rise of the regulatory state to replace the *dirigiste* state of the past' (Majone, 1994). Certainly, as Muller and Wright suggested (writing in 1994), 'it would be perfectly plausible to contend that the last 15 years have seen more "state reshaping" than "state retreat", with the state remaining a central policy actor, retaining "a nodal decision-making position"' even though 'their action is more indirect, more discreet and more bartered' (Muller and Wright, 1994: 7–8).

Similarly, Wyn Grant notes how, after an apparent 'rolling back' initially, 'the state starts to expand again, but in a more chameleon-like form', so that 'the emergence of a regulatory state does not mean that state power necessarily diminishes, but that its form changes ... becomes more diffuse ... becomes less direct, but also more penetrating. A regulatory state is in many ways a more fragmented state with responsibility divided amongst a host of different regulators or auditors' (Grant, 2003: 226–7).

This last point draws attention to the fact that 'regulation' requires constant evaluation, measurement and quantification, in order to gauge the extent to which performance indicators and targets are being met by service providers and 'street level bureaucrats' responsible for policy implementation. Consequently, the regulatory state fosters the 'audit society', as we will explain more fully in Chapter 9.

DEVOLUTION

The transition from government to governance was further enhanced by the first (1997–2001) Blair government's enactment of devolution, via the 1999 creation of the Scottish Parliament and Welsh Assembly. This, of course, had profound implications for Britain's hitherto 'unitary state' tradition and the empirical efficacy of the 'Westminster Model', in which political power and policies were assumed to emanate from Whitehall and Westminster in a top-down manner.

Ironically, it was the policies and policy style of the Thatcher-Major governments that did much to boost the demands for devolution in Scotland and Wales during the 1980s and 1990s. Not only was electoral support for the Conservatives rather lower than in England (giving rise to questions about Thatcherism's 'mandate' to impose unpopular polices on the Scottish and Welsh people), there was also a perception that Thatcherite Conservatism was a quintessentially, provincial, suburban, English phenomenon. Although Scotland already had its own educational and legal system, and thus a strong sense of distinctiveness from England, the Thatcher governments unwittingly reinforced this.

Meanwhile, in Wales, there had been growing concern in some quarters about the expansion of non-elected, ministerially-appointed bodies, often responsible for the allocation of significant sums of public monies (for a discussion of the growth of such bodies in general during the Thatcher-Major years, see Jenkins, 1995; Morris, 1994; Skelcher and Davis, 1996; Stewart, 1995; Stewart, 1996). For example, by 1996, there were more than 1,400 'quango' appointees in Wales, compared to 1,273 elected councillors. Furthermore, these 'quangos' presided over a combined annual budget of some £2 billion, which was almost equal to that spent by elected local authorities (Davies, 1999: 16, note 13).

The Thatcher-Major governments therefore prompted growing concern in Scotland and Wales about a 'democratic deficit', which, in turn, served to imbue the Labour Party's professed commitment to Scottish and Welsh devolution with greatly added relevance and resonance, even though there remained different views within the Labour Party about the precise form that devolution should take, and how much power should be devolved. For example, it was variously suggested that in spite of presiding over the actual enactment of devolution, Tony Blair was never enthusiastic about it, yet somehow felt obligated by a policy commitment inherited from his two predecessors, Neil Kinnock and John Smith.

Certainly, New Labour's devolution policies did not seem to be carefully thought through, either in terms of the constitutional implications, or the likely consequences for public policy, especially in the context of the professed commitment to 'joined-up government'. Instead, a combination of pragmatism and calculations of partisan or governmental advantage seem to have motivated much of New Labour's approach to constitutional reform (Dorey, 2008a: *passim*), which in turn ensured that the reforms which were enacted lacked 'any grand vision or underpinning framework' (Flinders, 2006: 130).

Devolution to Scotland

A referendum to gauge the degree of support in Scotland for its own Parliament was held in September 1997 (resulting in a convincing 'yes' vote), with the legislation then passed in 1998, and the Scottish Parliament itself finally established in 1999, accompanied by the devolution of a considerable range of legislative powers and policy competences, as listed below:

- agriculture, forestry and fishing
- crime (criminal and civil law, the prosecution system and the courts)
- culture (the arts and sport)
- economic development
- education
- health
- housing
- social work
- tourism
- transport.

The Scottish Parliament was also granted revenue-raising powers, permitting it to raise or reduce the basic rate of income tax to 3p in the £, although thus far it has not sought to exercise this particular power.

Central (Westminster) government and the core executive in London retained control of macro-economic strategy, monetary and fiscal policy, foreign affairs, defence, national security, national transport (air and rail services, and associated regulatory issues), and social security. In this respect, Tony Blair was adamant that ultimate sovereignty remained with the UK Parliament.

Comprising 129 Scottish Members of Parliament (SMPs), the Scottish Parliament is elected through the Additional Member System, with 73 SMPs directly elected on a first-past-the-post basis, using existing constituencies (although one additional constituency was created), with the remaining 56 SMPs selected from party lists, in accordance with their party's share of the vote, thus introducing a degree of proportionality into the system.

A major consequence of this last innovation was to ensure that no single party gained an overall majority in the Scottish Parliament in the first three elections: in 1999 and 2003, Labour was the single largest party (in terms of seats won), but was obliged to form a coalition, its partner on both occasions being the Liberal Democrats. Then, in the 2007 election, the Scottish National Party (SNP) emerged as the single largest party, but chose to rule as a minority government, prior to winning an overall majority in the 2011 Scottish Parliament election.

Scottish policy divergence

One important consequence of devolution has been the development or acceleration of 'policy divergence' in Scotland (and Wales), as the devolved institutions and their governments have pursued several policies that are distinct from those enacted in England. Due to the extensive range of powers devolved to Scotland, and the particular party configurations of the Scottish Executive (government) since 1999, devolution has resulted in a clear divergence from England in several spheres of public policy (for detailed accounts of policy divergence accruing from devolution, see: Adams and Robinson, 2002; Alcock, 2010; Birrell, 2009; Exworthy, 2001; Greer, 2004; Greer, 2010; Keating et al., 2003; Machin et al., 2013; Stewart, 2004; Trench and Jarman, 2007). However, it should be emphasized that, for various cultural and historical reasons, Scotland already enjoyed greater autonomy or policy distinctiveness *vis-à-vis* England, even before devolution (see, for example: Brown et al., 1998; Kellas, 1984).

The main policy areas where Scottish devolution has yielded either a divergence from corresponding policies in England, or a policy change that *preceded* a similar reform in England, are illustrated in Table 6.2.

It can be seen that most of these instances of policy divergence concern aspects of social policy, most notably education, health and social services. Of course, this reflects the fact that in matters pertaining to economic policy and foreign affairs, ultimate authority continues to reside in Westminster and Whitehall.

Much of this (social) policy divergence derives from two discrete, but interlinked and mutually reinforcing, aspects of politics and policy making in post-devolution Scotland.

Table 6.2   Examples of Scottish policy divergence *vis-à-vis* England under devolution

Policy	Divergence *vis-à-vis* England
Care for the elderly	Free personal/home care introduced for the elderly
Children's health	Free fruit distributed in schools
Health	1. 'Foundation hospitals' rejected, in favour of an integrated system of public healthcare 2. Minimum price (50p per unit) for alcohol to tackle problem/binge drinking 3. Cigarettes to be sold in plain packets
Fox hunting	Outlawed before it was banned in England
Nursery education	Pre-school provision for all three and four olds
Schools	1. Local (Education) Authorities continue to play a major role education provision 2. Less prescriptive, more flexible, curriculum 3. Key stage tests (at ages 7, 11, 14 and 16) replaced by assessments by teachers 4. School league tables abolished
University tuition/top-up fees	Abolished/rejected fees for Scottish students attending Scottish universities

First, the ideological stance and values of the various parties that have governed Scotland since 1999 have generally fostered a more collectivist or social democratic approach to many aspects of social policy (see, for example, Paterson, 2002). Bearing in mind that the Scottish Labour Party (like its Welsh counterpart) never really embraced 'New Labour', it is apparent that the parties which have thus far governed post-devolution Scotland are, to varying degrees, Left-leaning on many issues, and have consequently rejected much of the relentless neo-liberalism, marketization and individualism that have so strongly shaped public policy in England since the 1980s.

Instead, many post-devolution policies in Scotland have reflected 'a sense of shared responsibility and community ethos … of common or collective identity … social solidarity' (Keating, 2010: 49). One crucial consequence of this is that policy makers in Scotland have tended to view people first and foremost as citizens, whereas in England, Conservatives and New Labour alike view people primarily as consumers or customers who are permanently 'shopping around' for the 'best' public services. Certainly, with regard to education policy in particular, Bromley and Curtice have identified 'a distinctly Scottish policy', which reflects a 'distinctive strand of public opinion' north of the border (Bromley and Curtice, 2003: 10–11. See also Curtice, 2010).

Scotland's more social democratic and collectivist ethos also underpins the second factor that has fuelled policy divergence between Scotland and England, namely the *style* of both policy making and policy delivery (implementation) – notwithstanding that policies are often still being 'made' even while being implemented (as we will explain in Chapter 8). In England, marketization has been accompanied by the imposition of new public management (also discussed in Chapter 8) to ensure that professionals in the public sector comply with the objectives, priorities and targets stipulated by ministers in London. This in turn reflected and reinforced the political perspective in England since the 1980s that public sector professionals were (are) a self-serving and innately inefficient 'producer interest' who must be subject simultaneously to strong managerial control and the discipline of 'the market'.

By contrast, many spheres of public policy in post-devolution Scotland have been developed and delivered on the basis of partnership with those most directly involved or affected. In other words, whereas the Conservatives and New Labour (in England) view professionals such as doctors, nurses, police officers, social workers, teachers and university lecturers as adversaries who must be cajoled and coerced into compliance and conformity with governmental policies, these 'street level bureaucrats' have generally been viewed as allies or partners in Scotland, so that policy makers have sought to work with, rather than against, them as far as practicably possible. For example, with regard to healthcare, Greer notes how 'Scotland has opted ... for professionalism ... as against managers and markets', this entailing clinical networks that have sought to 'integrate professionals and their concerns'. Moreover, he points out, the Scottish civil service has worked closely with the leaders of the organized interests representing health professionals in Scotland in devising and delivering various policies (Greer, 2007: 146). In this respect, the health policy community that was deliberately weakened by successive British governments from the 1980s onwards (as we noted in Chapter 2) has been revived in post-devolution Scotland.

However, while this more consensual and partnership-based approach can largely be attributed to the prevailing ideological and political values in post-devolution Scotland, coupled with the party composition of Scottish governments since 1999, Keating (2010) has suggested another factor, namely the relatively small size of Scotland as a nation. Compared to England, where ministers have, since the 1980s, relied heavily on the imposition of central targets and 'managerialism' to secure compliance and conformity from large public sector organizations and their (sometimes) geographically remote front-line staff, Scotland's smaller size has made consultation and incorporation much more feasible and practicable.

As Keating explains:

> The small size of the Scottish system may also explain the tendency to work with professionals, local government and groups ... In Scotland, policy and delivery systems are small enough to allow short lines of communication and a dialogue among policy makers, administrators and service providers. This style of policy making is illustrated by reforms in health and higher education, which have taken strikingly divergent paths in England and Scotland.
>
> (Keating, 2010: 209)

Yet although Scotland's smaller size doubtless makes such collaboration and partnership easier to attain, the cultural proclivity, ideological preference and political will for pursuing consultative and consensual modes of policy making and delivery all need to exist in the first place. In Scotland, this desire and determination has been clearly evident; in England, it has been conspicuous by its absence.

Devolution to Wales

The first Blair government granted devolution to Wales in tandem with that granted to Scotland, with a referendum in Wales in 1997, followed by the relevant legislation the following year and the National Assembly for Wales launched in 1999. However, there remained important differences between the devolution granted to Wales and that which was enacted in Scotland.

First, the referendum in Wales was held a week later than that in Scotland, apparently in the expectation that Scotland's (envisaged) 'yes' vote would create a 'bandwagon effect', ensuring that Wales also endorsed devolution. It did, but only by the narrowest of margins, 559,419 (50.3 per cent) votes to 552,698 (49.7 per cent), a majority of just 6,721, and on a turnout of 50.1 per cent, which effectively meant that only one in four of the Welsh electorate actually voted for devolution. Of course, this immediately prompted a debate about whether this result reflected lack of enthusiasm for devolution *per se*, or dissatisfaction with the rather limited mode of devolution which Wales was being offered compared to Scotland.

Second, unlike the Scottish Parliament, the National Assembly for Wales was not established as a legislative institution, but as an executive body. It was not, therefore, empowered to introduce legislation pertaining to Wales, but, instead, was primarily responsible for administering 18 (later increased to 20) spheres of policy previously overseen by the Secretary of State for Wales and the Welsh Office, namely:

- agriculture, forestry, fisheries and food
- ancient monuments and historic buildings
- culture (including museums, galleries and libraries)
- economic development
- education and training
- the environment
- health and health services
- highways
- housing
- industry
- local government
- social services
- sport and recreation
- tourism
- town and country planning
- transport
- water and flood defence
- the Welsh language.

Crucially, though, this mode of executive devolution offered scope for adapting policies emanating from Westminster and Whitehall in order to tailor them to specific Welsh circumstances or needs.

Wales subsequently moved towards a stronger mode of devolution, entailing increasing legislative powers for the Welsh Assembly, in the wake of the recommendations in the 2004 Report of the Richard Commission (Commission on the Powers and Electoral

Arrangements of the National Assembly for Wales, 2004) and then the 2006 Government of Wales Act. The latter enabled the Welsh Assembly to enact legislation on *some* aspects of the devolved policy areas, subject to the approval of the UK Parliament at Westminster. A referendum was conducted in Wales in March 2011, in which the question was asked: 'Do you want the Assembly now to be able to make laws on all matters in the 20 subject areas it has powers for?'. The result was 517,132 (63.5 per cent) voting 'Yes' and 297,380 (35.5 per cent) voting 'No', albeit on a turnout of only 35.4 per cent.

Third, the National Assembly for Wales does not possess any tax-raising powers. It is permitted, however, to determine how its block grant will be apportioned between the various services in Wales, thereby enabling the Welsh Assembly to give greater priority to some policy areas rather than others in any financial year. However, like the Scottish Parliament, the National Assembly for Wales has used the Additional Member System. Of the 60 Assembly Members for Wales (ASMs), 40 are elected on a first-past-the-post basis, from existing Westminster constituencies, while the other 20 are recruited from party lists, according to their party's share of the 'top-up' vote. In all four elections to the Welsh Assembly so far (1999, 2003, 2007 and 2011), Labour has emerged as the single largest party, but not always with a majority. Consequently, Wales has been governed by Labour administrations (1999–2000, 2003–07 and since 2011), a Labour-Liberal Democrat coalition (2000–03) and a Labour-Plaid Cymru coalition (2007–11).

Welsh policy divergence

In spite of its hitherto limited powers, the National Assembly for Wales has, like the Scottish Parliament, pursued several policies and initiatives that diverge from corresponding policies in England, and which were also doubtless viewed with some displeasure by the Blair governments in London. The main examples of such policy divergence since 1999 are illustrated in Table 6.3.

One particular source of conflict that emerged virtually from the outset between the National Assembly for Wales and Westminster/Whitehall concerned Objective One funding. When the Welsh (former) mining regions and rural West of Wales were ascribed 'Objective One' status by the EU (due to their extreme socio-economic deprivation), the Treasury initially declined to provide the requisite 'match funding' – a refusal that ultimately prompted the 'no confidence' motion in Labour's then First Minister, Alun Michael, who was widely perceived to be 'too Blairite' to be able effectively to represent Welsh interests. Eventually, in the summer of 2000, and following Michael's enforced resignation, the Treasury relented and Wales was awarded the match funding upon which the EU monies depended.

However, the episode provided a clear indication of the limited powers of the Welsh Assembly, and the extent to which Wales lacked the degree of autonomy enjoyed by Scotland *vis-à-vis* Westminster and Whitehall.

Nonetheless, some writers have discerned an increasingly distinct Welsh dimension emerging, both with regard to an inclusive policy-making process and the substance of the policies pursued, particularly in the twin spheres of social policy and welfare provision,

Table 6.3　Examples of Welsh policy divergence *vis-à-vis* England under devolution

Policy	Divergence *vis-à-vis* England
Care for the elderly	Free home care for the first six weeks after leaving hospital
Children's welfare	Establishment of a Children's Commissioner (later adopted in England)
Health	1. Free NHS prescriptions for citizens under 25 and over 60 years of age 2. Rejection of foundation hospitals
Schools	1. League tables abolished 2. Abolition of tests for 7 year olds (these were subsequently abolished in England) 3. Free school milk for children under 7
Transport	Free bus travel for pensioners
University tuition/top-up fees	Considerable financial support for Welsh students to offset the cost of attending university. Welsh students will not personally have to pay £9,000 per year; much of this will be paid for them.

reflecting (historically) 'a greater willingness to embrace socialist and communitarian values at the ballot box than has been the case in England', whereupon:

> ... the Welsh Executive has attempted to articulate such values in the development of a social policy agenda based upon the following notions: universalism; a rejection of marketisation; and co-operation rather than competition in the provision of collective goods ... devolution ... has created an enabling context in which these values can be applied to social policy.
>
> (Chaney and Drakeford, 2004: 136)

For example, in ensuring that Welsh students were subsidized, so that they would only have to pay a proportion of the £9,000 fee charged by most UK universities from 2012 onwards, the Welsh Education Minister, Leighton Andrews, proudly declared that 'This is a "Made in Wales" policy which demonstrates the benefits of devolution. We are preserving the principle that the state will subsidise higher education and maintain opportunities for all' (BBC, 2013).

Of course, the scope for further divergence between Wales and England has increased considerably now the Welsh Assembly has acquired law-making powers in 20 policy areas. What also makes more policy divergence likely is the different political complexion of the Welsh and UK governments, with a Labour government in Cardiff (albeit occasionally relying on support from Plaid Cymru, due to Labour winning 30 out of the 60 seats in the 2011 Welsh Assembly election, and so not acquiring an overall majority) and a Conservative-dominated coalition at Westminster.

Devolution and the need for greater policy coordination

Devolution to Scotland and Wales has increased the importance of coordination in the core executive, and thus the need for ministers, departments, senior civil servants and Special Advisers to consider the implications for Scotland and/or Wales when developing policies. The Cabinet Office (2013a. See also Cabinet Office 2012) thus advises policy makers to:

- Consider the territorial impact or scope of each policy – 'you may be working on a policy that has an effect in England only, England and Wales, across Great Britain or UK-wide'.
- Consider the extent to which a 'reserved' (non-devolved) policy will nonetheless require the cooperation of Scottish and Welsh policy makers during implementation – 'you may need to work with the devolved administrations to successfully implement your policy or deliver your service'.
- Consider whether a policy being devised in London has been devolved to Scotland and/ or Wales, in which case – 'you have a good opportunity to learn from different approaches taken elsewhere and can share learning about common problems'.
- To assist in such considerations, and also to facilitate coordination, each government department has a designated 'Devolution Coordinator' to advise ministers and senior civil servants on the implications for Scotland and/or Wales of their proposed policies.

Other forms of coordination between the core executive and the devolved institutions are pursued primarily through the Cabinet Office, and a Joint Ministerial Committee that comprises various ministers from central government, including the Secretaries of State for Scotland and Wales, and also senior Members from the Scottish Parliament and the Welsh Assembly.

BLURRING PUBLIC–PRIVATE BOUNDARIES IN POLICY DELIVERY

A key characteristic and consequence of the shift to governance, particularly in the context of 'marketization', is that an increasingly diverse range of bodies are involved in 'delivering' many policies and public services at regional or local levels. Since the 1980s, there has been a steady expansion of organizations such as charities, not-for-profit organizations, private sector companies, 'social entrepreneurs' and voluntary bodies, all of whom are now playing a much greater or more direct role in providing public services, either instead of, or in partnership with, governmental institutions (see, for example, Macmillan, 2010).

This trend towards a mixed economy of policy delivery and public service provision has derived from numerous factors, the most notable of which have been attempts at: curbing public expenditure (particularly under the Thatcher-Major governments and the post-2010 coalition); the promotion of competition (to provide more choice and raise standards); reducing the role of 'vested interests' (professionals) in the public sector and weakening further the power of trade unions, whose membership is now overwhelmingly comprised of public sector workers.

Of course, all of these objectives are intrinsic to the neo-liberal ideological framework, which has prevailed in Britain since the 1980s – even under New Labour – in which the mantra has been 'private sector good, public sector bad'.

According to Vincent Wright, there has been:

a tendency ... towards the increased Balkanisation and privatization of the public domain, as the result of devolving authority to a diversified network of agencies, regulatory bodies, sub-contractors, third sector bodies, private companies,. This network is bound together by a 'nexus of contracts' which has replaced integrated hierarchies. Exchange or bartered relationships are slowly replacing authoritative command structures ... [all leading to an] increasing process of policy obfuscation, or 'boundary-blurring', in which public and private interact in inextricable ways.

(Wright, 1994: 127)

Or as Dryzek and Dunleavy (2009: 149) argue, governance 'entails the further blurring of the boundaries between state, economy and civil society (though those boundaries have never been completely clear-cut)'.

Similarly, Pierre and Stoker observe that with the advent and advance of governance:

Local, regional and national political elites alike seek to forge coalitions with private businesses, voluntary associations and other societal actors to mobilize resources across the public–private border in order to enhance their chances of guiding society towards politically defined goals.

(Pierre and Stoker, 2000: 29)

As a consequence, any study of the policy process in contemporary Britain has to acknowledge that there are:

... more actors involved, the boundaries between the public and the private sphere are less precise, and the Government's command over the policy process is seen to have receded ... the Government is only one actor (although a crucial one) among many others in the policy arena.

(Richards and Smith, 2002: 4)

Meanwhile, Goldsmith (1997: 7) emphasizes that governance 'places an emphasis on vertical co-operation between institutions and tiers or levels of government, and on horizontal co-operation between public, private and voluntary sectors at the local level.'

Certainly, with regard to local politics, Wilson notes that:

Governance refers to the development and implementation of public policy through a broader range of public and private agencies than those traditionally associated with elected local government. Partnerships, networks and contracts have therefore become integral parts of the local political scene.

(Wilson, 2000: 258. See also Stoker, 2004: 19)

Of course, much public policy has always been administered by local political actors and authorities, but the process of 'agencification' initiated by the Thatcher–Major governments, coupled with the increased role that was simultaneously ascribed to the private and voluntary sectors in service provision, have greatly accelerated and intensified this process.

The transition to governance was lent additional impetus by the first (1997–2001) Blair government's enactment of devolution to Scotland and Wales, via the establishment of a Scottish Parliament and Welsh Assembly in 1999. More recently, the Conservative-Liberal Democrat coalition government forged in May 2010 has further reinforced the transition from government to governance through its efforts at granting non-state actors a larger role in policy implementation and service delivery, particularly in the spheres of social policy and aspects of welfare provision.

Consequently, the contemporary policy process is increasingly 'fragmented into a maze of institutions and organizations', entailing 'many centres and diverse links between many agencies of government at local, regional, national and supranational level' and each of these discrete levels, in turn, 'has a diverse range of horizontal relationships with other government agencies, privatized utilities, private companies, voluntary organizations and community groups' (Pierre and Stoker, 2000: 30–1).

Under the Thatcher governments in the 1980s, for example, a range of services were transferred away from the public sector to private providers, such as hospital laundry and school dinners. At the same time, cleaning in many public sector organizations was 'contracted-out' to private firms. The 1980s also saw other local government services 'deregulated' or subjected to 'compulsory competitive tendering', as was the case with public transport, whereupon private transport companies could replace or compete alongside local authority buses.

The involvement of the private sector continued apace when New Labour was in Office from 1997 to 2010, with education and the NHS again experiencing the most notable transformations. During this period, private sector involvement was generally of two kinds: infrastructure and service provision.

With regard to infrastructure, New Labour was very enamoured with the use of the Private Finance Initiative (PFI) – albeit rebranded as Public–Private Partnerships (PPP) (see Flinders, 2004) – to fund the building of new schools and hospitals, or to provide equipment and technology in education and the NHS. This mode of funding entails private sector companies or consortiums building or equipping schools, hospitals and prisons, whereupon they are leased (rented) back to the relevant health, education or prison authority, until the costs have been recouped, often over a period of 20–30 years.

However, PPPs increasingly entail private companies managing or delivering services either under contract from public sector bodies, or being commissioned by central government. Moreover, this mode of private sector involvement can either entail competing against existing public sector 'providers' or through collaboration in service delivery. For example, in the early 2000s, the Blair government began promoting academy schools, in accordance with its professed goal of diversifying secondary education, and ensuring that 'bog standard' comprehensives faced much more competition, which would thus compel them to raise educational standards.

Crucially, these academies could be 'sponsored', meaning that a non-state body or business person could invest up to £2 million in the creation of such a school, and in return be granted considerable input into the appointment of senior staff (including the headteacher), as well as partly shaping both the school's 'vision' and some of its curriculum.

Meanwhile, the 1997–2010 Blair governments also encouraged the 'independent' (i.e., private) sector to provide various healthcare services, ostensibly to assist and support the NHS. To this end, Independent Sector Treatment Centres (ISTCs) were established, which were private healthcare providers commissioned to treat NHS patients, primarily in order to reduce waiting lists. Patients were not charged for such treatment, thus enabling New Labour to insist that in spite of this increasing private sector involvement in the NHS, treatment remained free at the point of access (for an overview of ISTCs, see Naylor and Gregory, 2009).

David Cameron's vision of a 'Big Society'

The formation of a Conservative-dominated coalition government in May 2010 heralded a further expansion of non-state actors in the delivery and management of sundry public services, particularly those pertaining to social and welfare policies. Prior to becoming Prime Minister, the Conservative leader, David Cameron, had canvassed the notion of the 'Big Society', which he posited as an alternative to the 'Big Government' apparently favoured by the Labour Party (in both its 'Old' and 'New' variants).

Cameron explained that the Big Society 'includes a whole set of unifying approaches – breaking state monopolies, allowing charities, social enterprises and companies to provide public services, devolving power down to neighbourhoods', all of which were deemed to herald a bold and stark alternative to Labour's paternalism and state control (Cameron, 2010).

This vision was reiterated in the foreword to the Conservative Party's 2010 election manifesto, which promised a change 'from big government to Big Society', and 'from state action to social action, encouraging social responsibility ... supporting social enterprises with the power to transform neighbourhoods' (Conservative Party, 2010: vii–viii). Among the specific 'Big Society' measures pledged in the manifesto were:

- To establish a Big Society Bank, funded from dormant bank accounts, to support neighbourhood groups, charities, social enterprises and other non-governmental bodies.
- Permit non-state organizations to share in the delivery and provision of public services.
- Give public sector workers ownership of the services they deliver, by allowing them to establish cooperatives and 'mutualization' in education and health, and letting them bid to take over the services they run.
- Allow parents to establish their own 'free' schools.
- Allow communities to take over the management of local amenities, such as libraries and parks.
- Transform the civil service into a 'civic service' by ensuring that participation in social action is recognized in civil servants' appraisals.
- Promote the creation and development of neighbourhood groups, which can take action to improve their local area. Cabinet Office funds were to be provided to train independent community organizers to establish and manage these neighbourhood groups.

These initiatives, it was claimed, would create or re-establish 'the "little platoons" of civil society – and the institutional building blocks of the Big Society' (Conservative Party, 2010: 27, 37–9). The notion of 'little platoons' had originally been articulated in 1790 by the Conservative philosopher, Edmund Burke (2004: 135), and referred to the plethora of 'intermediate institutions' that existed between individuals and the state.

Although the notion of the 'Big Society' was associated primarily with David Cameron, it was discernible in the ideas promoted by several other Conservative politicians and academics from the 1990s onwards, but more particularly in the first decade of the 21st century, ostensibly in pursuit of a post-Thatcherite variant of Conservatism (Blond, 2009: 33; Blond,

Table 6.4 Examples of private/voluntary sector involvement in the delivery or management of public services

Policy sector	Policy/Project	Non-state actors involved
Crime	1) Managing Belmarsh Prison	1) Serco (private company) Turning Point (social enterprise) Catch22 (charity)
	2) Managing Peterborough Prison (and three others)	2) Sodexo (private company)
	3) Managing several prisons	3) G4S (private company)
Defence	Managing facilities and security at various military bases in Britain	Sodexo (private company)
Education	Managing student accommodation at several universities	University Partnerships Programme (private company)
Health	1) Managing Hinchingbrooke Hospital	1) Circle (private company)
	2) Managing facilities at Norfolk and Norwich University Hospital	2) Serco (private company)
Housing	1) Managing 'social' housing in several areas	1) Capita (private company)
	2) Providing accommodation to 'vulnerable' women in Cheshire	2) Adullam Homes Housing Association (charity)
Immigration	Managing several detention centres	G4S (private company)
Local Government	Managing 13 public libraries in Croydon and various others elsewhere in England	John Laing Integrated Services (private company)
Welfare	1) Assessing social security claimants' 'fitness to work' in cases of disability	1) Atos Healthcare (private company)
	2) Managing child maintenance services (financial arrangements/ support in the case of separation by parents)	2) G4S (private company)
	3) Getting the unemployed into work/training (south-west England/Wales)	3) Interserve (private company) Rehab Group (not-for-profit organization)
	4) Getting the unemployed into work/training (east London)	4) Careers Development Group (charity)

2010: *passim*; Green, 2003: 5–6; Letwin 2002: 45–51; Letwin, 2003; Norman, 2010; Willetts, 1994: 23; see also Willetts, 2002: 55. For a general overview of the origins and development of the 'Big Society', see Dorey and Garnett, 2012).

Since becoming Prime Minister, Cameron has continued to extol the alleged virtues of the Big Society, entailing a major extension of private and voluntary sector involvement in the delivery and management of public services. Indeed, he asserts that: 'Instead of having to justify why it makes sense to introduce competition in individual public services … the state will have to justify why it should ever operate a monopoly' (Cameron, 2011. See also HM Government, 2011).

As a result of these changes, a wide range of public services are now delivered or managed, to varying degrees, by private companies or other non-state actors, as illustrated by Table 6.4.

Although private companies have been the prime beneficiaries of the 'contracting-out' of public services, many of these sub-contract the day-to-day management and provision of services to local social entrepreneurs and voluntary organizations, thereby creating an often highly complex and intricate web of institutional relationships in service delivery. Certainly, these developments have resulted in an increased blurring of the former formal distinction between the public and private sectors in Britain. With private companies often providing the buildings and technology in much of the public sector, and directly providing, strategically managing or sub-contracting key public services, the lines of demarcation are steadily dissolving. Not surprisingly, this also results in increasing obfuscation and opacity in terms of identifying responsibility and ensuring accountability.

THE PROBLEM OF ACCOUNTABILITY

One particular problem arising from the transition to governance is that of accountability – who is responsible when a policy is deemed to have failed? Of course, even before the era of governance, the doctrine of individual ministerial responsibility was often problematic in practice, for although ministers, not civil servants, were supposed to shoulder the blame (to the extent of resigning) if serious policy errors or failures ensued, such resignations were relatively rare. After all, it is not always clear whether, or how seriously, a policy has failed – an issue that we will return to in Chapter 9 when we examine policy evaluation.

Moreover, failure or serious errors might only become apparent *after* the minister who initiated the policy has moved to another department, or perhaps returned to the backbenches in Parliament. Should his/her successor at the department have been expected to take responsibility for the failings of their predecessor's policy to the extent of resigning?

In reality, therefore, ministerial resignations as a direct result of policy failure or other serious errors have been increasingly rare (for a fuller analysis, see Barker, 1998; Finer, 1956; Flinders, 2000; Gay, 2012; Gay and Powell, 2004; Marshall, 1989; Pyper, 1991; Woodhouse, 1994). Indeed, when ministers have resigned, particularly since the 1990s, it has often owed more to aspects of their private lives (such as financial improprieties or sexual scandals) and/or lack of support in their parliamentary party, rather than because of a serious policy failure *per se* (a point emphasized by a House of Commons Public Administration Select Committee (2011: 17) inquiry into the contemporary role of ministers).

The constitutional convention of individual ministerial responsibility has been rendered even more problematic in the era of governance, precisely because of the plethora of actors involved in the delivery of many policies and public services. Although a Secretary of State is still the political head of a department, and therefore officially both presides over policy development and provides strategic leadership, the combined effect of agencification, devolution and the increasing involvement of non-state actors in policy delivery and public service provision has been to obfuscate further the attribution of responsibility (and thus blame) when major errors or failures occur.

In an era of governance: 'Fragmentation erodes accountability because sheer institutional complexity obscures who is accountable to whom and for what' (Rhodes, 1997: 101). Two prominent cases in the 1990s, during the early years of 'agencification', clearly signalled these problems.

The first involved the Child Support Agency (CSA), which was established in 1993 to pursue 'absent fathers' in order to compel them to pay maintenance (child support) to their former wife or girlfriend. However, from the outset, the CSA was beset by numerous problems (as we will note in Chapter 8) and thus subject to widespread criticism, not least from the House of Commons Social Security Select Committee. These problems begged the question of whether the CSA and its remit had been badly designed by the Secretary of State for Social Security, or whether the ensuing problems derived from serious errors and general incompetence by the CSA itself in implementing the policy.

Actually, one academic suggested that the answer was 'both', for while the CSA itself was 'an administrative shambles', it was 'also handicapped by poorly designed policy and legislation' (Theakston, 1999a: 29). Ultimately, though, it was the chief executive of the CSA, Ros Hepplewhite, who resigned amidst relentless criticism of the CSA's failings, not the Secretary of State for Social Security.

Even more controversial was the case involving the Home Office and the Prisons Agency in 1995. When three prisoners escaped from the Isle of Wight's high-security Parkhurst Prison in January 1995, the question was raised about whether the government's – or more specifically, the Home Office's – prison policy was inadequate (possibly due to staff shortages and thus a lack of prison officers to maintain adequate security and supervision), or whether the escapes could be attributed entirely to incompetent management of the prisons and inadequate supervision of inmates by prison governors, and in this case, the Director of the Prisons Agency, Derek Lewis. What ensued was a highly public and protracted bitter dispute between Lewis and the then Home Secretary, Michael Howard.

Howard was emphatic that prison security (and in this instance, the apparent lack of it) was firmly the responsibility of those charged with routine management of Britain's prisons. A breakout by any prisoner(s) was deemed to be the consequence of lax security and thus ineffective management at prison level on a day-to-day basis; the Home Secretary could hardly be expected to be held responsible, and blamed, for a prison breakout 90 miles from London. Howard insisted that: 'With regard to operational responsibility, there has always been a division between policy matters and operational matters', and that as Home Secretary, his responsibility was for the former (House of Commons Debates, 1995a: vol. 252, col. 40).

Yet Derek Lewis begged to differ, maintaining that it was indeed the Home Office's policy on prisons that was at fault, coupled with ministerial interference, and which therefore impeded the ability of prison officers and managers to supervise inmates effectively and efficiently, and thereby ensure prison security (Lewis, 1997). The episode resulted in an inquiry into prison security, chaired by Sir John Learmont, whose Report in October 1995 scathingly observed that the Parkhurst Prison escapes had 'revealed a chapter of errors at every level and a naïvete that defies belief' (Learmont, 1995: para. 2.257). Yet Howard maintained that the Learmont Report did not attribute blame for the breakout to any decision of his, adding that the Director General of the Prison Service, Derek Lewis, had 'ceased to hold his post with effect from today' (House of Commons Debates, 1995b: vol. 264, cols. 31–3).

Thirteen years later, a Labour Cabinet Minister (David Blunkett) informed a parliamentary select committee that:

> We have shifted ... in the 1980s with the next steps, with the obsession with agencies and then with decentralization from trying to do too much from the centre to doing things through agencies or through local institutions without any clear accountability either administratively or politically at that level. So what we end up with is secretaries of state standing at the dispatch box declining to answer questions on things that are no longer directly their responsibility without anyone knowing who carries the responsibility publicly and who can legitimately be held to account. To give you an example, if you ask the Department of Health [DoH] about what a primary care trust [PCT] is up to in terms of its interpretation of regulations laid down by the DoH because the regulations have been devolved downwards to the PCT, it will be the PCT's fault, but the PCT will tell you that they are only following what they thought were the regulations that the DoH had laid down and the secretary of state at the dispatch box (although the present one I am sure would carry responsibility for whatever he felt was needed) would quite legitimately say, 'It's nothing to do with me, Guv'. In the end if 'it's nothing to do with me, Guv' and it is nothing to do with government and it is nothing to do with us as elected representatives to hold to account those who theoretically have their hands on more than just the distribution of resources, we are getting ourselves in a muddle. I think we need to take a deep breath; we need to try that balance between grabbing and implementing new levers that we tried to do from 1997 because, as Gillian Shepherd quite rightly put it in the Department of Education, she pulled levers that were not connected to anything, so nothing happened. We then move to laying down everything on God's earth and then we have to move back again. So if we could just get the pendulum into the centre, the clock might tick better.
>
> (House of Commons Public Administration Select Committee, 2009: Ev 38,
> Oral evidence given on 23 October 2008)

Yet thereafter, ministers still struggled to 'get the pendulum into the centre', for as a parliamentary select committee report noted a few years later:

> The old doctrine of ministerial accountability (by which ministers alone are accountable to Parliament for the conduct of their department) is being stretched to implausibility by

the complexity of modern government and by the increasing devolution of responsibility to civil servants and to arm's length bodies. It is important that Parliament should be able to hold to account those who are in reality responsible. However, we accept that it may not always be possible to distinguish clearly between responsibility for policy making and responsibility for delivery. These are not simple matters.

(House of Commons Liaison Committee, 2012: 41, para. 114. See also House of Commons Public Administration Select Committee, 2011: 17–18, para. 39)

The constitutional principle that ministers should be held responsible when a policy seemingly fails has always been problematic when applied to concrete cases, but the transition to governance has rendered the doctrine of individual ministerial responsibility even more difficult to adhere to or enforce.

CONCLUSION

The transition from government to governance thus entails not only the weakening of old notions of hierarchy and vertical chains of command, but also erodes the relative autonomy of many traditional policy sectors or 'silos'. With the administration or delivery of many policies and services now shared between a plethora of public, private and voluntary bodies, the role of partnerships, coordination and strategic oversight becomes ever more important.

Furthermore, as in other policy arenas, the emphasis is on shared resources and exchange relationships, with the devolved assemblies, their partnership groupings, regional and local service providers and delivery agencies obliged to work together and forge alliances in order to achieve policy objectives and performance indicators. Consequently, the various consultative and exchange relationships that characterize both the core executive and policy communities at national level are increasingly a key feature of regional and local policy making and delivery. Indeed, the contemporary policy process is now characterized by both vertical (between national, regional and local level policy actors), and horizontal (between policy actors at specific – national, regional or local – levels).

In the era of governance, the core executive is increasingly reliant on a mixed economy of policy actors to implement policies and deliver public services at regional and local levels. Of course, central government has always relied heavily on sub-national policy actors and street-level bureaucrats to put policies into practice, but whereas much of this implementation was previously carried out by public sector bodies, via local government, governance means that a much wider range of organizations are now involved, many of them from the private or voluntary sectors. Hence the shift in the state's own role, from rowing to steering; stipulating policy objectives and performance indicators, but relying heavily on other sub-national or non-state policy actors to achieve these.

However, we have also noted that the state, or more specifically, the core executive, has often found it difficult to relinquish control, especially when it has been dissatisfied or impatient with the implementation or outcomes of particular policies. In such instances, ministers have attempted to re-assert control from the centre, either by imposing more prescriptive policy objectives and performance indicators, or by altering the 'mix' of actors delivering policy. For example, successive Education Secretaries have intervened when unhappy with aspects of teaching provided by schools and teachers, whereupon some schools have been placed under 'special measures' or new management.

There have also been periodic changes to the content of the National Curriculum, or even the content of specific subjects within it, such as Michael Gove's attempts, in 2013, to change the history syllabus. Furthermore, Ofsted has variously had its role and remit modified by Education Secretaries in response to perceived failings in the education system.

In effect, although the transition from government to governance entails a corresponding shift to 'steering, not rowing' by the state, ministers still periodically attempt to seize the oars or change the crew in order to strengthen compliance with central government's policy objectives. Those formally doing the rowing will often be expected to row in a specified direction, towards a stipulated destination at a particular speed and often in a prescribed style.

QUESTIONS AND TOPICS FOR DISCUSSION

1. How does governance differ to government?
2. What factors have prompted the transition to governance?
3. What is the role of government in a system of governance?
4. Why has regulation increased since the 1980s?
5. In what ways has devolution resulted in policy divergence in Scotland and Wales *vis-à-vis* England?
6. Why has devolution resulted in this policy divergence?
7. Why have boundaries between the public and private sectors become less clear since the 1980s?
8. Why have strategic partnerships in policy delivery become more important since the 1980s?
9. How might governance result in problems concerning accountability?

RECOMMENDED TEXTS AND FURTHER READING

1. Derek Birrell (2009) *The Impact of Devolution on Social Policy*. Bristol: The Policy Press.

   Examines the degree of policy divergence in several spheres of social policy since 1999, but does so by organizing the chapters thematically. As such, specific policies are cited by way of examples, rather than constituting the topic of the chapter *per se*. This provides for an original, refreshing and somewhat more sophisticated approach to examining the policy impact of devolution.

2. Michael Keating (2010) *The Government of Scotland: Public Policy Making after Devolution*, second edition. Edinburgh: Edinburgh University Press.

   A marvellous account of how the first decade of devolution has impacted both on the policy-making process in Scotland, and the actual polices subsequently enacted. Notes a considerable degree of divergence from England, partly in terms of the greater involvement of public service professionals and policy communities in policy making on Scotland, and partly because Scottish policy makers have largely resisted the 'marketization' and free-market fetishism which have been inflicted on England's public services and social policies.

3. Guy Lodge and Katie Schmuecker (eds) (2010) *Devolution in Practice 2010*. London: Institute for Public Policy Research.

A very welcome and timely collection of essays spanning a wide range of policy areas, such as care of the elderly, child poverty, criminal justice, health and housing. Written by an academic expert in their field, each chapter examines both the extent to which policies are diverging, and what factors are fuelling policy differentiation within the UK.

4. Michael Moran (2001) 'The rise of the regulatory state in Britain', *Parliamentary Affairs* 54 (1): 19–34.

Very useful and well-written article, clearly delineating the emergence of a new mode of regulation by the State in Britain since the 1980s, one which is qualitatively different to the forms of *dirigiste* government regulation which characterized the 1960s and 1970s. Initially developed in the 1980s to regulate the privatized industries, but subsequently extended to the public sector, most notably education (at all levels) and the NHS, ostensibly to improve accountability, efficiency, performance and value-for-money. Ultimately, the State has not so much been 'rolled back' or 'hollowed out' as restructured, and intervenes in new guises.

5. Jon Pierre and Gerry Stoker (2000) 'Towards multi-level governance', in P. Dunleavy, A. Gamble, I. Holliday and G. Peele (eds) *Developments in Politics 6*. Basingstoke: Macmillan.

Useful essay discussing both the concept of (multi-level) governance, and the extent to which the concept provides a good characterization of the changes in the structure and functioning of Britain's political and policy-making institutions.

6. R.A.W. Rhodes (1997) *Understanding Governance: Policy Networks, Governance, Reflexivity and Accountability*. Buckingham: Open University Press.

Seminal text on how and why the government has increasingly been replaced by governance, as policy-making increasingly takes place at different levels, across sectors, and between a range of actors engaged in networks, strategic partnerships, exchange relationships and resource dependency. One major aspect of the transition towards governance has been a blurring of the erstwhile boundaries between the public and private sectors in policy implementation.

7 The Internationalization of Public Policy

In tandem with the transition from government to governance in Britain since the 1980s, as examined in the previous chapter, there has been a parallel trend towards a system of international governance, as an increasing number of policies are either formulated beyond Britain or are still formally developed within Britain, but shaped or prompted by developments, events and institutions at European or global level.

The most contentious aspect of the internationalization of 'British' policy making is that of Europeanization, which refers to the increasing influence or impact of the European Union on British public policy. However, we will explain that some policy areas or issues are more affected by Europeanization than others, which in turn shapes the stance of the various government departments; some of them resent the encroachment of the EU into their policy domain, viewing it as an infringement of departmental autonomy, while others actually welcome it, either because it has given some departments a new lease of life and actually enhanced their role, or because the department views the EU as aiding the pursuit of particular policy goals, which might be more difficult to pursue alone.

As well as impacting on the policies of some departments, there is another way in which Britain's key political institutions and the policy process have been Europeanized, namely their organizational responses to the EU's increased role in several policy areas. For example, within the 'core executive', not only do most departments now have a European Division or Directorate, the Cabinet Office also addresses EU issues through one of its Secretariats. Meanwhile, a select group of senior civil servants are seconded to Brussels, representing Britain's interests (although Eurosceptics might dispute this!) and regularly reporting back to senior ministers and the Cabinet Office in London.

Meanwhile, as noted in Chapter 5, Parliament has responded to Europeanization by establishing committees that focus exclusively on the impact or implications of EU policies on Britain. Indeed, the relevant committee in the House of Lords is often commended by some academics for the quality of its scrutiny of EU 'legislation' *vis-à-vis* Britain and the expertise that many peers can contribute when engaged in such scrutiny, often derived from the professional knowledge they acquired in their previous careers.

The second aspect of the internationalization of 'British' public policy is that of globalization, which is especially notable in economic affairs. Many policies are increasingly devised in the context of, or in response to, the perceived requirements of multinational companies, overseas investors, bond markets, and since 2008 especially, international credit ratings agencies. The ideological and intellectual hegemony of neo-liberalism and free trade in recent decades, and the consequent wealth and power that have been acquired by international companies and financiers, has meant that British policy makers have become increasingly mindful of the need to ensure that economic, employment and taxation policies will meet with international approval, and ensure that Britain remains a country that multinational corporations and global investors are happy 'to do business' with. The 'wrong' economic policies could result in a 'flight of capital' out of Britain, as companies and investors relocate to a more business-friendly country, taking jobs and tax contributions with them, thereby leaving Britain with even higher unemployment and fewer tax revenues to fund public services and welfare.

Of course, this imbues international big business and wealthy individuals with considerable ability to 'blackmail' British governments and 'hold them to ransom' by insisting that particular economic policies are pursued. True, large corporations and business tycoons have always been able to apply pressure on governments to enact favourable policies – pressure that ordinary citizens have been unable to match – but globalization has enormously enhanced the power of big business. However, many other issues and problems have become internationalized in recent decades, such as the drug trade, the environment, human trafficking/sex slavery, and – since 9/11 especially – terrorism. These too have prompted closer cooperation between Britain and other countries in formulating and implementing policies to tackle these new (or previously unacknowledged or hitherto less serious) problems, which, by their very nature, cannot be eradicated by one country alone.

The third manifestation of the internationalization of 'British' policy making has been the phenomenon of 'policy transfer', whereby the search for solutions to particular problems has entailed looking overseas to observe which policies other countries have enacted. Where these have been judged successful, Britain's policy makers have either adopted them, or at least adapted them in a manner that aims to render them more applicable to domestic circumstances. We will note that various key policy innovations since the 1990s can be attributed to policy transfer, namely the Child Support Agency, welfare into work, and 'zero tolerance' policing.

EUROPEANIZATION

Britain joined what was then the European Communities[1] (EC) on 1 January 1973, but which subsequently became the EU as a consequence of the 1992 Maastricht Treaty. This Treaty significantly enhanced or expanded the policy jurisdiction and responsibilities of the EU, the most obvious example being the pursuit of economic and monetary union, which ultimately led to the establishment of the single European currency – more commonly known as 'the euro', from which Britain secured an 'opt out'.

---

[1] The plural reflects the fact that the EC officially comprised three distinct bodies, namely the: European Economic Community (EEC); European Coal and Steel Community (ECSC); European Atomic Energy Community (Euratom). However, it was the EEC that Britain was primarily interested in joining and many commentators talked of British membership of the EEC, rather than the EC.

The Maastricht Treaty also sought to facilitate a common foreign and security policy, to provide the EU with a greater role in matters pertaining to European defence and foreign affairs. A further objective of the Maastricht Treaty was to promote closer cooperation between EU member states in dealing with asylum and illegal immigration, as well as tackling crime.

THE UNEVEN IMPACT OF THE EU ON PUBLIC POLICY IN BRITAIN

Yet in spite of the steady widening and deepening of the EU's policy jurisdiction, and the consequent warnings by Eurosceptics about the relentless loss of British sovereignty accruing from the alleged development of a European 'super-state', the direct impact on policies in Britain has been uneven; some spheres of policy, and *inter alia*, departments or ministries, have been more affected by Europeanization than others. This has meant that: 'For some departments, Europe provides an opportunity for increasing their role and autonomy whilst for others it is a constraint on their activities' (Marsh et al., 2001: 217).

As such, Watts and Pilkington (2005: 151) observe that: 'The picture is … a patchy one, with the nature and extent of EU involvement in policy making differing from issue to issue.' Indeed, Bache and Jordan (2006: 269) have suggested that even in policy spheres with a relatively strong EU input or impact, there will be nuances and variations within them, with some aspects of a particular policy sector more 'Europeanized' than others.

In this context, Bulmer and Burch (2009: Chapters 6 and 7) have suggested that there is an 'inner core' and 'outer core' of departments in Whitehall, with the former being those most directly affected by Europeanization, while the latter are affected more loosely, sporadically or only on a limited range of policy issues. However, we would add an 'intermediate layer', comprising the departments that fall somewhere in between the inner and outer core, due either to a slight increase in their EU obligations overall, or because some of their departmental responsibilities have been Europeanized, while others have retained considerable autonomy.

The inner core

The spheres of policy that have been most affected by Europeanization are those concerned with economic policy (particularly those pertaining to competition and trade), the environment, and agriculture (including fisheries). Consequently, the former Department of Trade and Industry (DTI) (now the Department of Business, Innovation and Skills (DBIS)), the Treasury, and what was the Ministry of Agriculture, Fisheries and Food (MAFF), but in 2001 was replaced by the Department for Environment, Food and Rural Affairs (DEFRA), have become Britain's most 'Europeanized' departments.

The DTI/DBIS

The former DTI was strongly 'Europeanized', due mainly to the primary economic objective of the EC/EU, namely the promotion of free trade between member states, and the concomitant removal of border controls and tariffs *vis-à-vis* imports and exports. This objective was given a major impetus by the 1986 Single European Act. Bulmer and Burch

(2009: 145) therefore note that the DTI was 'affected by the European integration process from the very outset.'

As we noted in Chapter 4, the 'trade' division of the DTI was strongly inclined towards liberalization, and as a consequence, the department was highly receptive towards the EC/EU's promotion of free trade, the single market, de-regulation, competition, and so on. Indeed, one departmental official claimed that 'in the areas that are core to the DTI, trade policy and Single Market policy, we are closer to the Commission probably than any other member state' (quoted in Buller and Smith, 1998: 174), while another DTI official acknowledged that the department had generally been in favour 'of a strong Commission which is capable of policing a single market ... and which is capable of devising and seeing through an effective liberal trade policy' (quoted in Marsh et al., 2001: 220. See also Buller and Smith, 1998: 174).

Certainly, in their major study entitled *The Europeanisation of Whitehall: UK Central Government and the European Union*, Bulmer and Burch (2009: 146) emphasize that:

> ... since the 1980s, the DTI has been in the front-line of most of the UK government's positive economic policies on the EU: advocating the single market from the 1980s, advancing the competitiveness agenda ... as well as advocating an open world trade policy on the part of the EU.

Evidently, the degree of compatibility between the DTI's in-house ideology of economic liberalism (noted in Chapter 4) and the EU's commitment to facilitating free trade and competition provided the department with opportunities to shape aspects of the EU's policy agenda. The DTI's more active and enthusiastic stance towards the EU was further enhanced by the often administratively complex or highly technical character of various policy issues, such as those pertaining to energy and telecommunications.

The Treasury

Meanwhile, the Treasury has also experienced considerable 'Europeanization', but unlike the DTI/DBIS, its stance towards the EU has generally been 'defensive' (Bulmer and Burch, 2009: 133), due to the vexatious nature of many key economic issues, most notably Britain's budgetary contributions, EMU (and Britain's opt-out from the single European currency – the euro) and the extent to which EU obligations impacting on other departments and policies might have expenditure implications.

Certainly, the Treasury has been embroiled in occasional clashes with Brussels over 'match funding', whereby EU money is allocated to an economically weak region in order to encourage industrial regeneration and generate employment, but on condition that the domestic government contributes the same amount of money, rather than cutting its own expenditure accordingly. Yet the Treasury's inclination has sometimes been to view EU regional funding as an alternative, rather than an addition, to the government's own expenditure.

According to Geddes, this stance derives from the 'the Treasury view that UK receipts from the EU budget are reimbursement for contributions made rather than fresh funding' (Geddes, 2004: 172), a perspective that has sometimes caused tension not just between the

Treasury and the EU, but between the Treasury and other departments (or regions of the UK), which would be the beneficiaries of this EU 'match funding'. As such, one senior civil servant in the Cabinet Office confessed that the Treasury tended to view the EU as 'a bloody nuisance' (quoted in Marsh et al., 2001: 217).

A further reason for the 'defensive' stance of the Treasury towards the EU has been identified by Dyson (2000: 902), namely the Treasury's determination to maintain the role of 'the City' (Britain's financial services and major banks) as a major global financial centre. One manifestation of this has been the Treasury's strong opposition to any EU initiatives to harmonize taxation in a manner that would have a negative impact on 'the City' and Britain's lucrative financial services industry.

This stance strongly underpinned the Treasury's strong resistance, in 2011–12, to EU proposals for a tax of 0.01 per cent on 'financial transactions', which could raise up to 57 billion euros (£47.3 billion) annually. Again, the Treasury's argument was that imposing new taxes on banks and financial services would be counter-productive, because they would probably relocate to countries with lower taxes, whereupon Britain (and other EU member states) would lose the taxes that the financial services industry currently contributed, most notably the corporation tax paid on their profits and the income tax paid by those employed in this sector.

MAFF/DEFRA

Another department that had a close relationship with the EU, but which generally viewed it in a positive manner, was the Ministry of Agriculture, Fisheries and Food (MAFF), which was superseded by the DEFRA in 2001. Although MAFF's Euro-enthusiasm could partly be attributed to the issue of subsidies for farmers and thus the operation of the Common Agricultural Policy (CAP), what also enhanced the Ministry's involvement in EU agricultural policy making was the specialist, and sometimes scientific, nature of many aspects of agricultural policy. As Kassim observes: 'Some departments have a monopoly over technical expertise which may make it difficult for other actors to challenge their positions' (Kassim, 2000: 28).

Consequently, MAFF enjoyed what Geddes characterizes as 'close and intensive ties with EU institutions and other member states'. Indeed, Geddes suggests that its role and relationship *vis-à-vis* the EU 'gave MAFF a *raison d'etre* … when its core functions centred on subsidies and marketising intervention had become deeply outmoded ideas in Whitehall' (Geddes, 2004: 164). This point is also emphasized by Marsh et al. (2001: 217) when they observe that: 'The impact of European agricultural policy has been to save [the] department', while in the late 1980s, a former senior mandarin in MAFF reflected that: 'In Whitehall terms, it has moved the Ministry from the periphery to the centre' (quoted in Bulmer and Burch, 2009: 128). Indeed, Bulmer and Burch suggest that by the mid-1990s, 'agriculture and fisheries had arguably become the most Europeanised policy areas' (Bulmer and Burch, 2009: 128).

Intermediate layer

Three particular departments have experienced either increasing Europeanization, or have found that some of their responsibilities have a strong European dimension, while others remain largely unaffected by the EU. As such, their degree of Europeanization has not been extensive enough to place them in the 'inner core', but they have definitely been more affected by the EU than the departments located in the 'outer' core.

The Home Office

The Home Office has often evinced an ambivalent stance towards the EU and the process of European integration, depending on the particular issues within the department's broad-ranging remit. On matters pertaining to international crime, drug trafficking, human trafficking/sex slavery and terrorism, the Home Office has often found it advantageous, or even essential, to cooperate with its EU counterparts in order to devise or administer policies to address these transnational issues, albeit through intergovernmental cooperation facilitated by the Justice and Home Affairs 'pillar' of the Maastricht Treaty. In this context, the Home Office is among the departments 'that have significantly enhanced their engagement' due to the need for collaboration and cooperation on problems which cannot be tackled by any one EU member state alone (Bulmer and Burch, 2006: 47. See also Geddes, 2013: 201).

However, with regard to EU policies that might impinge upon domestic control of Britain's borders (most notably asylum and immigration), criminal justice, penal policy and policing, the Home Office has been strongly 'concerned with limiting EU competence, maintaining sovereignty and protecting perceived national interests' (Buller and Smith, 1998: 176).

The Home Office's insistence on retaining policy autonomy and thus resisting further Europeanization in these spheres is particularly significant because of the political sensitivity surrounding emotive issues like asylum, immigration and crime; these are issues on which many people have strong, and often authoritarian, views and so the Home Office is deeply concerned to resist any EU measures that would (further) reduce the department's policy autonomy. As a result: 'The Home Office's aim is to keep decision-making at an intergovernmental level in order to oppose imposition from above' (Marsh et al., 2001: 222–3).

This intergovernmental approach was evident 13 years later when the Home Secretary Theresa May informed Parliament that Britain would be opting out of all pre-Lisbon Treaty EU police and criminal justice measures (due to come into effect in 2014), 'for reasons of principle, policy and pragmatism', whereupon 'we should seek to rejoin only those measures that help us co-operate with our European neighbours to combat cross-border crime and keep our country safe'. May reiterated her conviction that 'the UK's international relations in policing and criminal justice are first and foremost a matter for Her Majesty's Government' (House of Commons Debates, 2013: v. 566, c. 177).

Ministry of Defence

Similarly, the Ministry of Defence has broadly welcomed some EU developments, but been deeply sceptical about others; some EU initiatives have been viewed as opportunities, while others have been deemed to be threats. Like the Home Office, the Ministry of Defence became more affected by Europeanization as a consequence of the Maastricht Treaty, and in particular, the adoption of a common foreign and security policy (CFSP). To the extent that the CFSP facilitated intergovernmental cooperation between member states on military matters and security issues, albeit primarily concerned with peace-keeping expeditions and humanitarian intervention, the Ministry of Defence was generally supportive.

Moreover, the 1998 St. Malo Declaration heralded an agreement between the British and French government to establish a European 'Rapid Reaction Force' (RRF), which would enable the swift deployment of troops, military transport and weapons from member states to deal with armed conflict and/or 'failed states', although again this would usually be in the guise of providing humanitarian aid or peace-keeping. For the Blair government, part of the impetus for such an initiative was to ensure that the EU could respond effectively to another humanitarian disaster like that engendered by the war in Bosnia during the first half of the 1990s, following the break up of Yugoslavia.

However, the Ministry of Defence, and successive British governments and Prime ministers, have insisted that neither the CFSP nor the RRF will jeopardize or supersede Britain's 'special relationship' with the USA, nor will they supplant the central role of the North Atlantic Treaty Organization (NATO) as the primary institution for pursuing international peace, security and stability.

In this respect, the Ministry of Defence and British political leaders would emphasize that the RRF is not a European army (as it is sometimes referred to), because there is no permanent armed force or 'standing army' under central European command. For the RRF to be activated requires unanimous intergovernmental agreement (it cannot be ordered by the EU), and even in such an eventuality, any troops or other military resources are deployed by member states themselves. The fact that any activation of the RRF requires unanimity among member states means that Britain (or any other EU state) can veto a proposed deployment with which it disagrees.

The Ministry of Defence subsequently became somewhat more 'Europeanized' as a consequence of the post-1999 establishment of a European Defence and Security Policy (EDSP) – still under the auspices of the CFSP – since military representatives have served on the UK Permanent Representation (UKREP) in Brussels (discussed below). However, this particular mode of Europeanization has not generally proved problematic for the Ministry of Defence because 'the UK is in the vanguard of the EDSP's development' (Bulmer and Burch, 2009: 161), rather than the initiative being imposed by the EU.

Department of Work and Pensions

Since being established in 2001, the Department of Work and Pensions has experienced an uneven process of Europeanization, with the EU impacting on some spheres of the department's remit, but with others continuing to enjoy considerable autonomy. Probably the most notable aspect of the department's EU involvement concerns the administration of social security benefits, such as old age pensions, for British citizens who are now resident in a country with which Britain has a 'reciprocal agreement' *vis-à-vis* welfare payments. Many of these agreements, though, are with countries beyond the EU.

The other main sphere in which the EU has impacted upon the responsibilities of the Department of Work and Pensions is via the European Social Fund (ESF). This is intended to improve the skills, and thus employment opportunities, of individuals and communities experiencing serious socio-economic deprivation, most notably high levels of unemployment and poverty (or 'social exclusion'). The Department of Work and Pensions is responsible for administering these funds, which between 2007 and 2013 totalled £2.5 billion, with the British government contributing another £2.5 billion. This is another example of 'match funding'.

The outer core

Several departments have so far experienced only limited or occasional impact from Europeanization, particularly those concerned with social policy, such as the Department of Education, and the Department of Health. The Department of Transport has also retained considerable autonomy *vis-à-vis* the EU.

Department of Education

The Department of Education has been relatively unaffected by Europeanization to date, and to the extent that it has been obliged to respond to EU policies, the responses have usually pertained to employment-related issues when the department had a wider range of responsibilities in its earlier guises, or student exchange schemes (via SOCRATES and ERASMUS) when universities were within the jurisdiction of the department.

In terms of primary and secondary education, though, the department has retained considerable autonomy from the EU, with British policy makers still determining key aspects of curriculum content in Britain's schools, along with the range of qualifications attained by pupils, teacher training, and since the 1990s, the type of schools, coupled with the regime of inspections by Ofsted. None of these aspects have been much affected by, or enacted in response to, Directives emanating from the EU.

Department of Health

Similarly, the Department of Health 'is not ... especially Europeanised' (Bulmer and Burch, 2009: 166). Its main European-orientated activity concerns the administration of the E1/11 scheme, which has now been superseded by the European Health Insurance Card. These enable(d) EU citizens to obtain healthcare and treatment in other EU member states, thereby obviating the need to return home immediately in the event of illness or injury while on holiday.

One other issue that has compelled the Department of Health to engage with the EU is that of the long hours worked by junior doctors. This issue acquired a European dimension because of the EU's Working Hours Directive, which stipulated that employees could not be compelled to work more than 48 hours per week; any excess over this time limit had to be voluntarily pursued by workers, such as paid overtime. As junior doctors in Britain have traditionally worked more than 48 hours per week, this particular EU Directive caused considerable consternation for the Department of Health, until it secured an exemption for medics.

Department of Transport

Although some member states have experienced considerable EU influence over their transport policies, Britain has remained relatively unaffected (Glaister et al., 2006: 131), which means that the Department of Transport has retained most of its autonomy. Indeed, in some spheres of transport policy since the 1980s, most notably the liberalization both of air transport and the road haulage industry (Bulmer et al., 2007: 55–61; Glaister et al., 2006: 131), reforms in Britain have either acted as an impetus or exemplar for the EU itself, or have preceded similar reforms in other member states. In this context at least, far from being a laggard or 'reluctant' European seeking to slow down or opt-out of policy initiatives emanating from Brussels, Britain seems to have 'led the way' with regard to various transport policies, and thereby illustrated that in a European (or wider global) context, nation states do not always have policies imposed upon them in a top-down manner, but can themselves 'export' or promote policies in a bottom-up fashion.

Probably the most contentious issue pertaining to European transport policy was the requirement, in the 1980s, that tachographs (commonly known as the 'spy in the cab') be fitted in lorries and coaches in order to measure the movement of such vehicles. The purpose was to monitor the number of hours that drivers were being required to work and *inter alia*, how long they were being granted for breaks or other rest periods. In effect, tachographs were supposed to be linked to health and safety in the road haulage industry and passenger transport, by ensuring that drivers of commercial vehicles were not compelled to work for such long hours that they became unduly tired, and thus more likely to cause a serious accident by falling asleep at the wheel.

However, many British politicians and transport employers opposed the installation of tachographs, partly on the grounds of the costs that would be incurred in fitting them, but also because it was argued that Britain's drivers were already protected, via employment and other health and safety legislation, against 'excessive' working hours. Britain only accepted the installation of tachographs in commercial vehicles after the dispute was referred to the European Court of Justice, which overruled the objections of the British government.

Further aspect of uneven impact

It must be emphasized that while 'Europeanization' is widely perceived to be a top-down process affecting nation states, and arguably challenging their very viability and efficacy as geo-political institutions, it is also the case that the EU itself needs the cooperation and compliance of member nation states in order to achieve its objectives. In other words, Europeanization should not be simply viewed as a linear, one-way, top-down policy process, in which Britain always fatalistically or grudgingly accepts policy initiatives invoked and then imposed by the EU. Instead, opportunities exist for member states to influence to varying degrees, and according to circumstances, policies at European level through a process of 'uploading' policy proposals or preferences.

This indicates that 'Europeanization' is not always a one-way, top-down process – as Eurosceptics tend to imply – but a two-way process, whereby on certain policy issues or in certain policy sub-systems, domestic policy actors can seek to shape the EU policy agenda, or at least skilfully exploit that agenda to further their own policy objectives. In other words, Europeanization does not merely entail a top-down imposition of policies on Britain by the EU, but can also enable British policy actors to participate in a 'bottom-up' promotion of policies up to the EU.

In this context, one writer has discerned three broad responses by member states towards the EU with regard to public policy: pace-setting, fence-sitting and foot-dragging. This approach emphasizes the extent to which 'Europeanization is a two-way process. It entails a "bottom-up" and "top-down" dimension'. As such, member states will sometimes take the initiative, or seek to set the EU's institutional agenda, by 'actively pushing policies at the European level, which reflect a Member State's policy preferences' (Börzel, 2002: 194). In such instances, individual member states can act as pace setters in the EU, so that 'domestic policies are exported to the European level and subsequently adopted by other Member States' (Börzel, 2002: 197).

For example, it could be argued that the process of liberalization pursued by the EU since the 1980s, and enshrined in the 1986 Single European Act, was partly influenced by the neo-liberal economic policies and privatization programme pursued by the Thatcher governments in Britain during the 1980s. In this context, far from being the EU's foot-dragging member state, Britain acted as a pace setter within the EU, promoting policies of economic liberalization and deregulation that were subsequently adopted by other member states in the EU, and became primary objectives of the Commission (see Bulmer et al., 2007: 55–6, 185–9).

Certainly, a senior official in the Department of Trade and Industry once claimed that: 'We have … become one of the departments that has been arguing for deregulation in Europe, or at least better regulation', while another departmental official not only claimed that 'the EU has enhanced the autonomy of the DTI', it had also 'allowed the DTI to make policy at the EU level rather than in Whitehall' (Marsh et al., 2001: 220).

Even when a member state such as Britain is unable to influence the formulation of an EU policy in a particular manner, the EU will still be heavily dependent on the member state(s) to implement the policy in the manner intended, so that national or sub-national level policy actors become, in effect, the street level bureaucrats. Seen from this perspective, 'the interplay between the EU system and the British polity appears to be characterised by complex feedback loops', and 'European [policy] inputs rarely, if ever, enter Britain without modification' (Rosamond, 2000: 59).

COORDINATING EU POLICY

The impact of Europeanization on various government departments, albeit varied and uneven, has made it increasingly important to develop mechanisms and processes for coordinating EU-influenced policies, both within the core executive, mainly between affected departments, and between the core executive and the EU itself. Coordination within the core executive is primarily the responsibility of the Cabinet Committee on European affairs, aided by the Cabinet Office's European and Global Issues Secretariat (COEGIS) – we noted in Chapter 4 how the Cabinet Office services and supports the Cabinet and its sundry committees.

The Cabinet Committee on European Affairs

This particular Cabinet committee is responsible for discussing and coordinating governmental and ministerial responses to EU policies, mainly with regard to the latter's impact on, or implications for, departmental policies. As Box 7.1 shows, it naturally comprises those ministers whose departments are most directly involved in, or affected by, Europeanization. So, for example, the Secretary of State for Business, Innovation and Skills, the Secretary of State for Environment, Food and Rural Affairs and the Secretary of State for Energy and Climate Change are members, whereas the Secretaries of State for Health, and Transport are not.

Box 7.1   Membership of the Cabinet Committee on European Affairs by ministerial post

- Secretary of State for Foreign and Commonwealth Affairs (FCO) (Chair)
- Secretary of State for Energy and Climate Change (Deputy Chair)
- Chancellor of the Exchequer
- Secretary of State for Home Department
- Secretary of State for Business, Innovation and Skills
- Lord Chancellor, Secretary of State for Justice
- Secretary of State for Environment, Food and Rural Affairs
- Secretary of State for Communities and Local Government
- Chief Secretary to the Treasury
- Secretary of State for Scotland
- Minister of State – Cabinet Office
- Minister of State – Europe
- Minister of State – Ministry of Justice
- Minister of State – FCO/Business, Innovation and Skills
- Chief Whip.

(Source: Gov.UK, 2013b)

However, because of the broadness and generality of its remit (namely strategic oversight and coordination), this committee is served by a sub-committee, comprised entirely of Junior Ministers, which focuses on more detailed or day-to-day aspects of British public policy that are affected by the EU. In so doing, this sub-committee further facilitates interdepartmental/interministerial coordination of EU policies within the core executive. The functional membership of this sub-committee is listed in Box 7.2.

Box 7.2   Membership of the Cabinet Sub-committee on European Affairs

Minister of State – Europe (Chair)
Minister of State – Justice (Deputy Chair)
Minister of State – Environment, Food and Rural Affairs
Minister of State – Cabinet Office
Minister of State – Home Office

(Continued)

(Continued)

Minister of State – Work and Pensions
Minister of State for Energy and Climate Change
Minister of State – Transport
Minister of State – Foreign and Commonwealth Office/Business, Innovation and Skills
Financial Secretary to the Treasury
Parliamentary Under Secretary, Culture Media and Sport
Deputy Chief Whip

(Source: Gov.UK, 2013b)

Coordination and liaison between the core executive and the EU itself is facilitated by three bodies, namely the Cabinet Office's European and Global Issues Secretariat, the UK Permanent Representation to the European Union (UKREP) in Brussels, and the Foreign Office (Allen, 2013: 120). Bulmer and Burch (2009: 100) refer to these three bodies as 'the triad; they are at the heart of the handling of EU policy' within Whitehall.

The Cabinet Office's European and Global Issues Secretariat

Within the Cabinet Office, the Secretariat that has responsibility for dealing with EU issues has been subject to various restructuring and renaming over the years. For example, under New Labour, it was simply the Cabinet Office European Secretariat, but since the May 2010 formation of the Conservative-Liberal Democrat coalition, it has become the European and Global Issues Secretariat (COEGIS).

In fostering coordination of EU policy within the core executive, COEGIS performs several specific roles, namely:

- Supporting the Prime Minister, Deputy Prime Minister and the Cabinet Office Minister for Government Policy in their dealings with other political leaders *vis-à-vis* EU issues and policies, including attendance at meetings and summits, such as European Councils.
- Liaising with senior officials in other EU member states on aspects of EU policy that affect Britain and its interests.
- Servicing the Cabinet Committee on European affairs, which is chaired by the Foreign Secretary.
- Hold regular meetings with the UK's ambassador to the EU and other senior Whitehall officials involved in dealing with EU matters in their departments.

(Cabinet Office, 2013c)

As can be seen from these functions, COEGIS works closely with 10 Downing Street, liaising both with the Prime Minister directly and their staff in the Policy Unit.

The UKREP in Brussels

A vital conduit between London and Brussels, and thus the core executive and the EU, is provided by the UKREP in Brussels, which both conveys the policy preferences and concerns of British policy makers to key EU policy actors – especially the European Commission, and the Committee of Permanent Representatives (COREPER, although there are actually two of these bodies, as explained below) – and keeps British policy makers informed of policy developments and imminent proposals emanating from the EU.

As such, UKREP is a key two-way channel of information between British and EU policy makers, what Geddes (2013: 125) characterizes as 'the bridge between domestic and EU politics', and what Nugent has described as 'a sort of embassy to the EU ... the "eyes and ears" of the government in Brussels' (Nugent, 2000: 211).

Comprising approximately 130 staff overall (the precise figure fluctuates over time), and headed by a Permanent Representative and a Deputy Permanent Representative, UKREP includes 11 thematic 'teams', each dealing with a particular sphere of EU policy, while another team provides legal advice and support. The 11 thematic teams are listed in Box 7.3.

Box 7.3   The 'thematic' teams of UKREP

- Common Foreign and Security Policy/Common Security and Defence Policy (CSDP)
- CSDP/enlargement
- Competitiveness and markets
- Economics, finance and taxation
- EU aid projects
- External relations/trade, development, Africa, Asia and the Americas
- Justice and home affairs
- Legal advice
- Political and institutional affairs
- Regions and agriculture
- Social and environment
- UK Military Representative (UKMILREP)

(Source: Gov.UK, 2013c)

Most of these teams comprise between 10 and 16 staff, although legal advice, EU aid projects and UKMILREP have just 4–7 staff. In each team, individual staff are allocated a specific set of policy responsibilities; for example, in the Justice and Home Affairs team, one member deals with issues concerning cyber security, counter terrorism and data exchange issues, while in the Regions and Agriculture team, someone focuses on veterinary affairs and food, encompassing animal health and welfare, meat hygiene and veterinary medicines. These two examples also indicate the often highly specialist or technical character of much routine EU business, in contrast to the high profile disputes between British ministers and Brussels which are regularly reported in the media.

Most of the staff serving UKREP are civil servants who are seconded to Brussels as part of their career development. Of course, this means that when their secondment ends and they return to Whitehall, they will be able to utilize their expertise of EU policy issues within their department. This, in turn, will further contribute to the accretive Europeanization of the core executive. Indeed, the *Civil Service Management Code* (Cabinet Office, 2011b: Chapter 10, section 10.4.1) states that:

> Departments and agencies should encourage staff with potential to consider service with the European institutions as part of their developmental training. Work in the institutions should normally be regarded as experience which will be valuable to the department or agency on the officer's return.

Meanwhile, the UK Permanent Representative, a post of ambassadorial rank, sits on the Committee of Permanent Representatives (COREPER) II, which deals with matters of 'high politics' (Geddes, 2013: 126), most notably economic affairs, financial policy, foreign policy, defence and security. The Deputy Permanent Secretary serves on COREPER I, which focuses mainly on consumer rights, social affairs, energy, environmental issues and transport, along with aspects of the single market.

The work of both COREPERs is often highly administrative and technical, and plays a significant role in resolving detailed issues and problems behind the scenes, in advance of meetings of ministers who will formally take the final decisions, usually via the Council of the European Union (previously the Council of Ministers) (Wall, 2008: 194). The expertise acquired by UKREP, coupled with its cultivation of links and networks in Brussels, means that it also plays an important role in proffering advice to Britain's ministers when the latter are attending meetings of the Council of the EU.

In addition to these policy-orientated teams, each of the devolved governments have opened their own offices in Brussels and established close links with UKREP. Indeed, by virtue of their Brussels' staff, the devolved Scottish and Welsh governments are regarded as 'part of the UKREP family', thereby ensuring the maintenance of close relations, regular contact and attendance at relevant meetings (Bulmer and Burch, 2009: 175; Keating, 2010: 158).

The Foreign and Commonwealth Office

Britain's membership of the EC/EU initially had a broadly positive impact on the Foreign and Commonwealth Office (FCO), by imbuing it with a significantly enhanced and renewed role following Britain's loss of Empire and the decline of the Commonwealth. According to one senior mandarin in the FCO, 'I think we may be particularly conscious in the Foreign Office that the UK's future on the international stage is very much bound up with it being a major player in Europe' (quoted in Marsh et al., 2001: 226).

Initially, the FCO often took the lead in many of Britain's negotiations with the EC/EU, and in so doing, acted as something of a conduit between the core executive and Brussels. However, since the 1990s, as various departments have become increasingly Europeanized due to the expansion of EU policy competences, they have developed more direct links with officials in Brussels and their counterparts in other governments, linkages which were strengthened as the relevant ministers attended meetings of the Council of the European Union. This stronger departmental and ministerial role was also facilitated by the growing technicality or administrative complexity of many EU policies and regulations.

As a consequence, the FCO saw its former coordinating and diplomatic role (viz. the EU and Brussels) diminish slightly during the 1990s and early 2000s, partly because ministers and departments acquired experience and expertise in dealing directly with the EU, but also because coordination was increasingly undertaken both by the former Cabinet Office's European Secretariat (now the European and Global Issues Secretariat) and UKREP. Thus did a 2010–11 inquiry into the role of the Foreign Office, by the House of Commons Select Committee on Foreign Affairs, suggest that: 'The FCO's institutional position in the government's handling of EU business is ambiguous', for although it was 'officially the lead government department on the EU', the coordinating role had been increasingly shared with the COEGIS and UKREP (House of Commons Foreign Affairs Committee, 2011: 61, paras. 133–4).

However, the influence of the FCO might be exercised indirectly or in a more subtle manner, because the Foreign Secretary chairs the Cabinet Committee on European affairs, while its sub-committee on European affairs is chaired by the Minister for Europe, who is also based in the Foreign and Commonwealth Office.

Furthermore the FCO enshrines several Directorates concerned with EU matters, operating under the auspices of the Economic and Consular Division. The two largest European Directorates (in terms of their remit and policy responsibilities) are those on EU Internal affairs and EU External affairs respectively. The responsibilities of these two Directorates are listed in Boxes 7.4 and 7.5.

Box 7.4   Responsibilities of the FCO's Europe Directorate – Internal

- Multiannual financial framework and EU budget
- Relations with the EU institutions
- EU economic reform, including the growth agenda and financial services
- Common agricultural and fisheries policies
- European council coordination
- Justice and home affairs
- Her Majesty's Government (HMG) engagement with the EU institutions.

(Source: http://www.fco.gov.uk/en/about-us/who-we-are/our-directorate/europe-globalization)

Box 7.5   Responsibilities of the FCO's Europe Directorate – External

- Coordination of EU external relations
- General Affairs and External Relations Council
- Gymnich (informal meetings of EU Foreign Ministers)

(Continued)

(Continued)

- Political and Security Committee
- G8 foreign policy
- Developing an effective neighbourhood policy
- EU parliamentary scrutiny
- European external action service
- Common foreign and security policy institutional issues
- European security and defence policy missions
- EU external spending.

(Source: http://www.fco.gov.uk/en/about-us/who-we-are/our-directorate/europe-globalization)

Formal coordination between UKREP, COEGIS and the FCO is secured through meetings, on Friday mornings, held in the Cabinet Office. Until the mid-2000s, these meeting were held on a weekly basis, but since then, their frequency has declined somewhat. They still take place on a Friday, but not every week, partly because electronic communication (email, texting, and so on) has made regular contact between the three bodies easier, thus slightly obviating the necessity of a regular meeting *every* week (Wall, 2008: 191).

When they do take place, though, these meetings are attended by the head of COEGIS and other senior members of this Secretariat, the UK Permanent Representative – although s/he now sometimes participates via a televisual link, rather than in person (Allen, 2013: 121) and senior officials from the FCO and the Treasury. Officials from other departments will also attend on an *ad hoc* basis when EU business pertaining to their policy remit is on the agenda for discussion.

These Friday morning meetings, which have 'become a central part of the process for handling EU matters', are primarily concerned to 'consider issues coming up in Councils or elsewhere during the coming week, and to settle matters of negotiation strategy, tactics and, if necessary, further preparation of an issue before proceeding with it' (Bulmer and Burch, 2009: 105–6). In this regard, one former UK Permanent Representative has described it as 'a kind of steering body', while an erstwhile head of COES deemed it 'vital' to ensuring that British officials and ministers adopt a 'coordinated position' when dealing with EU business (quoted in Bulmer and Burch, 2009: 10–16. See also Geddes, 2013: 203; James, 2011: 55; Nugent, 2000: 212).

GLOBALIZATION

Although links between nation states, most notably in terms of imports, exports and trade generally, are centuries old, the concept of globalization is relatively new. It refers to the manner in which countries, and thus their economies, political institutions and many social problems appear to be increasingly interconnected in the contemporary world, to the extent of raising serious questions about the very notion of the autonomous nation state and national sovereignty.

Although capital(ism) has never recognized or confined itself to national borders and geopolitical boundaries, many commentators believe that the world has entered a qualitatively new phase of international economic interdependence, hastened – as well as symbolized – by the collapse of the former Soviet Empire during 1989–90.

However, some academics believe that the scope or conceptual significance of globalization has been exaggerated (Hardt and Negri, 2000; Hirst and Thompson, 1996), because nation states still retain relative autonomy over many policy areas, and even when policies are agreed or imposed internationally, implementation is still usually via the nation states themselves. In this regard, nation states could be likened to the 'street-level bureaucrats', which we will discuss in the next chapter; the often overlooked or underestimated policy actors who actually implement or 'deliver' policies that have been formulated or agreed at a higher level. These 'street-level bureaucrats', and in this context, nation states, can therefore still play a significant role in interpreting and applying policies as they deem appropriate, perhaps adapting them to 'local' circumstances and conditions.

Other writers suggest that globalization is, to a very considerable degree, an ideological phenomenon or discourse that both reflects and reinforces the apparent hegemony of neo-liberalism since the 1980s (see, for example, Watson, 2005: Chapter 9). By depicting globalization as inevitable and immutable, those societal actors or elites who either benefit most from free market economics, and/or are ideologically committed to neo-liberalism, seek to convince the rest of the population that its pervasiveness is now unavoidable and irrevocable. Crucially, this then 'legitimizes' a range of specific policy preferences, which are depicted as essential or unavoidable in order to ensure the competitiveness of the domestic economy.

However, the 'costs' of such policies are mostly incurred by ordinary citizens in terms of reduced employment protection – the much-vaunted 'labour market flexibility' – relentless attempts at driving down labour costs (via wage curbs or job losses) and the reduction of public expenditure and welfare provision, in order to fund tax cuts that disproportionately benefit wealthy individuals and corporations.

For the purpose of our discussion, globalization refers to:

> ... the multiplicity of linkages and interconnections that transcend the nation-states (and by implication the societies) which make up the modern world system ... Nowadays, goods, capital, people, knowledge, images, communications, crime, culture, pollutants, drugs, fashions, beliefs all readily flow across territorial boundaries ... the existence of global systems of trade, finance and production binds together, in very complicated ways, the prosperity and fate of households, communities and nations across the globe.
>
> (McGrew, 1992: 65–6)

As such, globalization is deemed to involve both a widening and deepening of 'interconnectedness' between countries and institutions of governance (Giddens, 1991: 187). It entails 'widening' by virtue of the increasing number of linkages between nation states, which are themselves increasingly mediated between international institutions, such as the EU (discussed above), G7 (or G8, as it has become since the accession of Russia), the IMF and NATO.

Although these particular organizations pre-date the current (or latest) phase of globalization, they nonetheless symbolize the manner in which countries, their governments and other national policy actors are increasingly forming or joining transnational bodies to coordinate economic, military and political activities and policy making. For example, in 1909, there existed 37 international governmental organizations (IGOs) and 176 international non-governmental organizations (INGOs), but by 1996, there were 260 IGOs and 5,472 INGOs (Held et al., 1999: 4).

It also entails a 'deepening' of these interconnections, though, as they become more complex and exert a correspondingly greater impact on the citizens and policy makers of particular countries. There is deemed to be a growing interdependence between countries and national governments, as they are increasingly obliged to confront common problems – AIDS, asylum seekers, drug trafficking, global warming, organized crime, pollution, terrorism, and so on – which cannot be effectively tackled independently by nation states or national governments acting in isolation. For example, since 9/11, the USA has repeatedly called upon the 'international community' to help defeat terrorism.

Although globalization manifests itself in a variety of ways and is evident in such spheres as cultural developments, military activity and social movements, it is often the economic aspects that are viewed as most important, or even the underlying impetus. According to Marxist writers such as Wallerstein, globalization is ultimately fuelled by capitalism's relentless expansionist tendencies, with companies and corporations constantly searching for new markets, raw materials, cheap labour, and ultimately, new sources of profit. He believes that during the latter part of the 20th century, capitalism became truly global to the extent that 'the entire globe is operating within the framework of … the capitalist world-economy' (Wallerstein, 1984: 13. See also Wallerstein, 1979; Wallerstein, 1983).

Not dissimilarly, Sklair, observes the establishment of a 'global system' in terms of 'transnational practices', of which the transnational corporation is the primary economic manifestation, 'the major locus of transnational economic practices', while a parallel 'transnational capitalist class is the major locus of transnational political practices'. As such, 'the global economic system, based on a variegated global capitalist class … unquestionably dictates economic transnational practices while also seeking to maintain ideological and political dominance' (Sklair, 1991: 5–6).

This view is shared by Robinson, who claims that an international capitalist class has developed, as a consequence of globalization, 'unifying the world into a single mode of production and a single global system, and bringing about the organic integration of different countries and regions into a global economy' (Robinson, 2001: 158).

Some writers have noted how the economic dynamics underpinning globalization have been enhanced by technological developments. For example, Castells notes that:

Capital is managed around the clock in globally integrated financial markets working in real time for the first time in history: billion dollars' worth of transaction take place in seconds in the electronic circuits through the globe. It is now the case that due to the expansion of capital and technological changes, savings, investments and currencies are now interconnected world-wide.

(Castells, 1996: 93. See also Urry, 1989: 97; Held, 1989: 193)

The development of an increasingly interconnected global economic system has, in turn, resulted in the development of new forms of international economic governance, as various nation states and national governments seek to secure a degree of order and predictability in a regime with the potential for considerable instability. In other words, the economic consequences of globalization have fostered attempts at political cooperation and coordination through sundry international organizations, as well as *ad hoc* summits attended by political leaders and/or finance ministers.

THE IMPACT OF GLOBALIZATION ON POLICY MAKING IN BRITAIN

Globalization has impacted – and continues to impact – upon Britain, both in institutional terms and with regard to various policies, particularly those of an economic character. However, there appears to have been less public and political concern about the impact of globalization on Britain compared to the anxiety about 'Europeanization', partly, perhaps, because the process and its ramifications are somehow more subtle and more difficult to discern, and partly because Britain has been one of the 'core' nations anyway, so that membership of various international institutions has not yielded the same fears about 'surrendering' sovereignty in quite the same manner as EU membership and integration have done.

Indeed, one might suggest that the psychological and historical legacy of formerly presiding over an Empire, and then, Commonwealth, which spanned the globe, has rendered Britain more at ease about involvement in global politics – particularly in view of the alleged 'special relationship' with the contemporary hegemon, the USA – whereas considerable unease continues to underpin Britain's relationship with Europe. For example, Britain is a member of several key economic, diplomatic and military bodies beyond the EU level, as illustrated by Figure 7.1.

However, it is with regard to economic and industrial policies that globalization seems to have imposed the greatest constraints on the autonomy of British policy makers. In an era of multinational corporations and international finance, coupled with the ability of large companies and financial institutions to shift billions of pounds from one location to another around the globe, it has been deemed axiomatic that Britain ensures that economic, employment and fiscal policies are conducive to attracting and then retaining overseas companies, thereby maintaining the flow of inward investment upon which so many jobs have come to depend.

In this context, policy makers in Britain have increasingly had to accept certain limits with regard to aspects of economic and employment policies, such as tax rates, the level of the statutory minimum wage, the scope of employment protection legislation, and so on,

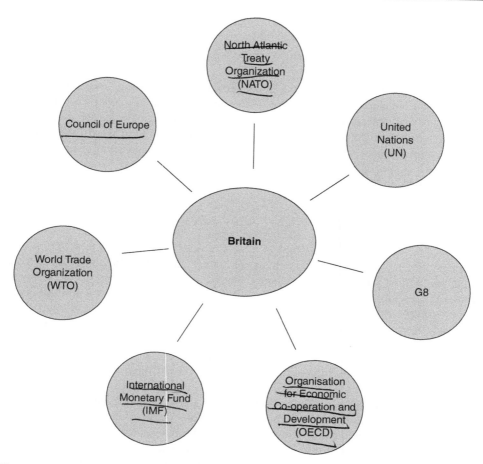

Figure 7.1   Britain's membership of key international bodies (beyond the EU)

for fear that setting any of these 'too high' will prompt a 'flight of capital' or a decision by a foreign company not to open a factory or headquarters in Britain. Or as one political theorist has expressed it:

> ... the internationalization of production, finance and other economic resources is unquestionably eroding the capacity of the state to control its own economic future. At the very least, there appears to be a diminution of state autonomy, and a disjuncture between the idea of a sovereign state determining its own future and the conditions of modern economies, marked as they are by the intersection of national and international economic processes.

(Held, 1989: 194)

The economic aspects of globalization also have ramifications for ostensibly non-economic policies and institutions, as evinced by political attempts at 'reforming' (invariably a euphemism for reducing) the welfare state. Many British policy makers seem to have readily accepted that the post-1945 welfare state is no longer economically viable, due to the 'punitive' level of taxation required to fund it and which is assumed to deter investment in Britain, both by domestic entrepreneurs and multinational companies.

Meanwhile, the post-1980 evisceration of trade unions and concomitant weakening of statutory employment protection (workers' rights) have often been justified partly on the grounds that 'labour market flexibility' is vital to securing inward investment, or to prevent companies currently located in Britain from transferring their operations and resources overseas to countries that offer lower taxes and/or weaker employment protection.

Similarly, British politicians will routinely exhort workers not to pursue 'excessive' pay claims, lest they either deter overseas companies from investing in Britain, or drive out companies already operating here, but who decide to relocate overseas in search of lower labour (wage) costs. In the context of globalization, holding down workers' wages is invariably deemed essential to ensure the 'competitiveness' of the British economy.

Of course, when the criterion of 'competitiveness' is applied to the salaries of bankers, company directors or chief executives, the result is often huge (six- or seven-figure) salaries, accompanied by warnings that they themselves will leave the country if they are not generously rewarded for their professed business acumen or leadership skills. For example, since the 2008 international banking crisis that precipitated the recent global recession, senior bankers in 'the City' (of London) have repeatedly threatened to emigrate if any curbs are imposed on their huge salaries or bonuses, or if ministers seek to curb the power and role of the banks in response to the 2008 financial crash.

In making such threats, 'the City' alludes to the jobs that it provides (directly or indirectly), the 'trickle down' effect of consumer spending by highly-paid bankers, and the taxes paid by the banks and their staff, all of which will be lost to the British government if it 'attacks' the banking industry. In view of the fluidity and mobility of finance – technology (and the absence of exchange controls) means that enormous sums of money can be moved across the globe with considerable ease and speed – ministers are invariably inclined to take such threats very seriously indeed.

Although, as we have noted above, some writers believe that the scale of globalization has been exaggerated, many policy makers act as if it were a self-evident fact that must be responded to, rather than refuted. Or as Higgott has remarked: 'The reconfiguration of UK politics, especially the management of the functions of the state, is … increasingly determined by – or at least influenced by – the perceptions of the impact of globalization' (Higgott, 1998: 20). Certainly, some of the most senior figures associated with New Labour insist on the need both to acknowledge the constraints imposed on Britain by globalization, and on the necessity of embracing the apparent opportunities that it offers.

For example, with regard to the constraints imposed on Britain's economic policies by globalization, the Chancellor Gordon Brown, in a July 1998 speech to a News International conference, explained that:

> The first objective national governments must have, in a global market place, is to maximise economic stability ... For in a global economy, funds will flow to those countries whose policies inspire confidence, and investors punish mistakes more quickly and severely than in the past. Both the old Keynesian fine-tuning, and the rigid application of fixed monetary targets were policies designed for sheltered national economies, and based on apparently stable and predictable relations which have now broken down in modern, liberalised and global capital markets.

However, while globalization is clearly placing certain constraints on the autonomy of national policy actors, this does not meant that the nation state and its political institutions are becoming obsolete (as some of the more extreme or utopian theorists of globalization sometimes assume). Instead, international policy responses to transnational problems are still mediated through national-level actors or representatives, both when policies are being developed via arenas such as NATO or G7(8), and when agreed policies are subsequently being implemented at national level. Or as Robinson observes, nation states increasingly function as 'transmission belts and filtering devices for the imposition' of policies and programs agreed at the global level (Robinson, 2001: 188).

At the same time, it is an exaggeration or over simplification to assume that the need to attract inward investment or prevent a flight of capital will automatically and inevitably lead policy makers to seek to dismantle the welfare state and constantly curb public expenditure (in order to minimize taxation and other economic costs). Such a highly reductionist or determinist account of the impact of globalization on domestic or national policy makers overlooks the extent to which companies might consider other factors when making decisions about investment and (re)location of production, such as education and training provision, and the skills of the indigenous labour force.

In other words, some investment decisions will involve a trade off between low taxes and low unit labour costs on the one hand, and the level of provision of collective or public goods, human capital and various supply side measures on the other. In this respect:

> ... the conventional view about the impact of the multi-nationalization of production and financial integration on national economic policy regimes is overly simplistic. Managers of multi-national enterprises and mutual funds are not unsophisticated capitalists whose reaction to interventionist government is everywhere and always the same. Mobile capital may well choose to invest and produce in economies with interventionist governments. As a result, governments may retain considerably more autonomy in the era of global markets than is often presumed.

(Garrett, 2000: 114)

Similarly, Holton has argued that, while globalization certainly places limits on what national governments and domestic policy makers can do, multinational companies 'remain dependent on nation-states for certain types of resources in a range of circumstances' (Holton, 1998: 92). The implication of this is that 'there is still room for a good deal of effective domestic economic management' (Thompson, 1992: 214).

It also remains the case that even when a country's policy makers are signatories to international agreements or commitments, the national government and/or other domestic policy actors will ultimately be responsible for the enactment of the programme or policy, often with at least some discretion about how to implement it. In this respect, the increasing involvement of states (such as Britain) in international organizations and summits represents something of a paradox, but one which itself reflects the uneven, dialectical and contradictory character of globalization itself (for a discussion of which, see Held and McGrew, 2002; Holton, 1998; McGrew, 1992; Smith, 1992).

On the one hand, such involvement and the obligation to abide by certain international agreements reflects the acknowledged erosion of national autonomy caused by globalization, and the extent to which many problems cannot be adequately addressed on a purely national basis. On the other hand, though, international cooperation and mutual agreements provide a degree of order and predictability in an otherwise unstable and insecure world. This enables states to retain a degree of efficacy and competence, without which they would probably be completely destabilized and rendered impotent, whereupon their legitimacy in the eyes of their citizens would be grievously undermined.

In this context, it has been suggested that: 'Reciprocal sovereignty still constitutes the basis of the international order, and nation-states ... have been empowered because of their status as constitutive parts of a recognised [international] order' (Axford, 1995: 139). Or as Tony Blair (1999) expressed it, in a speech in Chicago in April 1999: 'If sovereignty mean's control over one's destiny and strength, then strength and control, in today's world, means forging alliances or falling behind'.

As such, although globalization undoubtedly places certain limits and constraints on the autonomy of British policy makers, either in the sense that they need to secure international cooperation for the pursuit of certain policies, or in the sense that they are obliged to adopt particular policies that they might not otherwise have freely chosen, it can also be argued that globalization offers new opportunities to British policy makers: international cooperation and agreements can enable policy makers in Britain to tackle problems that they would otherwise have been unable to address in isolation. This is particularly evident with regard to issues such as climate change, international crime and tax evasion.

Since the 1990s, there have been several international agreements to tackle the underlying causes of climate change and environmental degradation, most notably reductions in the carbon emissions (greenhouse gases), which many scientists believe are primarily responsible for global warming. Such agreements derive from recognition that environmental policies enacted in isolation by an individual country will have a negligible impact on climate change, hence the need for as many countries as possible to cooperate and reach agreement, and thus share responsibility for tackling global warming and associated environmental problems.

Meanwhile, tackling various types of crime also increasingly necessitates international cooperation between nation states and their law and order agencies. Just as many companies now operate globally, so too do many criminals, as evinced by the increase in (or greater awareness of) such phenomena as drug smuggling, human trafficking/sex slavery, money laundering and terrorism.

There has also been a growing political awareness in recent years of tax evasion and the amount of lost revenue this represents for the Treasury. Certainly, since 2010, the coalition's austerity measures and public expenditure cuts, enacted in order to tackle Britain's fiscal deficit – whereby government spending exceeds tax and other revenues – have raised awareness (and public anger) about the scale of tax evasion engaged in by many wealthy individuals and companies.

Although estimates of the amount of money lost to the Treasury by tax evasion vary enormously, precisely because of the degree of guess work involved, it has often been suggested that the figures are far greater than the amount of taxpayer's money lost through social security fraud, even though the latter generally attracts far greater opprobrium and critical media coverage.

As tax evasion usually entails individuals secretly transferring their incomes or funds to a bank account in another country, or multinational companies purporting to be based in a low-tax country (even when most of their profit-making activities are conducted else-where), national governments wishing to tackle this problem invariably need to reach agreements with those countries that 'receive' most of this money. As such, the Treasury has established agreements with several foreign governments and/or banks to retrieve money that should originally have been paid as tax in Britain. One such agreement was signed with Switzerland in October 2011, reflecting the Treasury's calculation that about 80 per cent of Swiss bank accounts held by British citizens, totalling £40 billion, entails money that is liable to taxation, but has not been declared. It was estimated that the signing of this agreement would yield the Treasury £3.2 billion in previously unpaid tax (Coates, 2013).

Elsewhere, a June 2013 meeting in Northern Ireland of the G8 group of countries (comprising Canada, France, Germany, Italy, Japan, Russia, the United Kingdom, and the USA) formally agreed a set of core principles to tackle tax evasion and share relevant information. However, critics were quick to claim that this agreement lacked the power or sanctions to ensure compliance by the signatories, and as such, the professed principles were unlikely to be matched by action or significant achievements; they were largely symbolic.

The summer of 2013 also heralded a 15-point action plan by the Organisation for Economic Cooperation and Development (OECD) to tackle global tax evasion, would facilitate international cooperation and coordination against companies that exploited loopholes in international tax laws, and as a consequence, often paid only minimal amounts of (corporation) tax on their profits (Pitel, 2013).

Meanwhile, an inquiry by the House of Commons Public Accounts Committee (2013: 12–14, paras.15–22) was highly critical of HM Revenue & Customs (HMRC) for not being much more robust or vigourous in tackling tax evasion by companies operating in Britain, some of whom only paid a small fraction of what they ought to pay.

POLICY TRANSFER

Although globalization and Europeanization are the two most obvious manifestations of the internationalization of public policy, a third aspect has become increasingly prevalent since the 1980s, namely 'policy transfer'. Two of the British academics who have done most to develop and popularize the concept in Britain are David Dolowitz and David Marsh, who have defined policy transfer as:

The process by which knowledge about policies, administrative arrangements, institutions and ideas in one political system (past or present) is used in the development of policies, administrative arrangements, institutions and ideas in another political system.

(Dolowitz and Marsh, 2000: 5. See also Deacon, 2000; Dolowitz, 1998; Dolowitz and Marsh, 1996; Dolowitz, 2000a: 3; Walker 1998)

Dolowitz believes that 'many of the changes in British public policy in the 1980s and 1990s can be traced directly to the process of policy transfer', most of it from the USA, which has been 'a source of ideas, inspirations, policies and institutions for various aspects of British public policy over the past twenty years' (Dolowitz, 2000a: 1–2). Certainly, Dolowitz and Marsh (2000: 5) believe, 'policy makers appear to be increasingly relying upon policy transfer'.

There are two main reasons why British policy makers have evinced a growing propensity for looking overseas for policy ideas or inspiration. The first is that the policies previously adopted have failed to eradicate a problem (and which has returned to the institutional agenda), thereby prompting policy makers to look abroad to see if another country has devised a more successful or seemingly ready-made solution.

The second reason why policy makers might look overseas for a policy solution is that they have recently encountered a new problem (or an issue which has now been defined as a problem) for which there is no precedent. In such circumstances, policy makers might seek a quick or ostensibly ready-made solution imported from overseas, even if this is only to give the impression of responding to public or media demands to 'do something'.

Three of the most notable examples of policy transfer since the 1990s are the Child Support Agency (CSA), 'welfare into work' and 'zero tolerance' policing.

The Child Support Agency

The CSA was established in Britain in 1993, two years after the Child Support Act had received the Royal Assent. The CSA, and the legislation on which it was based (the 1991 Child Support Act), reflected concern amongst a number of senior Conservatives from the late 1980s onwards about Britain's growing number of 'lone parents' (from 570,000 in 1971 to 1,150,000 by 1989), particularly 'unmarried mothers'.

While many Conservatives disapproved of 'lone parents' on moral grounds alone (believing that only a heterosexual, monogamous, marital relationship provided the proper basis for raising children), what reinforced a 'moral panic' about 'unmarried mothers' from the late 1980s was partly the costs in terms of welfare expenditure and social security entitlements (some Conservatives even claimed that Britain's 'generous' welfare state was encouraging young women to have illegitimate children in order to qualify for Income Support, rather than undertake paid employment), and partly the alleged link between 'single parents', juvenile delinquency and urban decay. In short, 'unmarried mothers' were not only deemed to be a major consequence of the 'permissive society' and a key component of the 'dependency culture', they were also considered a significant element of the emerging 'underclass' and juvenile criminality/gang culture, which social commentators were turning their attention to during this period.

Charles Murray, a conservative American sociologist, especially became a prominent critic of the underclass, believing that the welfare state in Britain was providing a perverse incentive to young working-class women to have children outside of marriage, as a 'life-style choice' or *de facto* career option, due both to their consequent eligibility for welfare support, and their apparent 'priority status' with regard to local authority housing.

Meanwhile, Murray argued, young working-class males had no incentive to be sexually responsible, for not only had the stigma or shame of 'illegitimacy' and 'pregnancy outside marriage' virtually disappeared from most parts of British society, these males knew that the welfare state would support 'their' children if they made a woman pregnant; they could, quite literally, leave her 'holding the baby' while they left to pursue their next short-term or casual relationship, or returned to 'hanging out' with their gang, and quite likely, engaging in petty crime either as a means of securing an income (instead of earning a wage through legitimate employment) or to alleviate the boredom of their empty and direction-less day-to-day lives.

At the same time, though, the illegitimate children of the growing number of unmarried mothers were raised without the presence of a male role model. This meant that the boys of unmarried mothers lacked a father who could provide authority and discipline to com-plement the mother's love and tender care, and so instead were likely to acquire values and behaviour patterns from their (often delinquent) peers and fellow 'gang members', who effectively became a surrogate family: they became 'feral children'.

Consequently, the children of unmarried mothers were deemed particularly prone to juvenile crime and delinquency, whereupon the inner city or urban housing estates where such lone parents tended to be located or 'dumped' by local authorities often became 'sink estates'. In turn, 'respectable' families moved away to escape the crime, vandalism, drug-dealing and general delinquency, whereupon the estate's downwards spiral and descent into a lawless virtual 'no-go' area (for the authorities and the police) continued (Murray, 1989; Murray, 1994a; Murray 1994b).

For social commentators such as Murray and many Conservatives, Britain was thus fac-ing a socio-demographic crisis by the 1990s and it was in this context that Conservative ministers began looking at ways of tackling this issue (it had now moved onto the institu-tional agenda). Given that Murray was himself American, and claimed that the socio-demographic trends he discerned in Britain were closely following those that had already manifested in the USA a decade or two earlier, it was, perhaps, only natural that British policy makers wondered how their American counterparts had addressed the problem.

Consequently, the then Minister of State for Social Security, Tony Newton, accompa-nied by senior officials from his department, visited Wisconsin, to see how the Americans had established what was believed to be the first child support system in the world, and one which was also deemed to be highly efficient. Enthused by what it observed, 'the Thatcher government transferred the design and structure of the Child Support Agency from the United States', although many of the agency's ensuing problems reflected a fail-ure by Conservative ministers to investigate the operation of child support more widely in the USA; 'the British government … concentrated on the Wisconsin system', elements of which subsequently proved inappropriate or inapplicable to Britain (Dolowitz, 2000b).

For example, in the Wisconsin version, lone parents were often permitted to keep a proportion of their social security payment, even after the absent father had paid child support, in order to help combat child poverty, whereas in Britain, the Treasury insisted that a lone parent's Income Support would be reduced by £1 for every £1 of child support that was received. In other words, rather than imbuing the child support system with an anti-poverty component, the British version was viewed (by the Treasury) primarily as a means of reducing public expenditure via the social security budget.

The case of the Child Support Agency therefore provides a salutary lesson of the need either to investigate the wider operation or impact of a particular policy in another country or to recognize the problems that are likely to arise from attempts at wholesale policy transfer, which fail to take account of politico-administrative, legal or cultural differences between Britain and other countries, or the slightly different objective or rationale of the policy in its country of origin prior to being 'transferred'.

Welfare into work

The second contemporary example of 'policy transfer' concerned the 'welfare into work' programme, initiated in Britain in the mid-1990s by the same (Conservative) government that launched the CSA, but which was developed further – and became more widely associated with – the New Labour/Blair governments since 1997. In certain respects, of course, welfare into work derived from many of the same socio-political concerns that underpinned the child support initiatives delineated above, most notably anxiety among some intellectuals and policy makers that Britain was experiencing the emergence of an underclass, whose 'members' were not only unemployed and part of a growing 'dependency culture', but who were also, in many cases, virtually 'unemployable', either because they lacked the requisite qualifications or training, or because they were not sufficiently imbued with the 'work ethic' to start with.

For New Labour especially, 'welfare into work' was inextricably linked with its professed determination to tackle social exclusion, and re-integrate those who were economically inactive and socially marginalized. It was also explicitly linked to New Labour's proudly proclaimed principle (although it was one which many, if not most, Conservatives could readily agree with) that citizens' rights had to be matched by responsibilities; in this particular case, welfare rights had to be matched by corresponding social responsibilities (see, for example, Department of Social Security, 1998: 23).

There was also an assumption that by tackling the 'social exclusion' of this nascent underclass, crime would also be reduced. In this respect, the manner in which 'welfare into work' apparently dovetailed into other New Labour social objectives was lauded as an indication of the professed desire to pursue 'joined-up government'.

Yet while 'welfare into work' seemed to correspond neatly to many other New Labour objectives, the origins of the policy largely emanated from the USA (Annesley, 2003: 157–9; Deacon, 2000; Driver and Martell, 1997; King and Wickham-Jones, 1999). In noting the similarities between Britain and the USA concerning this policy, Deacon emphasises the extent to which 'the British approach follows the American in its redefinition of welfare as a period of temporary assistance during which claimants would be equipped with the skills and capacities to re-enter the labour force, and then required to do so'. In making this observation, and *inter alia* noting that New Labour's welfare policy was no longer concerned with raising the level of social security benefits *per se* in order to tackle poverty, Deacon suggests that 'welfare into work' appeared to be 'yet another candidate for the new holy grail of transatlantic politics' (Deacon, 2000: 130).

'Zero tolerance' policing

A third example of 'policy transfer' was discernible in some of the Blair governments' law and order policies, particularly New Labour's advocacy of a 'zero tolerance' policy towards inner-city crime and anti-social behaviour. Once again, ministers looked across the Atlantic for inspiration, impressed, it seems, by the apparent success of Rudolph Giuliani, the Mayor of New York during much of the 1990s. Giuliani became synonymous with the 'zero tolerance' form of policing, whereby even minor misdemeanours were prosecuted, the reasoning being that if individuals went unpunished for committing petty crimes, many of them would proceed, unchecked, to more serious crimes and thereby become serial offenders.

This perspective was closely associated with the 'broken windows' metaphor originally deployed by Wilson and Kelling (1982. See also Kelling, 1998; Kelling and Coles, 1996), who argued that if a broken window was left unrepaired, a sense that 'no-one cares' was likely to develop, whereupon other windows in the building, and then the neighbouring buildings, were likely to be smashed, until the whole street or area became dilapidated and run down, and no 'respectable' citizens would want to live there.

Applying this metaphor to petty crime (which is certainly not petty to the victims, for whom it can be a source of fear and misery seriously affecting their quality of life, and emotional or psychological well-being), it was believed that if minor acts of law breaking or anti-social behaviour were not tackled, then criminality would exponentially increase, as the perpetrators realized that they could 'get away with it'. Ultimately, whole neighbourhoods would become blighted by crime and delinquent behaviour, and in extreme cases, perhaps become 'no-go' areas for ordinary citizens and even the local police.

In this context, 'zero tolerance' policing was supposed to deal firmly with even ostensibly petty crime and low-level disorder, and thereby pre-empt a drift into more serious criminality. This was elaborated upon by Alun Michael, who was appointed a Minister of State in the Home Office when New Labour was first elected in 1997. He explained that:

> One interpretation of 'zero tolerance' is fast police action to stop crime in its tracks and to protect the public. That interpretation had its place. But another interpretation is to 'nip things in the bud' when they start to go wrong, to recognise the patterns of behaviour which, if left to grow, will go from bad to worse. If graffiti starts to creep along a wall, they will soon take it over; while one broken window left unrepaired will start to feed a sense of decay as others follow.

> (Quoted in Jones and Newburn, 2007: 109)

More generally, by making the streets safer and restoring public confidence in the police and criminal justice system, it was envisaged that a process of urban regeneration would be instigated, as formerly run-down, even 'no go' districts began to attract new businesses and residents. Such a 'zero tolerance' policy has been widely credited with having made New York a much safer city, to the extent that the once dangerous, crime-ridden, district known as Alphabet City in the (Lower) East Village in Manhattan, and which tourists were strongly advised to avoid, has now become a trendy, bohemian district, and undergone major regeneration and gentrification.

This apparent success so impressed many senior figures in New Labour that in 1995, Labour's Shadow Home Secretary, Jack Straw, visited New York to observe for himself the impact of 'zero tolerance' policing. Thereafter, the influence of 'zero tolerance policing' could be discerned in the raft of policy initiatives, announced from 1997 onwards, to tackle relatively minor forms of crime and public disorder, such as public drunkenness, noise nuisance, graffiti, vandalism and 'aggressive' begging. Meanwhile, local authorities were empowered to apply for 'after dark' curfews to be imposed on children under the age of 15, while both the police and local authorities were entitled to seek the imposition of ASBOs on troublesome individuals, the breach of which could result in a custodial sentence.

These three examples indicate that since the early 1990s, policy transfer has become more prevalent in Britain, both reflecting and reinforcing the trend towards more pro-active Cabinet Ministers, and their quest for alternative or additional (to that traditionally provided by senior civil servants) sources of policy advice and inspiration.

The most recent example of policy transfer is provided by the post-2010 coalition government's promotion of Free Schools (see Hatcher, 2011; Lundahl, 2011, Nelson 2008). Although 'liberating' schools from LEA control has been integral to Conservative education policy since the 1980s at least, the main impetus for Free Schools in particular emanated from Sweden (a country more usually cited as an exemplar of egalitarianism, gender equality and successful social democracy!). As a Conservative Party (2007: 16) policy document explained:

> The country that provides the closest model for what we wish to do is Sweden. Over the past fifteen years, Sweden has introduced a new system that has allowed the creation of many new high quality state schools that are independent of political control. All parents have the power to take their child out of a state school and apply to a new independent state school ... The results? Hundreds of new schools have been started. Thousands of children have been saved from failing schools, and given a chance in life. In particular, thousands of children from the poorest areas have been able to escape failing state schools. And, crucially, standards have risen across all state schools because failing state schools have been forced to reform. These are the basic dynamics we will introduce into the British school system.

While it would seem entirely natural that Britain's policy makers should sometimes look to other countries in order to ascertain how they have addressed particular issues or tackled specific problems, it should be borne in mind that the decision to look overseas in the first place, and then whether or not to adopt (or adapt) the policies observed, is not necessarily an objective or 'rational' process. This is because looking overseas for examples or evidence of 'best practice' usually reflects a government's own ideological inclinations or political objectives in the first place.

In other words, policy makers will usually look to another country because they expect to find a particular policy solution that is commensurate with their own political philosophy or values. They will rarely look at several countries to gauge which of them has the 'best' policy (as a more 'rational' form of policy making would imply), but will instead select the country (or two) that is expected to provide the most appropriate or attractive (ideologically or politically) policy for addressing a particular issue or problem, or which might 'legitimize' ministers' existing policy preference.

This would account for the tendency of British policy makers to look first and foremost at the USA when searching for ideas and policies pertaining to key aspects of economic management, penal policy and welfare reform. As such, the Conservative Party's recent penchant for Sweden's 'free schools' is something of an exception to the usual rule of looking across the Atlantic, rather than the North Sea (or the English Channel), for policies to adopt.

CONCLUSION

The messiness of the policy process that we have emphasized at various points in this book has been further reflected and reinforced by the manner in which many policies have become affected or shaped by international factors and forces. While some policies have been devolved within Britain, and others have been transferred to non-state actors in the private or voluntary sectors, so have other policies been increasingly subject to external developments and obligations.

In particular, Britain's membership of the EU, coupled with the latter's steadily expanding jurisdiction and objectives, have had significant implications for various policies and departments in the core executive. Crucially, though, we have emphasized the uneven impact of this process of Europeanization, with some policies and ministries being rather more affected than others. Furthermore, among those departments that have been most affected by Britain's membership of the EU, some resent the loss of autonomy or additional obligations that this entails, whereas a few ministries actually welcome it, due either to the enhanced or revived role and importance they have acquired as a consequence of British membership, or because they see Europeanization as a means of achieving policy objectives that could not be achieved in isolation. This is especially the case with regard to policies that are inherently international, such as some forms of crime, climate change, illegal immigration, security issues, and so on.

Similarly, globalization can be viewed as both a threat to national or departmental autonomy, particularly with regard to economic policies (viz. the need to attract multinational companies or other overseas investors who are assumed to want low taxes, low wages, minimal statutory employment protection and labour market flexibility – although many British politicians actually support such policies anyway), or as an opportunity for governments and departments to tackle international problems, such as climate change, in partnership with other countries, or via the various organizations that constitute an emerging system of global governance.

QUESTIONS AND TOPICS FOR DISCUSSION

1. In what way(s) is the impact of the EU on public policy in Britain uneven?
2. How might British policy makers seek to influence the policies of the EU?
3. How is coordination of EU policies pursued within the core executive?
4. Why do some departments have a more favourable or positive attitude towards the EU, viewing it as an ally rather than an adversary?
5. What factors are fuelling globalization?
6. How is globalization seemingly affecting policy making in Britain?
7. Why might some British policy makers view globalization as an opportunity rather than a threat?
8. Why might British policy makers seek to transfer policies from another country?
9. Which policies have been enacted via policy transfer since the 1990s?
10. Why might a policy transfer *not* prove successful?

RECOMMENDED TEXTS AND FURTHER READING

<u>Europeanization</u>

1. Simon Bulmer and Martin Burch (2009) *The Europeanization of Whitehall: UK Central Government and the European Union*. Manchester: Manchester University Press.

   Having interviewed over 200 (past and present) Ministers and civil servants, Bulmer and Burch provide a major and much needed study of the extent to which the core executive has been affected by Britain's membership of the European Union, and the latter's increased policy jurisdiction. Emphasizes that the impact of the EU is uneven, with some Departments rather more affected than others. Also notes that a few Departments have acquired a more positive view of the EU, because of the manner in which their role has actually been enhanced by Europeanization.

2. Andrew Geddes (2013) *Britain and the European Union*. Basingstoke: Palgrave Macmillan.

   Starting with an historical overview of Britain's often fraught or unenthusiastic relationship with Europe since 1945, this very recent and thus up-to-date text offers a clear and cogent account both of the institutional and policy impact of the EU on Britain. Also examines the origins and nature of Britain's renowned Euroscepticism, and how this affects British governments' stance and tactics in EU negotiations.

3. Philip Giddings and Gavin Drewry (eds) (2004) *Britain in the European Union: Law, Policy and Parliament*. Basingstoke: Palgrave Macmillan.

   Interesting and eclectic collection of essays written by an array of academic experts and senior parliamentary clerks, detailing both the institutional and policy impact of Britain's membership of the EU. The former includes an examination of Parliament's scrutiny of EU policies *vis-à-vis* their implications for Britain, and consideration of the relationship between the EU, Westminster and the devolved institutions. Among the policies analysed are employment/social protection, immigration and asylum, and defence/security.

4. Ben Rosamond (2003) 'The Europeanization of British politics', in P. Dunleavy, A. Gamble, R. Heffernan and G. Peele (eds) *Developments in Politics 7*. Basingstoke: Palgrave.

Highly informative essay detailing the ways in which European integration is impacting upon Britain's political and policy-making institutions, and in so doing, both reflects and reinforces trends towards multi-level governance.

Globalization

1. Paul Hirst and Grahame Thompson (1995) 'Globalization and the future of the nation state', *Economy and Society*, 24 (3): 408–42.

Intriguing article which adopts a more original and nuanced stance than most writers on globalization. Challenges the common notion (or fear) that globalization heralds the end of the nation state as a viable and effective geo-political entity, arguing that national-level economic processes remain central. Even though globalization impacts upon the autonomy and character of contemporary nation states, they remain the key institutions through which a system of global governance is sustained and mediated, and also the prime source of legitimacy.

2. Maria Gritsch (2005) 'The nation-state and economic globalization: soft geo-politics and increased state autonomy?', *Review of International Political Economy*, 12 (1): 1–25.

Another article which disputes the view that globalization heralds the death of the nation state. Argues that it is often Western nation states themselves who are actively promoting globalization in order to strengthen their economic advantages, international influence and political authority. Moreover, globalization enhances the autonomy of nation states, not *vis-à-vis* other counties and governments, but from their own people; polices such as labour market flexibility and reduced welfare can be imposed for ideological reasons, but justified to ordinary citizens on the grounds of international pressures. In other words, globalization enables many nation states and domestic governments to impose policies, on behalf of corporate capital and big business, which might not otherwise be accepted without the legitimating discourse provided by globalization.

3. Robert Holton (1998) *Globalization and the Nation-State*. Basingstoke: Macmillan.

Clear and concise overview of globalization, with particular attention paid to the economic manifestations and implications, and the impact on the contemporary nation state (and domestic policy makers).

4. Frank J. Lechner and John Boli (eds) (2011) *The Globalization Reader*, fourth edition. Oxford: Wiley-Blackwell.

Very good, comprehensive collection of abridged chapters outlining the widening and deepening of globalization, as well as discussing its causes and consequences. The 71 'essays' address such themes and issues as the economic and financial 'drivers' of globalization, the impact on nation states and political authority, crime, culture, environmentalism, religion, and transnational governance. An excellent overview of the issues and academic debates surrounding globalization.

Policy Transfer

1. David Dolowitz (1998) *Learning from America: Policy Transfer and the Development of the British Workfare State*. Brighton: Sussex Academic Press.

   Major contribution to the then emerging study of policy transfer, examining the extent to which, and the reasons why, key aspects of welfare reform in Britain were being 'imported' from the United States.

2. David Dolowitz, with Rob Hulme, Mike Nellis and Fiona O'Neill (2000) *Policy Transfer and British Social Policy*. London: Open University Press.

   Fine overview of the phenomenon of policy transfer, detailing what it entails, why it has occurred apace since the 1980s, and providing empirical case studies of particular policies by way of examples and illustration.

3. David Dolowitz and David Marsh (2000) 'Learning from abroad: The role of policy transfer in contemporary policy-making', *Governance*, 13 (1): 5–23.

   A broad-ranging yet still clearly focused article which initially identifies the extent of policy transfer in recent years, and the reasons for this phenomenon in public policy, before then developing a conceptual model for defining and explaining different types of policy transfer.

4. Trevor Jones and Tim Newburn (2007) *Policy Transfer and Criminal Justice*. Maidenhead: McGraw-Hill/Open University Press.

   Based on a series of cases studies and interviews, Jones and Newburn analyse the extent of various law-and-order policies – such as 'zero-tolerance policing' – have been 'imported' into Britain from the United States since the 1990s, and the reasons for such policy transfer. This valuable study also examines the practical processes and mechanisms of policy transfer.

8 Policy Implementation

It is only since the 1970s that implementation has become widely recognized as a significant subject of policy analysis in its own right. Previously, implementation was assumed to be a relatively straightforward end point in an apparently linear or 'stagist' policy process: agenda setting and problem recognition; policy formulation (involving the core executive and policy networks); policy endorsement and legislation (via Parliament); implementation, whereby the resultant policy was put into practice. Little academic attention was previously paid to the implementation 'stage', and the impact that this often has on the effectiveness of public policies. Yet a policy can be seriously undermined by problems occurring while it is being implemented; in common parlance, 'delivered' or 'rolled out'.

The linear, sequential or stagist model of the policy process also presupposed a top-down approach, whereby those responsible for implementing public policy simply acted in accordance with guidelines or instructions from above, as stipulated by formal policy makers at the centre, thereby reflecting a clear, hierarchical chain of command. This tacit assumption itself partly reflected and reinforced the notion that in modern societies, organizations operated on the basis of a 'rational-legal' mode of authority, as originally outlined by the German sociologist Max Weber (1947: 329–41).

According to Weber, modern bureaucracies symbolized this mode of rational-legal authority, and as such, had the potential for:

> … attaining the highest degree of efficiency, and is in this sense formally the most rational known means of carrying out imperative control over human beings. It is superior to any other form in precision, in stability, in the stringency of its discipline and in its reliability. It thus makes possible a particularly high degree of calculability of results … It is finally superior both in intensive efficiency and in the scope of its operations, and is formally capable of all kinds of administrative tasks.

> (Weber, 1947: 334)

This, of course, creates a clear tension between the process of democratization and the principle of 'people power' regularly expressed through the ballot box on the one hand, and the parallel trend towards bureaucratization and the power of senior administrators on the other. Expressed another way, democratization entails a decentralization or devolving of power downwards and outwards towards 'the people', whereas bureaucratization involves a centralization of power upwards towards the centre. This tension was clearly noted in the early 20th century by Robert Michels (1962 [1911]: 70), who observed that: 'With the advance of organization, democracy tends to decline', thereby establishing an 'iron law of oligarchy'.

However, quite apart from the perennial risk that 'expert' and permanent bureaucrats might assume that they are better-placed or more suitably qualified to make decisions than 'generalist' and transient (but democratically elected) politicians, such a mode of rational-legal authority can itself foster inefficiency. This is because although the strict application of rules and regulations, coupled with the strong imposition of top-down authority, reduces the potential for arbitrary decisions, or perhaps, decisions based on personal prejudices, such a system also risks embedding bureaucratic inflexibility into decision taking and policy implementation.

As B.C. Smith notes, 'rigid adherence to rules may impede efficiency by preventing organizations from changing in response to their "environments" or responding to special, unique, sets of circumstances'. Consequently, he suggests that: 'Efficiency may therefore depend less on formal rules and more on an official's ... ability to adapt behaviour to changing circumstances' (Smith, 1988: 7. See also, Peters, 1984: 135).

Yet regardless of how clear and precise a set of rules (or other criteria) might appear to be, they will still be open to a degree of interpretation by sub-national policy actors implementing policies on a daily basis. Deciding whether a specified rule applies to a specific case in a specific circumstance will still require a degree of judgement and the exercise of discretion by street level bureaucrats, which can, in turn, have a notable impact on the way that a policy is actually applied in the 'real world'.

While this might be advantageous, by enabling street level bureaucrats to implement a policy in accordance with individual or local circumstances, such discretion or relative autonomy might also have a detrimental impact on a policy, by undermining (either intentionally or inadvertently) its original objective(s), and yielding different results to those originally intended by those at the centre. In other words, policy outputs do not always yield the intended outcomes.

It was Pressman and Wildavsky's (1973) book *Implementation* that heralded a fundamental change in the academic approach to implementation. By studying the application of a particular policy, the Economic Development Administration programme in the American city of Oakland in California, Pressman and Wildavsky drew scholarly attention to the manner in which the implementation 'stage' often determined the ultimate success or failure of public policy, and as such, was an aspect of the policy process that was far more important than had previously been assumed.

In so doing, Pressman and Wildavsky effectively challenged two of the tacit assumptions of traditional policy analysis. First, they drew attention to the inadequacy of orthodox linear models of the policy process. The clear implication of Pressman and Wildavsky's study was that rather than assuming a policy process with a beginning (agenda setting and problem recognition), middle (policy formulation and formal endorsement) and end (implementation), the policy process was circular and continuous. The apparent 'end stage' of implementation actually contributed towards policy making, because the identification of practical problems, such as unenforceability, unintended consequences or administrative complexity, frequently led to subsequent revisions of policy, or even the replacement of the original policy by a new one.

Viewed from this perspective, there was no definite beginning, middle and end to the policy process, but instead, an ongoing process of refinement and reform arising from deficiencies or difficulties identified during the implementation 'stage'. In cases of serious policy failure, the problem that the policy was intended to ameliorate would probably move back onto the institutional agenda: the implementation stage did not represent 'closure' or the end of the policy process, but was an integral part of a continuous cycle.

The second tacit assumption of traditional policy analysis, which was challenged by Pressman and Wildavsky's study, concerned the role of the 'street level bureaucrats', the front-line professionals who actually implement much public policy 'on the ground' (on the role of 'street level bureaucrats' in policy implementation, see the classic study by Lipsky, 2010). The hitherto assumption (*pace* Weber) had been that these 'street level bureaucrats' were effectively passive functionaries, simply applying regulations, or enforcing legislation, as laid down by their political or organizational superiors in a clear hierarchical chain of command stretching back to central government or the core executive. This, of course, reflected a simplistic top-down view of the policy process.

A major consequence of Pressman and Widlavsky's work was the realization that sub-national policy actors and 'street level bureaucrats' themselves often play a significant role in determining how policies are actually applied in practice, and in so doing, can shape policy outcomes in ways that had not been envisaged or intended by formal policy makers at national or central level. Far from being mere administrative automatons, 'street level bureaucrats' are actually active participants in the policy process, to the extent that, by accident or design, by intention or inadvertence, they can shape the 'final' policy, even though ministers and senior civil servants (and maybe Special Advisers) assumed that what they had originally devised, and Parliament subsequently approved, represented the final policy. Yet what ultimately ensued was sometimes rather different to what had originally been envisaged.

Pressman and Wildavsky therefore served to galvanize wider academic interest in the implementation 'stage' of the policy process, prompting many other writers to devote attention to the dynamics of implementation and the ways in which policies either failed at implementation 'stage', or the manner in which deficiencies only became apparent while a policy was being implemented, thereby returning the issue or problem back on to the institutional policy agenda. As Michael Hill (a British academic expert on implementation) explains, a policy decision often 'sets off a long and complicated chain – the implementation process – full of opportunities for things to go wrong' (Hill, 1998: 233).

THE PREREQUISITES FOR 'PERFECT IMPLEMENTATION'

To understand the importance of the implementation 'stage' and appreciate why this is when and where problems often arise or become apparent, various writers have identified the criteria that would need to be met in order to achieve 'perfect implementation'. Their objective has not been to offer a normative or prescriptive model of how policy *ought* to be implemented, but instead, to provide a heuristic device (a social scientific model or paradigm used for illustrative purposes) against which empirical reality can be contrasted, and differences or discrepancies explained. As Brian Hogwood (1987: 169) once suggested:

> One of the best ways of understanding what goes wrong with policies at the implementation stage is to turn the question on its head and ask what would be necessary for implementation of a policy to be completely successful.

If the reader's response to the list (below) of criteria required to facilitate 'perfect implementation' is: 'They are unattainable in the real world', then s/he will readily understand why policies often prove to be only partially successful – when they do not end in disastrous failure (on 'policy disasters' and some of their causes, see Dunleavy, 1995). This is the intellectual purpose of listing the criteria, which would need to be met to facilitate 'perfect implementation'. However, these criteria can still be utilized by policy makers in order to improve the administration and delivery of policies, and thereby reduce as many problems as possible.

Although it was Hood (1976: 6) who originally compiled a model of 'perfect implementation', other writers have refined the list of criteria on which the model was based, and so what follows constitutes something of a synthesis, extrapolating not only from Hood's work on this topic, but also from: Gunn (1978); Hogwood (1987: 165–70); Hogwood and Gunn (1984: 199–206); Marsh and Rhodes (1992b: Chapter 11); Pressman and Wildavsky (1973); Sabatier (1986). The criteria are synthesized in Box 8.1, although we have added the final criterion.

Box 8.1   Criteria that would be needed for 'perfect implementation'

1. External factors do not impose major constraints or undermine policies.
2. Policies enjoy autonomy; they are not compromised or weakened by other policies.
3. Dependency relationships are minimal.
4. There are a minimal number of 'decision points'.
5. Understanding of the problem/policy is based on a valid theory of cause and effect.
6. The objectives are clear, coherent and consistent.
7. The objectives are fully understood and/or accepted by 'street level bureaucrats'.
8. Resources are adequate and policy tools are appropriate.
9. Those to whom a policy is applied or targeted respond in the anticipated manner.

By briefly examining some of these criteria, we can understand the problems that implementation often encounters in practice, which in turn will help us to appreciate how and why some policies are only partially successful, some prove to be wholly ineffective and a few degenerate into spectacular failures or disasters. That said, policy makers might be reluctant to acknowledge that one of their policies had failed, insisting instead that it is too soon to judge or that critics are being selective in the evidence they are citing.

This links back to the notion of agenda management, which we discussed in Chapter 1, and the manner in which policy makers sometime seek to deny a problem or redefine it in order to reduce its scale or significance and avoid taking action. In the case of alleged policy failure, they might insist that the policy needs more time to achieve its objectives, or that different measurements indicate that its alleged failings are rather less than critics are claiming, perhaps because the policy's critics are trying to promote their own agenda.

However, determining the success or shortcomings of a policy also raises questions pertaining to *what* is being measured, *who* is conducting the measurement and *how* they are measuring it. In short, these are matters pertaining to policy evaluation, which is the subject of our next chapter.

External events do not impose major constraints or undermine policies

This particular requirement would necessitate policies being self-contained entities, operating independently of wider economic, political or social developments and events. Clearly, however, in an increasingly complex society, characterized by a transition to governance on the one hand, and subject to the dual phenomena of Europeanization and globalization on the other, the chances of any policy enjoying such autonomy are small indeed. More than ever before, almost all policies are at least partly contingent both upon the behaviour of other actors and institutions, and on wider events and occurrences, any of which can seriously impede or undermine the successful implementation of particular policies.

One of the most obvious and important constraints upon the effective implementation of public policy in this context is that of the economy, both at domestic level and in an international or global context (as noted in the previous chapter). Not only are a Chancellor's macro-economic and fiscal policies based on assumptions and forecasts about a range of economic trends and indicators, but in turn, many of the government's programmes and policy goals are heavily dependent on continued economic growth and stability, for these will determine the extent to which the Treasury receives sufficient revenues to fund the various policy programmes and departments.

A good example of an economic policy being seriously affected by external events occurred in September 1992, just a few months after John Major's Conservative government had been re-elected in a general election in which his party's perceived economic competence (in stark contrast to the untrusted Labour Party) had been a crucial factor. Yet by September, heavy selling of sterling (the pound) by speculators in the currency markets led ultimately to Britain's enforced withdrawal from the EU's Exchange Rate Mechanism (ERM) on 16 September 1992, known widely as 'Black Wednesday' (for a full discussion of this episode, see Thompson 1995: 248–74; Thompson, 1996). One academic declared that Britain's ERM withdrawal 'consigned to the dustbin the most important components of the Major Court's [*sic*] domestic and external governing strategies' (Bulpitt, 1996: 248).

In response to Britain's departure from the ERM, the Major government hastily devised a new (or some might say, returned to the pre-ERM) fiscal and monetary policy, including an inflation target of 2.5 per cent, to be achieved by strict controls over both public expenditure and public sector pay awards. There were also various increases in indirect taxation. Even though the events were (arguably) beyond the government's control, the Conservatives nonetheless suffered serious damage to their hitherto reputation for economic competence and credibility. The ensuing loss of public and electoral popularity was compounded by the rises in indirect taxation, particularly as the Conservatives had warned, in their April 1992 election campaign, that it was the Labour Party that would impose higher taxes if elected.

More recently, of course, the 2005–10 Labour government suffered a disastrous loss of public support and trust in the wake of the 2008 global banking crisis. Much of the Blair-Brown government's public expenditure ('investment') had been predicated on a continually expanding economy, buoyed to a considerable extent by the health of the financial services sector and the City. This, it was assumed, would continue to provide both relatively high tax revenues for the Treasury, and cheap credit to underpin consumer confidence and personal spending, as evidenced, for example, by the rapid increase in house prices from the late 1990s onwards.

Consequently, Labour's economic strategy was dealt a mortal blow when the 2008 crash occurred (even though, arguably, it could have done little to prevent it). Like the Conservatives back in 1992, the 2008 crash fatally damaged the reputation for economic competence that New Labour had originally worked so hard and painfully to achieve during its 18 years (1979–97) in Opposition, and Gordon Brown's hubristic boast that there would be 'no more boom and bust' came back cruelly to haunt him.

More than three years after its consequent defeat in the May 2010 general election, and with millions of British people suffering financial hardship and job insecurity due to the recession and the coalition's austerity policies, Labour is still trusted rather *less* than the Conservatives and Chancellor, George Osborne, on the crucial issues of economic competence and which of the parties is most likely restore economic growth. Indeed, the coalition has successfully persuaded much of the British electorate that the recession has been primarily caused, not by the international financial collapse or reckless bankers, but by Labour's economic incompetence and fiscal irresponsibility while in Office for 13 years.

Policies enjoy autonomy; they are not compromised or weakened by other policies

Just as international events or crises can undermine the effectiveness of a policy, so too can the consequences of ostensibly unconnected policies. This problem is another manifestation of the increasingly interconnected character of contemporary society, where policies can have unforeseen or unintended repercussions elsewhere, thus making it even more important, yet more difficult, to achieve 'joined-up government'. For example, the coalition government has sought to curb expenditure on Housing Benefit, the total cost of which was forecast to rise to £24 billion by 2015. Yet the overall cost of Housing Benefit is not solely determined by the number of claimants at any given time (important though this is), but also by the rents charged by landlords. This, in turn, will reflect the state of the housing market in terms of the number of properties available and their cost.

In recent years, Britain has experienced both a shortage of housing, and record house prices (the two are closely linked, of course), which has meant that many people have been unable to buy a home of their own. As a consequence, many people have effectively been compelled to live in private rented accommodation, for which the weekly or monthly rent is often very high: in 2013, the weekly rent for most one-bedroom flats in London was between £300–500 (although at the highest end of the rental market, the weekly rents was in the £000s).

As tenants on low incomes, or who are not in work (due to unemployment, disability or long-term illness) are generally eligible for Housing Benefit – the exact amount varying according to individual circumstances – this has led to a marked increase in the total amount of Housing Benefit paid each year. In an era of austerity and public expenditure cuts, this has become a controversial political issue. Yet one of the reasons for the lack of cheaper or 'affordable' housing is that during the 1980s, when the Thatcher governments were implementing their popular right-to-buy scheme, which enabled council house tenants to purchase their own homes, local authorities were forbidden to build new homes to replace those that were sold. This subsequently led to a shortage of 'social' housing, which has still not been rectified.

Consequently, many people who cannot afford to buy a home of their own have little choice but to rent from a private landlord or letting agency. When their income is low, and their rent is above a certain level, many such tenants become eligible for Housing Benefit. In this respect, an important component of the social security budget is being affected by aspects of housing policy and parallel trends in the property market since the 1980s.

Dependency relationships are minimal

Ideally, the agency or policy actor(s) responsible for implementing a policy would enjoy maximum autonomy from others in the policy process, in order that they could administer the policy as intended, and without the need to seek the agreement or cooperation of others. Clearly, the more actors involved in the implementation or 'delivery' of a policy, the greater is the potential either for communication problems, or conflicts of interests, the latter invariably due to the actors seeking to pursue their own particular goals. For example, a major problem arising from the privatization of Britain's railways in 1996 was precisely the extent to which the industry was broken up into more than 100 companies, not only in the sense of regional railway companies being established, with a subsequent lack of coordination between train services and timetables in different parts of the country, but also in a functional sense, with different companies having different responsibilities, such as actually operating the trains, or maintaining tracks and signalling, or catering, and so on. The 25 regional train operators, therefore, have sometimes found that their ability to provide a punctual and reliable service has been undermined by the failure of those responsible for track maintenance – 19 rail engineering companies – to complete engineering works on time.

Similarly, the train operators lease rolling stock (carriages) from a small number of companies established to provide precisely this service, but the latter could be said, on commercial grounds, to have an interest in using existing rolling stock for as long as practically possible, thereby maximizing their financial returns and deferring investment in new, upgraded carriages that would provide rail 'customers' with more comfortable journeys (Haubrich, 2001: 322).

There is a minimal number of 'decision points'

One of the main findings to emanate from Pressman and Wildavsky's study concerned the number of 'decision points', which occurred *after* a policy had been formally adopted. It was discovered that policies will often encounter a number of situations and stages where sub-national policy actors and 'street level bureaucrats' need to consider how to proceed, or how to apply the policy in the particular circumstances facing them. The cumulative effect of such successive 'decision points' may well be to alter the policy in ways never envisaged or intended by those who originally formulated it originally, thereby impinging upon its effectiveness.

Certainly, the more decision points that arise during implementation, the more likely it is that a policy will be altered and amended, possibly in a manner or to a degree that impacts upon its ultimate effectiveness or success. In such circumstances, disputes and mutual recriminations might arise, as central policy makers allege that the policy has been misinterpreted or poorly administered by the street level bureaucrats, while the latter retort that the original policy was inherently flawed to start with, or inappropriate to the problem it was supposed to tackle.

As Pressman and Wildavsky's case study clearly illustrated, implementation problems arising from a plethora of actors, agencies and associated decision points are especially likely to occur in policies concerned with urban development or regeneration, for as John observes, those pursuing urban policies in particular have 'to negotiate the maze of central government departments, their regional organizations, the numerous government agencies, and private-sector and local-authority bodies' (John, 1998: 28). Since the late 1980s, in the context of the transition to a system of governance, this 'maze' has become considerably more complex, as we noted in Chapter 6.

Policy is based on a valid theory of cause and effect

Virtually any policy will be based, directly or indirectly, on an assumption that '*a* causes *b*', or that *b* is a consequence of *a*, so that if *b* is adjudged undesirable or unsustainable – is defined as a problem by policy makers – then it is likely that a policy will be devised to tackle *a*. Clearly, however, if policy makers' assumptions about the underlying cause of a particular problem are erroneous, then their subsequent policy is unlikely to be effective at the implementation stage. For example, many governments (but especially Conservative ones) in post-war Britain have assumed that a major cause of (rising) crime has been lax sentencing by 'soft' judges and an insufficiently harsh regime inside prisons, so that criminals are no longer afraid of being convicted: they would either escape a custodial sentence, perhaps by virtue of their lawyer offering a 'sob story' about the wretched life the defendant had endured, or even if they were imprisoned, would experience a comfortable regime inside; the prison as a holiday camp, according to some tabloids. This perspective has underpinned many initiatives to impose a tougher law and order regime over the years, involving longer prison sentences, coupled with granting the police greater powers of arrest. In 2003, meanwhile, the Blair government, concerned that too many defendants were escaping custodial sentences, attempted to place certain limits on trial by jury.

However, longer sentences and harsher regimes inside prison do not seem to have had much effect in themselves in reducing crime, not least because most criminals probably assume that they will not get caught in the first place. Given the conviction rates for various types of crime, linked to the number of crimes that go undetected or unsolved, some criminals seem to make a 'rational' calculation that they will not get caught, so that the potential prison sentence associated with their particular crime does not act as a deterrent. Moreover, some crimes seem to be opportunistic or 'spur-of-the-moment' in character, and so again, the perpetrator is unlikely to think calmly and rationally about the likely consequences of being caught and convicted.

Elsewhere, successive governments and their Education Secretaries since the 1980s have frequently alleged or implied that low levels of numeracy and literacy among school children, and/or disruptive behaviour by pupils in the classroom, is the fault of 'bad' teachers. It has variously been claimed that too many teachers are 'lax' in terms of imposing rigorous academic standards and/or discipline, possibly because of 'trendy' teaching methods and 'liberal' theories of child-centred learning. As a consequence, secondary education in Britain has been repeatedly reformed since 1988 right up until the present day, and schools subjected both to regular Ofsted inspections and league tables to measure and publicize their levels of success.

Yet the problems that are readily blamed on 'bad' or 'incompetent' teachers are likely to have their origins outside of the classroom and school gates. Teachers might struggle to interest some children in reading if they emanate from homes where their parents do not value literacy, and so do not encourage their children to read, or perhaps do not bother to read them a bedtime story. Similarly, bad behaviour by pupils in the classroom is likely to reflect problems at home. Indeed, some parents will even tell their children that if any teacher tries to discipline them in any way, the parent will visit the school to 'sort your teacher out'. Furthermore, some children from dysfunctional homes are more likely to become involved in gangs and thus succumb to peer pressure to behave in an anti-social manner. In such circumstances, the gang leader will probably become the wayward youngster's chosen role model or authority figure, rather than their teachers.

The objectives are clear, coherent and consistent

The greater the number of objectives attributed to a particular policy, the more likely it is that discrepancies or inconsistencies will become apparent at implementation stage. By way of illustration, Marsh and Rhodes cite the example of the Thatcher governments' privatization policies of the 1980s, which suffered from enshrining 'multiple and conflicting objectives' (Marsh and Rhodes, 1992b: 182).

One of the goals that Conservatives attributed to privatization was to increase competition and consumer choice, yet in many cases, nationalized industries were sold with only limited fragmentation into separate competitive companies. This was partly because some of the senior managers or potential managers successfully persuaded Conservative ministers against breaking up the industries, and partly because ministers themselves recognized that the potential value of shares in a national company would inevitably be higher than those of a regional company, thereby making the initial sale of shares more attractive to investors.

A further inconsistency arising from this particular aspect of privatization concerns the issue of regulation. A major feature of the Thatcherite critique of the pre-privatization British economy was the alleged degree of regulation to which industry was subjected, and as such, privatization was to herald a new era of freedom and autonomy for industries liberated from political meddling and bureaucratic interference. Yet because many of the privatized industries effectively retained their monopoly status, the Thatcher governments recognized that some mechanism was required to protect the interests of the consumer.

Privatization thus merely exchanged one mode of regulation for another, as each of the privatized industries became subject to a regulatory body, which was intended to ensure that certain standards of service were provided to consumers, and also to approve proposed price increases. Consequently, rather than resulting in a 'rolling back' of the state as apparently intended, the privatization programme of the 1980s and 1990s entailed a restructuring of the state; regulation was not so much reduced or removed as reintroduced in a different guise. As we noted in Chapter 6, this became a key feature of the development of 'governance' in Britain from the 1980s onwards and the rise of the 'regulatory state'.

Meanwhile, when Britain's railways were subsequently privatized by John Major's government in 1996 the opposite problem arose, namely a degree of fragmentation, both territorially and functionally, which rendered it virtually impossible to provide the promised improvement in services. Indeed, Britain's privatized railways became renowned for their delays, cancellations, overcrowding due to shortages of 'rolling stock' (carriages), speed restrictions or diversions due to engineering works and breakdowns *en route* (see, for example, Batchelor, 1999; Bennett, 1998; Department of the Environment, Transport and the Regions, 1999: Table 5; Groom, 2000; Haubrich, 2001: 321–2; Jowit, 2000).

Privatization was also depicted as a major means of extending share ownership to ordinary people, thereby embedding support for 'popular capitalism'. Yet while the initial sales of shares in key industries such as British Gas and British Telecom were oversubscribed, as millions of ordinary people sought to buy shares over the counter of their high street bank, for example, many people soon sold their shares in order to yield an instant profit, particularly when the sale price of the shares had been set at below their market value in order further to attract 'small investors'. For example, although 2,051,373 million people purchased shares in British Telecom when it was privatized in 1984, this figure had declined to 1,236,870 by 1990. Similarly, while 4,407,079 million people originally purchased shares during the 1986 privatization of British Gas, the number of people owning shares in British Gas had fallen to 2,780,813 by 1990 (although Conservatives could still claim that this was precisely 2.78 million more shareholders than before the industry was privatized).

Elsewhere, of the two million people who purchased shares in the 1986 privatization of Rolls-Royce, less than half still retained them by 1990. Similarly, during the same period, the number of shareholders in British Airways declined from 1,100,000 to 347,897 (Abromeit, 1988). Meanwhile, although individual shareholders owned 58 per cent of all shares in Railtrack Group PLC when the company was floated on the stock market in April 1996, only 30 per cent still did so just two years later (Haubrich, 2001: 325).

Once again, the CSA can be cited as an example of the problems that can arise at the implementation 'stage', as a consequence of unclear, incoherent or inconsistent objectives. When the CSA was established in 1993, it was widely envisaged that the primary targets when seeking child support payments would be those men who had fathered illegitimate children, but paid little or nothing towards their upbringing (apparently happy to leave their ex-girlfriend/wife to fend for herself, or become reliant on the welfare state/taxpayer).

However, because of the performance indicators and targets, which the CSA had been set, including figures for the amount of child support payments to be obtained in order to yield savings on social security payments of £530 million during its first year, it was either men who were already paying 'maintenance' to their ex-partners (and who could thus readily be contacted to secure increased payments) or higher-earning middle-class men who were initially targeted. Indeed, leaked internal memos sent to area managers within the CSA confirmed this strategy, with one such memo declaring:

> This is not the time for the cases we know should get early attention, but which will need a lot of effort to extract money. The name of the game is maximising the maintenance yield – don't waste a lot of time on non-profitable stuff!

> (Quoted in Brindle, 1993a)

This strategy was reiterated by a member of the CSA's management board, through another internal memo to divisional managers, which pointed out that: 'Higher savings can be achieved if we prioritise as follows', the subsequent list starting with 'absent parents in work with higher than average earnings', followed by 'absent fathers in regular contact with the parent with care' (quoted in Brindle, 1993b).

Such a prioritization, pursued in order to achieve targets set for social security savings, was in direct contrast to what had widely been deemed a key objective of the CSA, namely ensuring that most, and eventually all, 'absent fathers' made a financial contribution towards their children, but especially those deemed to be part of the irresponsible, 'feckless' underclass. Instead, those already paying maintenance were pursued for additional sums, sometimes £100s more than they were already paying, rather than those (often lower-income) men who were paying little, if anything, and who might take a long time to 'track down'.

The objectives are fully understood and accepted by 'street level bureaucrats'

The last example also illustrates the type of problems that can occur when the objectives of a particular policy are not fully understood or accepted by street level bureaucrats. As

Malpass and Murie (1999: 198) have noted: 'Sometimes, performance fails to match intentions, because the objectives are not shared by those responsible for implementation, or because they are unaware of what the objectives are.'

Furthermore, the extent to which 'street level bureaucrats' implement a policy in the manner intended by national-level policy makers will depend not only on whether they fully understand the objectives and purpose enshrined in the policy, but also, perhaps, on its compatibility with their own values or organizational goals. Just as government departments have often been characterized by a particular in-house philosophy or operational paradigm, so too might the organizations acting as 'street level bureaucrats' have their own particular ethos or institutional ideology, and this may have practical consequences for their interpretation or acceptance of a policy emanating from above. Or as Barrett and Fudge observe, public policy 'is mediated by actors who may be operating with different assumptive worlds from those formulating the policy and, inevitably, it undergoes interpretation and modification and, in some cases, subversion' (Barrett and Fudge, 1981b: 251). For example, the (1997–2007) Blair governments' policy initiatives to tackle antisocial behaviour were often hindered by the apparent reticence of the courts to fully use the powers available to them, in the guise of legislation enacted in 1998 and 2001, which empowered courts to impose ASBOs and night-time curfews on troublesome youths. Yet by November 2002, only 654 such ASBOs had actually been imposed in England and Wales, rather fewer than the 5,000, which the government had originally envisaged (Burney, 2002; Randall, 2004: 182).

With regard to another aspect of anti-social behaviour, autumn 2004 heralded the publication of a report, by Hazel Blears, a Minister of State at the Home Office, noting that local authorities and the police were failing to make full use of the powers vested in them (by the government) to tackle binge drinking, public drunkenness and related disorderly behaviour. Part of the problem, the report noted, was a lack of coordination and communication between the police and local authorities. Blears also reported that in spite of the government's efforts to tackle under-age drinking, 35 per cent of the off-licences that were tested, and 65 per cent of tested bars and clubs, were still selling alcohol to under-age drinkers (Cracknell, 2004: 13).

More recently, it has been claimed in spite of successive ministers extolling the virtues of flexible working practices, in order to facilitate a better work–life balance and enable parents to spend more time with their children, relatively few employers or companies were actually facilitating 'flexi-work' for their employees (Jones, 2013).

Resources are adequate

In this context, 'resources' refers not only to finance and funding, vital though these invariably are, but also other criteria, most notably sufficient time and adequate levels of staffing, or staff with requisite expertise and competence. The absence of any of these resources will invariably have a detrimental impact on the successful implementation of public policy.

Of course, finance and staffing are often inextricably linked, for the number – and calibre – of staff employed by any organization involved in policy implementation will be heavily dependent on its levels of funding. In this respect, a 'perfect' health service or education system is unattainable, because finance is finite and so only a certain number of doctors, nurses, surgeons and teachers can be employed. Similarly, only a certain number of police officers can ever be deployed at any given moment, hence attempts at eradicating crime or apprehending criminals will only ever be partially successful.

However, the staff shortages that might militate against perfect implementation are not always a direct consequence of limited financial resources, but sometimes the result either of an insufficient number of suitably qualified personnel. No government's desire to improve the health service will be wholly successful if hospitals cannot recruit enough qualified nurses, doctors or consultants, nor is a policy initiative to raise educational standards likely to be a resounding success if schools cannot attract enough qualified teachers.

Meanwhile, in October 2012, it was reported that Britain faced a potential future shortage of university lecturers, because the scale of graduate debt, caused by the student fees regime (which has seen the cost of studying for a degree increase from £3,000 per annum in 2006 to £9,000 in 2012) was deterring students from pursuing postgraduate study; a PhD traditionally being a prerequisite of obtaining an academic job (Swain, 2012).

In similar vein, summer 2013 heard a warning that Britain's schools faced an imminent shortage of qualified maths and science teachers, due largely to a decline in suitably-qualified graduates pursuing a career in teaching. It was noted that up to 30 per cent of places for would-be maths teachers on PGCE (teacher training) courses, due to commence in September 2013, remained vacant, with a similar shortfall affecting science subjects such as physics. Yet maths and science were deemed to be of the utmost importance by ministers; indeed, they were classified as 'national strategic priorities' by the Education Secretary, Michael Gove (Garner, 2013a).

Elsewhere, one of the many problems encountered by the CSA, immediately following its launch in 1993, was inadequate staffing – inadequate both in relation to the volume of case loads it was attempting to deal with, and the administrative complexities involved in the assessment of those cases. The 5,000 staff initially employed – half of them from outside of the civil service, and having received just 4–8 weeks' training (Garnham and Knights, 1994: 54) – immediately found themselves struggling to process the cases submitted to them, while the formulae devised to determine how much child support should be paid was so complex that 100 pieces of information was sometimes required to make the calculation for one case or application. Not surprisingly, erroneous calculations and lengthy delays ensued, and the CSA became the target of increasing criticism from a wide variety of sources, not least the 'lone parents' it purported to be serving.

Those to whom a policy is applied or directed respond in the anticipated manner

This is an aspect of policy implementation that has previously tended to be overlooked, yet which often has a crucial bearing on whether or not policies are effective and successful. When formulating and finalizing programmes and laws, policy makers will generally assume that the vast majority of people will accept the measure concerned and act accordingly. This clearly implies either a high level of compliance from those to whom a particular policy is targeted, or a positive response, in terms of potential recipients availing themselves of the provisions of a new policy (such as claiming a social security benefit to which they have become entitled). In this respect, the successful implementation of a particular policy may well be beyond the control of both formal policy makers and the street level bureaucrats, because the citizens who constitute the 'target audience' do respond as expected.

One of the most dramatic examples of a policy whose implementation was seriously affected by the failure of citizens to respond as anticipated was the 1990 (1989 for Scottish readers) Community Charge, or Poll Tax, as it was more commonly known. Conservative ministers could not have anticipated that so many citizens would refuse to pay the Poll Tax, even to the extent of 'disappearing' from the electoral register in order to avoid liability to pay. In Scotland, for example, about 600,000 people (representing 15 per cent of the Scottish population) had 'failed' to pay their poll tax by the autumn of 1989, at least six months after its introduction, while in England during the summer of 1990, it was becoming apparent that in Liverpool and some inner-London districts, about 50 per cent of eligible adults had not paid their poll tax (since the April introduction). In London as a whole, about 27 per cent of adults had still not paid their poll tax by August 1990 (Butler et al., 1994: 165, 167).

Rather more recently, it has become evident that the outlawing of fox hunting, via the Hunting Act 2004, has been a resounding failure, with most hunts continuing as before, and openly (and defiantly) too, with TV cameras and press photographers often invited to film the meeting of a Boxing Day hunt, for example. Meanwhile, the police seem often to have ignored most hunts, perhaps reasoning that their resources are already stretched and that they perhaps have more serious crimes to tackle. Furthermore, the relatively few prosecutions that have been pursued for unlawful hunting have often resulted in only small fines being imposed by the courts.

SEEKING TO OVERCOME THE 'IMPLEMENTATION GAP'

Although the Blair governments continued with many of the overall policies of the preceding Conservative governments – the primacy of the market, private sector involvement in financing capital projects in the public sector, refusal to raise income tax, close(r) links with employers rather than with the trade unions, public service reform, welfare reform, and so on – and the principles underpinning these, they seemed to acknowledge various of the problems enshrined in the top-down approach to policy implementation and tailored their policy style accordingly, at least initially.

Consequently, rather than seeking to marginalize sub-national policy actors, or impose policies on them by ministerial decree, the Blair governments initially opted for a more inclusionary policy style, whereby the importance of non-governmental or sub-national policy actors and street level bureaucrats was accepted, thus leading to greater consultation, dialogue and partnerships. Ministers still determined key policy objectives – although often depicted as 'aspirations' – but formally allowed sub-national policy actors to determine exactly how these were to be achieved.

New Labour seemed to recognize, at least in its early stage, that the transition to governance made it vital to pursue a more collaborative and coordinated approach. This manifested itself in Tony Blair's emphasis on 'joined-up government', and a corresponding need to foster partnerships between the plethora of sub-national organizations and individuals responsible for policy implementation. As many problems had a variety of causes or origins, the appropriate policy response necessitated the involvement of more than one department, while the implementation of the ensuing policies required the input of several sub-national actors and the crafting of a more holistic approach to policy 'delivery'.

In fact, this was being acknowledged back in 1994, with Malcolm Wicks (subsequently a minister in the Blair-Brown governments) noting that in:

> … many of the most crucial items of the policy agenda – the run-down of the inner cities, the need for urban regeneration, family policy – have characteristics and demand solutions which are not the province of any one department, central or local. Yet our whole system of government is riddled with specialism and departmentalism. Political reputations are made by civil servants defending departmental interests, safeguarding their budget and warding off intrusions from other fiefdoms …The House of Commons Select Committee system mirrors, not challenges, this departmental slicing of the cake of governance.
>
> (Wicks, 1994: 22)

Wicks' concerns were echoed in the 1999 White Paper, *Modernising Government*, which bemoaned that:

> In general, too little effort has gone into making sure that policies are devised and delivered in a consistent and effective way across institutional boundaries – for example, between different government departments, and between central and local government. Issues like crime and social exclusion cannot be tackled on a departmental basis. An increasing separation between policy and delivery has acted as a barrier to involving in policy-making those people who are responsible for delivering on the front line … Too often the work of departments, their Agencies and other bodies has been fragmented …
>
> (Cabinet Office, 1999a: Chapter 2, paras. 4 and 5)

Although this lack of coordination was a consequence of the phenomenon of departmentalism in the core executive, as noted in Chapters 3 and 4, it was compounded by the trend towards governance, for as we discussed in Chapter 6, the range of sub-national policy actors has increased significantly since the 1980s. Consequently, coordination became much more important, both within the core executive during the policy formulation stage and then among the sub-national institutions formally responsible for implementing or 'delivering' governmental policies.

In terms of enhancing coordination within the core executive and between departments, we observed in Chapter 4 the long-standing role of Cabinet committees and the enormously increased importance of the Cabinet Office (and its various 'units') in addressing issues, which cut across traditional departmental boundaries and policy remits. Certainly, the Blair governments' commitment to tackling 'social exclusion' entailed considerable interdepartmental cooperation and collaboration, some of which was facilitated or overseen by the Cabinet Office itself, particularly the Social Exclusion Unit.

However, this ostensibly more collaborative, partnership approach to implementation belied the fact that New Labour became increasingly obsessed with the setting of targets and other performance indicators in order to 'incentivize' policy actors to adhere to the Blair-Brown governments' objectives, and to ensure that the associated policies were successfully implemented. In this regard, the apparent discretion and empowerment of street level bureaucrats and local institutions responsible for 'delivering' New Labour's policies was progressively reduced, as targets and performance indicators not only became more numerous, but more prescriptive and detailed. Often, ministers not only set targets, but also sought to stipulate *how* these were to be achieved or reached, so that processes and strategies became increasingly important.

Thus has Moran noted that, since the 1990s, the fragmentation and consequent multiplicity of policy actors wrought by the transition to governance have resulted in ministers often seeking to re-assert tight control over sub-national policy actors and street-level bureaucrats, in order to ensure compliance with ministerial objectives and targets. As a result, policy implementation has often entailed 'increasing control over individual work practices and performance ... more emphasis on hierarchical controls and the micro-management of individuals' (Moran, 2007: 128).

So obsessed did New Labour become with ensuring the compliance of street level bureaucrats and front-line professions, especially in the sphere of social policy, that doctors, nurses, probation officers, social workers, teachers and university lecturers increasingly complained of being 'micro-managed', with preparations for, or participation in, an endless series of audits, appraisals and inspections almost becoming ends in themselves.

As we noted in Chapter 6, although senior Conservatives, during David Cameron's initial leadership of the party, pledged to dismantle much of the Blair-Brown governments' framework of central targets, and instead restore more autonomy and power to professionals and street level bureaucrats in the implementation of public policy, the post-2010 Conservative-dominated coalition has actually been characterized by a continuation of the targets and inspections regime throughout many public services. For many professionals in the public sector, the years since May 2010 have been a case of 'meet the new boss, same as the old boss'.

NEW PUBLIC MANAGEMENT

A crucial means of attempting to improve policy implementation is evident in the development of new public management, a concept and practice that has developed widely since the late 1980s, and which is inextricably linked to the transition to governance and the associated rise of the regulatory state, both of which we discussed in Chapter 6.

According to Christopher Hood (1995: 104–5), new public management enshrines seven main features and objectives, namely:

- 'hands-on' management in the public sector
- specified criteria and standards of performance, both by individuals and institutions
- stronger emphasis on 'output controls'
- disaggregation of monolithic public services into distinct units and 'cost centres'

- increasing competition, both with the private sector and within the public sector itself
- private sector styles of management
- greater financial discipline and 'parsimony in resource use'.

To this list might be added criteria or objectives such as 'accountability' and 'transparency'.

The new public management developed in response to concerns that the professionals 'delivering' public services were often failing to do so effectively or efficiently, and thus exerting a negative impact on successful policy implementation. This perspective was part of a more general New Right critique of the alleged inadequacies and incompetence of 'street level bureaucrats' in public sector organizations and services, and the consequent need to exercise much stronger managerial control over professionals.

It had previously been commonly assumed that most professionals pursuing careers in public services, such as education, health, policing and social work, were strongly motivated by a sense of altruism and civic responsibility; they wanted to serve the community or society rather than 'make money'. However, the New Right rejected this notion of noble public servants, and argued that public servants were themselves motivated by considerations of self-interest, most notably in terms of budget maximization and/or professional power, either of which meant that they did not necessarily provide the best service to their 'customers' or clients.

This unflattering characterization of selfish, self-serving, public servants and professionals was itself partly derived from 'public choice theory', a critique of public sector or governmental bureaucracies that was developed by neo-liberal economists during the 1970s and 1980s (for examples, see Buchanan and Tullock, 1962; Lee, 2012; Tullock et al., 2000). They claimed that many state employees were themselves 'rational actors' who were concerned to acquire more resources and power, even while claiming to be motivated by altruism and a desire to serve civil society.

Another way of depicting this apparent distinction between virtuous altruism and venal self-interest among public sector professionals and street level bureaucrats has been advanced by Julian Le Grand (2010: 2 and *passim*. See also Le Grand, 2007), who draws a distinction between 'knights', who are 'predominantly public-spirited or altruistic', and 'knaves' who are 'motivated primarily by their own self-interest'.

Needless to say, the perspective of successive governments since the 1980s has been to focus on the allegedly knavish motives of many public sector professionals and street level bureaucrats, whereupon they need to be exposed simultaneously to both managerial and market disciplines, in order to compel them to serve their 'customers' more courteously and efficiently.

What compounded this alleged problem, according to the New Right, was that many public services operated as virtual monopolies (the sole providers), which in turn meant that poor performance rarely incurred costs or sanctions for the professionals employed in such organizations; dissatisfied 'customers' of a monopoly service could rarely switch to another provider, while financial losses were invariably 'covered' by increased government subsidies using taxpayers' money (or debts were written off completely by ministers). In such circumstances, there was apparently little incentive for public sector professionals to become more efficient, cost-effective or responsive to those who used their services.

Since the 1980s, this critique of state employees has increasingly shaped governmental policies towards the management and funding of those public services, which have not (yet) been privatized. Successive governments have endeavoured to impose new modes of management on public service professionals and street level bureaucrats, in order to increase efficiency, productivity or value for money, and improve the quality of service provision by those implementing public policy. The enhancement of managerial authority, and the professed empowerment of 'consumers' of public services, has entailed a corresponding diminution of the authority and autonomy hitherto enjoyed by professionals and street level bureaucrats employed in education, the National Health Service, the police, the probation service, social services, and so on.

Certainly, a major aspect of this new public management is a much stronger, 'hands on', mode of management in public sector/service institutions' management. This is intended to counter the alleged proclivity of public sector professions and street level bureaucrats to prioritize their own interests over those of their clients or 'customers', or provide a service in a manner that is more convenient for the street level bureaucrats than those they are serving.

In this respect, 'hands on' management deliberately erodes or eliminates the autonomy and much of the discretion traditionally enjoyed by professionals and street level bureaucrats, and instead subjects them to much stronger managerial discipline from above. This, of course, is in addition to the discipline of 'the market', which public sector professional and street level bureaucrats have also been relentlessly subjected to since the late 1980s. For example, within public sector/service organizations, the new public management not only stipulates *which* policy outputs or outcomes are expected to be achieved, often in the form of targets and other performance indicators, but specifies *how* particular tasks are to be conducted in order to achieve the specified results. Professionals and street level bureaucrats therefore find themselves much more rigorously managed, with their performance being constantly and closely monitored (see, for example, Newman and Clarke, 2004).

Such performance management and monitoring exercises are usually conducted through regular appraisals of individual staff and/or detailed questionnaires about their achievements in the past year, and how these have contributed to the goals, objectives and targets of their organization or service. Staff are also likely to be asked what their objectives are for the next year (or whatever timeframe is being adopted), how they intend to achieve these and how these objectives will contribute to their organization's strategic goals or targets. This might well involve attaching a detailed 'action plan', against which their performance can then be gauged at their next appraisal.

Of course, with new public management, it is not only the individuals in public sector/service organizations whose performance is routinely monitored, but also the organizations themselves. After all, if the individuals employed in any organization are having their performance regularly measured to ensure compliance, efficiency and improvement, then it is assumed that *ipso facto* the organization in which they are employed will also improve its performance as a consequence and thus ensure a more effective implementation of policies. In this respect, public sector organizations and services have themselves been (and continue to be) subject to a plethora of targets and other performance criteria, as successive governments have endeavoured to ensure clear and measurable improvements in the implementation of policies.

Ironically, in spite of the Conservatives' and New Labour's neo-liberal discourse of 'the market' and empowering the 'customers' of public services, one academic expert on 20th century Russian history has compared the regime of targets, inspections and monitoring *in* the public sector to aspects of the former Soviet Union, the latter renowned for its often absurd five-year plans and dreaded inspections of sub-national institutions by zealous state officials to gauge compliance and progress in achieving goals and objectives stipulated by central government (Amann, 2003).

CONCLUSION

While the model of 'perfect implementation' was never remotely attainable (and was not intended to be, of course), many of the conditions enshrined within it have become even less feasible since it was originally devised. In an increasingly global, interconnected world, policies are even more subject to external constraints and agencies than ever before. Similarly, within Britain itself, there are more organized interests, agencies and sundry other policy actors than ever before, partly reflecting the increasingly cross-cutting or interconnected nature of many policy issues or problems, particularly as policies are increasingly formulated at different levels within the policy.

As such, implementation has increasingly been recognized as a dynamic, ongoing, two-way process: 'a policy/action continuum in which an interactive and negotiative process is taking place over time between those seeking to put policy into effect and those upon whom action depends' (Barrett and Fudge, 1981a: 25). Or as Malpass and Murie (1999: 199) note, in their study of housing policy:

> Central government policy outputs, often in the form of legislation, are then passed down to local authorities and housing associations, where there is a process of analysis and interpretation, leading up to local political decisions which provide the framework for another reinterpretation as policies are negotiated into practice by the street-level bureaucrats.

Consequently, 'there has been a growing trend towards multi-organizational forms of policy implementation' (Gray, 2000: 284). What this means, ultimately, is that much implementation in Britain reflects the transition from government towards governance, which we examined in Chapter 6. This further illustrates the limits of top-down models of implementation and the notion that implementation constitutes the final 'stage' in a linear or sequential policy process.

QUESTIONS AND TOPICS FOR DISCUSSION

1. Why was Pressman and Wildavsky's book *Implementation* so important in galvanizing interest in this 'stage' of the policy process?
2. What was the significance of 'decision points', according to Pressman and Wildavsky?

3. Who are 'street level bureaucrats', and why are they important to the success of policies?
4. Why might clear rules and regulations still cause problems in the implementation of policies?
5. If it cannot be achieved in reality, what use is a model of 'perfect implementation'?
6. Which particular implementation problems did the CSA encounter, ultimately leading to its failure?
7. How might the transition to governance have made implementation more difficult?
8. What are the main features of the new public management?
9. According to the new public management, why can't public sector professionals and street level bureaucrats be trusted?
10. How is new public management intended to produce more effective policy implementation?

RECOMMENDED TEXTS AND FURTHER READING

1. Susan Barrett and Colin Fudge (eds) (1981) *Policy and Action*. London: Methuen.

   Very good (albeit somewhat dated) series of essays which provides a judicious blend of empirical case studies from specific policy areas and events, and discussion of the academic literature on implementation studies.

2. Lewis Gunn (1978) 'Why is implementation so difficult?', *Management Services in Government*, 33:169–76.

   Seminal article succinctly identifying 10 reasons why policies often encounter problems during implementation. In so doing, Gunn greatly enhances our understanding of why policies may fail, or at least prove only partly successful.

3. Michael Hill and Peter Hupe (2002) *Implementing Public Policy*. London: Sage.

   Traces the development of 'implementation studies' to the present day, examining the key concepts and debates concerning both the theories and the practice of implementation. In many respects, a rich and in-depth literature review.

4. Christopher Hood (1995) 'Contemporary public management: A new global paradigm', *Public Policy and Administration*, 10 (2): 104–17.

   Very important article outlining the defining features of the New Public Management and examining its development as a major means of managing policy implementation and (purportedly) improving public service delivery. Essential to understanding why the public sector is has become subjected to so many targets, audits and inspections.

5. David Marsh and R.A.W. Rhodes (1992) 'The implementation gap: Explaining policy change and continuity', in D. Marsh and R.A.W Rhodes (eds) *Implementing Thatcherite Policies: Audit of an Era*. Buckingham: Open University Press.

Although focusing on policies pursued during the 1980s, draws more general and useful lessons about the factors which determine the success or failure of policy implementation.

6. Jeffrey Pressman and Aaron Wildavsky (1973) *Implementation: How Great Expectations in Washington Are Dashed in Oakland*. Berkeley, CA: University of California Press.

The original, ground-breaking, text which effectively established 'implementation studies' as a vitally important aspect of the policy process in its own right. Through a case study of the application of a particular policy in a specific city, Pressman and Wildavsky drew more general conclusions about the problems which policies often encounter when being put into practice 'on the ground', and which thus affect their success.

7. Paul Sabatier (1986) 'Top-down and bottom-up approaches to implementation research: A critical analysis and suggested synthesis', *Journal of Public Policy*, 6 (1): 21–48.

Important article which reviews the literature on implementation since the 1970s, comparing and evaluating the respective conceptual models, such as the 'top-down' and 'bottom-up' approaches, and then offers a new framework which synthesizes the best elements of each approach.

9 Policy Evaluation

Although the evaluation of policies has always been a feature of the policy process to some extent, with academics and practitioners alike variously seeking to gauge the success of particular policies, policy evaluation has assumed much more importance since the 1980s, as evinced by the scale of audits and monitoring alluded to in the previous chapter. The increased importance of policy evaluation in the contemporary policy process is both a response to growing recognition of the extent to which many policies have previously failed to achieve their professed objectives (*pace* the 'implementation gap'), and also derives from aspects of 'marketization', most notably the relentless pursuit of increased efficiency, improved cost-effectiveness and ensuring value for money (VFM) in the provision of public services.

Furthermore, having become enamoured with the potential or perceived benefits of formal evaluation, ministers have increasingly proclaimed their commitment to 'evidence-based policy' or 'what works' in an allegedly post-ideological era. This, in turn, has prompted increased interest in the adoption of 'pilot schemes', whereby new policies are tested in a particular community or town, or perhaps on a specific section of society, in order either to gauge a policy's likely effectiveness, or to identify potential problems, prior to implementing the problem nationally.

However, policy evaluation is also an integral component of the new public management, which we discussed in the previous chapter. As we explained, new public management entails two analytically distinct, but in practice, inextricably linked, aspects.

1. Stipulating what is to be achieved, through the setting of targets or other performance indicators. In many instances, this will also stipulate the mechanisms or processes of how these are to achieved: not merely stating what front-line staff or street level bureaucrats must do or achieve, but also how.
2. A system of audit, inspection and measurement to evaluate whether the specified goals, targets or other performance indicators have been attained. After all, as Burton notes: 'If a performance cannot be measured, it cannot be managed' (Burton, 2013: 219).

Having delineated the first aspect of new public management in the previous chapter, we now turn our attention to the second aspect, by outlining the role it plays in the evaluation of public policy, via audits.

THE ROLE OF AUDITS IN PUBLIC POLICY

The plethora of performance indicators and targets that have been imposed on public sector organizations and their staff since the 1990s, coupled with the consequent increase in evaluation to measure improvements or success, has resulted in what Michael Power refers to as 'audit explosion', to the extent that 'Britain has become an "audit society"' (Power, 1994: 1). As a consequence, public services, and the professionals or street level bureaucrats working within them have become enmeshed in an 'audit culture' (Power, 1997. See also Russell, 2009: 27).

Crucially, though, Power notes that some audits are not concerned solely with evaluating or measuring outputs and outcomes (crucial though these are), but with institutional processes themselves; to evaluate 'the systems in place to govern quality' (Power, 1994: 6). This, of course, reflects the new public management premise that if the correct organizational mechanisms and procedures are established and effectively managed, then improved performance, outputs and outcomes will naturally follow.

The rise of this 'audit society' means that since the early 1990s, all public sector organizations and service providers have been subject to regular audits to gauge their efficiency and success in performing their roles (see, for example, Burton, 2013: Chapters 14–15). This often entails measuring the extent to which they have achieved stipulated targets and other specified performance indicators, whereupon the results are likely to be published for public perusal, often in the form of league tables. Table 9.1 illustrates some of the main audits that various public service providers have been subject to during the last couple of decades or so, indicating which agency conducts the audits and what each one measures in its particular policy sector.

The various audits usually entail a combination of written documentation, in the form of detailed questionnaires or self-evaluation reports and on-site inspections, with officials

Table 9.1   Examples of audits of various public services since the early 1990s

Policy sector/Institutions	Agency conducting audit	Criteria – what is evaluated
National Health Service	Care Quality Commission (Department of Health)	Hospitals (and other health providers) measured against 16 criteria (outcomes), including:
		1. respecting and involving people who use services
		2. acquiring patients' consent to treatment
		3. meeting nutritional needs
		4. cooperating with other health or care providers
		5. cleanliness and infection control
		6. safety, availability and suitability of equipment
		7. adequate levels of staffing
		8. effective and safe management of medicines
		9. accurate and up-to-date patient records.

Policy sector/Institutions	Agency conducting audit	Criteria – what is evaluated
Probation Service	HM Inspectorate of Probation (Ministry of Justice)	Adult offenders; five main criteria: 1. assisting sentencing 2. delivering the sentence of the court 3. reducing the likelihood of reoffending 4. protecting the public 5. delivering effective work for victims. Inspections often thematic, focusing on a particular topic (drug abuse, violence, etc.)
Schools	Ofsted (Department of Education)	School inspections; four main criteria: 1. the achievement of pupils at the school 2. the quality of teaching in the school 3. the behaviour and safety of pupils at the school 4. the quality of leadership in, and management of, the school.
Social Work	Ofsted* (Department of Education)	Several aspects concerning 'at risk' children and children in care: 1. the quality, effectiveness and timeliness of assessment and risk management 2. the effectiveness of the help given to children, young people and their families 3. the consistency of the focus on the child/ young person's needs and best interests 4. the quality and effectiveness of inter-agency cooperation and communication 5. the extent to which social workers and other professionals working with the child/young person and their family have meaningful, consistent and direct contact with them 6. the effectiveness of quality assurance and management oversight of practice and decision making 7. the experiences of particularly vulnerable children/young people 8. how well the local authority takes account of, and responds to, the wishes and feelings of children and young people.
Universities	Quality Assurance Agency for Higher Education (Department of Business, Innovation and Skills) Higher Education Funding Councils (Department of Business, Innovation and Skills)	Three main types of audit: 1. Periodic Programme Review 2. Institutional Review 3. Research Excellence Framework.**

* Involved in social work inspection, because its full title is the Office for Standards in Education, Children's Services and Skills.

** Previously the Research Assessment Exercise (RAE).

from the relevant agency actually visiting (possibly for several days) the institutions being audited to observe directly that it is performing efficiently, and in accordance with relevant regulations and other performance criteria. These inspections will also usually entail interviews with front-line staff, management and service 'users'.

Following the audit and inspection, the agency conducting the evaluation will normally write a report, both grading the quality of service provision against benchmark criteria and highlighting the issues that need to be addressed in order to yield improvements. In some cases, such as inspections of schools, and universities' research, the results will be ranked, often in the form of published league tables. Needless to say, the publication of the results of audits and inspections has become an integral aspect of ensuring that public services should be 'accountable' and 'transparent' in their activities and operational efficiency.

Meanwhile, institutions that have been adjudged highly successful in their audit or inspection may be awarded additional funding. For example, universities that are deemed to have excelled in research audits (conducted every 6–7 years) may be awarded an increase in their subsequent research funding.

In a subtle but significant manner, of course, the allocation of additional funds in response to excellent performance is intended to imitate the profit motive, which prevails in the private sector. As such, the linking of funding to measured performance can be viewed as another manifestation of the 'marketization' of the public sector, and the determination of successive governments since the late 1980s to inculcate a business ethos into the remnants of the public sector.

CONSEQUENCES AND PROBLEMS OF AUDITS

As audits have become more pervasive throughout the public sector since the 1990s, they have engendered several criticisms, both from an intellectual or methodological perspective, and (not surprisingly) from the professionals and street level bureaucrats who have increasingly been subject to such performance monitoring and measurement.

A major issue that Power (1997: *passim*) has noted is that the contemporary 'audit culture' does not merely measure public policy outputs and outcomes, it serves to define or determine *what* can or should be measured, and *how* such measurement should be conducted. This can have subtle but nonetheless highly significant consequences for the implementation of public policy, and impinge upon the manner in which front-line professionals or street level bureaucrats actually perform their roles and responsibilities; the bureaucratic tail can start wagging the professional dog.

Stipulating what is to be measured

There are actually several, albeit closely related, issues here. The first is that audits actually define what is measurable, and thus steer professionals and public service institutions towards a focus on the activities that can be audited, whereas those that are less amenable to such empirical verification are likely to be ascribed a lower priority. For example, with regard to policing, 'bobbies on the beat' (police officers patrolling the street) may well serve to deter 100s of crimes each year, but of course, it is by definition impossible to measure how many crimes have been deterred by such 'preventative' policing. By contrast, the number of arrests and convictions can readily be measured as a consequence of 'reactive' policing, whereby the police either respond to a crime that is taking place and arrest the perpetrators in the act, or successfully investigate a crime that has already occurred and thereby convict the person(s) who carried it out.

What this means, therefore, is that an officer involved in preventative policing might be audited (via performance appraisal) and report that they have made zero arrests in the past three months, whereas a colleague engaged in reactive policing might report that they have made 20 arrests or solved 20 crimes during the same period. According to the logic of the audit culture, and its prioritization of what can be measured, the latter police officer will be deemed much more efficient or productive, even though the former police officer might have deterred 50 or 100 crimes; by definition, the latter cannot be proved and so is not audited.

Hence the criticism that by defining what is actually measurable, audits do not simply evaluate the performance of public service professionals, they effectively determine *how* staff do their jobs, and what they focus on. In the case of the police therefore, a 2010 survey revealed that barely 10 per cent of police officers were on front-line duty at any given time (HM Inspectorate of Constabulary, 2010: 15). This was in spite of opinion polls indicating that the vast majority of British people want to see more 'bobbies on the beat'. Ironically, too, that politicians routinely insist that public sector reform is intended to ensure that such services are much more responsive to the public and the wishes of service users.

Meanwhile, in higher education, the Research Assessment Exercise (RAE) (now replaced by the Research Excellence Framework (REF)), did not merely measure the number and quality of academic publications by each 'research active' member of staff in every university, but also stipulated which type of publications or 'research outputs' were worthy of evaluation. As a consequence, academic research has become increasingly pre-occupied by considerations of what would be eligible for submission to the next RAE/REF itself, rather than any intrinsic intellectual or educational value that a book or journal article might possess; 'tortuous bureaucracies assess[ed] the merits of the research produced by every department in all the 200 universities', the results of which would determine the subsequent allocation of up to £5 billion of research funding (Cohen, 2008: 30).

However, because the RAE prioritized scholarly research and 'cutting-edge' originality, a specialist monograph that only sold 300 copies was ascribed much more 'weight' than a textbook that might have been read or purchased by 10,000 undergraduates nationally, and which would presumably have been of far more use to them in educational or pedagogic terms. In other words, in an era of higher education expansion and record numbers of students attending university, lecturers were often discouraged from writing textbooks for students because these would not be acceptable for their department's RAE submission. Therefore, like many such audits in the public sector, the RAE was not 'innocent'; it did not merely evaluate a particular professional activity. On the contrary, it effectively defined what constituted 'quality' academic research and thereby influenced the type of research that academics pursued, and *inter alia* what type of publications they should direct their research towards. Or as Power notes, because of the RAE and its definition of original research: 'Editing books, organizing conferences and, paradoxically, reviewing and facilitating the publication efforts of others fall out of account' (Power, 1997: 100).

Quantity vs quality

The second problem accruing from the operation of audit in modern public services is that measurements are often quantitative rather than qualitative. Again, this can partly be attributable to methodological factors, and the priority ascribed to measuring what can actually be observed and quantified. Criteria such as 'how many', 'how often' or 'how quickly' can be, in most instances, readily counted, and then reported with ostensibly clear figures and statistical data. This data can subsequently be translated into user friendly or headline grabbing league tables, or cited by ministers to illustrate that a desirable activity or policy outcome has increased by *x* per cent, or that a problem has been reduced by *y* per cent.

However, it might sometimes be the case that the quality of a service or core activity is compromised by the focus on increasing the quantity of a specified performance indicator. For example, hospital managers or an NHS Trust might understandably boast that their surgeons are now operating on more patients each day, and thereby reducing waiting lists, to the obvious benefit of patients who would otherwise have a longer and often painful or physically debilitating wait for surgery. Yet surgeons themselves might complain that conducting more operations each day means that they are under pressure to 'rush' each operation, thereby increasing the chances of making mistakes during surgery – mistakes that could, in a few instances, prove fatal to the patient.

Meanwhile, in many hospitals, nurses are now instructed to spend only 15–20 minutes with each patient on 'ward rounds', in order that they can see more patients each day. This increase can then be cited as evidence both of the nurse's and the hospital's increased efficiency and productivity. Yet this can mean that a nurse might not have time to elicit all the relevant information about a patient's symptoms or medical history, even though such information will be vital when decisions are being taken about the patient's medical treatment or need for surgery. At the same time, patients themselves might consequently complain about the standard of nursing care, or even that the nurses were brusque in their manner; too eager to move on to their next patient.

Certainly, a 2012 survey by the Royal College of Nursing (RCN) revealed that '60% of respondents [nurses] were spending less time with patients than they did a year ago, with over a quarter (26 per cent) claiming their patient-facing time had significantly decreased.' As a consequence: 'Only a small minority of nurses (6 per cent) felt that they always had the time to deliver the level of care patients needed. Sometimes this lack of time resulted in the inability to properly discuss patients' concerns', with one nurse explaining that: 'It takes time for people to open up or discuss concerns, we don't have the time to give them', a concern echoed by another nurse who explained that there was 'not enough time to discuss patient concerns or deal with complex needs' (Royal College of Nursing, 2012: 14).

Similarly, probation offers and social workers alike increasingly find themselves under pressure to see more 'clients', such as young offenders or 'problem families' respectively, each day or each week, so that their managers or departments can show an increase in 'productivity' or efficiency. Yet this will often entail spending less time with each 'client', and therefore being unable to provide the degree of advice or support needed, or developing trust; the young offender might thus re-offend, or the 'problem family' might become more dysfunctional, with a correspondingly damaging impact on the children, and perhaps, wider or longer-term costs to society.

Elsewhere, if more pupils attain higher GCSE grades, does this in itself prove that the quality of education has improved, or could it be a consequence of teachers (understandably) 'teaching to the test', in order to ensure that their school improves its league table position, in order to continue attracting pupils, and ultimately, ensure that the teachers retain their jobs? Certainly, one writer has lamented that: 'The chief business of schools is no longer to produce educated people, but education statistics' (Russell, 2009: 27. See also Mansell, 2007).

Meanwhile, the police have sometimes complained that the need to increase the number of crimes solved and/or successful prosecutions can divert time and resources away from more complex cases that would take longer to solve, and thus mean lower, less impressive figures for 'clear-up' rates and detection. Instead, they are under pressure to solve 'easy' crimes, even though these are often less serious.

The increasing use of targets and their consequences

As audits and inspections for measuring operational performance, outputs and outcomes have become more widespread, and apparently more 'robust', so have ministers become increasingly enamoured with setting targets for public services and their staff. Certainly, the Blair-Brown governments seemed to be afflicted by a pathological mania for targets in the public sector, these being viewed as vital to increasing the efficiency of professionals and front-line staff and *inter alia* to improving the provision or 'delivery' of public services. At the same time, however, targets have been intended to provide objective or transparent criteria against which performance and improvements in public services can be measured; targets have thus become integral to the audit society.

However, many staff in Britain's public services have queried the efficacy or utility of many of these targets, partly on the grounds that they reinforce the measurement of quantitative criteria rather than the actual quality of service provision or performance, but also because they can serve to divert the attention of professionals and street level bureaucrats away from what their 'clients' or the public actually want, towards what politicians or managers deem important at any given time.

For example, a 2007–08 study of the social work profession revealed a growing concern among many social workers that their activities were 'too focussed on achieving national targets and ensuring that statutory processes were met at the expense of direct contact ... time given to developing a rapport and building a relationship with children and their families' (Holmes et al., 2009: 15).

At about the same time, a study of the impact of targets on policing outlined the scenario whereby:

> The commander goes to headquarters and gets, 'a bollocking in front of the others' for not hitting his targets. When he comes back 'that bollocking passes down the line'. In those circumstances justifying a failure to meet the target with: '"Well sorry but I was helping the public instead" just doesn't wash' ... Advising an old lady on better security; spending 'seven hours with a victim of crime' as one officer had done that week; giving a youth a stern talking to; comforting the family where someone has died suddenly. None of these fulfils a single target, yet for the public they are the essence of good policing.
>
> (Sergeant, 2008: 37, 42)

Certainly, the police have variously complained that they are compelled to 'chase targets' rather than criminals, and that as a consequence, they have not always been able to respond to the concerns of local communities about particular crimes in a neighbourhood, because of the pressure from above to prioritize targets stipulated by the Home Office. As the researcher for a BBC TV police drama *Line of Duty* discovered: 'Many dedicated officers now regard policing as an impossible job', in which 'procedures have been transformed by a target culture that dictates which crimes get investigated', and officers are often obliged to disregard 'reported crimes because they're under pressure to focus on cases that can be solved within a workable timeframe'. At the same time: 'Temporary initiatives prioritise certain offences; once targets are met, these are downgraded, so resources can be directed towards the next initiative' (Mercurio, 2012: 28).

The increasing use of targets can also foster institutional game playing or forms of creative accounting by professionals and street level bureaucrats under pressure to hit various targets. For example, the Blair-Brown governments stipulated that hospitals' accident and emergency (A&E) departments should admit and then discharge or transfer patients within four hours, as part of New Labour's more general commitment to reducing the time that NHS patients had to wait for hospital treatment. Consequently, there were various claims that when an A&E department was particularly busy, and unlikely to be able to 'process' a new patient within four hours, some ambulances waited outside A and E until staff were less busy, and then able to treat the patient within the four hours from the time of admission (see for example: Commission for Health Improvement, 2003: 2–26; Conservative Party, 2008: 10; Harris, 2011; Campbell 2008; Donnelly, 2009).

Elsewhere, it has been claimed that: 'In order to meet targets, police are now classifying incidents as crimes that would previously have been dealt with informally, classified differently or ignored … Many police complained senior officers were pressurising them to make arrests they considered unethical' (Sergeant, 2008: 39). Meanwhile, towards the end of 2013, some police officers admitted that they 'fiddled' crime figures in order to hit targets and improve 'performance indicators' (Ford, 2013).

Also under the auspices of the Home Office is the UK Border Agency, from where a 'whistleblower' has claimed that staff were sometimes stationed in airport departure lounges, so that when an illegal immigrant was voluntarily *leaving* Britain, they would be handed official 'removal' documentation, thereby enabling the agency to record this as a successful deportation (Oakeshott, 2011).

Meanwhile, in summer 2013, it was revealed that thousands of pupils were being entered for GSCE maths exams with different examination boards, in order to increase their chances of obtaining a grade C in at least one of them. This would then help to improve their school's pass rate, and *inter alia* its league table ranking (Garner, 2013b).

Bureaucratic overload and tick-box culture

The 'audit culture' not only shapes the manner in which professionals and street level bureaucrats actually implement policies and administer public services, it has also been criticized for resulting in 'bureaucratic overload'. This derives both from the sheer scale and scope of performance indicators and targets – often changing or being added to on a regular basis – which many professionals and service providers have been subjected to since the 1990s, and the often administratively complex and time-consuming character of preparing for, or participating in, the ensuing audits and inspections.

Certainly, a major complaint of many public sector professions since the 1990s concerns the seemingly inexorable increase in the volume and complexity of associated paperwork. Ministers who insist that the private sector is stifled by red-tape and bureaucratic meddling seem to think that the public sector will become more efficient and productive if it is subject to ever increasing bureaucracy and paperwork! There has been both a quantitative and qualitative increase in the box ticking, form filling and report writing that many professionals have to undertake in order to provide 'evidence' that they are performing their roles and responsibilities effectively, and hitting targets.

Much of the bureaucracy engendered by the audit culture is also linked to ministerial and media demands for 'accountability' and 'transparency' in Britain's public services. Virtually every public sector activity now has to be documented, often in considerable detail, otherwise there is no verifiable evidence that a task has been satisfactorily performed, the correct procedures followed or targets attained.

For example, Home Office figures revealed that in 2006–07, Britain's police officers spent more time on paperwork than they did actually 'on patrol', leading Sir Ronnie Flanagan, the then Chief Inspector of Constabulary, to remark that the amount of paperwork faced by contemporary police officers was 'truly staggering' (quoted in Johnston, 2007).

The Home Secretary at the time, Jacqui Smith, pledged that the Labour government would look for ways to cut the red tape imposed on the police, thereby freeing up more time directly to tackle anti-social behaviour and crime. Yet a Home Office consultative paper on the reform of policing, published three year later, suggested that little progress had been made:

> Over the years the amount of data central Government has collected to assess the police has piled up to the extent that it is getting in the way of common sense policing ... Too much police time is spent filling out forms and following procedures that are unnecessary ... Officers all too often collect information just in case it is needed rather than applying a common sense approach.
>
> (Home Office, 2010: 20, 22)

Even in 2012, police officers continued to complain about the volume of paperwork that they were required to complete for virtually every activity, however minor. While they readily acknowledged that some paperwork was necessary, and always would be, 'many officers feel the pendulum has swung too far in the direction of bureaucratic oversight'. For example, making an arrest still 'required the officer to fill in numerous forms to ensure correct protocols had been followed' (Mercurio, 2012: 28).

The police were certainly not alone in their exasperation and frustration about the volume and complexity of paperwork engendered by the audit society and associated target culture. Throughout the public sector since the 1990s, complaints from professionals have increased concerning the inexorable growth of bureaucracy, and the manner in which paperwork, including the recording or provision of data, has seemingly become a core activity in itself. For example, social workers have bemoaned that 'excessive' paperwork has prevented them from actually dealing with 'at risk' children or their parents (Herbert, 2004; Revans, 2007). At the same time, social workers have experienced 'an increase in statutory processes, and a tightening of timescales', which have further 'added to the volume of indirect work, particularly as staff take time to learn new procedures'. As a consequence, it is claimed that social workers are 'required to spend a substantial proportion of their time on routine administrative tasks' (Holmes et al., 2009: 15. See also: British Association of Social Workers and Social Workers Union, 2012: 9–13; Burton and Van der Broek, 2009; Lamb, 2010: 45; Morton, 2012).

Similarly, the nursing profession has increasingly bemoaned the volume and complexity of paperwork that nurses have to deal with, thereby reducing the actual amount of time spent with patients. This administrative burden derives from the range of activities that nurses are obliged to record, including: 'Lengthy admission forms, patient care plans, complex discharge planning documents ... a plethora of risk assessment ... [an] increasing number of audit reports, policy documents and evaluation sheets required to measure outcomes and care quality' (Lomas, 2012. See also Royal College of Nursing, 2008).

Doctors too have complained about the bureaucratization of the NHS, with one consultant oncologist claiming that the internal market has 'wreaked havoc ... spawned a nation of administrators'. Moreover, he claims that whereas the welfare state was originally intended to provide a system of universal care and support 'from cradle to grave', the contemporary NHS was more akin to 'a cradle rocked by accountants who are incapable of even counting the number of times they have rocked it' (Waxman, 2010: 28).

Meanwhile, academics (not least, this author!) have long complained about the burgeoning bureaucracy and repeated audits or monitoring exercises to which they have been subjected since the 1990s, invariably in the name of 'quality assurance' or 'research excellence'. Two American academics who were visiting British universities a few years ago confessed that they were:

> ... baffled by the level of monitoring, reporting, evaluating and bureaucratic hassling to which academics in this country are subjected. Our response is to ask: why doesn't Britain let its academics do what they do best, teach and carry out research, without government and university administrators breathing down their necks? ... Many British academics groan under the weight of administrative tasks ... US universities have [also] experienced an increase in paperwork in recent decades. But they can't compare with their UK counterparts in terms of sheer zeal for reporting and monitoring.
>
> The problem is that bureaucrats prefer to introduce monitoring and reporting in order to forestall problems that they expect, rather than dealing with the tiny number of such problems that might actually appear. This is evident in the constant reporting on all sorts of things. Instead of the central administration reacting to problems that come to their attention, they expect departments to spell out their activities in mind-numbingly detailed reports.

(Kord and Wilson, 2006)

Lest it be thought that such complaints only emanated from public sector professionals themselves, it should be noted that in 2011, the House of Commons Justice Select Committee deemed it 'staggering' that probation officers could spend as little as 25 per cent of their time supervising and helping to rehabilitate criminals and ex-offenders, because of the extent to which a 'tick-box, bean-counting culture' compelled probation offers to prioritize paperwork and form filling (House of Commons Justice Committee, 2011: 19, para. 40; 33, para. 83).

Another official inquiry that revealed the scale and deeply damaging consequences of box ticking, form filling and target chasing, this time in the NHS, was the Francis investigation into the Mid-Staffordshire NHS Trust scandal. Between 2005 and 2009, between 400 and 1,200 patients died in Stafford Hospital, apparently as a consequence of neglect by medical staff. Other patients were sometimes left crying out for pain relief medication, or lying in their own urine or excrement when there was no one to take them to the toilet or provide a bed pan. Sometimes, patients were left without food or drink, or were not washed regularly.

This tragic scandal prompted an official inquiry, chaired by Robert Francis, a Barrister, which commenced in November 2010 and published its final report in February 2013. Not surprisingly, given the scale of the tragedy at Stafford Hospital, the report identified major failings and derelictions of duty by staff at all levels, along with considerable organizational or institutional dysfunctionality. The main failings and problems identified in the report (Francis, 2013: *passim*) are outlined in Box 9.1.

Box 9.1   Key findings of the 2013 Francis Report on the Mid-Staffordshire NHS Trust scandal

- Senior management, both in the Trust and the hospital, seemed to prioritize finance and targets, with a consequent disregard or denial of concerns, and an isolation from practice elsewhere ... the Trust was operating in an environment in which its leadership was expected to focus on financial issues, and there is little doubt that this is what it did. Sadly, it paid insufficient attention to the risks in relation to the quality of service delivery this entailed ... The Trust prioritized its finances ... over its quality of care, and failed to put patients at the centre of its work.
- An organizational structure and ethos in which systems, processes and meeting targets were the main measures of performance. The focus of the system resulted in a number of organizations failing to place quality of care and patients at the heart of their work. Finances and targets were often given priority without considering the impact on the quality of care. This was not helped by a general lack of effective engagement with patients and the public, and failure to place clinicians and other healthcare professionals at the heart of decision making.
- Trust management had no culture of listening to patients. There were inadequate processes for dealing with complaints and serious untoward incidents (SUIs). Staff and patient surveys continually gave signs of dissatisfaction with the way the Trust was run, and yet no effective action was taken.

(Continued)

(Continued)

- As a result of poor leadership and staffing policies, a completely inadequate standard of nursing was offered on some wards in Stafford. The complaints heard … testified not only to inadequate staffing levels, but poor leadership, recruitment and training. This led in turn to a declining professionalism and a tolerance of poor standards. Staff did report many incidents, which occurred because of short staffing, exhibited poor morale in their responses to staff surveys, and received only ineffective representation of concerns from the RCN.
- Whistleblowing – it is clear that a staff nurse's report in 2007 made a serious and substantial allegation about the leadership of A&E. This was not resolved by Trust management.
- Savings in staff costs were being made in an organization, which was already identified as having serious problems in delivering a service of adequate quality, and complying with minimum standards. Yet no thought seems to have been given in any part of the system aware of the proposals to the potential impact on patient safety and quality … it is remarkable how little attention was paid to the potential impact of proposed [financial] savings on quality and safety.
- Constant reorganization of NHS structures often led to a loss of corporate memory and misunderstandings about an organization's functions and responsibilities.
- Ward sisters and nurse managers should operate in a supervisory capacity and should not be office bound. The ward manager should know about the care plans relating to every patient on their ward, and should be visible and accessible to patients and staff alike.

In the context of these findings, the Francis Report emphasized that, ultimately:

> … it should be patients – not numbers – which count … The demands for financial control, corporate governance, commissioning and regulatory systems are understandable and in many cases necessary, but it is not the system itself which will ensure that the patient is put first day in and day out. It is the people working in the health service and those charged with developing healthcare policy that need to ensure that is the case.
>
> (Francis, 2013: 5)

Among the many recommendations advanced by the Francis Report, it was proposed that:

> The professional voice needs to be strengthened … There should be at least one nurse on the executive boards of all healthcare organisations.
>
> (Francis, 2013: 76, para.1).

In effect, many of the problems that the Francis Report identified can readily be understood in the context of the new public management, whereby: chasing targets to achieve measurable or quantifiable outputs becomes a priority or end in itself; there is an excessive emphasis on institutional structures, administrative processes and top-down re-organization; front-line professional staff are increasingly deprived of autonomy or discretion as a consequence of stringent managerial or hierarchical control and the need to adhere to rigid bureaucratic procedures.

In such instances, the new public management, which purports to ensure accountability, cost-effectiveness, efficiency, 'quality' service delivery and transparency, all too often yields organizational dysfunctionality, bureaucratic game playing, blame avoidance, confusion over roles and responsibilities among staff, and a regime in which professionals are compelled to spend considerable amounts of time at desks writing reports and ticking boxes to ensure that there is an institutional paper trail that can then be audited. In extreme and tragic cases, such as the Mid-Staffs NHS Trust scandal, the result can be a major implementation gap resulting in a policy disaster, one entailing the cumulative loss of hundreds of lives.

Yet, if staff complain about such dysfunctional and demoralizing regimes, they risk being labelled 'troublemakers' by managers, and of being branded (by ministers and much of the media) as a self-serving 'vested interest' which is afraid of accountability. In some cases, professionals who become 'whistleblowers' (meaning that they 'go public' about what is happening in their organization because they are so appalled) are likely to be sacked and possibly accused of bringing their institution 'into disrepute'. This is why so many front-line professionals keep quiet about wrongdoing in public services; they fear the consequences of speaking out and so succumb to a conspiracy of silence.

Nonetheless, ministers seem to retain an unshakeable faith in new public management and its associated processes of audit and monitoring in Britain's public services, to the extent that when problems arise or scandals occur, the assumption is that a few individuals are to blame, not the regime itself. The response, therefore, is often to discipline or dismiss the 'guilty' individuals, and then impose even more 'robust' procedures for monitoring and measuring both individual and institutional performance.

Like the rulers of the former Soviet Union, Britain's senior politicians cannot accept or acknowledge that the regime – in this case, the new public management and the associated target-chasing audit culture – is itself inherently flawed or prone to dysfunctionality. Therefore, when problems periodically occur, they are assumed to be a 'one off' from which 'lessons will be learned', whereupon there is a redoubling of efforts, often entailing yet more bureaucratic procedures or managers, to make the regime work properly.

EVIDENCE-BASED POLICY MAKING

The increased importance of formal audit, monitoring and evaluation since the late 1980s also underpins the growing political emphasis on 'evidence-based policy', with an increasing insistence by ministers that their policies are predicated on 'what works', rather than deriving from ideology (Solesbury, 2001). This was certainly the case with the 1997–2010 (New) Labour governments, whereby Tony Blair was keen to present himself as a post-ideological Prime Minister who was only interested in pursuing policies that were clearly and demonstrably effective. This enabled him to distance New Labour from Old Labour, with the latter deemed to have pursued too many policies for ideological reasons, even when those policies were impracticable, ineffective or unpopular with mainstream voters.

In contrast to this alleged dogmatism, Blair and fellow New Labour acolytes insisted that they were public policy pragmatists, only concerned with pursuing policies if they were workable and feasible in practice, and could be proven to achieve their stated objectives. Or as the 1999 White Paper *Modernising Government* argued, policy makers should be concerned:

> ... to produce policies that really deal with problems; that are forward-looking and shaped by the evidence rather than a response to short-term pressures; that tackle causes not symptoms; that are measured by results rather than activity ... To meet people's rising expectations, policy making must also be a process of continuous learning and improvement.
>
> (Cabinet Office, 1999a: 15)

Similarly, a 'strategic policy-making team on professional policy making for the 21st century', located in the Cabinet Office, emphasized that 'policy making must be soundly based on evidence of what works' (Cabinet Office, 1999b). Similar claims have variously been made by ministers in the post-2010 Conservative-Liberal Democrat coalition government, with Danny Alexander and Oliver Letwin (Alexander and Letwin, 2013: 2), Chief Secretary to the Treasury and Minister for the Cabinet Office respectively, jointly asserting that: 'It is a fundamental principle of good public services that decisions are made on the basis of strong evidence, and what we know works'.

To this professed purpose, in March 2013, the Cabinet Office established four 'independent', 'What Works' centres whose objective would be to conduct empirical research that would then shape and underpin ministers' decisions and policies. The four policy areas covered by these What Works centres were: local economic growth; early intervention (education, children and families); 'ageing better'; and crime reduction. These were to work alongside two established 'evidence' centres, namely the Education Endowment Foundation (operated in partnership with the educational Sutton Trust) and the National Institute for Clinical and Health Excellence (NICE).

The precise role and *modus operandi* of these What Works centres, as envisaged by the Cabinet Office, is delineated in Box 9.2.

Box 9.2   Role and *modus operandi* of What Works centres established in 2013

1. Generate evidence synthesis, by undertaking systematic assessment of relevant evidence and produce a sound, accurate, clear and actionable synthesis of the global evidence base, which:

    a) assesses and ranks interventions on the basis of effectiveness and cost-effectiveness
    b) shows where the interventions are applicable

c) shows the relative cost of interventions
d) shows the strength of evidence on an agreed scale.

2. Translate the evidence to produce and apply a common currency for comparing the effectiveness of interventions.
3. Put the needs and interests of users at the heart of its work.
4. Promote 'evidence absorption' by publishing and disseminating findings in a format that can be understood, interpreted and acted upon.
5. Promote good evidence by identifying research and capability gaps, and work with partners to fill them.
6. Advise those commissioning and undertaking innovative interventions and research projects to ensure that their work can be evaluated effectively.

(Source: Cabinet Office, 2013b: 5)

One particularly notable aspect of such attempts at pursuing evidence-based policy making has been noted by Palfrey et al. (2012: 39–41), namely the apparent similarity to Herbert Simon's (1957) original model of 'rational' decision making, whereby policy makers were assumed or expected to respond to a problem by:

- deciding on their policy goal or objective
- identifying the possible means for achieving their goal or objective
- evaluating each of these options
- selecting the 'best' option
- implementing it.

This model has subsequently been subject to considerable criticism, particularly from Charles Lindblom (1959; 1979), for being simplistic or unrealistic; real world policy making is deemed to be much more messy, with budgetary constraints, cognitive limits, competing bureaucratic or political interests, conflicting values, multiplicity of policy actors, time constraints and uncertain or incompatible policy goals, all limiting or undermining the scope for 'rational' policy making.

Nonetheless, those policy makers who claim to be pursuing evidence-based policy and 'what works' seem to be convinced that they are purveyors and practitioners of a much more rational mode of decision taking and policy making than has previously been the case.

Yet a note of caution – or cynicism – must be sounded, for as Majone (1989: 25) recognizes, 'policy analysts and researchers are often deeply involved in the process of norm setting', which means that it is virtually impossible to eradicate values from rational analysis. In other words, the values or ideological perspective of policy makers will invariably shape their interpretation of the 'evidence', or even what counts as evidence in the first place.

Indeed, as we noted in Chapter 1, the very notion of what constitutes a problem warranting attention from policy makers is socially constructed and reflects political beliefs. This will therefore often pre-determine what 'problems' policy makers decide to conduct research into in the first place, how the research question is phrased (what is the research seeking to evaluate or measure?) and how the ensuing 'evidence' is interpreted.

For policy makers operating within, and broadly accepting, a neo-liberal paradigm or overarching ideological framework (as has prevailed in Britain since the 1980s, even when New Labour was in government), the 'evidence' of 'what works' invariably entails policies that extend and strengthen the role or 'the market' in public service delivery, and thus 'prove' that provision by the state is inherently, and thus always, less efficient or effective.

By depicting such policies as being evidence-based and derived from 'what works' (as gleaned from empirical observation and measurement), politicians like Tony Blair and David Cameron have sought to present themselves and their respective parties as being post-ideological, and thus as pragmatists and technocrats concerned merely with finding the most effective and workable policy solutions to tackle problems, based on an objective evaluation of the evidence.

Yet quite apart from the underlying or covert partisan perspectives and objectives of avowedly non-ideological policy makers, the type of rational approach to decision taking seemingly extolled by the Cabinet Office's 'What Works' programme is still likely to encounter practical problems. For example, what will be deemed 'relevant evidence' (as opposed to 'irrelevant' – or perhaps inconvenient – evidence)?

Also, in an era of marketization and privatization, coupled with the commitment to cutting public expenditure, the stipulation that evidence must be considered according to criteria such as 'effectiveness and cost-effectiveness' and the 'relative costs of interventions' will presumably have serious implications for the type of evidence that is considered, or deemed appropriate; 'effective' in actually tackling a problem, even if this entailed additional spending by government or an expanded role for the state, or 'effective' in cutting public expenditure and further reducing state intervention?

Two further potential problems of the Cabinet's 'What Works' initiative are, first, that it extols those conducting research and advocating evidence-based policies to 'put the needs and interests of users at the heart its work', yet those 'needs and interests' might not be compatible or commensurate with the government's own objectives, or the resource constraints that currently prevail in an era of austerity.

Second, in an era of governance and multi-agency delivery of public services, even an ostensibly rational, evidence-based, policy will need to be implemented by a range of subnational organizations and street level bureaucrats who might not always have the same objectives or values, or who might themselves lack adequate resources; problems which we noted in the previous chapter.

In this context, Geoff Mulgan, while fully supporting the goal of imbuing policy making with more scientific advice and evidence wherever possible, readily acknowledges that:

> The most brilliant advice may go wholly unheeded if it's not fitted to the social context of decision makers, the psychology of people making decisions in a hurry and under pressure, and the economics of organisations often strapped for cash.

> (Mulgan, 2013: 34)

For example, the Department of Education has, relatively recently, conducted empirical research into the impact of class sizes on pupils' educational attainment, in the context of common assumptions that if class sizes are 'too large', teachers find it more difficult to maintain the attention or discipline of pupils, with a corresponding decline in educational achievements. However, the report suggested that 'a smaller class size has a positive impact on attainment and behaviour in the early years of school, but this effect tends to be small and diminishes after a few years', and as such: 'It is therefore important to assess the value for money of reducing class size against other policy options as the costs could potentially outstrip the benefits'. Indeed, the report concluded that 'class size reduction policies are not the best option in terms of value for money to raising pupil attainment, compared to others such as increasing teacher effectiveness' (Department for Education, 2011: 46, 1). In other words, the Department for Education's research suggests that *better*, rather than *more*, teachers need to be employed, the clear implication being that a 'good' teacher will be able to teach a class containing more than 30 pupils, whereas a 'bad' teacher will struggle.

Another example of relatively recent research commissioned by the government, ostensibly in the context of evidence-based policy, concerned the relationship between alcohol prices and consumption. This research, commissioned by the Home Office, was pursued in the context of widespread concern that the availability of cheap alcohol was fuelling excessive or binge drinking, particularly among young people, which in turn resulted in behavioural problems and civil disorder in Britain's towns and cities at weekends.

Again, however, the findings were equivocal (or at least, were interpreted as such), it being argued that 'the relationship between increasing alcohol price and its impact on various harms is not always straightforward, as a linear relationship does not always exist.' With regard to alcohol consumption and civil disorder, the report claimed that 'available evidence does not indicate a straightforward linear relationship between alcohol consumption and crime; there is little evidence to suggest that drinking alcohol directly causes individuals to commit crime'. Moreover, even when crime *is* committed by people who are drunk, factors other than alcohol might be major influences, such as their cultural or social background or underlying personality (Home Office, 2011: 11–12). The report thus concluded that:

> Overall the evidence presented has shown that on balance increases in alcohol prices are linked to decreases in harms related to alcohol consumption. This suggests that policies designed to increase the price of alcohol may be effective in reducing alcohol harms. *However, alcohol price is only one factor that may affect levels of alcohol consumption, with individual, cultural, situational and social factors also influential.*
>
> (Home Office, 2011: 21, emphasis added)

Subsequently, in July 2013, the coalition government announced that it was *not* going to introduce a statutory minimum price for alcohol, claiming that there was insufficient incontrovertible evidence that minimum pricing would reduce the harmful effects of problem drinking without penalizing those who drank responsibly. As to the problem of civil disorder in Britain's city centres on Friday and Saturday nights, it was claimed that the solution was for pubs and clubs to act more responsibly, and for the alcohol industry itself to place a much higher priority on educating its customers about the need to practise responsible drinking, while also exercising greater responsibility in its marketing or promotional campaigns.

Incidentally, it is worth noting that the phenomenon of 'policy transfer', which we discussed in Chapter 7, can itself be viewed as a manifestation of evidence-based policy. Indeed, in addition to abandoning its plans for minimum alcohol pricing, July 2013 also heard the government announce that it was delaying legislation that would require cigarettes to be sold in plain packets only (and hence without the brands being displayed), pending an evaluation of the effects of similar legislation recently enacted in Australia. The Health Secretary, Jeremy Hunt, explained that although 'we take very seriously the potential for standardised packaging to reduce smoking rates, we have decided to wait until the emerging impact of the decision in Australia can be measured, and then we will make a decision in England' (Department of Health, 2013).

Pilot schemes

Another manifestation of the increased recourse to formal evaluation and evidence-based policy has been the greater propensity for ministers to conduct 'pilot schemes' prior to implementing a new policy nationally. Here, pilot schemes are defined as 'the phased introduction of major government policies or programmes, allowing them to be tested, evaluated and adjusted where necessary before being rolled out nationally' (Cabinet Office, 2003: 1).

The increasing recourse to pilot schemes is also a response to the 'implementation gap' identified in the previous chapter, as policy makers seek to identify the potential or actual problems which would otherwise undermine the success of a new policy. Furthermore, 'pilot schemes' can serve to avoid one of the causes of policy disasters identified by Dunleavy (1995), namely 'scale aggregation'. What he meant by this was that if a major new policy is implemented nationally (the Poll Tax and the CSA constituting two classic examples), then the consequences of any subsequent failures will be that much greater; more people will be affected, and the costs – either in terms of money wasted or loss of political credibility – will be correspondingly higher.

It was under New Labour that pilot schemes became a more significant feature of the policy process, not least because they could readily be linked to the Blair government's professed commitment to 'evidence-based policy' and post-ideological 'what works' criteria of policy efficacy. Thus did the previously mentioned 1999 White Paper *Modernising Government* pledge that:

> We will improve our use of evidence and research so that we understand better the problems we are trying to address. We must make more use of pilot schemes to encourage innovations and test whether they work. We will ensure that all policies and programmes are clearly specified and evaluated, and the lessons of success and failure are communicated and acted upon. Feedback from those who implement and deliver policies and services is essential too. We need to apply the disciplines of project management to the policy process.
>
> (Cabinet Office, 1999a: 17)

When a new policy is subject to a 'pilot scheme', this can either entail applying it at a local level, to gauge its effectiveness in a town or region, for example, or it can be applied to a particular section of society, such as victims of domestic violence, although this too will often be on a local basis. In either case, the pilot scheme will usually be a prelude to the policy being implemented more widely or nationally, once its effectiveness has been evaluated and any problems have been addressed. Some examples of recent or current pilot schemes are listed in Table 9.2.

Table 9.2   Examples of contemporary pilot schemes

Policy tested	Where conducted	When conducted	Outcome
Agriculture Culling of badgers to curb spread of bovine tuberculosis	Gloucestershire and Somerset	Summer 2013	DEFRA to review during Autumn 2013
Child protection 'Sarah's law'; allows parents to check if a convicted paedophile is living in their neighbourhood	Cambridgeshire; Cleveland; Hampshire; Warwickshire	2008–10	Extended throughout England and Wales in 2011
Crime/law and order Give police the power to evict partners suspected of domestic violence for up to 28 days	Manchester; West Midlands; Wiltshire	2011–12	Home Office evaluating results
Family Parenting classes for parents of children under five years of age	Camden (London); High Peak (Derbyshire); Middlesbrough	2011	Intention that parenting classes will be extended nationally from 2013, subject to funding
Health Extending patients' choice of GP; not confined to GP nearest to where they live	London (three areas – City/Hackney, Tower Hamlets, Westminster); Manchester; Nottingham	2012–13	Department of Health evaluating results
Higher Education Higher Education Achievement Report (HEAR), eventually to replace traditional university degree results	12 Universities, including Bristol, Leicester, Manchester, Newcastle, Plymouth and St Andrew's	2010–11	Extended to all universities from 2012 onwards
Urban regeneration Scheme to rejuvenate high streets in 12 economically deprived towns or urban districts. Pursued in partnership with retail expert and TV presenter, Mary Portas	Bedford; Bedminster (Bristol); Croydon; Dartford; Liskeard; Margate; Market Rasen; Nelson; Newbiggin-by-the-Sea; Stockport; Stockton-on-Tees; Wolverhampton	From Spring 2012	Ongoing

Of course, in exceptional cases, it might be that the policy proves so ineffective or beset with problems that ministers decide to abandon it entirely. In such circumstances, their disappointment will probably be alleviated by relief that its failings have been identified at an early stage, or only in a particular town or region, rather than after the policy had been implemented nationally; then, the economic – and possible political – costs would have been much higher. After all, the spectacular unravelling of, and backlash against, the Poll Tax was a major factor (albeit certainly not the only one) precipitating Margaret Thatcher's downfall as Conservative Party leader and Prime Minister in November 1990.

Although they are an integral part of the increasing penchant for evidence-based policy, the evaluation of 'pilot schemes' enshrines many of the potential methodological problems and risks of the modes of audit discussed above, in terms of what exactly is being measured, quantitative versus qualitative data, determining the relevant 'causes' of particular outcomes, identifying independent variables, the representativeness of the sample area or socio-demographic, and so on.

However, one other perennial problem that 'pilot schemes' might encounter pertains to the short timeframe usually involved, because a policy 'experiment' might really require a longer period of evaluation than ministers feel able to provide. Due to this (potential) dilemma, it has been deemed 'critical that pilots are seen to be only the first stage in a continuous process of evaluation that will provide information on which to base future policy' (Cabinet Office, 2003: 28).

This allusion to 'a continuous process' brings us back to the point that we emphasized in the Introduction, namely the circular, ongoing, never-ending character of the policy process, which contrasts starkly with the linear, sequential, stagist model of policy making. Most policies are subject to continual or periodic evaluation, whereby problems that are identified provide the impetus or rationale for reform, revision or repeal of the original policy.

CONCLUSION

The increased role of audit and evaluation is therefore both an attempt at improving the implementation of policies, and of instilling greater rationality into the making of public policy. The new public management, which we discussed in the previous chapter, not only entails the setting of targets and other performance indicators for those who 'deliver' public services, in order to improve efficiency, quality and value for money (for taxpayers and service users), it also begets an architecture of audit and appraisal, both of individuals and institutions involved in policy implementation.

At the same time, the increased recourse to evaluation both reflects and reinforces a belief among many policy makers that it is possible – and necessary, for reasons of efficiency and effectiveness – to develop a more rational and scientific approach to developing policies, based both on measuring statistical data and conducting experiments via 'pilot schemes' and consequently determining 'what works'. Ministers are also wont to depict evidence-based policies as non-ideological and thus based on a cool, calm, careful consideration of their effectiveness in achieving policy objectives.

Yet quite apart from the various methodological problems that this chapter has highlighted with regard to measuring either the performance of professionals involved in service delivery, or the policy outputs and outcomes, the recent penchant for evidence-based policy belies the fact that the policies themselves might still be inspired by ideological objectives or form part of a political project.

Moreover, the avowedly objective results of an audit or other mode of policy evaluation still need to be interpreted, which might well prove problematic if the 'evidence' is at variance with a minister's or government's ideological perspective or political objectives. Would the minister or government change its own views and objectives, or would it insist that the 'evidence' was flawed?

Besides, if policies really were, or could be, based on the results and evidence gleaned from genuinely impartial, objective and non-ideological audits and evaluation, Britain might as well be governed by expert administrators, scientists and technocrats. We could dispense with politicians altogether. Now there's a thought …

QUESTION AND TOPICS FOR DISCUSSION

1. Why has the evaluation of policies become more important in the past couple of decades?
2. In what ways are public services audited?
3. What criteria might be measured in an audit?
4. Why is it often easier to measure quantity rather than quality of public service provision?
5. How might audits inadvertently encourage organizational 'game playing' or produce 'perverse incentives'?
6. Why have many professionals and street level bureaucrats regularly complained about the manner in which audits are conducted?
7. Why has evidence-based policy seemingly become more important and widespread since the 1990s?
8. What problems might be encountered in gauging the 'evidence' when making policy?
9. Why have governments and ministers made increasing use of 'pilot schemes'?

RECOMMENDED TEXTS AND FURTHER READING

1. Michael Burton (2013) *The Politics of Public Sector Reform: From Thatcher to the Coalition*. Basingstoke: Palgrave Macmillan (Chapters 14 and 15).

   Two excellent chapters exploring the increased importance of measuring and monitoring institutional and individual performance in Britain's public services since the 1980s. Explains both why this regime of evaluation has developed, and the problems which it has created.

2. Colin Palfrey, Paul Thomas and Ceri Phillips (2012) *Evaluation for the Real World: The Impact of Evidence in Policy Making*. Bristol: Policy Press.

   An examination of the development of evidence-based policy making, highlighting not only the factors which have encouraged this phenomenon, but also the political and practical problems, coupled with economic pressures and constraints, which have affected this ostensibly empirical or more scientific approach to policy making.

3. Michael Power (1997) *The Audit Society: Rituals of Verification*. Oxford: Oxford University Press.

    Excellent account of the way in which public services in Britain have been subject to increasing regulation, inspections, monitoring exercises and performance indicators, in order to measure the performance of individuals and staff in the public sector, and their policy outputs or outcomes. Emphasizes that many institutions and professionals are compelled to focus on activities and processes which are 'measurable', and that it is often easier to measure quantity rather than quality.

4. Jill Rutter (2012) *Evidence and Evaluation in Policy Making*. London: Institute for Government.

    Notes that while a 'test, learn and adapt' model of policy making has considerable potential to improve the quality and effectiveness of policies and public service provision in many spheres, there remains a lamentable tendency for many senior policy makers to use 'evidence' largely for partisan purposes and to score political points, rather than genuinely to enhance decision taking and devise more effective policies.

References

Abromeit, H. (1988) 'British privatisation policy', *Parliamentary Affairs*, 41 (1): 68–85.

Adam Smith Institute (2013) Adam Smith Institute (online). Available at www.adamsmith.org (accessed 17 October 2013).

Adams, J. and Robinson, P. (eds) (2002) *Devolution in Practice: Public Policy Differences Within the UK*. London: Institute for Public Policy Research.

Adonis, A. (1990) *Parliament Today*. Manchester: Manchester University Press.

Alcock, P. (2010) 'Devolution or divergence? UK third sector policy since 2000', in G. Lodge and K. Schmuecker (eds), *Devolution in Practice 2010*. London: Institute for Public Policy Research.

Alexander, D. and Letwin, O. (2013) *What Works: Evidence Centres for Social Policy*. London: Cabinet Office.

Allen, D. (2013) 'The United Kingdom: towards isolation and a parting of the ways?', in S. Bulmer and C. Lequesne (eds), *The Member States of the European Union*, 2nd edn. Oxford: Oxford University Press.

Amann, R. (2003) 'A Sovietological View of Modern Britain', *The Political Quarterly*, 74 (4): 287–301.

Anderson, J.E. (2006) *Public Policy-Making*, 6th edn. Belmont, USA: Wadsworth.

Anderson, P. and Mann, N. (1997) *Safety First: The Making of New Labour*. London: Granta.

Annesley, C. (2003) 'Americanised and Europeanised: UK social policy since 1997', *British Journal of Politics and International Relations*, 5 (2): 143–65.

Armstrong, R. (1986) 'Keepers of the Cabinet', *The Daily Telegraph*, 8 December.

Ashley, J. (2002) 'Brains at the heart of Brownland: interview with Ed Balls', *The Guardian*, 4 November.

Axford, B. (1995) *The Global System: Economics, Politics and Culture*. Cambridge: Polity.

Bache, I. and Jordan, A. (2006) *The Europeanization of British Politics*. Basingstoke: Palgrave Macmillan.

Bachrach, P. and Baratz, M. (1970) *Power and Poverty: Theory and Practice*. Oxford: Oxford University Press.

Bachrach, P. and Baratz, M. (1963) 'Decision and nondecisions: an analytical framework', *American Political Science Review*, 57 (3), 632–42.

Bagehot, W. (2011) 'When the Conservative right is wrong-headed', *The Economist*, 20 October.

Baker, K. (1993) *The Turbulent Years: My Life in Politics*. London: Faber and Faber.

Baldwin, N. (1985) 'Behavioural changes: a new professionalism and a more independent house', in P. Norton (ed), *Parliament in the 1980s*. Oxford: Basil Blackwell.

Baldwin, N. (1990) 'The House of Lords', in M. Rush (ed.), *Parliament and Pressure Politics*. Oxford: Clarendon Press.

Bale, T. (1996) 'Demos: populism, eclecticism and equidistance in the post-modern world', *Contemporary British History*, 10 (2), 22–34.

Bale, T. (2010) *The Conservative Party: from Thatcher to Cameron*. Cambridge: Polity.

Ball, A.R. and Millward, F. (1986) *Pressure Politics in Industrial Societies*. Basingstoke: Macmillan.

Ball, S. (1990) *Politics and Policy Making in Education*. London: Routledge.

Barber, J. (1991) *The Prime Minister since 1945*. Oxford: Blackwell.

Barber, M. (2007) *Instruction to Deliver: Fighting to Transform Britain's Public Services*. London: Politico's.

Barker, A. (1998) 'Political responsibility for UK prison security – ministers escape again', *Public Administration*, 76 (1): 1–23.

Barnett, J. (1982) *Inside the Treasury*. London: Andre Deutsch.

Barrett, S. and Fudge, C. (1981a) 'Reconstructing the field of analysis', in S. Barrett and C. Fudge (eds), *Policy and Action: Essays on the Implementation of Public Policy*. London: Methuen.

Barrett, S. and Fudge, C. (1981b) 'Examining the policy-action relationship', in S. Barrett and C. Fudge (eds), *Policy and Action: Essays on the Implementation of Public Policy*. London: Methuen.

Batchelor, C. (1999) 'Railtrack denies cutting back on basic renewal', *Financial Times*, 9 June.

BBC (2013) 'Welsh uni fees decision expected' (online). Available at http://www.bbc.co.uk/news/uk-wales-11872671 (accessed 30 October 2013).

BBC Four (2011) *The Secret World of Whitehall*, 16 March.

Beckett, A. (2008) 'What can they be thinking?', *The Guardian g2*, 26 September.

Benn, T. (1980) 'The case for a constitutional premiership', *Parliamentary Affairs*, 33 (1): 7–22.

Bennett, N. (1998) 'The right way to run a railway', *The Sunday Telegraph*, 4 October.

Bentham, J. (2006) 'The IPPR and Demos: think tanks of the new social democracy', *The Political Quarterly*, 77 (2): 166–74.

Birrell, D. (2009) *The Impact of Devolution on Social Policy*. Bristol: The Policy Press.

Blackburn, R. and Kennon, A. with Wheeler-Booth, M. (2003) *Parliament: Functions, Practice and Procedures*, 2nd edn. London: Sweet and Maxwell.

Blair, T. (1996) *New Britain: My Vision of a Young Country*. London: Fourth Estate.

Blair, T. (1999) 'Doctrine of the International Community', speech delivered in Chicago, 24 April. Accessible via: http://www.britishpoliticalspeech.org/speech-archive.htm?speech=279

Blair, T. (2010) *A Journey*. London: Hutchinson.

Blick, A. (2004) *People Who Live in the Dark: The History of the Special Adviser in British Politics*. London: Politico's.

Blick, A. and Jones, G. (2010) *Premiership: The Development, Nature and Power of the Office of the British Prime Minister*. Exeter: Imprint Academic.

Blond, P. (2009) 'Rise of the red Tories', *Prospect*, 28 February: 32–6.

Blond, P. (2010) *Red Tory: How Left and Right Have Broken Britain and How We Can Fix It*. London: Faber.

Blondel, J. (1978) *Political Parties: A Genuine Case for Discontent?* London: Wildwood House.

Bochel, C. and Bochel, H.M. (2003) *The UK Social Policy Process*. Basingstoke: Palgrave.

Bochel, H. and Defty, A. (2007) *Welfare Policy Under New Labour: Views from Inside Westminster.* Bristol: Policy Press.

Boles, N. (2013) *Nick Boles MP for Grantham and Stamford* (online). Available at http://www.nickbolesmp.com/home (accessed 17 October 2013).

Börzel, T. (2002) 'Member state responses to Europeanization', *Journal of Common Market Studies*, 40 (2): 193–214.

Bosanquet, N. (1983) *After the New Right*. London: Heinemann.

Brack, D., Grayson, R.S. and Howarth, D. (eds) (2007) *Reinventing the State: Social Liberalism for the 21st Century*. London: Politico's.

Brand, J. (1992) *British Parliamentary Parties: Policy and Power*. Oxford: Clarendon Press.

Brazier, A. and Fox, R. (2011) 'Reviewing select committee tasks and modes of operation', *Parliamentary Affairs*, 64 (2): 354–69.

Brazier, A., Kalitowski, S., Rosenblatt, G. and Korris, M. (2008) *Law in the Making: Influence and Change in the Legislative Process*. London: Hansard Society.

Brindle, D. (1993a) 'Struggling child support agency targets better-off absent fathers', *The Guardian*, 13 September.

Brindle, D. (1993b) 'Child support body targets easy money', *The Guardian*, 13 September.

British Association of Social Workers and Social Workers Union (2012) *The State of Social Work 2012*.

Brocklehurst, A. (2008) *Peerage Creations, 1958–2008*. London: House of Lords Library Note/LLN 2008/019.

Bromley, C. and Curtice, J. (2003) 'Devolution: scorecard and prospects', in C. Bromley et al. (ed.), *Devolution – Scottish Answers to Scottish Questions?* Edinburgh: Edinburgh University Press.

Brown, A., McCrone, D. and Paterson, L. (1998) *Politics and Society in Scotland*. Basingstoke: Palgrave.

Brown, C. (1990) 'Thatcher rewards the defenders of her political faith', *The Independent*, 21 December.

Buchanan, J. and Tullock, G. (1962) *The Calculus of Consent: Logical Foundations of Constitutional Democracy*. Ann Arbor: University of Michigan Press.

Buller, J. and Smith, M.J. (1998) 'Civil service attitudes towards the European Union', in D. Baker and D. Seawright (eds), *Britain For and Against Europe: British Politics and the Question of European Integration*. Oxford: Oxford University Press.

Bulmer, S. and Burch, M. (2006) 'Central government', in I. Bache and A. Jordan (eds), *The Europeanization of British Politics*. Basingstoke: Palgrave Macmillan.

Bulmer, S. and Burch, M. (2009) *The Europeanisation of Whitehall: UK Central Government and the European Union*. Manchester: Manchester University Press.

Bulmer, S., Dolowitz, D., Humphreys, P. and Padgett, S. (2007) *Policy Transfer in European Governance*. London: Routledge.

Bulpitt, J. (1996) 'The European question', in D. Marquand and A. Seldon (eds), *The Ideas that Shaped Post-War Britain*. London: Fontana.

Burch, M. (1988a) 'The British cabinet: a residual executive', *Parliamentary Affairs*, 41 (1): 34–48.

Burch, M. (1988b) 'The United Kingdom', in J. Blondel and F. Muller-Rommel (eds), *Cabinets in Western Europe*. Basingstoke: Macmillan.

Burch, M. and Holliday, I. (1996) *The British Cabinet System*. Hemel Hempstead: Prentice Hall/Harvester Wheatsheaf.

Burch, M. and Holliday, I. (1999) 'The Prime Minister's and Cabinet Offices: An Executive Office in All But Name', *Parliamentary Affairs*, 52 (1): 32–45.

Burke, E. (2004) *Reflections on the Revolution in France*. London: Penguin Classics (first published in 1790).

Burney, E. (2002) 'Talking tough, acting coy: what happened to the anti-social behaviour order?', *Howard Journal of Criminal Justice*, 41 (5): 469–84.

Burton, J. and Van der Broek, D. (2009) 'Accountable and countable: information management systems and the bureaucratization of social work', *The British Journal of Social Work*, 39 (7): 1326–42.

Burton, M. (2013) *The Politics of Public Sector Reform: From Thatcher to the Coalition*. Basingstoke: Palgrave Macmillan.

Butler, D., Adonis, A. and Travers, T. (1994) *Failure in British Government: The Politics of the Poll Tax*. Oxford: Oxford University Press.

Cabinet Office (1997) *Ministerial Code: A Code of Conduct and Guidance on Procedures for Ministers*. London: The Stationery Office.

Cabinet Office (1999a) *Modernising Government*. The Stationery Office, Cm 4310.

Cabinet Office (1999b) *Professional Policy Making for the Twenty First Century*. London: Cabinet Office Strategic Policy Making Team.

Cabinet Office (2003) *Trying it Out: The Role of 'Pilots' in Policy-Making*. London: Government Chief Social Researcher's Office.

Cabinet Office (2010a) *Ministerial Code*. London: The Stationery Office.

Cabinet Office (2010b) *Code of Conduct for Special Advisers*. London: The Stationery Office.

Cabinet Office (2011a) *The Cabinet Manual*. London: The Stationery Office.

Cabinet Office (2011b) *Civil Service Management Code* . Only accessible online: http://webarchive. nationalarchives.gov.uk/20110112043301/civilservice.gov.uk/about/resources/csmc/index.aspx.

Cabinet Office (2012) *Devolution: Memorandum of Understanding and Supplementary Agreements*. London: The Stationery Office.

Cabinet Office (2013a) *Guidance on Devolution* (online). Available at https://www.gov.uk/guidance-on-devolution (accessed 4 October 2013).

Cabinet Office (2013b) *What Works: Evidence Centres for Social Policy*. London: The Stationery Office.

Cabinet Office (2013c) *What We Do* (online). Available at: http://www.cabinetoffice.gov.uk/content/ european-and-global-issues-secretariat (accessed 9 November 2013).

Callaghan, J. (1996) 'The Fabian Society since 1945', *Contemporary British History*, 10 (2): 35–50.

Cameron, D. (2007) 'The Conservative approach to improving public services' (online), speech delivered on 26 January. Available at http://www.conservatives.com/News/Speeches/ 2007/01/ David_Cameron_The_Conservative_approach_to_improving_public_services.aspx.

Cameron, D. (2010) 'Speech: our Big Society plan' (online), 31 March. Available at http://www. conservatives.com/News/Speeches/2010/03/David_Cameron_ Our_Big_Society_plan.aspx.

Cameron, D. (2011) 'How we will release the grip of state control', *The Daily Telegraph*, 20 February.

Campbell, C. and Wilson, G. (1995) *The End of Whitehall: Death of a Paradigm*. Oxford: Blackwell.

Campbell, D. (2008) 'Scandal of patients left for hours outside A&E', *The Observer*, 17 February.

Castells, M. (1996) *The Information Age: Economy, Society and Culture: The Rise of the Network Society*. Oxford: Blackwell.

Castle, B. (1993) *Fighting All The Way*. London: Pan Books.

Catterall, P. and Brady, C. (1998) 'Cabinet committees in British governance', *Public Policy and Administration*, 13 (4): 67–84.

Chaney, P. and Drakeford, M. (2004) 'The primacy of ideology: social policy and the first term of the National Assembly for Wales', in N. Ellison, L. Bauld and M. Powell (eds), *Social Policy Review 16*. Bristol: Policy Press (with the Social Policy Association).

Chitty, C. (2002) 'Why New Labour shouldn't be touched with a bargepole', *Forum*, 44 (2): 45.

Chitty, C. (2009) *Education Policy in Britain*, 2nd edn. Basingstoke: Palgrave Macmillan.

Clark, A. (2012) *Political Parties in the UK*. Basingstoke: Palgrave Macmillan.

Coates, D. (2005) *Prolonged Labour: The Slow Birth of New Labour in Britain*. Basingstoke: Palgrave Macmillan.

Coates, S. (2013) 'Treasury nets £3.2bn from Britons with Swiss bank accounts', *The Times*, 22 June.

Cobb, R.W. and Elder, C.D. (1972) *Participation in American Politics: The Dynamics of Agenda-Building*. Boston: Allyn and Bacon.

Cockett, R. (1994) *Thinking the Unthinkable: Think-Tanks and the Economic Counter-Revolution 1931–83*. London: HarperCollins.

Cohen, M., March, J. and Olsen, J. (1972) 'A garbage can model of organizational choice', *Administrative Science Quarterly*, 17 (1): 1–25.

Cohen, N. (2008) 'The failings that mark down academia', *The Observer*, 8 June.

Commission for Health Improvement (2003) *NHS Performance Ratings: Acute Trusts, Specialist Trusts, Ambulance Trusts 2002/2003*. London: Commission for Health Improvement.

Commission on the Powers and Electoral Arrangements of the National Assembly for Wales (2004) *Report of the Richard Commission*,

Connell, A. (2011) *Welfare Policy under New Labour: The Politics of Social Security Reform*. London: I.B. Tauris.

Conservative Party (1979) *The Conservative Manifesto*.

Conservative Party (2007) *Raising the Bar, Closing the Gap, Responsibility Agenda*; Policy Green Paper, No.1.

Conservative Party (2008) *Delivering Some of the Best Health Care in Europe: Outcomes, Not Targets*, Responsibility Agenda; Policy Green Paper No.6.

Conservative Party (2010) *Invitation to Join the Government of Britain: The Conservative Manifesto 2010*. London: The Conservative Party.

Cortell, A. (1997) 'From intervention to disengagement: domestic structure, the state and the British information technology industry. 1979–1990', *Polity*, 30 (1): 107–31.

Cortell, A. and Peterson, S. (1999) 'Altered states: explaining domestic institutional change', *British Journal of Political Science*, 29 (1), 177–203.

Cowley, P. (2005) *The Rebels: How Blair Mislaid his Majority*. London: Politico's.

Cowley, P. (2007) 'Parliament', in A. Seldon (ed.), *Blair's Britain 1997–2007*. Cambridge: Cambridge University Press.

Cracknell, D. (2004) 'Police fail to use powers to tackle binge drinking', *The Sunday Times*, 17 October.

Crosland, A. (1956) *The Future of Socialism*. Jonathan Cape.

Crossman, R.H.S. (1963) 'Introduction', in Walter Bagehot (ed.), *The English Constitution* (originally published in 1867). London: Fontana.

Crossman, R. (1975) *The Diaries of a Cabinet Minister, Volume One: Minister of Housing, 1964–66*. London: Hamish Hamilton and Jonathan Cape.

Curtice, J. (2010) 'Policy divergence: recognising difference or generating Resentment?', in G. Lodge and K. Schmuecker (eds), *Devolution in Practice 2010*. London: Institute for Public Policy Research.

Dahl, R. (1961) *Who Governs? Democracy and Power in an American City*. New Haven (US): Yale University Press.

Daugbjerg, C. (1998) *Policy Networks Under Pressure: Pollution Control, Policy Reform and the Power of Farmers*. Aldershot: Ashgate.

Davies, R. (1999) *Devolution: A Process not an Event*. Cardiff: Institute of Welsh Affairs.

Deacon, A. (2000) 'Learning from the US? The influence of American ideas upon "New Labour" thinking on welfare reform', *Policy and Politics*, 28 (1): 5–18.

Dell, E. (1980) 'Some reflections on cabinet government', *Public Administration*, bulletin 32: 17–33.

Denham, A. and Garnett, M. (1996) 'The nature and impact of think tanks in contemporary Britain', *Contemporary British History*, 10 (1): 43–61.

Denham, A. and Garnett, M. (1998) *British Think Tanks and the Climate of Opinion*. London: UCL Press.

Denham, A. and Garnett, M. (1999) 'Influence without responsibility?: Think tanks in Britain', *Parliamentary Affair*, 52 (1): 46–57.

Denham, A. and Garnett, M. (2004) 'A "hollowed out" tradition?: British think tanks in the twenty first century', in D. Stone and A. Denham (eds), *Think Tank Traditions: Policy Research and the Politics of Ideas*. Manchester: Manchester University Press.

Denham, A. and Garnett, M. (2006) '"What works"? British Think Tanks and the "end of ideology"', *The Political Quarterly*, 77 (2): 156–65.

Department for Education (2011) *Class Size and Education in England Evidence Report*, DFE-RR169. London: Department for Education.

Department of the Clerk of the House of Commons (2010) *The European Scrutiny System in the House of Commons*. London: Department of the Clerk of the House of Commons.

Department of the Environment, Transport and the Regions (1999) *Bulletin of Rail Statistics – Quarter 4, 1998/9*. London: The Stationery Office.

Department of Health (2013) Statement by the Secretary of State for Health, Jeremy Hunt, 12 July. Available at: https://www.gov.uk/government/news/consultation-on-standardised-packaging-of-tobacco-products

Department of Social Security (1998) *A New Contract for Welfare*, Cmnd 3805. London: Stationary Office.

Desai, R. (1994) 'Second hand dealers in ideas: think tanks and Thatcherite hegemony', *New Left Review*, 203: 27–64.

Directgov (2010) *Public Bodies Reform – Proposals for Change*. Available at: www.direct.gov.uk/prod_consum_dg/groups/dg_digitalassets/@dg/@en/documents/digitalasset/dg_191543.pdf (accessed 9 November 2013).

Dolowitz, D. (1998) *Learning from America: Policy Transfer and the Development of the British Workfare State*. Brighton: Sussex Academic Press.

Dolowitz, D. (2000a) 'Introduction: a new face to British public policy', in D. Dolowitz with R. Hulme, M. Nellis and F. O'Neill (eds), *Policy Transfer and British Social Policy*. Buckingham: Open University Press.

Dolowitz, D. (2000b) 'Welfare: the Child Support Agency', in D. Dolowitz with R. Hulme, M. Nellis and F. O'Neill (eds), *Policy Transfer and British Social Policy*. Buckingham: Open University Press.

Dolowitz, D. and Marsh, D. (1996) 'Who learns what from whom: a review of the policy transfer literature', *Political Studies*, 44 (2): 343–57.

Dolowitz, D. and Marsh, D. (2000) 'Learning from abroad: the role of policy transfer in contemporary policy-making', *Governance*, 13 (1): 5–23.

Donnelly, L. (2009) 'Patients forced to wait hours in ambulances parked outside A&E departments', *The Daily Telegraph*, 30 May.

Donoughue, B. (1987) *Prime Minister: The Conduct of Policy under Harold Wilson and James Callaghan*. London: Jonathan Cape.

Dorey, P. (1998) 'The new "enemies within": the Conservative attack on single parents, 1989–1997', *Revue Française de Civilisation Britannique*, 7 (3): 79–92.

Dorey, P. (1999) 'The 3 Rs – Reform, Reproach and Rancour: education policies under John Major', in Peter Dorey (ed.), *The Major Premiership: Politics and Policies under John Major, 1990–1997*. Basingstoke: Macmillan.

Dorey, P. (2000) 'Public policy: the Child Support Act and Agency', in Steve Lancaster (ed.), *Developments in Politics 11: An Annual Review*. Ormskirk: Causeway Press.

Dorey, P. (2002a) 'Industrial relations as "human relations": Conservatism and Trade Unionism, 1945–1964', in S. Ball and I. Holliday (eds), *Mass Conservatism: The Conservatives and the Public since the 1880s*. London: Frank Cass.

Dorey, P. (2002b) 'Britain in the 1990s: the absence of policy concertation', in S. Berger and H. Compston (eds), *Social Partnership in the 1990s*. Oxford: Berghahn.

Dorey, P. (2003) 'Margaret Thatcher's taming of the trade unions', in S. Pugliese (ed.), *The Legacy of Margaret Thatcher: Liberty Regained?*. London: Politico's.

Dorey, P. (2006a) 'Homosexual Law Reform', in Peter Dorey (ed.), *The Labour Governments, 1964–1970*. London: Routledge.

Dorey, P. (2006b) '1949, 1969, 1999: the Labour Party and House of Lords reform', *Parliamentary Affairs*, 59 (4): 599–620.

Dorey, P. (2007) 'A new direction or another false dawn? David Cameron and the crisis of British Conservatism', *British Politics*, 2 (2): 137–66.

Dorey, P. (2008a) *The Labour Party and Constitutional Reform: A History of Constitutional Conservatism*. Basingstoke: Palgrave Macmillan.

Dorey, P. (2008b) 'Stumbling through "stage two": New Labour and House of Lords reform', *British Politics*, 3 (1): 22–44.

Dorey, P. (2009a) *British Conservatism and Trade Unionism 1945–1964*. Aldershot: Ashgate.

Dorey, P. (2009b) 'Individual liberty versus industrial order: Conservatives and the Trade Union closed shop, 1946–1990', *Contemporary British History*, 23 (2): 219–42.

Dorey, P. (2009c) '"Sharing the proceeds of growth": Conservative economic policy under David Cameron', *The Political Quarterly*, 80 (2): 259–69.

Dorey, P. (2009d) 'Change in order to conserve: explaining the Conservatives' decision to introduce the 1958 Life Peerages Act', *Parliamentary History*, 28 (2): 246–65.

Dorey, P. (2009e) 'The House of Lords since 1949', in C. Jones (ed.), *A Short History of Parliament*. London: Boydell Press.

Dorey, P. (2010a) 'A poverty of imagination: blaming the poor for inequality', *The Political Quarterly*, 81 (3): 333–43.

Dorey, P. (2010b) 'Faltering before the finishing line: The Conservative Party's performance in the 2010 general election', *British Politics*, 5 (4): 402–35.

Dorey, P. (2011a) 'Thatcherism and the Anti-Egalitarian backlash, 1979–1990', paper presented at the Political Studies Association conference, London.

Dorey, P. (2011b) *British Conservatism: The Politics and Philosophy of Inequality*. London: I.B. Tauris.

Dorey, P. (2011c) 'A conservative "Third Way"? British Conservatives and the development of post-Thatcherite conservatism', in Doğancan Özsel (ed.), *Reflections on Conservatism*. Newcastle: Cambridge Scholars' Publishing.

Dorey, P. (2014) 'Education policies: markets, managerialism and malice (towards teachers)', in C. Hay and S. Farrall (eds), *The Legacy of Thatcherism*. Oxford: Oxford University Press.

Dorey, P. and Denham, A. (2011) '"O, brother, where art thou?" The Labour Party leadership election of 2010', *British Politics*, 6 (3): 286–316.

Dorey, P. and Garnett, M. (2012) 'No such thing as the "Big Society"? The Conservative Party's unnecessary search for "narrative" in the 2010 general election', *British Politics*, 7 (4): 389–417.

Dorey, P. and Honeyman, V. (2010) 'Ahead of his time: Richard Crossman and House of Commons reform in the 1960s', *British Politics*, 5 (2): 149–78.

Dorey, P. and Kelso, A. (2011) *House of Lords Reform since 1911: Must the Lords Go?* Basingstoke: Palgrave Macmillan.

Dorey, P., Garnett, M. and Denham, A. (2011) *From Crisis to Coalition: The Conservative Party, 1997–2010*. Basingstoke: Palgrave Macmillan.

Downs, A. (1972) 'Up and down with ecology – the issue attention cycle', *The Public Interest*, 28 (Summer): 38–50.

Drewry, G. (ed.) (1989) *The New Select Committees*. Oxford: Oxford University Press.

Drewry, G. and Butcher, T. (1991) *The Civil Service Today*, 2nd edn. Oxford: Blackwell.

Driver, S. (2011) *Understanding British Party Politics*. Cambridge: Polity.

Driver, S. and Martell, L. (1997) 'New Labour's communitarianism', *Critical Social Policy*, 17 (3): 27–46.

Driver, S. and Martell, L. (2006) *New Labour*. Cambridge: Polity.

Dryzek, J. and Dunleavy, P. (2009) *Theories of the Democratic State*. Basingstoke: Palgrave Macmillan.

Dunleavy, P. (1995) 'Policy disasters: explaining the UK's record', *Public Policy and Administration*, 10 (2): 52–70.

Dunleavy, P. and Rhodes, R.A.W. (1990) 'Core executive studies in Britain', *Public Administration*, 68 (1): 3–28.

Dyson, K. (2000) 'Europeanization, Whitehall culture and the treasury as institutional veto player: a Constructivist approach to economic and monetary union', *Public Administration*, 78 (4): 897–914.

Easton, D. (1965) *A Systems Analysis of Political Life*. Chicago: Chicago University Press.

Edwards, J. (ed.) (2012) *Retrieving the Big Society*. Oxford: Wiley-Blackwell.

Efficiency Unit (1988) *Improving Management in Government: The Next Steps*. London: HMSO.

Elgie, R. (1995) *Political Leadership in Liberal Democracies*. London: Macmillan.

Englefield, D. (ed.) (1984) *Commons Select Committees: Catalysts for Progress?* Harlow: Longman.

Exworthy, M. (2001) 'Primary care in the UK: understanding the dynamics of devolution', *Health and Social Care in the Community*, 9 (5): 266–78.

Feigenbaum, H., Henig, J. and Hamnett, C. (1998) *Shrinking the State*. Cambridge: Cambridge University Press.

Finer, S.E. (1956) 'The individual responsibility of ministers', *Public Administration*, 34: 377–96.

Finlayson, A. (2003) *Making Sense of New Labour*. London: Lawrence and Wishart.

Fisher, J. (1996) *British Political Parties*. Hemel Hempstead: Prentice Hall/Harvester Wheatsheaf.

Flinders, M. (2000) 'The enduring centrality of individual ministerial responsibility within the British constitution', *Legislative Studies*, 6 (3): 73–92.

Flinders, M. (2004) 'The politics of public–private partnerships', *British Journal of Politics and International Relations*, 7 (2): 215–39.

Flinders, M. (2006) 'The half-hearted constitutional revolution', in P. Dunleavy, R. Heffernan, P. Cowley and C. Hay (eds), *Developments in British Politics 8*. Basingstoke: Palgrave Macmillan.

Flinders, M. (2008) *Delegated Governance and the British State*. Oxford: Oxford University Press.

Flinders, M. and Skelcher, C. (2012) 'Shrinking the quango state: five challenges in reforming quangos', *Public Money and Management*, 32 (5): 327–34.

Flynn, A., Gray, A. and Jenkins, W. (1990) 'Taking the next steps: the changing management of government', *Parliamentary Affairs*, 43 (2): 159–78.

Foley, M. (1992) *The Rise of the British Presidency*. Manchester: Manchester University Press.

Foley, M. (2000) *The Blair Presidency*. Manchester: Manchester University Press.

Ford, R. (2012) 'Lock 'em up, let 'em out: it's the May and Clarke show', *The Times*, 24 February.

Ford, R. (2013) 'We fiddled the crime figures to look good, admit police', *The Times*, 20 November.

Foster, C. and Plowden, F. (1996) *The State under Stress*. Buckingham: Open University Press.

Francis, R. (2013) *Report of the Mid-Staffordshire NHS Foundation Trust Public Inquiry*, HC 947. London: The Stationery Office.

Freeden, M. (1986) *The New Liberalism: An Ideology of Social Reform*. Oxford: Oxford University Press.

Friedman, M. (2002) *Capitalism and Freedom*, 40th Anniversary Edition (first published in 1962). Chicago: University of Chicago Press.

Gamble, A. (1997) 'Conclusion: politics 2000', in P. Dunleavy, A. Gamble, I. Holliday and G. Peele (eds), *Developments in British Politics 5*. Basingstoke: Macmillan.

Garner, R. (2013a) 'UK faces desperate shortage of science and maths teachers', *The Independent* 13 August.

Garner, R. (2013b) 'Schools ask pupils to sit GCSE maths exams twice to boost league table scores, warns Ofqual', *The Independent*, 1 August.

Garnham, A. and Knights, E. (1994) *Putting the Treasury First*. London: Child Poverty Action Group.

Garrett, G. (2000) 'Globalization and national autonomy', in N. Woods (ed.), *The Political Economy of Globalization*. Basingstoke: Palgrave.

Gash, T., Rutter, J., Magee, I. and Smith, N. (2010) *Read Before Burning: How to Increase the Effectiveness and Accountability of Quangos*. London: Institute for Government.

Gay, O. (2012) *Individual Ministerial Accountability*. London: House of Commons Library, standard note SN/PC/06467.

Gay, O. and Powell, T. (2004) *Individual Ministerial Responsibility – Issues and Examples*. London: House of Commons Library, research paper 04/31.

Geddes, A. (2004) *The European Union and British Politics*. Basingstoke: Palgrave Macmillan.

Geddes, A. (2013) *Britain and the European Union*. Basingstoke: Palgrave Macmillan.

Giddens, A. (1991) *Modernity and Self-Identity*. Cambridge: Polity.

Giddens, A. (1998) *The Third Way: The Renewal of Social Democracy*. Cambridge: Polity.

Giddings, P. (1993) 'Questions and departments', in M. Franklin and P. Norton (eds), *Parliamentary Questions*. Oxford: Clarendon Press.

Giddings, P. (1995) 'Prime Minister and Cabinet', in D. Shell and R. Hodder-Williams (eds), *Churchill to Major: The British Prime Ministership Since 1945*. London: Hurst.

Gilmour, I. (1978) *Inside Right: A Study of Conservatism*. London: Quartet.

Gilmour, I. (1992) *Dancing with Dogma: Britain under Thatcherism*. London: Simon and Schuster.

Glaister, S., Burnham, J., Stevens, H. and Travers, T. (2006) *Transport Policy in Britain*, 2nd edn. Basingstoke: Palgrave Macmillan.

Goldsmith, M. (1997) 'Changing patterns of local government', *ECPR News*, 9 (1).

Gould, P. (1999) *The Unfinished Revolution: How the Modernisers Saved the Labour Party*, revised edition. London: Little Brown.

Government Statisticians' Collective (1979) 'How official statistics are produced: views from the inside', in J. Irvine, I. Miles and J. Evans (eds), *Demystifying Social Statistics*. London: Pluto Press.

Gov.UK (2013a) 'Departments, agencies and public bodies' (online). Available at: https://www.gov.uk/government/organisations (accessed 10 November 2013).

Gov.UK (2013b) 'The Cabinet Committees system and list of Cabinet Committees' (online). Available at: http://www.cabinetoffice.gov.uk/resource-library/cabinet-committees-system-and-list-cabinet-committees (accessed 9 November 2013).

Gov.UK (2013c) 'Our governance: UK Ambassadors and Counsellors' (online). Available at: https://www.gov.uk/government/world/organisations/uk-representation-to-the-eu/about/our-governance (accessed 10 November 2013).

Grant, W. (1989) *Pressure Groups, Politics and Democracy in Britain*. Hemel Hempstead: Philip Allan.

Grant, W. (1997) 'BSE and the politics of food', in P. Dunleavy, A. Gamble, I. Holliday, and G. Peele (eds), *Developments in British Politics 5*. Basingstoke: Macmillan.

Grant, W. (2000) *Pressure Groups and British Politics*. Basingstoke: Macmillan.

Grant, W. (2003) 'Economic Policy', in P. Dunleavy, A. Gamble, R. Heffernan and G. Peele (eds), *Developments in British Politics 7*. Basingstoke: Palgrave.

Grantham, C. and Moore Hodgson, C. (1985) 'Structural changes: the use of committees', in P. Norton (ed.), *Parliament in the 1980s*. Oxford: Basil Blackwell.

Gray, C. (2000) 'A "Hollow State"?', in R. Pyper and L. Robins (eds), *United Kingdom Governance*. Basingstoke: Palgrave.

Grayson, R. (2007) 'Social democracy or social liberalism? Ideological sources of Liberal Democrat policy', *The Political Quarterly*, 78 (1): 32–9.

Grayson, R. (2009) 'Social liberalism', in Kevin Hickson (ed.), *The Political Thought of the Liberals and Liberal Democrats Since 1945*. Manchester: Manchester University Press.

Grayson, R. (2010) *The Liberal Democrat Journey to a Lib-Con Coalition – and Where Next?* London: Compass.

Green, D. (2003) *More Than Markets*. London: Tory Reform Group.

Greenleaf, W.H. (1983) *The British Political Tradition: Volume 1, the Rise of Collectivism*. London: Routledge.

Greer, A. (1999) 'Policy co-ordination and the British administrative system: evidence from the BSE Inquiry', *Parliamentary Affairs*, 52 (4): 598–615.

Greer, S.L. (2004) *Territorial Politics and Health Policy: The United Kingdom in Comparative Perspective*. Manchester: Manchester University Press.

Greer, S.L. (2007) 'The fragile divergence machine: citizenship, policy divergence and devolution in health policy', in A. Trench (ed.), *Devolution and Power in the United Kingdom*. Manchester: Manchester University Press.

Greer, S.L. (2010) 'Devolution and health: structure, process and outcomes since 1998', in G. Lodge and K. Schmuecker (eds), *Devolution in Practice 2010*. London: Institute for Public Policy Research.

Grice, A. (2004) 'Brown shuffles advisers to prepare for Balls' departure', *The Independent*, 10 January.

Grice, A. (2010) 'Cable threatens to use tax to bring the banks to heel on bonuses', *The Independent*, 22 September.

Grice, A. (2011) 'Chris Huhne to launch attack on "Tea Party Tories"', *The Independent*, 20 September.

Groom, B. (2000) 'Rail industry structure set to remain', *Financial Times*, 21 October.

Gruhn, Z. and Slater, F. (2012) *Special Advisers and Ministerial Effectiveness*. London: Institute for Government.

Gunn, L. (1978) 'Why is implementation so difficult?', *Management Services in Government*, 33: 169–76.

Hall, S. and Jacques, M. (eds) (1989) *New Times: The Changing Face of Politics in the 1990s*. London: Lawrence and Wishart.

Hansard Society (2004) *Pre-Legislative Scrutiny, Issues in Law Making*, Briefing Paper 5, July.

Hanson, A.H. (1956) 'The Labour Party and House of Commons Reform – 1', *Parliamentary Affairs*, 10 (4): 454–68.

Hardt, M. and Negri, A. (2000) *Empire*. Cambridge, USA: Harvard University Press.

Harris, C. (2011) 'Ipswich: Ambulances kept waiting to meet A&E targets, says MP', *The Ipswich Star*, 7 October.

Harris, M. (1996) 'The centre for policy studies: the paradoxes of power', *Contemporary British History*, 10 (2): 51–64.

Hatcher, R. (2011) 'The Conservative-Liberal Democrat Coalition government's "free schools" in England', *Educational Review*, 63 (4): 485–503.

Haubrich, D. (2001) 'UK rail privatisation five years down the line: an evaluation of nine policy objectives', *Policy and Politics*, 29 (3): 317–36.

Hawkes, A., Garside, J. and Kollewe, J. (2011) 'UK riots could cost taxpayer £100m', *The Guardian*, 9 August.

Hayton, R. (2012) *Reconstructing Conservatism? The Conservative Party in Opposition, 1997–2010*. Manchester: Manchester University Press.

Headey, B. (1974) *British Cabinet Ministers*. London: Allen and Unwin.

Healey, D. (1990) *The Time of My Life*. Harmondsworth: Penguin.

Heffernan, R. (1996) '"Blueprint for a Revolution"? The Politics of the Adam Smith Institute', *Contemporary British History*, 10 (1): 73–87.

Heffernan, R. (2000) *New Labour and Thatcherism: Political Change in Britain*. London: Palgrave.

Held, D. (1989) 'The decline of the nation state', in S. Hall and M. Jacques (eds), *New Times: The Changing Face of Politics in the 1990s*. London: Lawrence and Wishart/Marxism Today.

Held, D. and McGrew, A. (2002) *Globalization and Anti-Globalization*. Cambridge: Polity.

Held, D., Goldblatt, D., McGrew, A. and Perraton, J. (1999) *Global Transformations: Politics, Economics and Culture*. Cambridge: Polity.

Helm, T. (2011) 'Right-wing squares up to fight battle for soul of the Conservative Party', *The Observer*, 9 January.

Hennessy, P. (1986) *The Great and the Good: An Inquiry into the British Establishment*. London: Policy Studies Institute.

Hennessy, P. (1990) *Whitehall*. London: Fontana.

Hennessy, P. (2000) 'Why Mr Blair's premiership will end in tears', *The Independent* (*Weekend Review*), 20 May.

Hennessy, P. (2001) *The Prime Minister: The Office and its Holders Since 1945*. London: Penguin.

Hennessy, P. and Donnelly, L. (2012) 'Cabinet split over plan to introduce alcohol levy', *The Daily Telegraph*, 25 September.

Hennessy, P., Hughes, R. and Seaton, J. (1997) *Ready, Steady, Go! New Labour and Whitehall*. London: Fabian Society.

Herbert, I. (2004) 'Pressure of paperwork stops social workers from working', *The Independent*, 30 April.

Higgott, R. (1998) 'Review of "globalisation"', paper presented to the Economic and Social Research Council, 20 November.

Hill, M. (1998) *Understanding Social Policy*, 3rd edn. Oxford: Blackwell.

Hindmoor, A., Larkin P. and Kennon, A. (2009) 'Assessing the influence of select committees in the UK: the education and skills committee, 1997–2005', *Journal of Legislative Studies*, 15 (1): 71–89.

Hirst, P. and Thompson, G. (1996) *Globalisation in Question*. Cambridge: Polity.

HM Government (2011) *Open Public Services*, Cm 8145. London: The Stationery Office.

HM Inspectorate of Constabulary (2010) *Valuing the Police: Policing in an Age of Austerity*. London: HM Inspectorate of Constabulary.

HM Treasury (2010) *Reforming Arm's Length Bodies*. London: HM Treasury. Available at www.direct.gov.uk/prod_consum_dg/groups/dg_digitalassets/@dg/@en/documents/digitalasset/dg_186443.pdf (accessed 22 January 2014).

Hobhouse, L.T. (1911) *Liberalism*. London: Williams and Norgate.

Hodder-Williams, R. (1995) 'The Prime Ministership, 1945–1995', in D. Shell and R. Hodder-Williams (eds), *Churchill to Major: The British Prime Ministership Since 1945*. London: Hurst.

Hogg, S. and Hill, J. (1995) *Too Close to Call: Power and Politics – John Major in No. 10*. London: Warner Books.

Hogwood, B. (1987) *From Crisis to Complacency: Shaping Public Policy in Britain*. Oxford: Oxford University Press.

Hogwood, B. and Gunn, L. (1984) *Policy Analysis for the Real World*. Oxford: Oxford University Press.

Hogwood, B. and Mackie, T. (1985) 'The United Kingdom: decision sifting in a secret garden', in T. Mackie and B. Hogwood (eds), *Unlocking the Cabinet: Cabinet Structures in Comparative Perspective*. London: Sage.

Holliday, I. (2000) 'Executives and administrations', in P. Dunleavy, A. Gamble, I. Holliday and G. Peele (eds), *Developments in British Politics 6*. Basingstoke: Macmillan.

Holmes, L., McDermid, S., Jones, A. and Ward H. (2009) *How Social Workers Spend Their Time*. Loughborough: Loughborough University Centre for Child and Family Research.

Holton, R. (1998) *Globalization and the Nation-State*. Basingstoke: Macmillan.

Home Office (2010) *Policing in the 21st Century: Reconnecting Police and the People*, Cm 7925. London: The Stationery Office.

Home Office (2011) *The Likely Impacts of Increasing Alcohol price: A Summary Review of the Evidence Base*, HO_01728_G. London: The Stationery Office.

Hood, C. (1976) *The Limits of Administration*. London: Wiley.

Hood, C. (1995) 'Contemporary public management: a new global paradigm', *Public Policy and Administration*, 10 (2): 104–17.

Hood, C., Scott, C., James, O., Jones, G. and Travers, T. (1999) *Regulation Inside Government: Waste-Watchers, Quality Police and Sleaze-Busters*. Oxford: Oxford University Press.

Hoskyns, J. (2000) *Just in Time: Inside the Thatcher Revolution*. London: Aurum.

House of Commons (2011) *Standing Orders of the House of Commons*, London: The Stationery Office.

House of Commons (2012) *Sessional Returns, Session 2010–12, 25 May 2010–1 May 2012*, HC1. London: The Stationery Office.

House of Commons (2013) *Guide for Witnesses Giving Written or Oral Evidence to a House of Commons Select Committee*, London: The Stationery Office.

House of Commons Debates (1995a) Statement by the Home Secretary, Michael Howard, 10 January.

House of Commons Debates (1995b) Statement by the Home Secretary, Michael Howard, 16 October.

House of Commons Debates (2001) Debate on Second Reading of the Anti-terrorism, Crime and Security Bill, 19 November.

House of Commons Debates (2003) Debate on the Second Reading of the Female Genital Mutilation Bill, 21 March.

House of Commons Debates (2006) Written Answers, Vol.446, 985W, 17 May.

House of Commons Debates (2013) Statement by the Home Secretary, Theresa May, 9 July.

House of Commons Foreign Affairs Committee (2011) *The Role of the FCO in UK Government: Seventh Report of Session 2010–12, Volume 1*, HC 665. London: The Stationery Office.

House of Commons Health Committee (2010) *Alcohol: First Report of Session 2009–10, Volume I*, HC 151–I. London: The Stationery Office.

House of Commons Information Office (2010) *The Success of Private Members' Bills*, Factsheet L3, Legislation Series. London: The Stationery Office.

House of Commons Justice Committee (2011) *The Role of the Probation Service – Eighth Report of Session 2010–12, Volume I*, HC 519–I. London: The Stationery Office.

House of Commons Liaison Committee (2003) *Annual Report 2002*, HC 558. London: The Stationery Office.

House of Commons Liaison Committee (2012) *Second Report of Session 2012–13; Select Committee Effectiveness, Resources and Powers, Volume I*, HC 697. London: The Stationery Office.

House of Commons Modernisation Committee (2006) *The Legislative Process*, HC 1097. London: The Stationery Office.

House of Commons Public Accounts Committee (2011) *Sixty-First Report – HM Revenue and Customs 2010–11 Accounts: Tax Disputes*, HC 1531. London: The Stationery Office.

House of Commons Public Accounts Committee (2013) *Twenty-ninth Report of Session 2012–13; Tax avoidance: tackling marketed avoidance schemes*, HC 788, London: The Stationery Office.

House of Commons Public Administration Committee (2002a) *The New Centre*, minutes of evidence for 1 November 2001, HC 262-ii, published 18 January 2002. London: The Stationery Office.

House of Commons Public Administration Committee (2002b) *The New Centre*, minutes of evidence for 11 July 2002, HC 262-iii, published 29 July 2002. London: The Stationery Office.

House of Commons Public Administration Committee (2009) *Good Government, Eighth Report of Session 2008–09; Volume II, Oral and Written Evidence*. London: The Stationery Office.

House of Commons Public Administration Committee (2011) *Smaller Government: What do Ministers do? Seventh Report of Session 2010–11*, Volume 1, HC 530. London: The Stationery Office.

House of Lords Constitution Committee (2004) *Parliament and the Legislative Process*, HL 173. London: The Stationery Office.

House of Lords Constitution Committee (2010) *Fourth Report: The Cabinet Office and the Centre of Government, Minutes of Evidence*, HL Paper 30. London: The Stationery Office.

Howlett, M. and Ramesh M. (1995) *Studying Public Policy*. Toronto: Oxford University Press.

Hulley, T. and Clarke, J. (1991) 'Social problems: social construction and social causation', in M. Loney, R. Bocock, J. Clarke, A. Cochrane, P. Graham and M. Wilson (eds), *The State or the Market: Politics and Welfare in Contemporary Britain*. London: Sage/Open University.

Hurst, G. (2004) 'Abandon sofa-style informal Cabinet, says Butler', *The Times*, 8 September.

Irvine, J., Miles, I. and Evans, J. (eds) (1979) *Demystifying Social Statistics*. London: Pluto Press.

James, S. (1993) 'The idea brokers: the impact of think tanks on British government', *Public Administration*, 71 (4): 491–506.

James, S. (1999) *British Cabinet Government*, 2nd edn. London: Routledge.

Jenkins, S. (1995) *Accountable to None: The Tory Nationalization of Britain*. London: Hamish Hamilton.

James, S. (2011) *Managing Europe from Home: The Changing Face of European Policy-making Under Blair and Ahern*. Manchester: Manchester University Press.

Jenkins-Smith, H. and Sabatier, P. (1993) 'The Study of the Public Policy Process', in P. Sabatier and H. Jenkins-Smith (eds), *Policy Change and Learning: An Advocacy Coalition Approach*. Boulder (Colorado), USA: Westview Press.

John, P. (1998) *Analysing Public Policy*. London: Pinter.

Johnson, N. (1988) 'Departmental select committees', in M. Ryle and P. G. Richards (eds), *The Commons Under Scrutiny*. London: Routledge.

Johnston, P. (2007) 'We are strangled by red tape, say police', *The Daily Telegraph*, 13 September.'

Jones, A. (2013) 'Firms "not implementing flexi-work"', *The Independent*, 22 February.

Jones, D.S. (2012) *Masters of the Universe: Hayek, Friedman and the Birth of Neoliberal Politics*. Princeton: Princeton University Press.

Jones, G.W. (1965) 'The prime minister's power', *Parliamentary Affairs*, 18: 167–85.

Jones, K. (2003) *Education in Britain: 1944 to the Present*. Cambridge: Polity.

Jones, T. and Newburn, T. (2007) *Policy Transfer and Criminal Justice*. Maidenhead: McGraw-Hill/ Open University Press.

Jordan, A.G. and Richardson, J.J. (1982) 'The British policy style or the logic of negotiation?', in J.J. Richardson (ed.), *Policy Styles in Western Europe*. London: George Allen and Unwin.

Jordan, G. (1990) 'Sub-governments, policy communities and networks: refilling the old bottles', *Journal of Theoretical Politics*, 2 (3): 319–38.

Jordan, G. (1994) *The British Administrative System: Principles Versus Practice*. London: Routledge.

Joseph, K. (1975) *Reversing the Trend: A Critical Re-appraisal of Conservative Economic and Social Policies*. London: Barry Rose.

Joseph, K. (1976) *Stranded on the Middle Ground*. London: Centre for Policy Studies.

Joseph, K. (1987) 'Escaping the chrysalis of statism', *Contemporary Record*, 1 (1): 26–31.

Jowit, J. (2000) 'Britain's overstressed railways', *Financial Times*, 21 October.

Judge, D. (1990) 'Parliament and interest representation', in M. Rush (ed.), *Parliament and Pressure Politics*. Oxford: Clarendon Press.

Judge, D. (1993) *The Parliamentary State*. London: Sage.

Judge, D. (2005) *Political Institutions in the United Kingdom*. Oxford: Oxford University Press.

Kakabadse, A.P. and Kakabadse, N.K. (2011) 'Eleven sides to the Minister of the Crown', *British Politics*, 6 (3): 345–78.

Kalitowski, S. (2008) 'Rubber stamp or cockpit? The impact of Parliament on government legislation', *Parliamentary Affairs*, 61 (4): 694–708.

Kassim, H. (2000) 'The United Kingdom's co-ordination of European Union policy', in H. Kassim, G. Peters and V. Wright (eds), *The National Coordination of EU Policy: The Domestic Level*. Oxford: Oxford University Press.

Kaufman, G. (1997) *How to be a Minister*. London: Faber.

Kavanagh, D. (1987) *Thatcherism and British Politics: The End of Consensus?* Oxford: Oxford University Press.

Kavanagh D. and Seldon, A. (2000) 'Support for the Prime Minister: the Hidden Influence of No.10', in R.A.W. Rhodes (ed.), *Transforming British Government, Volume 2: Changing Roles and Relationships*. Basingstoke: Macmillan.

Keating, M. (2010) *The Government of Scotland: Public Policy Making after Devolution*, 2nd edn. Edinburgh: Edinburgh University Press.

Keating, M., Stevenson, L., Cairney, P. and Taylor, K. (2003) 'Does devolution make a difference? Legislative output and policy divergence in Scotland', *Journal of Legislative Studies*, 9 (3): 110–39.

Kellas, J. (1984) *The Scottish Political System*. Cambridge: Cambridge University Press.

Kelling, G. (1998) 'The evolution of Broken Windows', in M. Weatheritt (ed.), *Zero Tolerance: What Does It Mean and Is It Right for Policing in Britain?* London: The Police Foundation.

Kelling, G. and Coles, C. (1996) *Fixing Broken Windows: Restoring Order and Reducing Crime in our Communities*. New York: Simon and Schuster.

Kelly, R. (2010) *Pre-legislative Scrutiny*. London: House of Commons Library, SN/PC/2822.

Kelso, A. (2009) *Parliamentary Reform at Westminster*. Manchester: Manchester University Press.

King, A. (1985) 'Margaret Thatcher: the style of a prime minister', in A. King (ed.), *The British Prime Minister*, 2nd edn. Basingstoke: Macmillan.

King, D. and Wickham-Jones, M. (1999) 'From Clinton to Blair – the Democratic (Party) origins of Welfare to Work', *The Political Quarterly*, 70 (1): 62–74.

Kingdon, J. (1984) *Agendas, Alternatives and Public Policies*. London: Longman.

Kingdon, J. (1995) *Agendas, Alternatives and Public Policies*, 2nd edn. London: HarperCollins.

Klein, N. (2007) *The Shock Doctrine: The Rise of Disaster Capitalism*. London: Penguin.

Kooiman, J. and Van Vliet, M. (1993) 'Governance and public management', in K. Eliassen and J. Kooiman (eds), *Managing Public Organisations*, 2nd edn. London: Sage.

Kord, S. and Wilson, D. (2006) 'Drowning in bureaucracy', *The Guardian*, 27 December.

Korris, M. (2011) 'Standing up for Scrutiny: how and why Parliament should make better law', *Parliamentary Affairs*, 64 (3): 564–74,

Lamb, H. (2010) 'Response: we'll never protect children through box-ticking and checklists', *The Guardian*, 26 March.

Laws, D. (2004) 'Reclaiming Liberalism: a liberal agenda for the Liberal Democrats', in P. Marshall and D. Laws (eds), *The Orange Book: Reclaiming Liberalism*. London: Profile Books.

Lawson, N. (1992) *The View from No. 11: Memoirs of a Tory Radical*. London: Bantam.

Le Grand, J. (2007) 'The politics of choice and competition in public services', *The Political Quarterly*, 78 (2): 207–13.

Le Grand, J. (2010) *Motivation, Agency and Public Policy: Of Knights and Knaves, Pawns and Queens*. Oxford: Oxford University Press.

Leach, R. (2009) *Political Ideology in Britain*, 2nd edn. Basingstoke: Palgrave Macmillan.

Learmont, J. (1995) *The Learmont Report: Review of Prison Service Security in England and Wales and the Escape from Parkhurst Prison on Tuesday 3 January 1995*, Cm 3020. London: Stationery Office.

Lee, D.R. (2012) *Public Choice, Past and Present: The Legacy of James M. Buchanan and Gordon Tullock*. Dallas: Springer.

Lee, J.M., Jones, G.W. and Burnham, J. (1998) *At the Centre of Whitehall: Advising the Prime Minister and Cabinet*. Basingstoke: Palgrave.

Lee, S. (2000) 'New Labour, New Centralism: the centralisation of policy and the devolution of administration in England and its regions', *Public Policy and Administration*, 15 (2): 96–109.

Letwin, O. (2002) 'For Labour, there is no such thing as society, only the state', in G. Streeter (ed.), *There is Such a Thing as Society: Twelve Principles of Compassionate Conservatism*. London: Politico's.

Letwin, O. (2003) *The Neighbourly Society: Collected Speeches 2001–2003*. London: Centre for Policy Studies.

Letwin, S.R. (1992) *The Anatomy of Thatcherism*. London: Fontana.

Levy, J. (2009) *Strengthening Parliament's Powers of Scrutiny? An Assessment of the Introduction of Public Bill Committees*. London: The Constitution Unit.

Lewis, D. (1997) *Hidden Agendas: Politics, Law and Disorder*. London: Hamish Hamilton.

Liberal Democrats (2011) 'Nick Clegg's speech to Spring Conference' (online). Available at http://www.libdems.org.uk/latest_news_detail.aspx?title=Nick_Clegg%E2%80%99s_speech_to_Spring_Conference&pPK=9296205b-d75b-40b1-bbb1-72e74181473f (accessed 17 October 2013).

Lindblom, C. (1959) 'The science of "muddling through"', *Public Administration Review*, 19 (2): 79–88.

Lindblom, C. (1979) 'Still muddling, not yet through', *Public Administration Review*, 39 (6): 517–26.

Lipsky, M. (2010) *Street-Level Bureaucracy: Dilemmas of the Individual in Public Services*, 30th Anniversary edition (first published in 1980). New York: Russell Sage Foundation.

Lomas, C. (2012) 'The burden of bureaucracy', *Nursing Standard*, 28 March.

Loughlin, M. and Scott, C. (1997) 'The regulatory state', in P. Dunleavy, A. Gamble, I. Holliday and G. Peele (eds), *Developments in British Politics 5*. Basingstoke: Macmillan.

LSE GV314 Group (2012) 'New life at the top: special advisers in British government', *Parliamentary Affairs*, 65 (4): 715–32.

Lukes, S. (1974) *Power: A Radical View*. Basingstoke: Macmillan.

Lundahl, L. (2011) 'The emergence of a Swedish school market', in R. Hatcher and K. Jones (eds), *No Country for the Young: Education from New Labour to the Coalition*. London: The Tufnell Press.

Machin, S., McNally, S. and Wyness, G. (2013) *Education in a Devolved Scotland: A Quantitative Analysis Report to the Economic and Social Research Council*. London: Centre for Economic Performance.

Mackintosh, J. (1977) *The British Cabinet*, 3rd edn. London: Stevens.

Maclure, S. (1988) *Education Re-formed: A Guide to the Education Reform Act 1988*. London: Hodder and Stoughton.

Macmillan, R. (2010) *The Third Sector Delivering Public Services: An Evidence Review*, working paper 20. Birmingham: Third Sector Research Centre.

Madgwick, P. (1991) *British Government: The Central Executive Territory*. Hemel Hempstead: Philip Allan.

Maer, L. (2011) *Quangos*. London: House of Commons Library, SN/PC/05609.

Maer, L., Gay, O. and Kelly, R. (2009) *The Departmental Select Committee System*. London: House of Commons Library, research paper 09/55.

Majone, G. (1989) *Evidence, Argument and Persuasion in the Policy Process*. New Haven (US): Yale University Press.

Majone, G. (1994) 'The rise of the regulatory state', *West European Politics*, 17 (3): 77–101.

Major, J. (1992) *The Next Phase of Conservatism: The Privatisation of Choice*. London: Conservative Political Centre.

Major, J. (1993) *Conservatism in the 1990s: Our Common Purpose*. London: Carlton Club/ Conservative Political Centre.

Major, J. (1997) *Our Nation's Future*. London: Conservative Political Centre.

Malpass, P. and Murie, A. (1999) *Housing Policy and Practice*, 5th edn. Basingstoke: Palgrave.

Mandelson, P. and Liddle, R. (1996) *The Blair Revolution: Can New Labour Deliver?* London: Faber.

Mansell, W. (2007) *Education by Numbers: The Tyranny of Testing*. London: Politico's.

Marsh, D. and Read, M. (1988) *Private Members' Bills*. Cambridge: Cambridge University Press.

Marsh, D. and Rhodes, R.A.W. (1992a) 'Policy communities and issue networks: beyond typology', in D. Marsh and R.A.W. Rhodes (eds), *Policy Networks in British Government*. Oxford: Oxford University Press.

Marsh, D. and Rhodes, R.A.W. (1992b) 'The implementation gap: explaining policy change and continuity', in D. Marsh and R.A.W Rhodes (eds), *Implementing Thatcherite Policies: Audit of an Era*. Milton Keynes: Open University Press.

Marsh, D. and Smith, M.J. (2000) 'Understanding policy networks: towards a dialectic approach', *Political Studies*, 48 (1): 4–21.

Marsh, D., Richards, D. and Smith, M.J. (2001) *Changing Patterns of Governance in the United Kingdom: Reinventing Whitehall?* Basingstoke: Palgrave.

Marsh, R. (1978) *Off the Rails*. London: Weidenfeld and Nicolson.

Marshall, G. (ed.) (1989) *Ministerial Responsibility*. Oxford: Oxford University Press.

Marshall, P. and Laws, D. (eds) (2004) *The Orange Book: Reclaiming Liberalism*. London: Profile Books.

Marx, K. (1963) *The Eighteenth Brumaire of Louis Bonaparte*. New York: International Publishers (first published in 1852).

McClory, J. (2010) *Oiling the Machine: Thoughts for Special Advisers Working in Government*. London: Institute for Government.

McConnell, A. and Stark, A. (2002) 'Foot-and-mouth 2001: the politics of crisis management', *Parliamentary Affairs*, 55 (4): 664–81.

McGee, S. and Ungoed-Thomas, J. (2011) 'Huhne fights 80mph limit', *The Sunday Times* 29 May.

McGrew, A. (1992) 'A global society?', in S. Hall, D. Held and A. McGrew (eds), *Modernity and its Futures*. Cambridge: Polity/Open University Press.

Mercurio, J. (2012) 'Paperwork and a target culture have taken their toll on our police', *The Guardian*, 27 June.

Michels, R. (1962) *Political Parties: A Sociological Study of the Oligarchical Tendencies of Modern Democracy*. New York: The Free Press (first published in 1911).

Middlemas, K. (1979) *Politics in Industrial Society*. London: Andre Deutsch.

Mirowski, P. (2013) *Never Let a Serious Crisis Go To Waste: How Neoliberalism Survived the Financial Meltdown*. London: Verso.

Mitchell, A. (1986) 'A house buyer's bill: how not to pass a Private Member's Bill', *Parliamentary Affairs*, 39 (1): 1–18.

Montgomerie, T. (2010) 'Falling short: key facts that contributed to the Conservative Party's failure to win a parliamentary majority' (online). Available at http://conservativehome.blogs.com/files/electionreviewlee.pdf (accessed 8 October 2013).

Monypenny, W. and Buckle, G. (1929) *The Life and Times of Benjamin Disraeli: Earl of Beaconsfield*, vol. 2. London: John Murray.

Moran, M. (2000) 'From command state to regulatory state', *Public Policy and Administration*, 15 (4): 1–12.

Moran, M. (2001) 'The rise of the regulatory state in Britain', *Parliamentary Affairs*, 54 (1): 19–34.

Moran, M. (2007) *The British Regulatory State: High Modernism and Hyper-Innovation*. Oxford: Oxford University Press.

Morris, N. (2011) 'Ken Clarke in rift with Theresa May over knife-crime children', *The Independent*, 26 October.

Morris, N. (2012) 'Cabinet split over plans for levy on alcohol', *The Independent*, 25 November.

Morris, R. (1994) 'New magistracies and commissariats', *Local Government Studies*, 20 (2): 177–85.

Morton, K. (2012) 'Social workers overloaded with paperwork warn of risks to Children', *Nursery World*, 17 May.

Mount, F. (2009) *Cold Cream: My Early Life and Other Mistakes*. London: Bloomsbury.

Mucciaroni, G. (1992) 'The garbage can model and the study of policy making: a critique', *Polity*, 24 (3): 460–82.

Mulgan, G. (2006) 'Thinking in tanks: the changing ecology of political ideas', *The Political Quarterly*, 77 (2): 147–55.

Mulgan, G. (2013) 'Experts and experimental government', in R. Doubleday and J. Wilsdon (eds), *Future Directions for Scientific Advice in Whitehall*. Cambridge/Sussex: University of Cambridge's Centre for Science and Policy/Science Policy Research Unit (SPRU), and ESRC STEPS Centre at the University of Sussex/Alliance for Useful Evidence/Institute for Government/Sciencewise.

Mulholland, H. and Wintour, P. (2011) Liberal Democrats will be more assertive, says Nick Clegg', *The Guardian*, 11 May.

Muller, C. (1996) 'The Institute of Economic Affairs: undermining the post-war consensus', *Contemporary British History*, 10 (1): 88–110.

Muller, W. and Wright, V. (1994) 'Reshaping the state in western Europe: the limits of retreat', *West European Politics*, 17 (3): 102–37.

Mullin, C. (2011) *Decline and Fall: Diaries 2005–2010*. London: Profile.

Murray, C. (1989) 'Underclass', *The Sunday Times (Magazine)*, 26 November.

Murray, C. (1994a) 'Underclass: the crisis deepens', *The Sunday Times*, 22 May.

Murray, C. (1994b) 'The New Victorians and the New Rabble', *The Sunday Times*, 29 May.

Nakamura, R. (1987) 'The Textbook Process and Implementation Research', *Policy Studies Review 1*.

Naughtie, J. (2001) *The Rivals: The Intimate Story of a Political Marriage*. London: Fourth Estate.

Naylor, C. and Gregory, S. (2009) *Independent Sector Treatment Centres*. London: The King's Fund.

Nelson, F. (2008) 'Made in Sweden: the new Tory education revolution', *The Spectator*, 27 February.

Newman, J. and Clarke, J. (1994) 'Going about our business? The Managerialisation of public services', in J. Clarke, A. Cochrane and E. McLaughlin (eds), *Managing Social Policy*. London: Sage.

Newsnight (2011) BBC 2, 12 August (online). Available at http://www.bbc.co.uk/news/uk-14513517 (accessed 11 October 2013).

Norman, J. (2010) *The Big Society: The Anatomy of the New Politics*. Buckingham: University of Buckingham Press.

Norton, P. (1979) 'The organization of parliamentary parties', in S.A. Walkland (ed.), *The House of Commons in the Twentieth Century*. Oxford: Clarendon Press.

Norton, P. (1981) *The Commons in Perspective*. Oxford: Martin Robertson.

Norton, P. (1985) 'The House of Commons: behavioural change', in P. Norton (ed.), *Parliament in the 1980s*. Oxford: Basil Blackwell.

Norton, P. (1990) 'Parliament and policy in Britain: the House of Commons as a policy influencer', in P. Norton (ed.), *Legislatures*. Oxford: Oxford University Press.

Norton, P. (1991) 'Parliament since 1945: a more open institution?', *Contemporary Record*, 5 (2): 217–34.

Norton, P. (1993a) *Does Parliament Matter?* Hemel Hempstead: Harvester Wheatsheaf.

Norton, P. (1993b) 'Questions and the role of parliament', in M. Franklin and P. Norton (eds), *Parliamentary Questions*. Oxford: Clarendon Press.

Norton, P. (1998) 'Old institutions, new institutionalism? Parliament and government in the UK', in P. Norton (ed.), *Parliaments and Governments in Western Europe*. London: Frank Cass.

Norton, P. (2000) 'Barons in a shrinking kingdom: senior ministers in British government', in R.A.W. Rhodes (ed.), *Transforming British Government, ii: Changing Roles and Relationships*. Basingstoke: Macmillan.

Norton, P. (2005) *Parliament in British Politics*. Basingstoke: Palgrave Macmillan.

Norton, P. (2013) *Parliament in British Politics*, 2nd edn. Basingstoke: Palgrave Macmillan.

Nugent, N. (2000) 'The European Union and UK governance', in R. Pyper and L. Robins (eds), *United Kingdom Governance*. Basingstoke: Macmillan.

Oakeshott, I. (2011) 'Insider reveals border chaos', *The Sunday Times*, 13 November.

Oliver, J. (2010) 'Cabinet revolt over "blunderbuss" cuts', *The Sunday Times*, 1 August.

Osborne, D. and Gaebler, T. (1992) *Reinventing Government: How the Entrepreneurial Spirit is Transforming the Public Sector*. Boston, MA: Addison Wesley.

Pahl, R. and Winkler, J. (1974) 'The coming corporatism', *New Society*, 10 October: 72–6.

Palfrey, C., Thomas, P. and Phillips, C. (2012) *Evaluation for the Real World*. Bristol: The Policy Press.

Parker, G. (2008) 'Policy exchange powers party's "liberal revolution"', *The Financial Times*, 21 May.

Parliament (2013a) 'Private Members' Ballot Bills First Reading: 19 June 2013' (online). Available at http://www.parliament.uk/business/news/2013/june/private-members-ballot-bills-first-reading-19-june-2013/ (accessed 10 November 2013).

Parliament (2013b) 'Draft Bills before Parliament' (online). Available at http://www.parliament.uk/business/bills-and-legislation/draft-bills/ (accessed 10 November 2013).

Paterson, L. (2002) 'Scottish social democracy and Blairism: difference, diversity and community', in G. Hassan and C. Warhurst (eds), *Tomorrow's Scotland*. London: Lawrence and Wishart.

Patten, C. (1983) *The Tory Case*. London: Longman.

Patten, J. (1995) *Things to Come*. London: Sinclair-Stevenson.

Pautz, H. (2010) 'Think tanks in the United Kingdom and Germany: actors in the modernisation of social democracy', *British Journal of Politics and International Relations*, 12 (2): 274–94.

Pautz, H. (2012a) 'The think tanks behind "Cameronism"', *British Journal of Politics and International Relations*, 14 (2): 362–77.

Pautz, H. (2012b) *Think-Tanks, Social Democracy and Social Policy*. Basingstoke: Palgrave Macmillan.

Perry, B. and Dorrell, S. (2006) *The Well-Being of the Nation: Interim Report of the Public Service Improvement Policy Group*. London: The Conservative Party.

Peters, B.G. (1984) *The Politics of Bureaucracy*, 2nd edn. New York: Longman.

Pierre, J. and Stoker, G. (2000) 'Towards multi-level governance', in P. Dunleavy, A. Gamble, I. Holliday and G. Peele (eds), *Developments in Politics 6*. Basingstoke: Macmillan.

Pirie, M. (1988) *Micropolitics: The Creation of Successful Policy*. Aldershot: Wildwood House.

Pirie, M. (2012) *Think Tank: The Story of the Adam Smith Institute*. London: Biteback.

Pitel, L. (2013) 'Leaders agree global tax plan, but it may create new loopholes', *The Times*, 20 July.

Policy Exchange (2013) 'About us' (online). Available at http://www.policyexchange.org.uk/about-us (accessed 17 October 2013).

Potter, A.M. (1961) *Organized Groups in British National Politics*. London: Faber.

Power, M. (1994) *The Audit Explosion*. London: Demos.

Power, M. (1997) *The Audit Society: Rituals of Verification*. Oxford: Oxford University Press.

Pressman, J. and Wildavsky, A. (1973) *Implementation: How Great Expectations in Washington Are Dashed in Oakland*. Berkeley, USA: University of California Press.

Prior, J. (1986) *A Balance of Power*. London: Hamish Hamilton.

Pryce, S. (1997) *Presidentializing the Premiership*. London: Macmillan.

Pym, F. (1984) *The Politics of Consent*. London: Hamish Hamilton.

Pyper, R. (1991) 'Ministerial departures from British governments, 1964–90: a survey', *Contemporary Record*, 5 (2): 235–56.

Randall, N. (2004) 'Three Faces of New Labour: Principle, Pragmatism and Populism in New Labour's Home Office', in S. Ludlam and M.J. Smith (eds), *Governing as New Labour: Policy and Politics under Blair*. Basingstoke: Palgrave.

Ranelagh, J. (1992) *Thatcher's People: An Insider's Account of the Politics, the Power and the Personalities*. London: Fontana.

Rawnsley, A. (2001) *Servants of the People: The Inside Story of New Labour*. London: Penguin.

Read, M. (1992) 'Policy networks and issue networks: the politics of smoking', in D. Marsh and R.A.W. Rhodes (eds), *Policy Networks in British Government*. Oxford: Clarendon Press.

Reeves, R. and Wintour, P. (1999) 'Help the poor? Well we'll have to find them first', *The Observer*, 19 September.

Revans, L. (2007) 'Finding the time', *Community Care*, 26 April.

Rhodes, R.A.W. (1995) 'From prime ministerial power to core executive', in R.A.W. Rhodes and P. Dunleavy (eds), *Prime Minister, Cabinet and Core Executive*. Basingstoke: Macmillan.

Rhodes, R.A.W. (1996) 'The new governance: governing without government', *Political Studies*, 44 (4): 652–67.

Rhodes, R.A.W. (1997) *Understanding Governance: Policy Networks, Governance, Reflexivity and Accountability*. Buckingham: Open University Press.

Rhodes, R.A.W. (2011) *Everyday Life in British Government*. Oxford: Oxford University Press.

Rhodes, R.A.W. and Marsh, D. (1992) 'Policy networks in British politics', in D. Marsh and R.A.W. Rhodes (eds), *Policy Networks in British Government*. Oxford: Clarendon Press.

Richards, D. (1997) *The Civil Service Under the Conservatives 1979–97: Whitehall's Political Poodles?* Brighton: Sussex Academic Press.

Richards, D. and Smith, M.J. (1997) 'How departments change: windows of opportunity and critical junctures in three departments', *Public Policy and Administration*, 12 (2): 62–79.

Richards, D. and Smith, M.J. (2002) *Governance and Public Policy in the UK*. Oxford: Oxford University Press.

Richards, P.G. (1988) 'The role of the commons', in M. Ryle and P.G. Richards (eds), *The Commons Under Scrutiny*. London: Routledge.

Richards, S. (2000) 'Yes, Minister, it's safer to leave it to us ...', *The Independent on Sunday*, 29 October.

Richards, S. (2011) 'If free schools were really free, then they wouldn't be fair', *The Independent*, 8 September.

Richardson, J. (2000) 'Government, interest groups and policy change', *Political Studies*, 48 (5): 1006–25.

Richardson, J.J. and Jordan, A.G. (1979) *Governing Under Pressure: The Policy Process in a Post-Parliamentary Democracy*. Oxford: Martin Robertson.

Riddell, P (1991) *The Thatcher Era*. Oxford, Blackwell.

Riddell, P. (2001) 'Blair as Prime Minister', in A. Seldon (ed.), *The Blair Effect: The Blair Government 1997–2001*. London: Little, Brown and Co.

Riddell, P., Gruhn, Z. and Carolan, L. (2011) *The Challenge of Being a Minister: Defining and Developing Ministerial Effectiveness*. London: Institute for Government.

Ridley, N. (1991) *My Style of Government: The Thatcher Years*. London: Hutchinson.

Robinson, N. (2000) *The Politics of Agenda Setting: The Car and the Shaping of Public Policy*. Aldershot: Ashgate.

Robinson, W. (2001) 'Social theory and the globalization: the rise of a transnational state', *Theory and Society*, 30 (2): 157–200.

Rochefort, D.A. and Cobb, R.W. (1994) 'Problem definition: an emerging perspective', in D.A. Rochefort and R.W. Cobb (eds), *The Politics of Problem Definition: Shaping the Policy Agenda*. Kansas: University Press of Kansas.

Rogers, R. and Walters, R. (2004) *How Parliament Works*, 5th edn. London: Pearson Education.

Rosamond, B. (2000) 'The Europeanization of British politics', in P. Dunleavy, A. Gamble, R. Heffernan and G. Peele (eds), *Developments in British Politics 7*. Basingstoke: Palgrave.

Rose, R. (1984) *Do Parties Make a Difference?*, 2nd edn. London: Macmillan.

Rose, R. (2001) *The Prime Minister in a Shrinking World*. Oxford: Polity.

Rose, R. and Davies, P. (1994) *Inheritance in Public Policy: Change Without Choice in Britain*. New Haven (USA):Yale University Press.

Rowan, D. (2003) 'Profile: Matthew Taylor – ideas man', *The Observer*, 7 September.

Royal College of Nursing (2008) *Nurses Spend More than a Million Hours Every Week on Mountain of Paperwork*, press release, 28 April.

Royal College of Nursing (2012) *The Community Nursing Workforce in England*, policy briefing, September.

Ruben, P. (1996) 'The Institute for Public Policy Research: policy and politics', *Contemporary British History*, 10 (2): 65–79.

Rush, M. (1990) 'Select committees', in M. Rush (ed.), *Parliament and Pressure Politics*. Oxford: Clarendon Press.

Rush, M. (2000) 'Parliamentary Scrutiny', in R. Pyper and L. Robins (eds), *United Kingdom Governance*. Basingstoke: Macmillan.

Rush, M. (2001) *The Role of the Member of Parliament Since 1868*. Oxford: Oxford University Press.

Russell, J. (2009) 'Where, they ask, is all the gratitude? Well, it's the experience stupid', *The Guardian*, 15 July.

Russell, M. (2013) *The Contemporary House of Lords: Westminster Bicameralism Revisited*. Oxford: Oxford University Press.

Russell, M. and Benton, M. (2011) *Selective Influence: The Policy Impact of House of Commons Select Committees*. London: The Constitution Unit.

Sabatier, P. (1986) 'Top-down and bottom-up approaches to implementation research: A critical analysis and suggested synthesis', *Journal of Public Policy*, 6 (1): 21–48.

Sabatier, P. (1999) 'The Need for Better Theories' in Paul Sabatier (ed) *Theories of the Policy Process*, Boulder (Colorado), USA: Westview Press.

Savage, M. (2011) 'Bank bonuses still offensive, argues Cable in defiance of Osborne', *The Times*, 14 February.

Schattschneider, E.E. (1960) *The Semi-Sovereign People*. New York: Holt, Rinehart and Winston.

Secretary of State for Health (2010) *The Government Response to the Health Select Committee Report on Alcohol*, Cm 7832. London: The Stationery Office.

Seldon, A. (1996) 'Ideas are not enough', in D. Marquand and A. Seldon (eds), *The Ideas that Shaped Post-War Britain*. London: Fontana.

Seldon, A. (2004) *Blair*. London: Free Press.

Sergeant, H. (2008) *The Public and the Police*. London: Civitas.

Sewill, B. (1975) 'A view from the inside: in place of strikes', in R. Harris and B. Sewill, *British Economic Policy 1970–74: Two Views*. London: Institute of Economic Affairs.

Shell, D. (1985) 'The House of Lords and the Thatcher government', *Parliamentary Affairs*, 38 (1): 16–32.

Shell, D. (2007) *The House of Lords*. Manchester: Manchester University Press.

Sherman, A. (2005) *Paradoxes of Power: Reflections on the Thatcher Interlude* (edited by Mark Garnet). Exeter: Imprint Academic.

Simon, H. (1957) *Administrative Behaviour*. London: Macmillan.

Sklair, L. (1991) *Sociology of the Global System*. Brighton: Harvester Wheatsheaf.

Skelcher, C. and Davis, H. (1996) 'Understanding the new magistracy: a study of characteristics and attitudes', *Local Government Studies*, 22 (2): 8–21 .

Smith, B.C. (1988) *Bureaucracy and Political Power*. London: Longman.

Smith, M. (1992) 'Modernization, globalization and the nation-state', in A. McGrew and P. Lewis (eds), *Global Politics*. Cambridge: Polity.

Smith, M. (2011) 'The paradoxes of Britain's strong centre: delegating decisions and reclaiming control', in C. Dahlström, B.G. Peters and J. Pierre (eds), *Steering from the Centre: Strengthening Political Control in Western Democracies*. Toronto: University of Toronto Press.

Smith, M.J. (1990) *The Politics of Agricultural Support in Britain: The Development of the Agricultural Policy Community*. Aldershot: Dartmouth.

Smith, M.J. (1991) 'From policy community to issue network: salmonella in eggs and the new politics of food', *Public Administration*, 69 (2): 235–55.

Smith, M.J. (1993) *Pressure, Power and Policy: State Autonomy and Policy Networks in Britain and the United States*. Hemel Hempstead: Harvester Wheatsheaf.

Smith, M.J. (1999) *The Core Executive in Britain*. Basingstoke: Macmillan.

Smith, M.J. (2003) 'The core executive and the modernization of central government', in P. Dunleavy, A. Gamble, R. Heffernan and G. Peele (eds), *Developments in British Politics 7*. Basingstoke: Palgrave.

Smith, M.J., Marsh, D. and Richards, D. (1995) 'Central government departments and the policy process', in R.A.W. Rhodes and P. Dunleavy (eds), *Prime Minister, Cabinet and Core Executive*. London: Macmillan.

Smith, M.J., Richards, D. and Marsh, D. (2000) 'The changing role of central government departments', in R.A.W. Rhodes (ed.), *Transforming British Government, Volume 2: Changing Roles and Relationships*. Basingstoke: Macmillan.

Smookler, J. (2006) 'Making a difference? The effectiveness of pre-legislative scrutiny', *Parliamentary Affairs*, 59 (3): 522–35.

Solesbury, W. (2001) *Evidence Based Policy: Whence it Came and Where it's Going*. London: ESRC Centre for Evidence Based Policy and Practice, Queen Mary, University of London.

Stanley, M. (2000) *How to be a Civil Servant*. London: Politico's.

Stationery Office (2001) *The House of Lords: Completing the Reform*, Cm 5291. London: Stationery Office.

Stewart, J. (1995) 'Appointed boards and local government', *Parliamentary Affairs*, 48 (2): 226–41.

Stewart, J. (1996) 'Reforming the new magistracy', in L. Pratchett and D. Wilson (eds), *Local Government and Local Democracy*. London: Macmillan.

Stewart, J. (2004) '"Scottish solutions to Scottish problems"? Social welfare in Scotland since devolution', in N. Ellison, L. Bauld and M. Powell (eds), *Social Policy Review 16*. Bristol: Policy Press with the Social Policy Association.

Stewart, J.D. (1958) *British Pressure Groups*. Oxford: Oxford University Press.

Stoker, G. (2004) *Transforming Local Governance: From Thatcherism to New Labour*. Basingstoke: Palgrave Macmillan.

Stone, D. (1996) 'From the margins of politics: The influence of think tanks in Britain', *West European Politics*, 19 (4): 675–92.

Stratton, A. (2011) 'Vince Cable and Chris Huhne clash over carbon emissions', *The Guardian*, 9 May.

Straw, J. (2007) *The Governance of Britain*. London: The Stationery Office, Cm 7170.

Strickland, P. and Cracknell, R. (2001) *House of Lords Reform: Developments Since 1997*, House of Commons research paper 01/77, October.

Swain, H. (2012) 'Postgraduate study is the next social mobility timebomb', *The Guardian*, 22 October.

Thatcher, M. (1975) 'Let our children grow tall' (online), speech to the Institute of SocioEconomic Studies, New York, 15 September. Available at http://www.margaretthatcher.org/document/102769 (accessed 8 October 2013).

Thatcher, M. (1983) Interviewed by Brian Walden for London Weekend Television, *Weekend World*, broadcast 16 January. Available at http://www.margaretthatcher.org/document/105087 (accessed 8 October 2013).

Thatcher, M. (1993) *The Downing Street Years*. London: HarperCollins.

Thatcher, M. (1995) *The Path to Power*. London: HarperCollins.

Theakston, K. (1987) *Junior Ministers in British Government*. Oxford: Blackwell.

Theakston, K. (1999a) 'Junior Ministers in the 1990s', *Parliamentary Affairs*, 52 (2): 230–45.

Theakston, K. (1999b) 'A permanent revolution in Whitehall: the Major governments and the civil service', in P. Dorey (ed.), *The Major Premiership: Politics and Policies under John Major, 1990–1997*. Basingstoke: Macmillan.

Theakston, K., Gill, M. and Atkins, J. (forthcoming) 'The ministerial foothills: Labour government junior ministers 1997–2010', *Parliamentary Affairs*. Currently only accessible online: http://pa.oxfordjournals.org/content/early/2012/09/06/pa.gss054.full.pdf+html

Thompson, G. (1992) 'Economic autonomy and the advanced industrial state', in A. McGrew and P. Lewis (eds), *Global Politics*. Cambridge: Polity Press.

Thompson, H. (1995) 'Joining the ERM: analysing a core executive policy disaster', in R.A.W. Rhodes and P. Dunleavy (eds), *Prime Minister, Cabinet and Core Executive*. Basingstoke: Macmillan.

Thompson, H. (1996) *The British Conservative Government and the European Exchange Rate Mechanism, 1979–1994*. London: Pinter.

Thompson, L. (2013) 'More of the same or a period of change? The impact of Bill committees in the twenty-first century House of Commons', *Parliamentary Affairs*, 66 (3): 459–79.

Toye, R. (forthcoming) '"Perfectly Parliamentary"? The Labour Party and the House of Commons in the inter-war years', *Twentieth Century British History*.

Travis, A. (2010) 'Prison works, says Theresa May', *The Guardian*, 14 December.

Treanor, J. (2013) 'Vince Cable prepares to launch crackdown on executive pay', *The Observer*, 29 September.

Trench, A. and Jarman, H. (2007) 'The practical outcomes of devolution: policy-making across the UK', in A. Trench (ed.), *Devolution and Power in the United Kingdom*. Manchester: Manchester University Press.

Tressell, R. (2012) *The Ragged Trousered Philanthropists* (first published in 1914). London: Wordsworth Classics.

Tullock, G., Seldon, A. and Brady, G.L. (2000) *Government: Whose Obedient Servant? A Primer in Public Choice*. London: Institute of Economic Affairs.

Tyrie, A. (2011) *Government by Explanation: Some ideas from the Select Committee Corridor*. London: Institute for Government.

Urry, J. (1989) 'The end of organised capitalism', in S. Hall and M. Jacques (eds), *New Times: The Changing Face of Politics in the 1990s*. London: Lawrence and Wishart/Marxism Today.

Vance, C. (1989) 'Social Construction Theory: problems in the history of sexuality', in A. van Kooten Niekerk and T. van der Meer (eds), *Homosexuality, which Homosexuality?* London: Routledge.

Vincent, A. (2009) *Modern Political Ideologies*, 3rd edn. Oxford: Wiley-Blackwell.

Walker, R. (1998) 'The Americanisation of British welfare: a case-study of policy transfer', *Focus*, 19 (3): 32–40.

Wall, S. (2008) *A Stranger in Europe: Britain and the EU from Thatcher to Blair*. Oxford: Oxford University Press.

Wallerstein, I. (1979) *The Capitalist World-Economy*. Cambridge: Cambridge University Press

Wallerstein, I. (1983) *Historical Capitalism*. London: Verso.

Wallerstein, I. (1984) *The Politics of the World-Economy: The States, the Movements and the Civilizations*. Cambridge: Cambridge University Press.

Ward, L. (2001) 'Spending row deepens Blair-Brown split', *The Guardian*, 19 November.

Wass, D. (1983) *Government and the Governed*. London: Routledge and Kegan Paul.

Watson, M. (2005) *Foundations of International Political Economy*. Basingstoke: Palgrave Macmillan.

Watson, R. (2010) 'Tories hope public sector co-ops will pay dividends', *The Times*, 16 February.

Watts, D. and Pilkington, C. (2005) *Britain in the European Union Today*, 3rd edn. Manchester: Manchester University Press.

Waxman, J. (2010) 'Scalpel! This NHS red tape needs removing', *The Times*, 30 April.

Webb, P. (2000) *The Modern British Party System*. London: Sage.

Weber, M. (1947) *The Theory of Social and Economic Organisation*. New York: The Free Press.

Weeks, J. (1992) 'The body and sexuality', in R. Bocock and K. Thompson (eds), *Social and Cultural Forms of Modernity*. Cambridge: Polity/Open University.

Whitelaw, W. (1989) *The Whitelaw Memoirs*. London: Aurum.

Whiteley, P. and Winyard, S. (1987) *Pressure for the Poor*. London: Methuen.

Whiteley, P. and Winyard, S. (1988) 'The poverty lobby in British politics', *Parliamentary Affairs*, 41 (2): 195–208.

Wicks, M. (1994) *The Active Society: Defending Welfare*. London: The Fabian Society.

Wicks, M. (2012) 'What ministers do', *The Political Quarterly*, 83 (3): 585–98.

Widdecombe, A. (2005) 'The role of an MP: an opposition view', in N. Baldwin (ed.), *Parliament in the 21st Century*. London: Politico's.

Willetts, D. (1987) 'The Prime Minister's policy unit', *Public Administration*, 65 (winter): 443–54.

Willetts, D. (1994) *Civic Conservatism*. London: Social Market Foundation.

Willetts, D. (2002) 'The new contours of British politics', in G. Streeter (ed.), *There is Such a Thing as Society: Twelve Principles of Compassionate Conservatism*. London: Politico's.

Williams, Z. (2010) 'Brains for hire: the think tank', *The Guardian*, G2, 28 October.

Williams, Z. (2012) 'On the money', *The Guardian* (*Weekend* magazine), 31 March.

Williamson, L. and Sparrow, A. (2010) 'Ken Clarke: There is no dissent over my prison reforms', *The Guardian*, 15 December.

Wilson, D. (2000) 'New Labour, new local governance?', in R. Pyper and L. Robins (ed.), *United Kingdom Governance*. Basingstoke: Macmillan.

Wilson, J.Q. and Kelling, G. (1982) 'Broken windows: the police and neighborhood safety', *Atlantic Monthly*, March: 29–38.

Wintour, P. (1997) 'Angry Blair hits back at "cynicism"', *The Observer*, 23 November.

Wintour, P. (2001) 'Blunkett rejects "airy fairy" fears', *The Guardian*, 12 November.

Wintour, P. (2011) 'Cable and Huhne attack Tory right', *The Guardian*, 20 September.

Wintour, P. (2012) 'David Cameron backpedals on bonuses with late call for restraint', *The Guardian*, 31 January.

Wistow, G. (1992) 'The Health Service Policy Community: professional pre-eminent or under challenge', in D. Marsh and R.A.W. Rhodes (eds), *Policy Networks in British Government*. Oxford: Oxford University Press.

Woodhouse, D. (1994) *Ministers and Parliament: Accountability in Theory and Practice*. Oxford: Clarendon.

Woodward, W. (2006) 'Tories admit past mistakes over public service workers', *The Guardian*, 6 September.

Worth, S. (2013) *Better Public Services: A Roadmap for Revolution*. London: Policy Exchange.

Wright, V. (1994) 'Reshaping the state: implications for public administration', *West European Politics*, 17 (3): 102–37.

Yee, A.S. (1996) 'The causal effect of ideas on policies', *International Organization*, 50 (1): 69–108.

Young, D. (1990) *The Enterprise Years: A Businessman in the Cabinet*. London: Headline.

Young, H. (1990) *One of Us*. London: Pan.

Index